CIVIL PROCEDURE

Cavendish
Publishing
Limited

London • Sydney

CIVIL PROCEDURE

Stephen M Gerlis
District Judge and Recorder

Paula Loughlin
LLB, LLM, Solicitor

Cavendish
Publishing
Limited

London • Sydney

First published in Great Britain 2001 by Cavendish Publishing Limited,
The Glass House, Wharton Street, London WC1X 9PX, United Kingdom
Telephone: +44 (0)20 7278 8000   Facsimile: +44 (0)20 7278 8080

Email: info@cavendishpublishing.com
Website: www.cavendishpublishing.com

Gerlis, SM (Stephen M)
Civil procedure
1 Civil procedure – England   2 Civil procedure – Wales
I Title   II Loughlin, Paula

347.4'2

ISBN 1 85941 497 4

Printed and bound in Great Britain

For our families.

FOREWORD

The modern Civil Procedure Rules (CPR) pioneered by Lord Woolf are proving to be one of the real success stories in the history of English law. It was not written in the stars that this would be so. One of their early critics, Professor Michael Zander, predicted that passive resistance by the legal profession could and probably would wreck them. A combination of judicial enforcement and voluntary culture change within the profession has proved him wrong. But old habits die hard, and courts and practitioners still have things to learn and problems to work out under the new dispensation. English justice, while now speedier and generally simpler, can still be unacceptably expensive.

These changes, however, are not taking place in isolation. They form part of the most important tectonic shift in our legal system since the reforms of the 1870s. It is a shift which includes a fundamental reform of the legal aid system, with implications for access to justice, changes in the structure of the legal profession, and - arching over all of these - the Human Rights Act 1998 which, by bringing the effect of Article 6 of the European Convention on Human Rights into our law places on every court a duty to ensure proper access and a fair hearing for everyone.

The tension between this fundamental obligation and the need for speed and simplicity runs through the CPR. It is what makes a book like this so necessary for anyone who is brought either by their work or by misfortune (for nobody in their right mind willingly goes to law) into a legal system which hopes it has finally exorcised the ghost of Jarndyce. But the combination of rules, practice directions, protocols and residual sources of procedural law is already creating an editorial maze, as a glance at the standard volumes will show. The way this book is organised and presented is therefore especially welcome. Instead of simply tracking the rules numerically, it reallocates the disparate materials into subject headings, explaining each as it goes. Instead of a detailed map on which you have first to get your bearings, here is a user-friendly guidebook.

Like other guidebooks, it does not make maps unnecessary. Practitioners will always do well to consult both. The unexpected, as any lawyer will confirm, keeps happening, and occasional anomalies or omissions are bound to be revealed from time to time in the CPR. But for those who need a clear, readable and practical guide to the new terrain of litigation, which tells them what to do, what to expect, and where to look for details, this book performs an invaluable service.

Stephen Sedley

The Rt Hon Lord Justice Sedley

Royal Courts of Justice

London

PREFACE

Two years after the CPR 1998 were introduced, the LCD published a report evaluating the success of the civil justice reforms brought into effect by the CPR. The report, *Emerging Findings: An Early Evaluation of the Civil Justice Reforms*,[1] a mixture of anecdotal and statistical evidence, concludes that 'there is a feeling that the new system is running smoothly and that all the participants – court staff, judges, lawyers and other users – are working to fulfil Lord Woolf's vision of a new civil justice system.[2]

It is indeed remarkable how 'Lord Woolf's vision of a new civil justice system' set out in his two reports,[3] has been assimilated into and revolutionised our civil procedural system. Concepts such as the 'overriding objective' and 'proportionality', which were almost irrelevant under the old system, are now of the utmost importance to every claim litigated under the CPR 1998 and have brought about a corresponding change of culture in the legal profession. Although the CPR are by no means complete and numerous revisions and amendments have already been made since they came into force in April 1999,[4] the key principles of the Woolf reforms enshrined in the CPR have remained constant throughout.

The *Emerging Findings* report gives a warm welcome and positive assessment of important innovative procedures initiated by the Woolf reforms, namely pre-action protocols, Part 36 offers and payments, single joint experts and case management conferences. The report refers to a 'new settlement culture' encouraged by pre-action protocols[5] and a drop in the number of claims issued by the courts since the introduction of the CPR 1998.[6] Unfortunately the report is unable to provide definitive views on whether a key objective of the rules – making the cost of litigation more affordable and more proportionate to the value and complexity of the case – has been achieved. Further research is being undertaken.

In writing this book we aim to provide not just an exposition of the CPR but have also attempted to explain the principles and purpose behind them so that the reader comes away with a clear understanding of how the CPR operate in practice and how the rules are likely to affect the case or set of circumstances they are dealing with. One of Lord Woolf's aims in drafting the new rules was to provide a core code setting out basic practice which the courts were to apply in the light of the overriding objective to deal with cases

---

1   www.lcd.gov.uk/civil/emerge/emerge.htm.
2   *Ibid*, para 9.8.
3   See Access to Justice, Interim Report and Final Report available on the LCD website, www.lcd.gov.uk/civil/finalfr.htm and www.lcd.gov.uk/civil/interfr.htm.
4   At the time of writing the 23rd update to the CPR 1998 has just been published.
5   *Ibid*, para 3.15.
6   *Ibid*, para 3.1.

justly.[7] Therefore, although there are various important guideline cases promulgated by the appellate courts, often presided over by Lord Woolf himself, the principle still remains that each case is dealt with by the case management judge according to its unique facts and circumstances and not according to binding case law precedent. Therefore, although we would always recommend that the reader consult the most current version of the rules[8] we feel that this book will remain relevant despite the continuing changes to the CPR as it is written with the intention of explaining the purpose of the rules and how the principles are applied in practice rather than simply attempting to convey the substance of the rules themselves.

We would like to thank everyone at Cavendish Publishing and in particular Jo and Cara for their hard work, patience and encouragement. Paula wishes to thank Edward, Frances and Noah for their love, support and understanding. Stephen extends the same wishes to Ann and Maggie.

We attempt to state the rules as of May 2001 and include a brief summary of CPR Rules 55 and 56 which are to come into force in October 2001.

Stephen Gerlis and Paula Loughlin
June 2001

---

7   See Access to Justice, Final Report, Chapter 20, p 274, para 10. (*Ibid*.)
8   Available free of charge on the LCD website (www.lcd.gov.uk).

CONTENTS

Contents

Contents

Contents

Contents

Contents

Contents

Contents

Contents

Contents

Contents

TABLE OF CASES

TABLE OF STATUTES

TABLE OF STATUTORY INSTRUMENTS

Civil Procedure

TABLE OF INTERNATIONAL INSTRUMENTS

CHAPTER 1

INTRODUCTION

THE WOOLF REFORMS

On 28 March 1994, Lord Woolf was appointed by the Lord Chancellor, Lord Mackay of Clashfern, to carry out a review of our civil litigation system. The aims of the review were:

- to improve access to justice and reduce the cost of litigation;
- to reduce the complexity of the rules and modernise technology; and
- to remove unnecessary distinctions of practice and procedure.[1]

The findings and recommendations for reform following this review were published in two reports under the heading *Access to Justice*, consisting of the Interim Report, published in June 1995, and the Final Report, published in July 1996, along with a set of draft civil procedure rules.

In his reports, Lord Woolf recommended fundamental changes to the whole basis of our civil litigation system and his recommendations were substantially adopted. The resulting reforms are very much identified with the main author of them, reference being made to the Woolf Report, the Woolf reforms and a litigation climate which is 'post-Woolf'.

As a result of the implementation of the Woolf reforms, the former civil procedure rules which applied separately to the High Court and county courts were abolished and replaced by a single set of rules, the Civil Procedure Rules 1998 (CPR), applying to both courts. The CPR contain the substance and detail of most of our civil procedure system and are the main means through which the Woolf reforms have been put into effect.

FUNDAMENTAL REFORM

The background to the commissioning of the report was apparently a concern felt throughout the common law world that civil litigation was too expensive, too slow and too complex resulting in inadequate access to justice and an inefficient and ineffective system. The concern was not with judicial decisions at trial, but with the 'processes leading to the decisions made by the courts',[2] that is, civil procedure.

---

1   See *Access to Justice*, Interim Report, Introduction (www.lcd.gov.uk/civil/interfr.htm).
2   See Interim Report, Chapter 2, para 1. (*Ibid.*)

Before publishing his findings, Lord Woolf conducted a wide consultation programme and held public seminars in order to canvass opinion from a broad spectrum of the population. He perceived a widespread dissatisfaction with the existing system and a belief that the defects with it were impeding access to justice. He found that even lawyers specialising in litigation 'accepted that the situation [could not] continue' as it did under the old civil procedure system.[3]

Prior to the publication of Access to Justice there had been 60 reports on aspects of civil procedure and the organisation of the courts. Yet, despite this, our civil litigation system was felt to be in crisis. Lord Woolf believed that the failure of previous attempts to reform the system was not due to the inadequacy of the previous reforms, but because they were only partially [and not completely] implemented.[4] He put forward his reform programme as a 'whole' and argued that unless it was implemented as a whole, it would not achieve the results it was designed to produce.[5] In the event, Lord Woolf's proposed reforms were accepted and implemented with only minor exceptions and adjustments. Moreover, some of his proposals which have not been immediately implemented are likely to be implemented at a later date.[6]

THE PROBLEMS AND THEIR CAUSES

In his reports, Lord Woolf set out the problems with the existing civil litigation system, the causes of those problems and his proposed solutions.

The ideal system

Lord Woolf provided a list of the basic principles which a civil justice system should meet in order to ensure access to justice. He stated that the system should:

- be just in the results it delivers;
- be fair in the way it treats litigants;
- offer procedures and costs proportionate to the nature of the issues involved;
- deal with cases with reasonable speed;
- be understandable to those who use it;
- be responsive to the needs of those who use it;

---

3   See Interim Report, Chapter 3, para 17. (*Ibid.*)
4   See Interim Report, Chapter 3, para 1. (*Ibid.*)
5   See Interim Report, Chapter 4, para 29. (*Ibid.*)
6   Eg, pre-trial fixed costs for fast track cases: *Access to Justice*, Final Report, Section 2, Chapter 4 (www.lcd.gov.uk/civil/finalfr.htm).

- provide as much certainty as the nature of particular cases allows; and
- be effective, adequately resourced and organised so as to give effect to the above principles.[7]

He did not believe that the former civil litigation system was fulfilling these basic principles.

The problems

The adversarial system

Lord Woolf concluded that the unrestrained adversarial culture of the former civil justice system was largely to blame for the fact that that system did not conform with the basic principles he believed were necessary to ensure access to justice.[8]

Under the operation of the old civil procedure rules, our adversarial system placed responsibility for the conduct of proceedings with the parties to the case. The judge acted solely in the role of umpire adjudicating on the issues selected by the parties when they chose to present them to the court.

Lord Woolf believed that where only the parties are in control of the pace and conduct of litigation, 'the litigation process is too often seen as a battlefield where no rules apply. In this environment, questions of expense, delay, compromise and fairness may have only low priority. The consequence is that expense is often excessive, disproportionate and unpredictable; and delay is frequently unreasonable'.[9] Examples cited of the resulting evils were the failure to establish the real issues in dispute in the case, excessive and inefficient disclosure of documents and the exertion of partisan pressure on experts.[10]

It was also felt that the timetables and other requirements in the previous rules were flouted on a vast scale and only complied with when convenient to the interests of one of the parties.[11]

The expense of litigation

Lord Woolf believed that for 'individual litigants the unaffordable cost of litigation constitutes a denial of access to justice'.[12] Lord Woolf took into

---

7   See Interim Report, Chapter 1, para 3 (*ibid*), and Final Report, Section 1, para 1. (*Ibid.*)
8   See Interim Report, Chapter 4, para 1. (*Ibid.*)
9   See Interim Report, Chapter 3, para 4. (*Ibid.*)
10 See Interim Report, Chapter 3, paras 8–11. (*Ibid.*)
11 See Interim Report, Chapter 3, para 6. (*Ibid.*)
12 See Interim Report, Chapter 3, para 13. (*Ibid.*)

account the cost not only in financial terms, but also in terms of time and the diversion from normal activities. He felt that the problem of expense included the problem of the uncertainty as to the amount that would be incurred in legal costs and this in turn was caused by the uncontrolled nature of the litigation process.

He also raised the issue of disproportionate costs, particularly in smaller cases where 'the costs of litigation, for one side alone, frequently equal or exceed the value of what is at issue'.[13]

Lord Woolf ultimately believed that under the system existing at the time he wrote his report 'there can be no effective control of costs because there is no effective control of the work'.[14]

Delay

Lord Woolf was scathing in his criticism of the legal profession in the context of delay. He said that delay was 'of more benefit to legal advisers than to parties' as it allowed 'litigators to carry excessive caseloads in which the minimum possible action occurs over the maximum possible timescale'.[15] He also believed that most delays were caused by the legal profession arising from 'failure to progress ... case[s] efficiently, wasting time on peripheral issues or procedural skirmishing to wear down an opponent or excuse failure to get on with the case'.[16] He also blamed excessive discovery and the use of sought-after experts as a cause of delays.[17]

Lord Woolf believed that the practice of reaching a settlement at a very late stage in proceedings was endemic throughout the system, but involved the parties in substantial additional costs.[18]

He also lamented the fact that there was no certainty as to the time that a hearing would take with parties' time estimates bearing insufficient relation to reality. He believed this was due to the fact that there was no plan or programme for the hearing or any attempt to concentrate on key issues and key evidence.[19]

Complexity

Lord Woolf believed that the complexity involved in bringing civil proceedings was caused by: the state of the rules of court; the existence of

---

13 See Interim Report, Chapter 3, para 18. (*Ibid.*)
14 See Interim Report, Chapter 3, para 24. (*Ibid.*)
15 See Interim Report, Chapter 3, para 31. (*Ibid.*)
16 See Interim Report, Chapter 3, para 36. (*Ibid.*)
17 *Ibid.*
18 See Interim Report, Chapter 3, para 38. (*Ibid.*)
19 See Interim Report, Chapter 3, paras 42–43. (*Ibid.*)

different procedures and jurisdictions for the High Court and county courts, as well as for the different divisions of the High Court; the variety of ways of initiating proceedings; multiplicity of practice directions; and obscure and uncertain substantive law.[20]

According to Lord Woolf, in the light of the fact that legal advice and assistance were increasingly unavailable to litigants, due to their excessive cost, and due to the limited availability of legal aid, more litigants were being forced to act in person. However, owing to its complexity, most litigants in person could not understand the procedure and so they and the courts had problems when litigants acted in person.[21]

The solutions

Judicial case management

If an unrestrained adversarial culture was the main reason why our civil litigation system failed to provide access to justice, then judicial case management was primarily the answer to this problem. Lord Woolf did not advocate the abolition of our adversarial system in favour of an inquisitorial system; what he proposed was to keep our adversarial system, but give a more interventionist management role to the court in order to control what he described as the excesses of the adversarial system.[22]

Lord Woolf believed that there was now 'no alternative to a fundamental shift in the responsibility for the management of civil litigation from litigants and their legal advisers to the courts'[23] and that this would require a radical change of culture for all those involved in the civil justice system.[24]

Judicial case management would mean not only that the court could control the progress of proceedings, but also that the court could determine how much of the court's resources should be allotted to the resolution of a particular case and that all of this would be achieved primarily through the allocation of cases to a case management track with case management by the courts thereafter.[25]

He believed that judicial case management would 'facilitate and encourage earlier settlement through earlier identification and determination of issues and tighter timetables'.[26]

---

20 See Interim Report, Chapter 3, para 44. (*Ibid.*)
21 See Interim Report, Chapter 3, paras 45–47. (*Ibid.*)
22 See Interim Report, Chapter 5, para 15. (*Ibid.*)
23 See Interim Report, Chapter 4, para 2. (*Ibid.*)
24 Interim Report, Chapter 4, para 4. (*Ibid.*)
25 Interim Report, Chapter 4, para 8. (*Ibid.*)
26 Interim Report, Chapter 4, para 12. (*Ibid.*)

Judicial case management would be enforced by the use of sanctions, intended to deter breaches of the rules, rather than impose punishment. A range of sanctions would be introduced tailored to fit the seriousness of a party's breach. Lord Woolf's proposals under the new rules was for sanctions to have effect unless the party in breach of the rules applied for relief rather than following the previous practice of obliging the other party to apply for an order that the offending party comply with the rules and be punished for breach.[27]

Proportionality

Proportionality is a key concept to the new civil litigation system. In Lord Woolf's view, it involves the recognition that '[t]he achievement of the right result needs to be balanced against the expenditure of the time and money needed to achieve that result'.[28] It also means that the amount and importance of what is at stake will govern how much time and cost should be allotted to the resolution of a dispute both in terms of recoverable legal costs and the use of court time, resources and procedures.

If proceedings are commenced, they should be subject to a predetermined timetable from which it will be difficult to depart. The courts should consider the needs not only of the litigants before it at any given time, but those of the other litigants in the court system.[29]

Moreover, through judicial case management, disclosure and evidence should be limited to that which is just and appropriate for the disposal of a dispute.[30]

A single procedural code

In order to address the complexity of the present rules of procedure, Lord Woolf proposed a single set of rules applying to the High Court and county courts. The rules would be more simply drafted in plain English, and special rules for specific types of litigation would be reduced to a minimum.[31]

The overall aim was for the rules to be understandable to those who used them, which would include litigants in person. In furtherance of this, Lord Woolf also recommended that terminology and expressions would not be used in the new rules that were meaningless or confusing to non-lawyers. Examples of replacements for such terminology were: claimant for plaintiff; statement of case for pleading; disclosure for discovery; remedy for relief; and

---

27 Final Report, Section 2, Chapter 6. (*Ibid.*)
28 Interim Report, Chapter 4, para 6. (*Ibid.*)
29 Interim Report, Chapter 4, para 7. (*Ibid.*)
30 *Ibid.*
31 See Final Report, Section 1, para 9. (*Ibid.*)

'a claim' for the various terms for methods of starting an action such as writ, summons and originating application. Lord Woolf also believed that a change of terminology, and one which in particular shunned legal jargon, would help to underpin a change of attitude and culture within the legal profession itself'.[32] In order to further the simplification of the litigation process itself, all proceedings would be commenced in the same way, by claim form.[33]

An important and distinctive innovation of the new rules was the introduction of the overriding objective; the overriding objective of the new rules being to enable the court to deal with cases justly. The CPR are not meant to be definitive of civil procedure and, instead, the court is given a discretion in the application and interpretation of the rules to a particular case in accordance with the overriding objective.[34] This is meant to facilitate the operation of the rules in order to do justice in a particular case and in order to prevent a complex procedural system growing up around the rules based on a plethora of case law precedent.

Change of culture

In order to give full effect to the reforms, Lord Woolf believed it was necessary not only to reform the rules and procedures, but also to bring about a fundamental change in the culture of civil litigation. In place of the traditional adversarial approach to litigation, there would be an expectation of openness and co-operation between the parties from the outset and a principle that litigation would be a last resort for the resolution of a dispute. This new culture would be supported by the introduction of pre-action protocols setting standards for reasonable pre-action behaviour which parties would be expected to follow and which would include voluntary pre-action exchange of information and the identification of the issues in dispute at the earliest stage.[35]

In furtherance of this new culture, there would be an emphasis on pre-commencement resolution of disputes whilst, if proceedings become necessary, an onus on the parties to work to achieve a settlement at as early a stage as possible.[36] Moreover, where an alternative method of resolving disputes otherwise than through court proceedings exists, then this should be used before court proceedings are resorted to.[37]

Lord Woolf also proposed new procedures designed to encourage settlement and the early resolution of disputes. These include claimants' offers

---

32 See Final Report, Section 5, Chapter 20, paras 13 and 14. (*Ibid.*)
33 See Final Report, Section 1, para 9. (*Ibid.*)
34 See Final Report, Section 5, Chapter 20. (*Ibid.*)
35 See Final Report, Section 1, para 9. (*Ibid.*)
36 Interim Report, Chapter 4, para 7. (*Ibid.*)
37 See Interim Report, Chapter 4, para 7. (*Ibid.*)

to settle,[38] defendants' applications for summary judgment[39] and the obligation on legal representatives to provide costs information to their clients and to their opponents at various stages of the proceedings.[40]

It should be noted that references in the text to the rules and practice directions are references to the CPR 1998 unless otherwise specified. The work is up to date as at 31 May 2001.

---

38 See Interim Report, Chapter 4, para 27 (*ibid*) and Final Report, Section 3, Chapter 11. (*Ibid.*)
39 See Interim Report, Chapter 4, para 28 and Chapter 6, paras 17–21. (*Ibid.*)
40 Interim Report, Chapter 4, para 7. (*Ibid.*)

CHAPTER 2

SOURCES OF CIVIL PROCEDURE: STRUCTURE AND JURISDICTION OF THE CIVIL COURTS

SOURCES OF CIVIL PROCEDURE

The Civil Procedure Rules 1998

The Civil Procedure Rules (CPR) 1998 came into force on 26 April 1999.[1] The rules are a single procedural code applying to both the High Court and county courts and replace the Rules of the Supreme Court (RSC) and the County Court Rules (CCR). The statutory basis of the CPR is the Civil Procedure Act 1997. The CPR are a form of delegated legislation and are drafted by the Civil Procedure Rule Committee which replaced the Supreme Court Rule Committee and the County Court Rule Committee.

The main body of the CPR consists of rules and practice directions. The rules are divided into parts dealing with a different aspect of procedure and most parts are accompanied by a practice direction. Although, in theory, the rules and practice directions are supposed to be different in nature, the reality is that it is often difficult to distinguish their respective roles. In any event, no rule should be read without considering its relevant practice direction and vice versa.

The CPR also contain a number of pre-action protocols[2] which set standards for reasonable pre-action behaviour. There is also a short glossary, defining some of the terms referred to in the rules, which is meant for assistance only, particularly to litigants in person, and is not meant to provide a meaning to any term which it otherwise would not have.[3] Also, unlike terms which are defined within the main body of the rules, the terms in the glossary are not meant to affect the way the rules operate.[4]

The schedules to the CPR

Although the CPR abolished the former RSC and CCR, some of these former rules were brought back into force in the form of schedules to the CPR. The remaining RSC are contained in Sched 1 and the remaining CCR in Sched 2. The old rules still cover such matters as enforcement and a number of other aspects of procedure which have not yet been drafted into the form of the new

---

1   SI 1998/3132 as amended by the Civil Procedure (Amendment) Rules SI 1999/1008, SI 2000/221, SI 2000/940, SI 2000/1317, SI 2000/2092, SI 2001/256 and SI 2001/1388.

2   See Chapter 4, Pre-Action Protocols.

3   See the explanation at the beginning of the glossary to the CPR. (*Ibid.*)

4   See *Access to Justice*, Final Report, Chapter 20, para 16 (www.lcd.gov.uk/civil/finalfr.htm).

rules. However, some aspects of the retained RSC and CCR have been brought into line with the CPR so, for instance, if an application must be made under any of the RSC or CCR in the schedules, in many cases it must be made in accordance with Part 23 of the CPR.[5]

The overriding objective of the rules

The CPR describe themselves as 'a new procedural code with the overriding objective of enabling the court to deal with cases justly' (r 1.1(1)). The court must seek to give effect to this overriding objective when exercising any power under the rules or interpreting any rule (r 1.2). In the Final Report Lord Woolf said: 'As part of a comprehensive package of reforms ... modernised and improved rules have a major part to play.'[5a] The rules are meant to cover the main principles of the matter dealt with whilst the practice directions supply the detail. The intention was to move away from the old civil procedure system where the rules had become dense and convoluted, covering every eventuality and bound by case law precedent, to a system of procedural rules drafted in plain English and which give the court a wide discretion to make decisions in order to deal justly with a particular case in accordance with the overriding objective. As Lord Woolf expressed it: 'Every word in the rules should have a purpose, but every word cannot sensibly be given a minutely exact meaning. Civil procedure involves more judgment and knowledge than the rules can directly express.'[6]

In this way, cases decided under the previous system are not binding under the new rules[7] and the intention is that judges can exercise their discretion to deal with a case justly without necessarily being bound by decisions in other cases under the new rules.[8] However, in reality, there have already been a number of guideline cases decided by the court of appeal on the interpretation of the rules and significantly, when sitting in such appeals, Lord Woolf has often taken the opportunity to provide general guidance on the operation of the rules.[9]

Proceedings to which the CPR apply

The CPR apply to all proceedings in the county courts, the High Court and the Civil Division of the Court of Appeal apart from some important exceptions such as family and insolvency proceedings.[10] However, following a practice

---

5   See Chapter 19, Making Applications for Court Orders.
5a See Final Report, Chapter 20, para 29. (*Ibid.*)
6   See Final Report, Chapter 20, para 10. (*Ibid.*)
7   See judgment of Lord Woolf MR in *Biguzzi v Rank Leisure plc* [1999] 1 WLR 1926; [1999] 4 All ER 934, CA.
8   See *Hamblin v Field* (2000) *The Times*, 26 April and *Purdy v Cambran* (1999) Lawtel, 17 December, CA.
9   See, eg, *Ford v GKR Construction* [2000] 1 All ER 802.
10 There is a practice direction relating to insolvency proceedings.

direction issued by the President of the Family Division on 24 October 2000, costs directions under the CPR now apply to family proceedings and Family Division proceedings[11] and the principles of the overriding objective and proportionality now apply to ancillary relief proceedings. The following types of proceedings are also not covered by the CPR: non-contentious or common form probate proceedings; proceedings in the High Court when acting as a Prize Court, proceedings before the judge within the meaning of Part VII of the Mental Health Act 1983, and adoption proceedings (PD 2, para 2.1).

Enforcement of judgments has not yet been reformed, but is likely to be in the near future.

THE CIVIL COURTS

Our civil litigation system is administered through the civil courts, consisting of the Supreme Court and the county courts.

The Supreme Court

The Supreme Court consists of the High Court, the Court of Appeal and the Crown Court. In the Supreme Court, civil cases are heard only in the High Court, with appeals being heard in the civil division of the Court of Appeal. The High Court consists of the Queen's Bench Division, Chancery Division and Family Division. The Queen's Bench Division deals with contract and tort matters and includes the Commercial Court and the Admiralty Court. The Chancery Division deals with equity and trusts matters, contentious probate, tax, partnerships and bankruptcy and includes the Companies Court and the Patents Court. The Family Division deals with dissolution of marriages, matrimonial proceedings and proceedings relating to children.

In London, the High Court sits at the Royal Courts of Justice. In other areas of the country, the High Court sits at district registries. The High Court judiciary consists of the Vice Chancellor (Head of the Chancery Division), the Lord Chief Justice (Head of the QBD), the President (Head of the Family Division), the Senior Presiding Judge, High Court (or *puisne*) judges and masters and district judges.

The county courts

The county court is held for a geographical district (s 1 of the County Courts Act 1984). The county courts deal with the majority of civil litigation. Circuit

---

11   Although it is still not possible to enter into an enforceable conditional fee agreement in family proceedings, see Chapter 38, Funding Litigation.

judges, Recorders and district judges preside over the business of the county courts.

JURISDICTION OF THE HIGH COURT AND COUNTY COURTS

The High Court and county courts have concurrent jurisdiction over most actions and, as a general rule, proceedings in which both the county courts and High Court have jurisdiction may be commenced in either court. However, there are some important exceptions to this rule, as detailed below.

Jurisdiction of the High Court

The High Court has almost unlimited jurisdiction over most matters.[12] However, the intention is to reserve the High Court for only the most valuable, complex and important cases.

Unless the value of a monetary (non-personal injury) claim is worth more than £15,000, it cannot be commenced in the High Court.[13] In order to start such proceedings in the High Court, a party must state on the claim form that the value of the claim is worth more than £15,000 (PD 7). For personal injury claims, the value of the claim must be more than £50,000[14] and this must also be stated on the claim form before proceedings can be commenced in the High Court (PD 7). The financial value of a claim is calculated in accordance with r 16.3(6).[15]

Also, if a claim with an estimated value of less than £50,000 is issued in the Royal Courts of Justice, unless it is required by a statutory enactment to be tried in the High Court, it falls within a specialist list,[16] or is a type of claim suitable for trial in the Royal Courts of Justice, it will be transferred to a county court (PD 29, para 2.6). The type of claim suitable for trial in the Royal Courts of Justice include professional negligence claims, Fatal Accidents Act 1976 claims, fraud or undue influence claims.

Apart from these provisions, a claim should only be started in the High Court if by reason of its financial value and the amount in dispute, and/or the complexity of the facts, legal issues, remedies or procedures involved, and/or

---

12 Supreme Court Act 1981, s 19.
13 High Court and County Courts Jurisdiction Order 1991 SI 1991/724, Art 4A.
14 *Ibid*, Art 5.
15 *Ibid*, Art 9; see Chapter 11, Statements of Case.
16 See below, p 18, Specialist proceedings.

the public importance of the outcome, the claimant believes that the claim ought to be dealt with by a High Court Judge (PD 7, para 2.4).

Jurisdiction of masters and district judges in the High Court

Most of the case management[17] of cases in the High Court is dealt with by judges known as masters in the Royal Courts of Justice and district judges in the District Registries. As a general principle, a master or district judge can exercise any function of the court except where an enactment, rule or practice direction provides otherwise (r 2.4). PD 2B includes details where masters and district judges have no jurisdiction and where a judge must make the order instead. This includes[18] the power to:

- make search orders, freezing orders, an ancillary order under r 25.1(g) or an order authorising a person to enter land to recover, inspect or sample property;[19]
- make an order for an injunction, except where the terms are agreed by the parties, where it is in connection with a charging order or appointment of a receiver by way of equitable execution or in proceedings under RSC Ord 77 r 16 (order restraining person from receiving sum due from the crown). Also a master or district judge may make an order varying or discharging an injunction or undertaking if the parties consent to the variation or discharge;
- try a multi-track case unless all the parties consent or where the case is treated as allocated to the multi-track because it is proceeding under Part 8 (PD 2B, paras 2.1–2.4).

However these restrictions on jurisdiction do not prevent masters or district judges from:

- hearing applications for summary judgment or, if the parties consent, the determination of a preliminary issue;
- assessing damages due to a party under a judgment without limit as to the amount (PD 2B, paras 4.1–4.2).

Jurisdiction of the county courts

The county courts have general jurisdiction to hear and determine any action founded on contract or tort whatever its financial value, complexity or importance (s 15(1) of the County Courts Act 1984). However, there are certain

---

17 See Chapter 5, Judicial Case Management: The Overriding Objective.
18 PD 2B must be consulted for further details.
19 See Chapter 20, Interim Remedies.

contract/tort actions over which the county courts have no jurisdiction, the most important of which being most actions for libel or slander (s 15(2) of the County Courts Act 1984).

The county courts have unlimited jurisdiction to hear actions for the recovery of land (s 21 of the County Courts Act 1984).

The county courts have jurisdiction in equity and contentious probate proceedings where the estate, fund or assets involved do not exceed £30,000 (ss 23 and 32 of the County Courts Act 1984 and County Courts Jurisdiction Order 1981).[20] However, the county court will have jurisdiction to hear equity claims exceeding this amount if the parties agree that it should have jurisdiction, except in respect of proceedings under the Variation of Trusts Act 1958 (s 24 of the County Courts Act 1984).

Although, as a general principle, the county courts have the same jurisdiction as the High Court to award remedies and relief, this is apart from the remedies or relief of judicial review, freezing injunctions or search orders, which must be obtained in the High Court (County Court Remedies Regulations 1991).[21]

Jurisdiction of district judges in the county court

All district judges in the county court outside of London are also appointed district judges of the High Court so they can sit in the district registry. The trial jurisdiction of district judges includes:

- trials of cases allocated to the small claims and fast track or with exceptions, certain proceedings[22] which are treated as allocated to the multi-track under r 8.9(c) and Table 2 of the Practice Direction to Part 8;[23]
- proceedings for the recovery of land;
- the assessment of damages or other sum due to a party under a judgment without any financial limit;
- any other case with the consent of all the parties and the permission of the designated civil judge (PD 2B, para 11.1).

The district judge has jurisdiction to grant an injunction where:

- the injunction is to be made in proceedings where a district judge otherwise has jurisdiction;[24]

---

20 SI 1981/1123.
21 SI 1991/1222 (as amended by SI 1995/206).
22 PD 2B must be consulted for the exceptions.
23 See Chapter 14, Part 8 Claims.
24 See above.

- where the injunction is sought in a money claim where the claim has not yet been allocated to a track where the amount claimed does not exceed the fast track financial limit;
- in the circumstances where a High Court master or district judge has jurisdiction to grant an injunction[25] (PD 2B, paras 8.1–8.2).

Penalties for commencing proceedings in the High Court rather than the county court

If a claimant commences proceedings in the High Court which should have been commenced in the county court, the court has a discretion to penalise the claimant in costs by reducing the costs he would otherwise have been awarded by a maximum of 25% (s 51(8) and (9) of the Supreme Court Act 1981).

However, if proceedings are brought in the High Court and the court is satisfied that the person bringing them knew that they should have been brought in a county court instead, the court can strike out the proceedings (s 40(1)(b) of the County Courts Act 1984) provided it is a proportionate response, bearing in mind the right to a fair trial preserved by Art 6(1) of the European Convention on Human Rights (ECHR).[26]

TRANSFER OF PROCEEDINGS

Transfer of proceedings between the High Court and county courts

If proceedings are brought in the High Court which should have been brought in the county court, or brought in the county court but should have been brought in the High Court, either court can transfer the proceedings to the other court (ss 40(1)(a) and 42(1)(a) of the County Courts Act 1984).

The High Court and county courts have general jurisdiction, subject to specific jurisdictional rules, to transfer proceedings to the other court either of its own motion or on the application of a party (ss 40(2), (3) and 42(2), (3) of the County Courts Act 1984).

The High Court has general jurisdiction to order the transfer of any proceedings from the county court to the High Court (s 41 of the County Courts Act 1984).

---

25 See above, PD 2B, para 2.4.
26 See Chapter 37, The Human Rights Act 1998.

When deciding whether to transfer proceedings between the High Court and a county court, between county courts, or between the Royal Courts of Justice and district registries, the court must having regard to the matters referred to in r 30.3(2).[27]

Transfer between county courts

A county court may order the proceedings before it, or any part of them, such as a counterclaim or application, to be transferred to another county court if it considers it justified having regard to the matters referred to in r 30.3(2),[28] or if proceedings for the detailed assessment of costs or for the enforcement of a judgment or order could be more conveniently or fairly taken in that other county court (r 30.2(1)).

If proceedings have been started in a county court which is not the correct county court according to the CPR, a judge may: order that the proceedings be transferred to the county court in which they ought to have been started; continue in the county court in which they have been started; or be struck out (r 30.2(2)).

However, where proceedings must be started in a particular county court in accordance with an enactment, other than the CPR, r 30.2 does not give the court the power to transfer the proceedings to a county court which is not the court in which they should have been started or order them to continue in the wrong court (r 30.2(7)).

A transfer to another county court can be made by the court of its own motion or on the application of a party to the county court where the claim is currently being heard (r 30.2(3)).

Transfer between Royal Courts of Justice and a district registry[28a]

The High Court may, having regard to the matters referred to in r 30.3(2),[29] order proceedings, or any part of them, such as a counterclaim, in the Royal Courts of Justice to be transferred to a district registry, or those in a district registry to be transferred to the Royal Courts of Justice or another district registry (r 30.2(4)). The transfer may be made by the court of its own motion or on the application of a party and if the claim is currently proceeding in a district registry the application must be made to that registry (r 30.2(6)).

---

27 See below, p 17, Matters in r 30.3(2) to which the court should have regard when transferring proceedings.

28 *Ibid.*

28a See above, p 11, The Supreme Court.

29 *Ibid.*

Transfers between district registries[29a]

In the case of proceedings for the detailed assessment of costs, a district registry may order that the proceedings be transferred to another district registry if satisfied that they could be more conveniently or fairly heard in that other registry (r 30.2(5)). The transfer may be made by the court of its own motion or on the application of a party to the district registry where the proceedings are currently being heard (r 30.2(6)).

Transfers between divisions[29b] and to and from a specialist list[29c]

The High Court may order proceedings in any Division of the High Court to be transferred to another Division. Also, the court may order proceedings to be transferred to or from a specialist list. If a party wishes to transfer proceedings to or from a specialist list, an application must be made to a judge dealing with claims in that list (r 30.5).

Matters in r 30.3(2) to which the court should
have regard when transferring proceedings

The matters to which the court should have regard when transferring proceedings between the High Court and a county court, or between county courts, or between the Royal Court of Justice and the district registries include such matters as: the financial value of the claim or the amount in dispute (if different); the convenience or fairness of hearings being held in another court; the availability of a judge specialising in the type of claim in question; the complexity of the facts, legal issues, remedies or procedures; the public importance of the claim; the facilities available at the court where the claim is being dealt with, in particular with regard to any disabilities of a party or witness; and where there is a real prospect that the making of a declaration of incompatibility under s 4 of the Human Rights Act 1998 may arise (r 30.3).

In addition, when considering whether to make a transfer, the financial limits of the county courts and High Court under the High Court and County Courts Jurisdiction Order 1991 must be taken into account as well as the matter referred to in PD 29, para 2 (PD 30, para 1).[30]

29a See above, p 11, The Supreme Court.
29b *Ibid.*
29c See below, p 18, Specialist proceedings.
30 See above, p 12 onwards, Jurisdiction of the High Court and county courts.

Appeal against an order of transfer

A party may appeal against an order of transfer in accordance with the procedure set out in PD 30, para 5.

SPECIALIST PROCEEDINGS

Certain types of proceedings are treated as specialist proceedings under the CPR. These are admiralty proceedings, arbitration proceedings, commercial and mercantile actions, Patents Court business, Technology and Construction Court business, proceedings under the Companies Acts 1985 and 1989 and contentious probate proceedings (r 49.2). Although the CPR apply to these specialist proceedings, they do so only in so far as they are not inconsistent with separate practice directions for each type of specialist proceedings (r 49.1).

Prior to the introduction of the CPR, such specialist proceedings were conducted in accordance with a separately developed procedure which was felt to be efficient and effective and suited to the nature of the specialist proceedings and was accordingly retained. Therefore, although the CPR purports to provide a unified system of procedure for all types of civil action, in fact many variations and differences remain depending on the nature of the action litigated. Part 49 should be consulted for details as to the variations in procedure for specialist proceedings.

Various guides are produced by committees of the specialist courts, such as the Commercial Court Practice which gives further guidance about bringing proceedings of this type. Although chancery proceedings are not treated as specialist proceedings under the CPR, there is a guide published to proceedings in the Chancery Division which contains a number of practice directions relating to procedure for such actions. A similar guide has now been produced for the Queen's Bench Division.

COMPUTATION OF TIME UNDER THE CPR

Clear days

Where a period of time for doing any act is specified by the rules, practice directions or a judgment or order of the court as a number of days, it is computed as *clear days*. Clear days mean that in computing the number of days, the day on which the period begins is excluded and, if the end of the period is defined by reference to an event, such as a hearing, the day on which the event occurs is excluded (r 2.8(1), (2) and (3)). Accordingly, if the end of the period of time is not defined by reference to an event, for example if a rule specifies that a statement of case must be served within a period of time, then the last day of the period is included. Rule 2.8 gives a number of examples showing how a calculation of clear days operates in practice.

Periods of time of five days or less

If the specified period is five days or less, if the period of time includes a Saturday, Sunday, Bank Holiday, Christmas Day or Good Friday that day does not count (r 2.8(4)).

Court office

If a rule, practice direction, judgment or order specifies a period of time for doing any act at the court office, if that period of time ends on a day when the court office is closed, that act shall be in time if done on the next day on which the court office is open (r 2.8(5)).

Meaning of month

Where a judgment, order, direction or other document refers to a 'month' it means a calendar month (r 2.10).

Dates for compliance

Rule 2.9 provides that where the court gives a judgment, order or direction which imposes a time limit for doing any act, the last date for compliance must, whenever practicable, be expressed as a calendar date and include the time of day by which the act must be done.

Time limits varied by the parties

Rule 2.11 states that as a general rule, unless the rules, a practice direction or the court directs otherwise, the time specified for a person to do any act may be varied by the written agreement of the parties. However, there are quite widespread restrictions in the CPR on agreeing to a different time period to that specified.

If a rule, practice direction or court order requires a party to do something within a specified time and also specifies the consequences of failure to comply, the time for doing the act may not be extended by agreement of the parties (r 3.8(3)).

Also, for cases allocated to the fast track[31] or multi-track,[32] the parties cannot agree to vary certain key dates. In the fast track, these key dates are the date for the return of the listing questionnaire, the trial or the trial period. In the multi-track, the key dates are the same as for the fast track, but also include the date of a case management conference or a pre-trial review. If a party wishes to vary these dates, an application must be made to the court (rr 28.4 and 29.5).

The parties can agree to extend the period of time within which a defence is served, but only for a maximum period of a further 28 days. If such an agreement is reached, the defendant must notify the court of it in writing (r 15.5).

COURT FORMS

Court forms are specified for use by the parties in proceedings. Where a form is specified in a practice direction, that particular form must be used (r 4.1). Although a form may be varied if this is required by the circumstances of a particular case, such variations cannot leave out any information or guidance intended for the recipient (r 4.2 and 4.3). Also, if a form is sent by the court or by one party for use by another, it must be sent without any variation except that which is required for the circumstances of the particular case (r 4.4). A party does not have to use the actual versions printed by HMSO and in fact can fill in interactive forms downloaded from the court service website or those provided by commercial publishers on computer disks. If a form has the Royal Arms at the head of the first page, this must be replicated on the form used by the party (r 4.5).

The Practice Direction to Part 4 lists all the forms to be used in civil proceedings since the introduction of the CPR. The Practice Direction is divided into three tables. Table 1 lists forms required by the main body of the CPR. Table 2 lists the High Court forms previously in use under the old rules and still retained for certain matters. Table 3 lists the former county court forms which are still required for certain matters (see PD 4).

The Practice Direction also refers to the fact that other forms may be authorised for use in specialist proceedings[33] by the practice directions relevant to the specialist proceedings in question (PD 4, para 2.1).

---

31 See Chapter 17, The Fast Track.
32 See Chapter 18, The Multi-Track.
33 See above, p 18, Specialist proceedings.

Filing of documents at court

The rules indicate when documents must be filed at court and the time for doing so. Filing a document at court means simply delivering it to the court. This can be achieved by a number of methods, the most common being by post, but it can also be delivered by hand or by fax.

In relation to documents delivered at court by means of fax, the document is not filed until it is delivered by the court's fax machine; the time of transmission from the party's fax machine is not taken into account. If the document is delivered by fax after 4 pm, it will be treated as filed on the next day the court office is open. The party is not required to send a 'hard' copy by post or document exchange. Fax can be used to file such documents as statements of case, but should not be used to send letters or documents of a routine or non-urgent nature to court (PD 5 paras 5.3(1)–(6)), as there is a danger that they will not be placed before the judge in time for the matter to which they relate.

As a general rule fax should not be used, except in an unavoidable emergency, to deliver the following: a document which attracts a court fee; a Part 36 payment notice, a document relating to a hearing less than two hours ahead; or trial bundles or skeleton arguments. In the case of a document which attracts a court fee or a Part 36 payment notice, the fax should explain the nature of the emergency and include an undertaking that the fee or money has been dispatched that day by post or will be paid at the court office counter the following business day (PD 5, para 5.1(9) and (10)).

The date of filing will be recorded on the document by the court office (PD 5, para 5.1). On filing, particulars such as the date of delivery at the court and the title of the proceedings will be entered in the court records (PD 5, para 5.2).

CHAPTER 3

LIMITATION OF ACTIONS

INTRODUCTION

If a person has grounds to bring proceedings against another person, depending on the nature of the cause of action, he must do so within a limited period of time from when the cause of action arose. The time limits for bringing proceedings are entirely statutory and most are contained in the Limitation Act 1980. Although the periods of time are relatively long, a balance is struck between a person's right to sue a person for harm caused and the right not to be perpetually exposed to the risk of proceedings.

If proceedings are brought outside of these periods they will not be a nullity, it being incumbent on the defendant to raise a defence based on expiry of the limitation period for that cause of action.[1] The defendant is required to give details in his defence showing that the limitation period has expired (PD 16, para 14.1). Where a limitation period has expired, the proceedings are often referred to as 'statute-barred' in reference to the fact that the defendant will have a complete defence under the Limitation Act 1980. However, for some types of proceedings, such as certain personal injuries actions, the court has a discretion to disapply the limitation period and allow the action to continue.[2] On the other hand, for other types of action such as an action to recover land, or an action based on defective products brought under the Consumer Protection Act 1987, the cause of action will be extinguished and not just statute-barred, following the expiry of the limitation period.[3]

In this chapter, references to sections are to sections of the Limitation Act 1980.

Time when proceedings are brought

Proceedings are brought when the court issues a claim form at the request of the claimant (r 7.2(1)). However, if the claim form is received at the court office on an earlier date than that on which it was issued, the claim is brought on that earlier date for the purposes of the Limitation Act 1980 (PD 7, para 5.1).[4]

---

1   See *Dismore v Milton* [1938] 3 All ER 762, CA.
2   See below, p 32, Discretion to disapply limitation period.
3   See below, p 28, Actions to recover land, and p 33, Defective products.
4   For further details see Chapter 7, Starting an Action.

TIME LIMITS

The Limitation Act is divided into two parts. Part I gives the 'ordinary' time limits for actions (often referred to as the primary limitation period), that is, a basic limitation period within which proceedings should be commenced. Part II deals with the circumstances where the ordinary time limits can be extended or excluded for certain causes of action.

CONTRACT AND TORT

Contract

The time limit for bringing an action based on simple contract is six years from the date on which the cause of action accrued (s 5).

Simple contracts

A simple contract is a contract which is not a contract of record or a contract under seal.

Contracts under seal

In the case of a contract under seal, or other speciality, the time limit for bringing an action is 12 years from the date on which the cause of action accrued (s 8).

Tort

The time limit for bringing an action based in tort is six years from the date on which the cause of action accrued (s 2). However, certain actions based on tort have different limitation periods, for example, personal injury actions based on negligence, nuisance or breach of duty.[5]

Latent damage

A separate limitation period applies to negligence actions, except for personal injury actions, where the damage caused by the negligence is latent. In such

---

5   See below, p 29, Personal injury and death claims.

cases, the limitation period runs either six years from the date on which the cause of action accrued, or three years from the date when the claimant had the right to bring an action and knowledge of certain facts if those are discovered later (s 14A(4) and (5)). Knowledge under this section is defined in a similar way to that under s 14[6] in respect of personal injury and death claims, covering such matters as knowledge of the identity of the defendant, that the damage was caused by the defendant's negligence, and that the damage was sufficiently serious to justify instituting proceedings against the defendant.

Negligence actions based on latent damage which fall under the above provisions are subject to a long stop period of 15 years from the date of the negligent act or omission which is alleged to have caused the damage (s 14B).

Section 14A does not apply to actions based solely on contract.[7] However, where there is concurrent liability in contract and tort, for instance, in cases of professional negligence, the claimant can frame his case in tort in order to take advantage of the latent damage provisions.[8]

Also, a subsequent owner of property is entitled to rely on the alternative limitation period of three years from the date of knowledge if the property is disposed of before the damage is discovered by the original owner. The three years run from the date when the subsequent owner acquires an interest in the property (s 3(1) of the Latent Damage Act 1976). However, the primary limitation period of six years and the 15 year long stop period runs from the date when the damage occurred.

Date when cause of action accrues

In an action based on contract, the cause of action accrues from the date of breach of the contract even if damage is not suffered until a later date.[9]

For the type of tort which is established only if damage occurs, such as in negligence actions, the cause of action accrues from the date of damage.[10] If the tort is actionable without proof of damage, such as in the case of intentional trespass, the cause of action accrues on the date the tort was committed.[11]

---

6   See below, p 29, Personal injury and death claims.

7   See *Société Commerciale de Réassurance v ERAS (International) Ltd* [1992] 2 All ER 82.

8   See *Henderson v Merrett Syndicates Ltd* [1994] 3 WLR 761, HL.

9   See *Gibbs v Gibbs* (1881) 8 QBD 296.

10 See *Pirelli General Cable Works Ltd v Oscar Faber and Partners (A Firm)* [1983] 1 All ER 65, HL.

11 See *Granger v George* (1826) 5 B & C 149.

Equitable remedies

The time limits under the Limitation Act 1980 do not apply to any claim for specific performance of a contract, an injunction or any other equitable relief, except in so far as the court may apply any time limit by analogy (s 36(1)). Instead, the court applies equitable principles such as laches and acquiescence when deciding whether to refuse to grant such remedies and the Act does not interfere with the court's equitable jurisdiction to do so (s 36(2)).

OTHER CAUSES OF ACTION

Special time limit for actions in respect of certain loans

In the case of a contract of loan which does not provide for the repayment of the debt on or before a fixed or determinable date and which does not make repayment conditional on a demand for repayment, the cause of action to recover the debt will run from the date on which a written demand for repayment is made, and not from the date the contract of loan was made (s 6(1), (2) and (3)). This provision is meant to cover the making of loans between family and friends, although it is not limited to such circumstances.

Acknowledgment or part payment of debts

In the case of a claim to recover a debt or other liquidated pecuniary claim, if the person liable to repay it makes any payment in respect of it or makes an acknowledgment of the claim in writing and signed by him, the cause of action to recover the money shall be treated as running from the date of the acknowledgment or part payment and not before (ss 29 and 30).

Although the limitation period may be repeatedly extended by further acknowledgments or payments, once the limitation period has expired it shall not be revived by any subsequent acknowledgment or payment (s 29(7)).

Sums recoverable by statute

If a sum of money is recovered by virtue of any statute, it shall not be recoverable after the expiration of six years from the date on which the cause of action accrued (s 9).

Conversion

An action in conversion, being an action in tort, must be brought within six years from the date the cause of action accrued (s 2). The owner's title in the converted goods is extinguished if the goods are not recovered within the time limit for bringing an action (s 3(2)). If goods are converted and, before the owner recovers possession, a further action of conversion takes place, the limitation period of six years runs from the date of the original conversion (s 3(1)).

Theft

If goods are stolen, rather than converted, the limitation periods under ss 2 and 3 do not apply and there is no limitation on the period within which the owner of the goods can bring an action to recover the goods from the thief. If goods are stolen and then disposed of to someone who is not a purchaser in good faith, the owner can bring an action against the thief and/or the person to whom the goods are disposed without limitation as to time. If goods are stolen and then sold to someone who purchases them in good faith, the owner will not be able to bring an action against the purchaser after the expiry of six years following the purchase, although the right to bring an action against the thief will continue without limitation as to time. However, if goods are converted and then subsequently stolen by another person, the owner will not be able to bring an action against either the person who converted the goods or the thief after the expiry of six years following the conversion (s 4).

Defamation or malicious falsehood

An action for libel, slander or malicious falsehood must be brought within one year from the date on which the cause of action accrued (s 4A).

The court has a discretion if it appears equitable to do so to allow such an action to proceed notwithstanding the expiry of the one year limitation period (s 32A).[12]

Claim for a contribution

Under s 1 of the Civil Liability (Contribution) Act 1978, any person liable in respect of any damage suffered by another person may recover a contribution from any other person liable in respect of the same damage (whether jointly

---

12 See *Oyston v Blaker* [1996] 2 All ER 106 for an example of the exercise of this discretion.

liable or otherwise). An action for a contribution must be brought within two years of the date on which the right accrues (s 10(1)). In the case of proceedings which result in judgment, the right to claim a contribution accrues from the date of the judgment (s 10(3)). In the case of an agreement to provide compensation, without judgment being obtained, the right to claim a contribution accrues from the date the agreement is made (s 10(4)).

Actions to recover land

An action to recover land must be brought within 12 years from the date the cause of action accrued (s 15). Therefore, if an owner allows land to be occupied by a squatter for at least 12 years he will lose his right to recover the property from the squatter, who will have acquired title to the land by means of adverse possession. In this way, the owner's title will be extinguished (s 17).

The same period of 12 years applies to actions to recover money secured on land by a mortgage or charge or to recover the proceeds of the sale of land, for example, under a trust for sale (s 20).

Actions to recover rent

An action to recover arrears of rent, or damages in respect of arrears of rent, must be brought within six years from the date on which the arrears became due (s 19).

Actions to redeem a mortgage

The mortgagor's legal or equitable right to redeem the mortgage is barred if the mortgagee remains in possession of the mortgaged land for 12 years or more without giving any written acknowledgment of the title of the mortgagor or of his equity of redemption and without receiving any payment on account of principal or interest made by or on behalf of the mortgagor (s 16). Again, in this way the mortgagor's title will be extinguished (s 17).

Actions in respect of trust property

An action by a beneficiary to recover trust property or in respect of any breach of trust must be brought within six years from the date on which the cause of action accrued (s 21(3)).

However, no period of limitation under the Act will apply where the action by the beneficiary under the trust is in respect of any fraud or fraudulent breach of trust to which the trustee was a party or was privy to or where the trustee has converted trust property to his own use (s 21(1)).

Actions to enforce a judgment

An action to enforce a judgment must be brought within six years from the date on which the judgment became enforceable (s 24(1)).

It should be noted that the word 'action' does not include processes of execution which are procedural matters,[13] although leave is often required to issue such processes of execution where more than six years has elapsed since the judgment was obtained.[14]

However, although procedural steps to execute a judgment may be taken more than six years after the judgment was obtained, arrears of interest accruing in respect of any judgment debt are not recoverable more than six years after the date on which the interest became due (s 24(2)).

PERSONAL INJURY AND DEATH CLAIMS

Personal injury claims

An action brought for damages which consist of or include damages in respect of personal injuries to the claimant or any other person, whether the action is based on negligence, nuisance or breach of duty, must be brought within three years from either:

- the date on which the cause of action accrued; or
- the date of knowledge[15] (if later) of the person injured (s 11(1), (3) and (4)).

Time limits if person suffering personal injuries dies

If a person suffering personal injuries caused by another person's negligence, nuisance or breach of duty, dies from those injuries, two independent causes of action will potentially arise. One is the injured person's own cause of action for his personal injuries which may be brought following his death on behalf of his estate under the Law Reform (Miscellaneous Provisions) Act 1934. The other is an entirely separate cause of action which can be brought by the deceased's dependants for financial loss caused by the death under the Fatal Accidents Act 1976.

---

13 See *Lowsley v Forbes (t/a Le Design Services)* [1998] 3 All ER 897, HL.
14 See Chapter 39, Enforcement of Judgments and Orders.
15 Defined below, p 31, Knowledge.

Action on behalf of the estate

If the person injured dies before the time limit for bringing a personal injuries action expires, the time limit within which an action must be brought on behalf of his estate under s 1 of the Law Reform (Miscellaneous Provisions) Act 1934 is three years from either:

- the date of death; or
- the date of the personal representative's knowledge,[16] whichever is later (s 11(5)).

Action by dependants

For an action to be brought by the dependants it is necessary that the circumstances of the death are such that the deceased himself could have brought an action against the person responsible had he not died.

The time limit within which an action must be brought by the dependants under s 1 of the Fatal Accidents Act 1976 is three years from either:

- the date of death; or
- the date of knowledge[17] of the dependent, whichever is later (s 12(2)).

Where there are two or more dependants, the time limit under s 12(2) is applied separately for each person, such that the court will direct that any dependent for whom the action would be outside the time limit shall be excluded from bringing an action (s 13).

Breach of duty

The words 'breach of duty' refer to a breach of a duty not to cause personal injury to a person, rather than breach of an obligation not to infringe another person's legal rights.[18] Therefore, damages for personal injuries arising from actions for trespass to the person, false imprisonment, malicious prosecution or defamation of character would be actions for tort under s 2 and subject to a six year limitation period rather than actions under s 11 and subject to a three year limitation period. However, this also means that there is no discretion to disapply the limitation period in the case of personal injuries actions based on intentional harm.[19]

---

16 Defined below, p 31, Knowledge.
17 Defined below, *ibid.*
18 See *Stubbings v Webb* [1993] 1 All ER 322.
19 See below, p 32, Discretion to disapply limitation period.

Date of knowledge

The date of knowledge is defined in s 14 as the date on which the injured person had knowledge of all of the following facts:

- that the injury was significant; and
- that the injury was attributable, in whole or in part, to the action or omission which is alleged to constitute the negligence, nuisance or breach of duty;
- the identity of the defendant; and
- if it is alleged that the act or omission was that of a person other than the defendant, the identity of that person and the additional facts supporting the bringing of an action against the defendant.

However, knowledge that the act or omission in question amounted as a matter of law to negligence, nuisance or breach of duty is irrelevant (s 14).

Knowledge

A person's 'knowledge' is not entirely subjective, as it includes knowledge a person would reasonably have been expected to acquire from facts observable or ascertainable by him or from facts ascertainable with the help of medical or other appropriate expert advice which it is reasonable for him to seek (s 14(3)).

However, s 14(3) goes on to provide that a person will not be fixed with knowledge of a fact ascertainable only with the help of expert advice so long as he has taken all reasonable steps to obtain and, where appropriate, act on that advice. Therefore, in the case of *Ali v Courtaulds Textiles Ltd*,[20] where the claimant sought a medical opinion as to whether his deafness was noise-induced or age-induced, it was held that the claimant would not be fixed with the knowledge that his deafness was noise-induced at the time that he was aware of his deafness, as the issue as to the cause of his deafness was only ascertainable by means of expert advice, which was not only reasonable, but essential for him to obtain.

Significant injury

A significant injury is defined as one that a person would reasonably consider to be sufficiently serious to justify him instituting proceedings for damages against a defendant who did not dispute liability and was able to satisfy a judgment (s 14(2)).

---

20   (1999) *The Times*, 28 May.

Discretion to disapply limitation period

For personal injury and death claims under ss 11 and 12, the court has a wide discretion to disapply the limitation period so that an action can be brought even though the limitation period has expired if it appears equitable to the court to allow the action to proceed (s 33(1)). The court balances the prejudice that would be suffered to the claimant if it decides to hold that the limitation period should apply against the prejudice that would be suffered to the defendant if the court decides to disapply the limitation period (s 33(1)).

It is only those personal injuries or death claims arising from negligence, nuisance or breach of duty where the court has a discretion to disapply the limitation period, the court has no discretion to disapply the limitation period for other types of personal injuries actions such as those arising from intentional trespass to the person.[21]

Although the action on behalf of the estate or a dependant's action will be statute-barred if the injured person's claim was statute-barred at the time of his death, the court has a discretion to disapply the limitation period under s 33 for the benefit of the estate or the dependants (s 12(3) and s 33).

Matters that the court will take into account when deciding whether to disapply the limitation period

The court will take all the circumstances into account when deciding whether to disapply the limitation period and in particular it will take the matters specified in s 33(3) into account. These include: the length of and reasons for the claimant's delay in bringing proceedings; the effect the delay is likely to have on the evidence; the conduct of the defendant since the cause of action arose in co-operating with any requests from the claimant to provide information or access for inspection of property; the duration of any disability[22] of the claimant since the cause of action arose; whether the claimant acted reasonably and promptly once he was aware that he had a good cause of action against the defendant and the steps (if any) the claimant took to obtain medical, legal or other expert advice and the nature of any such advice he received.

When considering the relative prejudice to the parties, the court can take into account in deciding not to disapply the limitation period the fact that the claimant has a good cause of action against his legal advisers for failing to commence proceedings in time. However, although the existence of such a remedy is a highly relevant factor, this has to be offset by the fact that such a

---

21 See *Stubbings v Webb* [1993] 1 All ER 322.

22 By s 38(2) of the Limitation Act 1980, a person under a disability is a child or a person who has a mental disorder within the meaning of the Mental Health Act 1983.

person would be prejudiced to some degree by having to bring a fresh action against his solicitor as his advisers will be aware of all the difficulties and weaknesses with his personal injuries claim.[23]

Second action brought after limitation period expired

If a claimant brings a personal injuries or death claim which for any reason is struck out or discontinued and the limitation period expires, the court will not exercise its discretion under s 33 to disapply the limitation period in order to allow the second action to go ahead,[24] apart from where there are exceptional circumstances.[25] The rationale for this rule is that the claimant was not prejudiced by the limitation period because he was able to bring his first action within time, rather, he was prejudiced by his own, or his legal adviser's delay in prosecuting his action.

Defective products

The Consumer Protection Act 1987 introduced strict liability for damage caused by defective products. A special limitation period applies to actions brought under the Consumer Protection Act (s 11A). In the case of actions for personal injuries or death or damage to property (other than the defective product itself) the same limitation period of three years as under s 11 and 12[26] of the Act applies (s 11A(4) and (5)).

Section 11A(3) provides that there shall be a long stop period of 10 years from the date that the product was supplied to the consumer within which to bring an action under the Consumer Protection Act 1987. Further, s 11A(3) provides that the cause of action shall be extinguished, rather than simply becoming 'statute-barred',[27] once this 10 year period has expired. This long stop period is absolute, and once it has expired it overrides the court's power to disapply the limitation period for personal injury and death claims under s 33,[28] the extension of the limitation period under s 28 in cases of disability[29] and the postponement of the limitation period under s 32 where there has been deliberate concealment of facts.[30]

---

23 See *Thompson v Brown Construction (Ebbw Vale) Ltd and Others* [1981] 2 All ER 296, HL.
24 See *Walkley v Precision Forgings Ltd* [1979] 2 All ER 548, HL.
25 See *White v Glass* (1989) *The Times*, 18 February, CA.
26 See above, p 29, Personal injury and death claims.
27 See above, p 23, Introduction.
28 See above, p 32, Discretion to disapply limitation period.
29 See below, p 34, Time limits for children and patients.
30 See below, p 34, Extension of the limitation period in cases of fraud, concealment or mistake.

TIME LIMITS FOR CHILDREN AND PATIENTS

In the case of a child (a person under 18) or a patient (a person who, by reason of a mental disorder within the meaning of the Mental Health Act 1983, is incapable of managing and administering his own affairs), limitation periods do not begin to run until the child dies or comes of age, or the patient dies or recovers (s 28).

This is subject to a long stop period of 30 years for an action to recover land or money charged on land from the date on which the cause of action accrued (s 28(4)).

Also, for claims under the Consumer Protection Act 1987, this extension of limitation periods for children and patients shall not override the long stop period of 10 years prescribed by s 11A(3) which runs from the time the defective product was supplied[31] (s 28(7)). Nor will it override the long stop period of 15 years in the case of latent damage in negligence actions prescribed by s 14B[32] (s 28A).

EXTENSION OF THE LIMITATION PERIOD IN CASES OF FRAUD, CONCEALMENT OR MISTAKE

In the case of a cause of action based on fraud or mistake, or where the defendant has deliberately concealed facts relevant to the claimant's cause of action, the limitation period shall not begin to run until the claimant has discovered the fraud, concealment or mistake, or could with reasonable diligence[33] have discovered it (s 32(1)). Similarly, any intentional act which amounts to a breach of duty amounts to a deliberate commission of a breach of duty and triggers s 32(2) which does not require there to be concealment of facts rather than law.[34] The long stop period of 15 years prescribed for latent damages claims in negligence actions shall not apply where there has been deliberate concealment of facts relevant to the claimant's cause of action by the defendant (s 32(5)).

---

31 See above, p 33, Defective products.
32 See above, p 24, Latent damage.
33 See *Peco Arts Inc v Hazlitt Gallery Ltd* [1983] 1 WLR 1315.
34 *Liverpool RC Archdiocese Trustees v Goldberg* [2000] Lloyd's Rep PN 836.

NEW CLAIMS IN EXISTING PROCEEDINGS

A new claim in existing proceedings is a claim by way of set off or counterclaim and any claim involving the addition of a new cause of action or the addition or substitution of a new party (s 35(2). Section 35 specifies when such new claims are deemed to be commenced for the purposes of the limitation period.

Although permission may need to be sought to amend a statement of claim to plead a new claim or join a new party once proceedings have started and have reached a certain stage, the court has only very limited powers to allow a party to join a new party to the proceedings or to add a new cause of action once the relevant limitation period has expired.[35]

FOREIGN LIMITATION PERIODS

In general terms, where, in any proceedings, in accordance with rules of private international law, the law of any other country is to be taken into account in the determination of any matter, the law of that other country relating to limitation shall apply in respect of that matter for the purposes of the proceedings (s 1(1) of the Foreign Limitation Periods Act 1984).

---

35 See Chapter 13, Adding or Substituting a Party and Chapter 11, Statements of Case.

CHAPTER 4

PRE-ACTION PROTOCOLS

INTRODUCTION

In *Access to Justice*, Lord Woolf said:

> My approach to civil justice is that disputes should, wherever possible, be resolved without litigation.[1]

This statement was made in the context of his proposals for pre-action protocols and it could be argued that pre-action protocols epitomise, more than any other aspect of the new rules, Lord Woolf's approach to reforming our civil justice system, since the main purpose of a pre-action protocol is to facilitate the settlement of a dispute without litigation. Along with this, Lord Woolf emphasised that the quality and timing of a settlement are also important, not just the fact that a settlement has been made.[2]

Pre-action protocols are designed to enable the parties to be well informed about the other side's case in order to reach a mutually satisfying settlement or to make meaningful offers to settle, and to this end the protocols include schedules of documents that each side should voluntarily disclose. Also, the protocols expect identification of the issues and voluntary disclosure of relevant documents before litigation is begun in order to encourage the early resolution of a dispute. In Lord Woolf's opinion, a dispute settled at the door of a court is the most inappropriate time for it to settle as, by that stage, maximum cost and delay will have been incurred.[3]

Lord Woolf was also dissatisfied by the knowledge that many disputes settle because the claimant is tired of waiting and does not have the energy or resources to pursue the claim further; often, this is as a result of deliberate delaying and wearing down tactics adopted by the opponent.[4] The hope is that pre-action protocols, which encourage parties to behave in a reasonable and less adversarial way, even before proceedings have started, will help to curtail such tactics and save costs. One important and controversial example of this emphasis on co-operation is the encouragement to the parties to select a single joint expert.

Critics of the reforms complain that things such as pre-action protocols result in the 'front-loading' of litigation, making many disputes more

---

1   See *Access to Justice*, Final Report, Chapter 10, p 107, para 2 (www.lcd.gov.uk/civil/finalfr.htm).
2   See Final Report, Chapter 10, p 107, para 3. (*Ibid.*)
3   See Final Report, Chapter 10, p 107, para 3. (*Ibid.*)
4   See Final Report, Chapter 10, p 107, para 3. (*Ibid.*)

expensive and time-consuming rather than less. They argue that if a dispute settles, time and costs spent preparing a case to a standard as if it were ready for trial will be wasted. Lord Woolf's response to such criticism is that bringing work forward on a case will enable some cases to settle earlier. He feels that if that doesn't happen, early defining of issues and disclosure of documents will increase the likelihood of a settlement being reached and if that doesn't happen, such early work will enable the case to proceed more quickly and smoothly if litigation is started.[5]

The pre-action protocols were described by Lord Woolf as 'codes of sensible practice which parties are expected to follow'.[6] Although the protocols cannot be enforced, if proceedings are started the rules allow the court to take compliance with the protocols into account when exercising case management powers or awarding costs and to impose sanctions for failure to comply. The sanctions include indemnity costs and penalty interest. Moreover, if a protocol is not applicable to a particular dispute, then litigants should behave, or at least appear to behave, reasonably in the conduct of the dispute, as though an appropriate pre-action protocol were in place.

A clear message from the reforms is that litigation is an act of last resort and parties should be able to demonstrate from their pre-action conduct that they made a concerted effort to settle the dispute before issuing proceedings. Moreover, if litigation is started, the parties should approach it with a view to settlement at the earliest opportunity.

TYPES OF DISPUTE COVERED BY A PRE-ACTION PROTOCOL

It was never Lord Woolf's intention that there be a pre-action protocol for every type of dispute. Instead, he believed that they should cover specific types of dispute such as personal injury, clinical negligence[7] and housing.[8] There are now pre-action protocols applying to the following types of action:

- personal injury;
- clinical negligence;
- construction and engineering disputes; and
- defamation (PD – Protocols, para 5.1).

---

5   See Final Report, Chapter 10, p 108, para 6 and p 111, para 16. (*Ibid.*)
6   See Final Report, Chapter 10, p 108, para 6. (*Ibid.*)
7   'Clinical negligence' is the new phrase for what would formerly have been known as medical negligence disputes. The phrase was felt to be more accurate and understandable, as it covers not just medical negligence disputes, but also disputes involving dentists and nurses, etc.
8   See Final Report, Chapter 10, p 108, paras 6–8. (*Ibid.*)

Pre-action behaviour in cases not covered by a pre-action protocol

In accordance with the overriding objective, the parties to all disputes will be expected to act reasonably in exchanging relevant information and documents and in generally trying to avoid the necessity for the start of proceedings, whether a case is covered by a pre-action protocol or not (PD – Protocols, para 4).

The expectation is, in fact, that there will eventually be pre-action protocols for many more types of dispute than Lord Woolf intended. There is a practice direction which applies to pre-action protocols, and when other pre-action protocols are drafted they will be specified in the schedule to the Protocols Practice Direction (PD – Protocols, para 1.2). Only the substance of the personal injury pre-action protocol is covered here.

INFORMATION ABOUT FUNDING ARRANGEMENTS[9]

Funding arrangements include conditional fee agreements, which provide for a success fee and after the event legal expenses insurance. Success fees and after the event insurance premiums fall within the definition of an additional liability and are potentially recoverable from an unsuccessful opponent under an order for costs so long as notification of the funding agreement has been given to the opponent in accordance with the relevant rules and practice directions. Under para 4A of the Protocols Practice Direction, the notification requirements include an obligation, even before proceedings are commenced, to inform an opponent that such an arrangement has been entered into.

This obligation applies whether the type of action involved is covered by a pre-action protocol or not (PD – Protocols, paras 4A1 and 4A2). The time within which the notification must be given is not specified, but it is likely that the same consequences will apply as where proceedings have been started and notification has not been given, namely that a party will not be able to recover any additional liability for any period in which he failed to provide information about the funding arrangement.[10]

---

9   See Chapter 38, Funding Litigation, for information about funding arrangements.
10   See r 44.3B(1)(c).

PRE-ACTION PROTOCOL FOR PERSONAL INJURY CLAIMS

Definition

The Practice Direction to the pre-action protocols simply states that pre-action protocols 'outline the steps parties should take to seek information from and provide information to each other about a prospective legal claim' (PD – Protocols, para 1.3). This is a modest definition, as the personal injury pre-action protocol not only outlines the steps that should be taken, but specifies in detail the information that should be provided at each step and recommends a standard format for the letter notifying the claim. It sets down a timescale within which those steps should be taken and includes schedules containing lists of documents that should be disclosed according to the type of personal injury claim brought.

Aims

The personal injury protocol states that its aims are to achieve:
- more pre-action contact between the parties;
- better and earlier exchange of information;
- better pre-accident investigation by both sides;
- to put the parties in a position where they may be able to settle cases fairly and early without litigation;
- to enable proceedings to run to the court's timetable and efficiently, if litigation does become necessary (Protocol, para 1.2).

The effect of the protocol

The personal injury pre-action protocol has an introduction and notes of guidance which explain the purpose and operation of the protocol. The introduction explains that one of the purposes of the protocol is to initiate good litigation and pre-litigation practice by introducing standard timescales for pre-litigation steps such as the notification of a claim and the response to that claim. It also aims to standardise the format in which claims are notified and which documents are disclosed (Protocol, para 1.3).

Viewed in this light, rather than being a mechanism for avoiding proceedings, the protocol could be seen as bringing proceedings, and more importantly, court control of an action, forward. If the court expects a standard format letter of claim to be used, then such a document becomes more akin to a statement of case.[11] If the court expects a particular timescale to be followed, then this is akin to the timetable laid down by the rules. The presumption is that, unless there is a good reason to depart from it, parties should follow the protocol and they can be penalised for an unreasonable failure to do so if proceedings are started. The introduction of the pre-action protocols results in a real blurring of the pre-issue and post-issue stage of proceedings. Although compliance with the protocol cannot be enforced, the potential consequences of non-compliance if proceedings are issued are such that it would be a very brave or foolhardy party that chooses, without good reason, not to comply.

Scope of the protocol

The notes of guidance to the protocol state that it is intended to apply to all actions which include a claim for personal injury and to the entirety of those claims, not just the personal injury element of them (Protocol, para 2.2). So, for instance, if there is a claim for personal injury and property damage, then the protocol will apply to the whole claim even if the personal injury claim forms only a small element of the whole action.

However, the notes of guidance then go on to say that the protocol is primarily intended for road traffic, tripping and slipping and accident at work cases which include an element of personal injury with a value of less than £15,000 and are likely to be allocated to the fast track (Protocol, para 2.3). The expressed reasoning for this is that, owing to the short timetable of 30 weeks between the start of proceedings and trial on the fast track, in order realistically to comply with the timetable and ensure that the case is ready for trial, the parties will need to have exchanged relevant information and narrowed the issues between them before proceedings are started.

The notes of guidance then proceed to widen the scope of the protocol again by stating that 'the spirit, if not the letter of the protocol, should still be followed for multi-track type claims' (para 2.4). From all of this it might be concluded that, although there is a new expectation of high levels of pre-action co-operation and transparency between the parties, it is only for those disputes which specifically fall under the auspices of a pre-action protocol that the detailed provision of the protocol, covering such matters as time limits for responding and specified disclosure, should be followed. In so far as personal injury actions are concerned, although the position is by no means certain, one interpretation could be that only fast track actions of the type specified are strictly covered by the protocol.

---

11 Although the notes of guidance to the protocol expressly state that it is not intended to have the same status as a statement of case.

Settling and stocktaking

The parties and their legal representatives are encouraged by para 2.13 to enter into discussions and/or negotiations prior to starting proceedings. The protocol does not specify when or how this might be done, but parties should bear in mind that the courts increasingly take the view that *litigation should be a last resort*, and that claims should not be issued prematurely when a settlement is in reasonable prospect.

Where settlement is not achieved, it is suggested by para 2.14 that the parties might wish to carry out a stocktake of the issues in dispute, and the evidence that the court is likely to need to decide those issues, *before proceedings are started*. Where the defendant is insured and the pre-action steps have been conducted by the insurer, the insurer would normally be expected to nominate solicitors to act in the proceedings and the claimant's solicitor is recommended to invite the insurer to nominate solicitors to act in the proceedings and do so 7–14 days before the intended issue date.

SUMMARY OF THE PERSONAL INJURY
PRE-ACTION PROTOCOL

Early notification

The notes of guidance to the protocol refer to the fact that in some cases, the claimant's legal representative may wish initially to notify the defendant of the likelihood of a claim being brought against him without sending a detailed letter of claim. This may be the case if the claimant is not yet in a position to send a detailed letter of claim, but wishes to give the defendant early notification of a potential claim. Examples given are where, for instance, the defendant is unlikely to have any, or only limited knowledge of the incident giving rise to the claim or if the claimant is incurring significant expense as a result of the accident which he expects to claim from the defendant. The protocol states that such early notification will not activate the timetable for responding (Protocol, para 2.6).

The letter of claim

The protocol sets out, at Annex A, a standard format of a letter of claim that should be used, or amended to suit a particular case. The letter of claim should contain a clear summary of the facts on which the claim is based, an indication of the nature of the injuries suffered and any financial loss incurred (Protocol, para 3.2). The only guidance as to how much detail should be provided about the claim at this stage is that 'sufficient information should be given in order to enable the defendant's insurer/solicitor to commence investigations and at least put a broad valuation on the "risk"' (Protocol, para 3.5).

Parties may naturally be wary about how they define their claim and response to claim in correspondence at this early stage, as it may differ from their later pleaded case and there is a risk that any inconsistencies may be used against them if the case goes to court. As a limited measure to protect the parties in this respect, and presumably to encourage openness, the notes of guidance, under the heading of 'status of letters of claim and response' expressly states that letters of claim and response are not intended to have the same status as a statement of case in proceedings.

Moreover, it is recognised that matters may come to light as a result of investigation after the letter of claim has been sent, or after the defendant has responded, and the notes of guidance state that 'these circumstances could mean that the "pleaded" case of one or both parties is presented slightly differently than in the letter of claim and response. It would not be consistent with the spirit of the protocol for a party to "take a point" on this in the proceedings, provided that there was no obvious intention by the party who changed their position to mislead the other party' (Protocol, para 2.9). However, intentional misleading aside, parties should still draft their letters of claim and responses with great care, as it would presumably be open to a party to 'take a point' when the presentation of the pleaded case is more than *slightly different* to how it is presented in this early correspondence.

Sending the letter of claim

As soon as sufficient information is available to substantiate a realistic claim, a claimant should send two copies of a letter of claim to the defendant, one for passing on to his insurers. The protocol states that this should be done before issues of quantum are addressed in detail (Protocol, para 3.1). Therefore, a letter of claim should be sent as soon as a potential claim is identified, even though the extent of the loss suffered is not yet fully quantified or quantifiable.

If the claimant knows the identity of the defendant's insurer, he should send a copy of the letter of claim directly to the insurer as well as to the defendant (Protocol, para 3.4). If the claimant does not know the identity of the defendant's insurer, he should ask for details in the letter of claim as well as including another copy of the letter of claim for the defendant to forward to his insurer (Protocol, para 3.1).

In road traffic accident claims, the letter of claim should provide the name and address of the hospital where treatment has been obtained and the claimant's hospital reference number (Protocol, para 3.2). The claimant's

National Insurance number and date of birth only need to be supplied once the defendant has responded to the letter of claim and confirmed the identity of the insurer (Protocol, para 3.4).

It is recognised in the notes of guidance to the protocol that the defendant may have no personal financial interest in the outcome of the dispute because he is insured. In those circumstances, court imposed sanctions will be ineffective against the defendant. For these reasons the draft letter of claim emphasises the importance of the defendant passing the letter of claim on to their insurers and warns the defendant that their insurance cover may be affected if they fail to do so. The notes of guidance also state that in those circumstances where the defendant has delayed passing the letter of claim on to his insurers, the insurers would be justified in asking the claimant for more time to respond to the letter of claim (Protocol, para 2.7).

The defendant's response

The protocol allows the defendant a two stage response to the claimant's claim. The initial response can be simply an acknowledgment of the claim, which indicates to the claimant that the matter is being investigated and that the claimant should hold off from issuing proceedings. The defendant then has a period of time to investigate, after which a full letter of response should follow.

The defendant should reply within 21 calendar days of the date of posting of the letter of claim, identifying the insurer (if any). The protocol states that if there is no reply within that time limit, either from the defendant or insurer, the claimant will be entitled to issue proceedings (Protocol, para 3.6). The defendant (or his insurers) has a maximum of three months from the date of acknowledgment of the claimant's letter of claim to investigate the claim. The defendant or his insurers should reply within that three month time limit stating whether liability is denied and giving reasons for any denial (Protocol, para 3.7). Where liability is admitted, it will be presumed that the defendant is bound by this admission for all claims with a total value of up to £15,000.

Disclosure of documents

The protocol encourages voluntary early disclosure of relevant documents which would be likely to be the subject of an order for disclosure either through an application for pre-action disclosure or by disclosure in the course of proceedings (Protocol, para 3.10). To this end, Annex B to the protocol contains standard disclosure lists identifying types of document which are likely to be material to the types of dispute specifically covered by the protocol. So, there are standard disclosure lists for road traffic accident, tripping and slipping and workplace claims. The idea is that when the defendant receives a letter of claim in respect of one of these types of disputes, he should consult the list and voluntarily disclose, with the letter of reply, any documents he may have which are identified on the list. The lists are not intended to be exhaustive, so the defendant should also disclose any other relevant 'disclosable' documents even if they are not on the list (Protocol, para 3.10).

Where the claimant's investigation of the claim is well advanced, the notes of guidance state that the claimant's letter of claim could indicate which classes of document are considered relevant for early disclosure by the defendant (Protocol, para 3.11). In the absence of this degree of preparedness by the claimant, the implication is that the defendant will identify the relevant documents and voluntarily disclose them without any specific request from the claimant.

Where the defendant alleges contributory negligence of the claimant, he should give reasons for this and disclose any documents from the list relevant to this issue and the claimant should respond to these allegations before proceedings are issued (Protocol, para 3.12).

Although Lord Woolf recommended that disclosure be enforced through practice directions, in fact that recommendation was not followed, and disclosure under the protocol is entirely voluntary. However, if a party refuses to disclose relevant documents without good reason, the other party may be able to make use of the provisions on pre-action disclosure under s 33 of the Supreme Court Act 1981 and s 53 of the County Courts Act 1984 to enforce compliance with their request.[12] It should always be remembered also that any unreasonable conduct and failure to follow an appropriate protocol can be taken into account by the court and makes a party vulnerable to sanctions if proceedings are commenced.

Single joint expert

One of the most controversial aspects of the introduction of the personal injury pre-action protocol and the reforms to expert evidence in the fast track was the introduction of provisions for a single joint expert. The idea is that rather than both parties instructing their own expert, the selection of a single joint expert is agreed between the parties; when the report is obtained by the instructing party, it is disclosed to the other side, but relied upon by both parties. In order to make such a provision fully effective, the single joint expert needs to be instructed before either party instructs their own expert. If a party goes ahead and instructs their own expert, before trying to agree a single joint

---

12 See Chapter 29, Disclosure of Documents.

expert with the other side, they run the risk that the court will order the appointment of a single joint expert and that party will be unable to recover the costs of their own expert.

The pre-action protocol sets out steps a party should follow in order to agree to the instruction of a single joint expert. Annex C to the pre-action protocol contains a draft letter of instruction to a medical expert.

The notes of guidance set out the aims of the protocol for the instruction of a single joint expert. The intention is for this to apply in relation to medical experts, but the protocol does not rule out the possibility of it applying to other types of experts, such as engineers (Protocol, para 2.11). In the vast majority of personal injury cases, the only expert evidence will be medical evidence. The notes of guidance explain that the idea is for the claimant to obtain the medical report from the agreed joint expert, and disclose it to the defendant, who can agree it or ask questions. This will then be the agreed medical evidence in the case and the expectation is that the defendant will not obtain his own expert report (para 2.11). The notes of guidance also refer to the fact that some solicitors obtain experts through medical agencies rather than from a specific doctor or hospital. In those circumstances, the protocol states that if the defendant so requests, the agency should be asked to provide the names of the doctors whom they are considering instructing (para 2.12).

The expert evidence provisions of the protocol apply to both parties, not just the claimant. Therefore, the instruction of a single joint expert could come through the initiative of the defendant rather than the claimant. The protocol refers to the 'first party' as the party proposing and eventually instructing the expert, and the 'second party' as the party asked to agree to the proposal and instruction of the expert. Paragraph 3.14 of the protocol provides that:

> Before any party instructs an expert he should give the other party a list of the *name(s)* of *one or more experts* in the relevant speciality whom he considers are suitable to instruct.

Where it is a medical expert, the protocol states that the claimant's solicitor will obtain access to the claimant's medical records (para 3.15).

The second party will then have 14 days in which to object to one or more of the named experts. The first party should then instruct a mutually acceptable expert (para 3.16). If the second party objects to all the listed experts, the parties may then instruct experts of their own choice. However, such a course of conduct runs the risk of the court finding that one or both parties behaved unreasonably in not agreeing an expert (para 3.17).

Once an agreed expert has been nominated, the second party is not entitled to rely upon his own expert evidence within that speciality unless the first party agrees, the court so directs or the first party's expert report has been amended and the first party is not prepared to disclose the original report (para 3.18).

Either party can send written questions on the report via the first party's solicitors. The expert should send the answers to the questions separately and directly to each party (para 3.19).

The instructing first party usually pays the fee for the agreed expert's report. However, if a party asks questions of the expert, the party asking the questions usually meets the cost of the expert replying to the questions (para 3.20).

The protocol also provides that if the defendant admits liability in whole or in part, before proceedings are issued, any agreed medical report should be disclosed to the defendant. The claimant should postpone issuing proceedings for 21 days from disclosure of the report to see if a settlement can be reached (para 3.21).

SUMMARY OF CLINICAL NEGLIGENCE PRE-ACTION PROTOCOL

Purpose

The purpose (as stated in the protocol) is:
- to maintain/restore the patient health care provider relationship;
- to resolve as many disputes as possible without recourse to litigation to encourage openness and awareness of options; and
- to reduce delay and costs.

The protocol contains fairly detailed advice to healthcare providers and patients as to reporting procedures, the supply of hospital records and referral to ADR.

Contents of the protocol

As with the personal injury protocol above, there is a letter of claim (Protocol, Appendix C1). This must contain a clear summary of the facts; the main allegations of negligence; details of the patient's injuries; the claimant's financial losses in outline; and, in more complex cases, a chronology of events. There should be reference to any relevant documents plus copies if they are not already in the defendant's possession. It is also advised that the letter also contains an offer to settle, if relevant.

As far as the defendant's response is concerned (Protocol, Appendix C2), this should acknowledge receipt of the letter of claim within 14 days of its receipt. It should be followed by a reasoned answer within three months, with an admission, or part admission, or specific denial, together with any documents relied on. The full response should also respond to any claimant's offer to settle.

Experts

The protocol states that 'it is recognised that in clinical negligence disputes the parties and their advisers will require flexibility in their approach to expert evidence'. Expert opinions may be needed on breach of duty and causation; on patient's condition and prognosis; to assist in valuing the claim.

SANCTIONS FOR FAILURE TO FOLLOW THE PROTOCOLS

The pre-action protocols are 'codes of sensible practice which parties are expected to follow when they are faced with the prospect of litigation in an area to which a protocol applies'.[13] For proceedings to which a protocol applies, the court will expect the parties to comply in substance with the relevant protocol (PD – Protocols, para 2.2). Although a party cannot be compelled to comply with a pre-action protocol, any non-compliance may be penalised in a variety of ways if proceedings are commenced.

Under the case management powers set out in Part 3, the court can take into account the compliance or non-compliance with a pre-action protocol when giving directions for the management of proceedings (r 3.1(4)). So, the court may refuse to grant additional time for the doing of any act which should have been complied with under a pre-action protocol. Also, the power of the court, once proceedings are begun, to order a party to pay a sum of money into court, includes the circumstances where a party has refused, without good reason, to comply with a relevant pre-action protocol (r 3.1(5)). When making such an order, the court must have regard to the amount in dispute and the costs which the parties have incurred or may incur (r 3.1(6)).

The court must also take into account the conduct of the parties when making an order for costs and the conduct of the parties includes conduct before, as well as during proceedings and, in particular, whether a party has followed any relevant pre-action protocol (r 44.3(5)(a)). Therefore, although the general rule is that the unsuccessful party will be ordered to pay the successful party's costs (r 44.3(2)), the successful party may be deprived of some or all of his costs, or ordered to pay costs to the unsuccessful party, if he has failed to comply with a pre-action protocol.

As well as the above powers, the court has the powers set out in the Pre-action Protocol Practice Direction. The test as to whether these sanctions

---

13 See Final Report, Chapter 10, p 108, para 6. (*Ibid.*)

should be imposed is whether the defaulting party's conduct caused proceedings to be commenced or costs to be incurred which would otherwise not have been (PD – Protocols, para 2.3). The court will aim to place the innocent party in no worse a position than if the protocol had been complied with (PD – Protocols, para 2.4). Therefore, the court will only impose the following sanctions if non-compliance with a protocol has made a difference to the conduct or outcome of proceedings, something which in some circumstances may be very difficult to weigh up.

The sanctions that may be imposed are:

- an order that the party at fault pay all or part of the other party's costs of the proceedings (PD – Protocols, para 2.3(1));
- If the above order is made, the court can order that those costs are paid on an indemnity basis (PD – Protocols, para 2.3(2));
- If the party at fault is a claimant who has been awarded damages, an order depriving that party of interest for a specified period or awarding interest at a lower rate than would otherwise have been awarded (PD – Protocols, para 2.3(3));
- If the party at fault is a defendant who has been ordered to pay damages to the claimant, an order that that party pay interest for a specified period at a higher rate, not exceeding 10% above base rate, than would otherwise be awarded (PD – Protocols, para 2.3(4)).

The Practice Direction to the protocols gives examples of how each party may have failed to comply with a protocol. So, for instance, a claimant may have failed to provide sufficient information to the defendant or failed to follow the procedure for the instruction of a single joint expert (para 3.1). On the other hand, a defendant may have failed to make a preliminary response to the letter of claim within the specified time of 21 days, or failed to make a full response within the specified time of three months or failed to disclose relevant disclosable documents (para 3.2). However, from the wording of the protocol, mere failure to follow the protocol itself will not be enough to invoke the court's powers to impose a penalty on the defaulting party; the court will still have to be satisfied that the failure caused proceedings to be commenced or costs incurred which would otherwise not have been.

Compliance with a protocol is therefore not mandatory, and in some circumstances a party may escape any penalty even if they did not comply. However, there is an expectation that the substance of a relevant protocol will be followed and unless a party has a good reason for not doing so, a party who has not complied is likely to face a penalty subsequently if proceedings are commenced, either during the course of proceedings or at the end of proceedings when costs and other orders are made. However, given the fact that a sanction is not automatic for failure to follow the protocol and the court has to be satisfied that the failure had some effect on the commencement of proceedings or the incurring of costs, it is likely that much time and costs will be incurred in arguing that issue if a party asks for such a penalty to be imposed.

Transitional provisions

The court will not take into account compliance or non-compliance with any relevant pre-action protocol for actions started before the relevant protocol came into force (PD – Protocols, para 5.2). For actions started after the date a relevant protocol came into force, the court will take compliance or non-compliance into account except where the parties did not have sufficient time to comply with any requirements of the protocol between the publication date and the coming into force of the protocol (PD – Protocols, para 5.4). Both parties are asked in the allocation questionnaire[14] whether they have complied with a relevant pre-action protocol, and if not, why not.

PRE-ACTION BEHAVIOUR IN ALL CASES

It has long been acknowledged that most cases settle and only a small minority of cases make it to a court hearing, and in fact the court system would probably collapse if that were not the case. It could be said that, unless publicity was an aim of the client, a lawyer's function is to settle a dispute without litigation. The old rules contained a number of devices to aid the settlement of disputes without litigation, by means of, for example, 'without prejudice' offers, and payments into court. Also, under the old rules, if a party commenced proceedings without at least sending a 'letter before action', he could be penalised in costs. The rationale was that it was wasteful to incur the costs of issuing proceedings in circumstances where, if the defendant had been formally requested to pay the damages or provide the relief claimed, he would have complied. However, although the settlement of disputes was an aim supported under the old rules, and procedures were in place to encourage it, the requirement to try and settle a dispute, or the quality or length of the negotiations devoted to this end were not something that the courts were concerned with.

In commenting on the change of ethos brought about by the new rules when considering the policy behind without prejudice negotiations, Laddie J, in *Unilever v Procter & Gamble*,[15] said:

Although the courts have always been prepared to encourage settlement of proceedings, in the past that encouragement was of a hands-off variety. The current climate is very different. It is no longer sufficient to hope that the

---

14 See Chapter 15, Judicial Case Management: Allocation.
15 [1999] 2 All ER 691.

parties have the sense to resolve their disputes without litigation. Now parties are to be penalised if they commence proceedings without first trying to resolve their differences.

Although the old approach had begun to change even before the new rules came into force (see, for instance, the Commercial Court Practice Note [1994] 1 All ER 34, which led to changes in the Guide to Commercial Court Practice so as to include questions in the 'Pre-Trial Check List' as to whether the parties had considered ADR), it is clear that the ethos under the new rules is profoundly different from that under the old. Now parties in all types of case must make, or at least appear to make, strenuous efforts to settle the action before starting proceedings or risk facing costs and other penalties. Encouraging settlement of actions is a fundamental aim of the new rules.

PRE-ACTION PROTOCOLS AND COSTS

When it comes to assessment of costs, the costs rules provide[16] that in deciding whether costs were reasonably incurred or are proportionate, the court may take into account the efforts made, if any, before and during the proceedings in order to try to resolve the dispute. Both sides may make offers to settle at the pre-proceedings stage with consequent sanctions for failure to accept if the case is unnecessarily prolonged.

Strictly, there are no costs within the pre-action protocols themselves except on a retrospective basis, that is, if proceedings do not settle and litigation ensues, then the court can consider any costs incurred as part of the pre-action process. More recently, the rules have been amended to allow proceedings to be issued where all other matters apart from costs have been resolved.[17] These proceedings may, however, be defeated by a defendant filing an acknowledgment disputing the use of such proceedings. Thereafter, the claimant has to issue proceedings for the whole of the claim and not just the costs.

---

16 See Chapter 33, Costs.
17 See r 44.12A and Chapter 33, Costs.

CHAPTER 5

JUDICIAL CASE MANAGEMENT: THE OVERRIDING OBJECTIVE

INTRODUCTION

The essence of case management is that the court, rather than litigants or their legal advisers, exercises responsibility for the control of litigation. Although our system is still an adversarial one, case management gives the court an interventionist role. Case management covers such matters as identifying the issues in the case; summarily disposing of some issues and deciding what order issues should be resolved; setting timetables for steps to be taken in the proceedings; controlling the amount of disclosure of documents necessary for a case; limiting the amount of expert and other evidence that should be heard and setting timetables for the conduct of the trial.

Notwithstanding these specific aspects, the overall purpose of case management is to encourage settlement of disputes at the earliest opportunity and, if this is not achieved, and a trial is necessary, for this to take place as soon as possible by means of a cost-effective hearing strictly limited to resolution of the true issues in dispute and strictly limited in duration.[1]

THE OVERRIDING OBJECTIVE

The overriding objective of the new rules is to enable the court to deal with cases justly (r 1.1(1)). The court has a duty to give effect to the overriding objective when exercising any power under the CPR or when interpreting the CPR (r 1.2).

It was thought that the old civil procedure system had become too rigid, being bound by case precedent, and the new rules were designed to give the court more flexibility in dealing with individual cases. In this way, it is not intended that case precedents as such will be part of the new system and the case management judge will be free to decide what action is necessary for the case before him simply by applying the rules in the light of the overriding objective. This view was reiterated by the Court of Appeal in *Hamblin v Field*[2] when they said that excessive quoting of authorities was not of much assistance in applications to strike out in view of the wide discretion now

---

1   See *Access to Justice*, Interim Report, Chapter 5 (www.lcd.gov.uk/civil/interfr.htm).
2   (2000) *The Times*, 26 April.

given to the courts when dealing with such matters.[3] In any event, it has been held that earlier authorities on matters of civil procedure decided before the CPR came into effect are no longer generally of any relevance to the application of the CPR.[4]

The parties also have a duty to help the court to further the overriding objective (r 1.3). An obvious example of this would be an obligation on the parties to co-operate in providing information to the other party about their case and in actively seeking ways to settle the dispute. However, the obligation seems to go further in that in one case, it was said to include an obligation to alert your opponent to the fact that they are using the wrong forms and procedure to pursue a case.[5] Further, it may no longer be appropriate for one party (usually the defendant) to sit back and allow the other party to do nothing.[6]

The rules contain a list of what dealing justly with cases includes. These are:

- ensuring that parties are on an equal footing;
- saving expense;
- dealing with the case in ways which are proportionate:
  (a) to the amount of money involved;
  (b) to the importance of the case;
  (c) to the complexity of the issues; and
  (d) to the financial position of each party;
- ensuring that the case is dealt with expeditiously and fairly; and
- allotting to it an appropriate share of the court's resources, while taking into account the need to allot resources to other cases (r 1.1(2)).

A common theme is the concept of proportionality which could indeed be said to be one of the cornerstones of the CPR. The message is that excessive amounts of time, money and resources should not be expended in pursuing proceedings out of proportion to the value and importance of the matter in dispute. Whilst it is obviously for a party to decide how much time and money to devote to pursuing a case, if the costs are disproportionate they may not all be recovered from an unsuccessful opponent. Also, if court proceedings are started, the court will be able to exert case management control over the conduct of the proceedings and the amount of court resources devoted to resolving the dispute.

---

3   See also *Purdy v Cambran* (1999) Lawtel, 17 December, CA (unreported elsewhere).
4   See judgment of Lord Woolf MR in *Biguzzi v Rank Leisure plc* [1999] 1 WLR 1926; [1999] 4 All ER 934, CA.
5   *Hannigan v Hannigan* [2000] 2 FCR 650; (2000) *The Independent*, 23 May, CA; [2000] ILR, 3 July, CA.
6   *Khalili v Christopher Bennett and Others* (2000) EMLR 996, CA.

Note that the application of proportionality is both subjective – are the resources being spent on the particular case proportionate? – and objective – are the resources being spent on the case proportionate in relation to other cases that the court has to deal with? Thus, the court may feel that it is not worth devoting a lot of court time and resources to a case where the value of the claim does not warrant it, for example, neighbour disputes over small strips of land.

The court's duty set out in Part 1 to deal with cases justly in accordance with the overriding objective does not refer to its decision making role at trial. It is the way the court deals with the case *en route* to trial and the organisation of the trial hearing that the overriding objective is aimed at. The rules expressly oblige the court to further the overriding objective through active case management (r 1.4(1)).

Active case management

Specific case management functions are set out in the CPR for each procedural stage of a case, for example, allocation to one of the case management tracks. However, apart from these specific case management functions, the court is also given a general list of what active case management involves. Active case management therefore includes:

- encouraging the parties to co-operate with each other in the conduct of the proceedings;
- identifying the issues at an early stage;
- deciding promptly which issues need full investigation and trial and accordingly disposing summarily of the others;
- deciding the order in which issues are to be resolved;
- encouraging the parties to use an alternative dispute resolution procedure if the court considers that appropriate and facilitating the use of such procedure;
- helping the parties to settle the whole or part of the case;
- fixing timetables or otherwise controlling the progress of the case;
- considering whether the likely benefits of taking a particular step justify the cost of taking it;
- dealing with as many aspects of the case as it can on the same occasion;
- dealing with the case without the parties needing to attend at court;
- making use of technology; and
- giving directions to ensure that the trial of a case proceeds quickly and efficiently (r 1.4(2)).

GENERAL POWERS OF CASE MANAGEMENT

Part 3 of the CPR contains a list of general powers of judicial case management. These powers, as with all the court's powers under the rules, must be exercised in accordance with the overriding objective.[7] This general list is expressly stated to be in addition to any powers given to the court by any other rule, practice direction, enactment or any other powers the court may have (r 3.1(1)). It should therefore be recognised that, although wide ranging, these powers are not the extent of the court's judicial case management powers and r 3.1 expressly preserves the court's inherent jurisdiction to protect its process from abuse.

On the other hand, it should also be recognised that the court's general powers cannot be applied to vary the operation of a rule, practice direction or court order if the particular rule, practice direction or court order is expressed not to be subject to such variation (r 3.1(2)). Further, where the court makes an order, the court can also vary or revoke the order it has made (r 3.1(7)).

Rules as to time

The court has the power to extend or shorten the time for compliance with any rule, practice direction or court order. For example, in *George Barker v Joyce Jane Casserly and Others*[8] it was said that it would be extraordinary (and contrary to a claimant's rights under Art 6 of the ECHR) for the court to have no power to extend the period for service of a CPR Part 8 claim.

Although a party is more likely to be successful in seeking extra time for compliance if the application is made before the original time for compliance has expired, the court also has the power to grant extra time even if the application is made *after* the time for compliance has expired (r 3.1(2)(a)).

The circumstances in which a party may wish to apply to shorten time for compliance are, for instance, if he is required to serve a document on a party within at least a minimum time period before a hearing, but he has failed to do so.

Although the CPR were drafted on the premise that parties should carry out procedural steps within the time specified by the Rules or the court, this rule ensures that the court has the power to grant a party an indulgence if justice requires.

The court also has the power to adjourn or bring forward a hearing (r 3.1(2)(b)).

---

7   See r 1.2.
8   (2000) Lawtel, 24 October, Fam (Johnson J) (unreported elsewhere).

Attendance at and form of hearing

The court has a general power to order a party or their legal representative to attend court (r 3.1(2)(c)). For instance, the court may require attendance at an allocation hearing in order to assist the court to decide which track to allocate a case to. This is particularly true of case management conferences where the person attending must be familiar with the case and able to deal with all issues which may arise,[9] in default of which a wasted costs order may be made if an adjournment is necessitated.[10]

The court can decide to receive evidence or hold a hearing by means of a video link or the telephone (r 3.1(2)(d)). This power is being more and more regularly used as it is recognised to be more cost effective for parties and the court to hold hearings by such means rather than require parties to attend oral hearings at court. The new form of General Application[11] contains provision for the applicant to request a telephone conference and many judges' chambers are provided with suitable equipment for the purpose.

Managing the issues in a case

Part of the general powers of case management enable the court to direct the order in which issues are heard and whether parts of the case should be heard separately or at a different time.

Therefore, the court can:

- direct that part of any proceedings (for example, a counterclaim) is dealt with as separate proceedings (r 3.1(2)(e));
- stay the whole or part of any proceedings or judgment either generally or until a specified date or event (r 3.1(2)(f));
- consolidate proceedings (r 3.1(2)(g));
- try two or more claims on the same occasion (r 3.1(2)(h));
- direct a separate trial of any issue (r 3.1(2)(i));
- decide the order in which issues are to be tried (r 3.1(2)(j)).

Active case management also requires the court to exercise decisions as to which are the real issues in dispute between the parties despite how a party has presented his case. Therefore, the court has the power to:

- exclude an issue from consideration (r 3.1(2)(k));
- dismiss or give judgment on a claim after a decision on a preliminary issue (r 3.1(2)(l)).

---

9   CPR, r 29.3(2) and PD 29, para 5.2(2).
10 PD 29, para 5.3 and see *Baron v Lovell* (1999) *The Times*, 14 September, CA and Chapter 18, The Multi-Track, p 200 and Chapter 33, Costs, p 413.
11 Form N244.

Further powers

As a reflection of the fact that the court is not limited in its role of managing cases in order to achieve a just result, there is also provision in the list of general powers for the court to take any other step or make any other order for the purpose of managing the case and furthering the overriding objective (r 3.1(2)(m)).

ORDERING SUMS TO BE PAID INTO COURT

Power to impose conditions on orders

The court has the power to make an order subject to conditions, including the payment of a sum of money into court (r 3.1(3)(a)). The court also has the power to specify the consequences of failure to comply with an order or any condition (r 3.1(3)(b)).

Payment into court on failure to comply with a rule, practice direction or court order

If a party without good reason fails to comply with a rule, practice direction or applicable pre-action protocol, the court may order that party to pay a sum of money into court as punishment (r 3.1(5)). When deciding whether to exercise this power, the court, however, must have regard to the amount in dispute and the costs which the parties have incurred or may incur (r 3.1(6)). The court is likely to be proportionate when deciding on the amount a party must pay into court and should ensure that the imposition of this penalty does not make it impossible for a party to continue with the litigation.[12] However, a party cannot complain that the amount ordered is difficult for him to pay and a party is likely to have to be prepared to provide full and frank disclosure of his financial circumstances in order to avoid or reduce the amount ordered to be paid into court.[13]

Where a party is ordered to pay a sum of money into court, the money shall be security for any sum payable by that party to any other party in the proceedings. However, a defendant can instead elect to treat any ordered payment in as a Part 36 payment (r 3.1(6A)).[14]

---

12 See *Chapple v Williams and Others* (1999) Lawtel, 8 December, CA (unreported elsewhere).

13 See *Training in Compliance Ltd (T/A Matthew Read) v Christopher Paul Dewse (T/A Data Research Co)*, CA, unreported.

14 See Chapter 24, Offers to Settle and Payments into Court.

COURT MAKING ORDERS OF ITS OWN INITIATIVE

A major innovation of the CPR was to give power to the court to make orders of its own initiative instead of only being able to exercise powers on the application of a party. Rule 3.3(1) provides, therefore, that the court can exercise its powers either on an application or of its own initiative, unless expressly restricted from doing so by a rule or some other enactment.

When making an order of its own initiative the court can either:

- notify any party likely to be affected by the order that it is proposing to make the order and give that party an opportunity to make representations *before* the order is made (r 3.3(2)(a)). If the court decides to hear representations before making the order, it must notify the affected parties of the specified time and the manner by which their representations must be made (r 3.3(2)(b)). The court does not have to hold a hearing to decide whether to make the order and can order written representation to be made instead. Where a hearing is to be held, the court must give any affected party at least three days' notice of the hearing (r 3.3(3)(b)); or

- make the order without hearing the parties or giving them an opportunity to make representations (r 3.3(4)). If the court makes an order of its own initiative without hearing the parties or giving them an opportunity to make representations, a party affected by the order has the right to apply to have it set aside, varied or stayed, and the court order must inform the party of his right to do so (r 3.3(5)). The application challenging the order must be made within the time period specified by the court in the order or, if none is specified, not more than seven days after the date on which the order was served on the party (r 3.3(6)).

SANCTIONS FOR NON-PAYMENT OF CERTAIN FEES

It was recognised that with the introduction of case management, judicial and court staff would have a greater burden imposed upon them in carrying out their new functions and that parties may be asked to contribute to the additional costs resulting from the reforms. Since the introduction of the CPR, it is no coincidence that there has also been a dramatic rise in the level of court fees in bringing a civil action as well as the introduction of new fees at various stages in the proceedings, most noticeably at allocation and listing.

Allocation and listing fees

A fee is payable by the claimant when the allocation questionnaire[15] and listing questionnaire[16] are filed unless the claimant successfully applies for an exemption from or remission of payment of the fee.[17] However, even in those cases where the court has dispensed with the need for an allocation or listing questionnaire, or one is not required under the rules, the fee will still be payable. In those circumstances, the fee will be payable either within 14 days of the date the notice of allocation to track has been sent to the parties by the court, or where there is automatic allocation or no allocation to a track, within 28 days of the filing of the defence, or if there is more than one defendant, the last defence, or within 28 days of expiry of the time for filing all defences if sooner.[18]

An allocation fee will not be payable when the only claim is to recover a sum of money which does not exceed £1,000. Also, no listing fee is payable for a case allocated to the small claims track as listing questionnaires are not normally used.[19]

In the usual course of events, the court serving the allocation or listing questionnaire on the claimant will also remind the claimant of the fee that is due on filing of that document. If the claimant does not pay the relevant fee at the time that it is due, or apply for exemption from or remission of payment, the court will, in the first instance, serve a notice on the claimant requiring payment of the fee (r 3.7(2)). The court will also give a deadline by which the fee must be received (r 3.7(3)).

Sanction for non-payment

If the claimant does not pay the fee, or make an application for exemption from or remission of the fee, by the date specified in the court notice, the claim will be struck out and the claimant will be liable for the defendant's costs of the action unless the court orders otherwise (r 3.7(4)).

If the claimant has made an application for exemption from or remission of payment of the allocation or listing fee, but the application is refused, the court will serve a notice on the claimant requiring payment of the relevant fee by a specified date (r 3.7(5)). Again, if the fee is not paid by the specified date, the claim will be struck out and the claimant will be liable for the defendant's costs of the action unless the court orders otherwise (r 3.7(6)).

---

15 See Chapter 15, Judicial Case Management: Allocation, p 155.
16 See Chapter 17, The Fast Track, p 191 and Chapter 18, The Multi-Track, p 201.
17 See County Court Fees Order 1999 SI 1999/689, r 5.
18 *Ibid*, r 2.1.
19 *Ibid*, rr 2.1 and 2.2.

A claimant whose claim has been struck out will be able to apply to have his claim reinstated under the court's general powers to grant relief from sanctions under r 3.9.[20] If the court grants relief and reinstates the claim, this will be conditional on the claimant paying the relevant fee or filing evidence of exemption from payment or remission of the fee within two days of the date of the order granting such relief (r 3.7(7)).

If a claim is struck out for failure to pay the relevant fee, the court will notify the defendant that this has occurred (PD 3B, para 1).

In a case where an interim injunction has been obtained, the interim injunction will cease to have effect 14 days after the date the claim is struck out under r 3.7 (r 25.11 and PD 3B, para 2). However, if the claimant applies to reinstate the claim before the interim injunction ceases to have effect, the injunction will continue until the hearing of the application unless the court orders otherwise (r 25.11(2) and PD 3B, para 2).

SANCTIONS

A major change under the CPR was the introduction of the rule that a sanction specified by a rule would have effect unless a party obtained relief from the sanction (r 3.8). Under the old rules, if a party failed to comply with a rule or practice direction, the other party would have to apply to the court for any sanction to be imposed. Lord Woolf was of the opinion that this practice was one of the causes of delay under the old system, was a disincentive to compliance with the rules and allowed a party to act oppressively towards his opponent. He also believed that in order for the new system of case management to work, there must be an effective system of sanctions in operation designed to prevent and deter breaches of the rules rather than to punish.[21]

Sanctions applying automatically

Rule 3.8 states that where a party has failed to comply with a rule, practice direction or court order, any sanction for failure to comply imposed by the rule, practice direction or court order has effect unless the party in default applies for and obtains relief from the sanction.

Moreover, where the sanction is the payment of costs, the party in default can only obtain relief by appealing against the order for costs (r 3.8(2)).

---

20 See below, p 62, Relief from sanctions.
21 See *Access to Justice*, Final Report, Chapter 6 (www.lcd.gov.uk/civil/finalfr.htm).

Parties agreeing extra time for compliance

It was very common under the old rules for parties to agree to provide extra time to each other for compliance with the rules. So, for instance, it was very common for the parties to grant each other extra time to file pleadings (statements of case). Such agreements were common because, if a party did not agree, the court would, in most cases, grant extra time for doing the act in any event (unless the delay was inordinate and inexcusable, had caused prejudice to the other party and the limitation period for the cause of action had expired).

Under the CPR, if a rule, practice direction or court order requires a party to do something within a specified time and specifies the consequences of failure to comply, the time for doing it may not be extended simply by agreement between the parties (r 3.8(3)).

Although it is possible for the parties to agree to grant each other extra time to do something (if the rule does not include the time and consequences elements set out in r 3.8(3)), such agreement can always be overridden by the court in the exercise of its general powers of case management.[22]

RELIEF FROM SANCTIONS

In accordance with the general scheme of the CPR, the court has a wide discretion, in accordance with the overriding objective, to decide whether to grant relief to a party from any sanction imposed for failure to comply with a rule, practice direction or court order.

Rule 3.9 states that when hearing any application for relief from a sanction imposed for failure to comply with any rule, practice direction or court order, the court will consider all the circumstances of the case. However, the rule also goes on to provide a list of the matters that will be considered by the court when exercising its discretion to grant relief and it has been held that the court should consider each matter in this list systematically.[22a] This list is broadly based on the test set out in the case of *Rastin v British Steel*,[22b] a decision made before the CPR came into effect, but endorsed and adopted by Lord Woolf in his drafting of the rules.[23] The following matters will be included among the circumstances the court will consider:

---

22   See above, p 56, General powers of case management.
22a See *Bansal v Cheema* (2000) unreported, 2 March; CA transcript 358 of 2000.
22b [1994] 1 WLR 732.
23   See Final Report, Chapter 6, p 75, para 14. (*Ibid.*)

- the interests of the administration of justice;
- whether the application for relief was made promptly;
- whether the failure to comply was intentional;
- whether there is a good explanation for the failure;
- the extent to which the party in default has complied with other rules, practice directions, court orders and any relevant pre-action protocol;
- whether the failure to comply was caused by the party or his legal representative;
- whether the trial date or the likely trial date can still be met if relief is granted;
- the effect which the failure to comply had on each party; and
- the effect which the granting of relief would have on each party (r 3.9(1)(a)–(i)).

The application for relief should be made under Part 23[24] and must be supported by evidence (r 3.9(2)). Any sanction imposed should be proportionate.[25]

It is likely that the court will order summary assessment and immediate payment (that is, within 14 days) of the costs of the application by the party in default.

ERRORS OF PROCEDURE

If a party makes an error in procedure, for instance, fails to use the correct prescribed form, the court has a general power to remedy the error (r 3.10).

This power to correct an error in procedure should be distinguished from the power to grant relief from a sanction. In any event, this rule only applies for a failure to comply with a rule or practice direction, and not for failure to comply with a court order.

Technical defects, for example, the use of an incorrect form, should be considered in the light of the overriding objective.[26]

---

24 See Chapter 19, Making Applications for Court Orders.
25 *Luttenberger v Prince* (2000) Lawtel, 3 April, QBD (Nelson J) (unreported elsewhere); *Keith v CPM Field Marketing Ltd* (2000) *The Times*, 29 August, CA.
26 *Hannigan v Hannigan* [2000] 2 FCR 650; (2000) *The Independent*, 23 May, CA; [2000] ILR, 3 July, CA.

CHAPTER 6

PARTIES TO AND TITLE OF PROCEEDINGS

INTRODUCTION

The issue of whom a party may sue in respect of a cause of action is a question of substantive law. However, having decided upon the person or body to sue, rules of procedure govern how that person or body must be identified in the title of the proceedings.

TITLE OF PROCEEDINGS

The claim form and every other statement of case must be headed with the title of the proceedings. Practice Direction 7 includes provisions as to the title of the proceedings. In respect of the claim form, for which the prescribed forms N1[1] or N208[2] must be used, the notes for guidance on completing the claim form should also be taken into account. The title should state:

- the number of the proceedings;
- the court or division in which they are proceeding;
- the full name of each party and his status in the proceedings (that is, claimant/defendant);
- where there is more than one claimant (and/or more than one defendant), the parties should be numbered and described as follows, as the case may be:

(1) AB

(2) CD Claimants (PD 7, para 4.1).

The number of the proceedings

Obviously, when completing the claim form for filing and issue at court, the claimant will not be in a position to know the number of the proceedings, so at this stage the relevant part of the claim form and any statement of case is left blank. Once proceedings are issued, the court will give the proceedings a number and send a notice of issue to the claimant on which the number of the

---

1 See Chapter 7, Starting an Action, p 75.
2 See Chapter 14, Part 8 Claims, p 145.

proceedings will be entered. The court will also enter the number onto the claim form, a copy of which will be served on the defendant.

The heading of statements of case

Despite the reforms brought about by the CPR to the content of statements of case (formerly known as pleadings), and the absence of detailed rules as to how the heading of statements of case must be presented, a conventional heading is usually adopted by legal representatives which is the same as was formerly used under the old rules. The convention is for the court or division in which the matter is proceeding to appear on the top left hand corner of the document in capital letters. The number of the proceedings appears on the same line but at the right hand side of the document. On the next line appears the word 'between' and the names of the parties appear beneath this, in the centre, separated with the word 'and', while the party's status appears alongside at the far right hand side and underlined. The type of statement of case is presented in capital letters beneath the title and enclosed in tramlines.

An example is as follows:

IN THE CHELTENHAM COUNTY COURT   **Claim no: CH123**

Between

MARY SMITH   <u>Claimant</u>

-and-

ANN BROWN   <u>Defendant</u>

PARTICULARS OF CLAIM

PARTIES TO PROCEEDINGS

Different rules apply to such matters as how a party is described in proceedings and how he is served[3] with documents depending on the capacity of that party. The various capacities in which a party can be sued are set out below.

Individuals

The notes for the claimant on completing a claim form (attached to the claim form) provide that when a party is suing or being sued as an individual, the

---

3   See Chapter 9, Service of Documents.

title of the party must be provided, such as Mr, Mrs, Miss, Ms etc. The claimant must also provide all known forenames and the surname of the defendant along with a residential address in England and Wales, including the postcode and telephone number.

For other statements of case, such as particulars of claim, it is conventional just to give the details of the full name (excluding the title) of the person who is suing and being sued (as in the example above). However, in accordance with the accompanying notes to the claim form, the claimant must also provide, among other things, his address for service on the statement of case, as well as the claim form, if the former is a separate document.

Children and patients[4]

Where the party suing or being sued is a child, the child's full name should be given but the following words should appear in brackets after the name: (a child by [Mr] AB [his father] and litigation friend). Where the child is conducting proceedings on his own behalf, the words (a child) should appear after the child's name.

Where the party suing or being sued is a patient, the patient's full name should be given but the following words should appear in brackets after the name: (by [Mr] AB [his] litigation friend).

Trading names

If the person suing is the sole proprietor of a business, his full name should be given followed by the words 'trading as' and the trading name. If such a person is the person being sued, the claimant can either sue him in his own name with the words 'trading as' and the trading name given, or sue him simply in his trading name, followed by the words in brackets 'a trading name'.

If the person is sued in his trading name alone, he is treated as if he is a partner and the name in which he carries on business is the name of his firm (CCR Ord 5 r 10). Whether such a person is sued as an individual or in his trading name is significant because, if he is sued in his trading name, the rules on the automatic transfer of proceedings[5] on the filing of a defence by an individual would appear not to apply to that defendant.

---

4   See Chapter 26, Special Rules on Children and Patients.
5   See Chapter 15, Judicial Case Management: Allocation, p 153.

Deceased's estate

Where the estate of a deceased person is suing or being sued, the full name of the deceased's personal representative (either executor or administrator) should be given, followed by the words, 'as the representative of x (deceased)'.

Change of party by reason of death or bankruptcy

Where a party to a claim dies or becomes bankrupt but the cause of action survives, the proceedings are not a nullity because of the death or bankruptcy (RSC Ord 15 r 7). An order should be sought for the substitution of the appropriate representative party (r 19.4).

In the case of the death of a party, an order should be sought for a person in whom the claim may be vested to be substituted as a party or an application may be made for the claim to be struck out as against the claimant or defendant who has died (RSC Ord 15 r 9 and CCR Ord 5 r 12).

Clubs/unincorporated associations

If a club or other unincorporated association is suing or being sued, the full name of one or more members of the committee or trustees of the club or other unincorporated association should be given followed by the words 'suing/sued on behalf of' and the name of the club or other unincorporated association.

Partners

Two or more persons carrying on business as a partnership may sue or be sued in the name of the firm (RSC Ord 81 r 1 and CCR Ord 5 r 9). The firm's name should be given followed by the words, 'a firm'. The individuals who make up the firm can sue or be sued individually instead.

The claimant should also provide an address for service of the firm on the claim form which should be either a partner's residential address or the principal or last known place of business of the firm.

Corporations

A company is a separate legal entity and can sue or be sued as such. In the case of a company registered in England and Wales, the full name of the company should be given including the words 'Limited' or 'plc'. In the case of a corporation other than a company, the full name of the corporation should be given. In the case of an overseas company as defined by s 744 of the Companies Act 1985, the full name of the company should be given.

The claimant should also provide an address for service of the corporation on the claim form. In the case of a company registered in England and Wales it should be either the company's registered office or any place of business which has a real, or the most, connection with the claim. In the case of a corporation other than a company, it should be either its principal office or any other place where the corporation carries on activities and which has a real connection with the claim. In the case of an overseas company, it should be the address registered under s 691 of the Act or the address of the place of business having a real, or the most, connection with the claim.

Representative parties

If there is more than one person who has the same interest in a claim, the claim may be begun, or the court may order that the claim be continued, by or against one or more of the persons who have the same interest, as representatives of any other persons who have that interest. Unless the court orders otherwise, any judgment or order given in such a claim is binding on all persons represented in the claim but may only be enforced against a person who is not a party to the claim with the permission of the court (r 19.6).

It is more efficient to sue or be sued in a representative capacity where there are numerous people all having the same interest. An example is the case of *Moon v Atherton*[6] where one of 11 tenants in a block brought an action on behalf of herself and the tenants in a block of flats against their landlord for failing to carry out repairs. The full name of the representative or representatives should be given followed by the words 'on behalf of himself/herself/themselves' and then the description of the group represented.

6   [1972] 2 QB 43.

GROUP LITIGATION

Where there are a number of either claimants or defendants whose claims or defences give rise to common or related issues of law or fact, but who do not have the same interest in an action, such as in the case of product liability relating to a particular drug, a group litigation order may be made so that all the different cases can be managed together. This type of order will be appropriate where there are a substantial number of such claimants or defendants (Section III of Part 19 of the CPR should be consulted for details).

CHAPTER 7

STARTING AN ACTION

INTRODUCTION

One of the fundamental principles of the civil justice reforms was that there should be a single means of starting proceedings. Lord Woolf argued that the complexity of the old rules of court were an obstacle to access to justice, citing as a prime example of that complexity the multiplicity of forms that could be used to start an action. In his view, the rules on starting proceedings needed simplification and should be the same for both the High Court and county courts.[1]

The former rules offered a number of different forms to choose from to start proceedings. Thus, when commencing proceedings in the High Court, a choice had to be made between a writ, originating summons, originating motion or a petition, depending on the type of action. In the county courts the choice was a summons, originating application, petition and notice of appeal. There were further variations within those categories, for instance, there were three types of form of originating summons and several different forms of summons.

The new rules provide for one basic form to be used in both the High Court and the county courts: the claim form – the term 'summons' for an originating process has now gone. Although, superficially, this makes the process of starting a claim simpler (one form fits all), the claim form is modified to take account of differences in the nature of certain types of proceedings. Therefore, although there is a 'standard' claim form that is used for most actions, this is modified for specialised proceedings.

So, for example, in actions about the construction of a document, where there is no dispute of fact, it would not be appropriate to use a standard claim form followed by a particulars of claim and a defence. Instead, the claim form contains the question of construction the court is asked to decide along with a witness statement from the claimant containing any evidence in support. So, although called a claim form, a claim form for this type of action is in a different form and follows a different procedure that is known as the alternative procedure for claims (Part 8).[1a] It is used for those types of action formerly commenced by Originating Summons. Practice Direction 8B was issued in late March 1999 and sets out a list of all those proceedings where the

---

1   See *Access to Justice*, Final Report, Chapter 12 (www.lcd.gov.uk/civil/finalfr.htm).
1a See Chapter 14, Part 8 Claims.

Part 8 procedure and therefore the Part 8 claim form must be used.[2] Also, for specialist proceedings[3] such as commercial and admiralty actions, practice directions specify practice forms which must be used to start those proceedings. A new procedure for possession matters commences from 15 October 2001. Details are set out below on (see Chapter 14, Part 8 Claims, p 146).

Thus, although the reforms profess to simplify the rules on starting an action and introduce only one form by which to do so, the reality is different. On the surface, there is now only one form to start an action, but scratch the surface and the complexities demanded by the peculiarities of proceedings reappear. In theory, a single claim form seems desirable, but even at this early stage of the life of the rules, the necessity for variations to smooth the path of actions of a different nature or specialism is clear. It may not be surprising to find that as time progresses, the need for more variations becomes apparent and, paradoxically, the fact that substantially different forms come under the single name of a claim form makes starting an action more confusing rather than less.

Issuing proceedings[4]

Proceedings are started when the court issues a claim form at the request of the claimant (r 7.2(1)). On issue, the court will stamp the claim form with the court seal. The claim form is issued on the date entered on the form by the court (r 7.2(2)). The claimant can either post or deliver the claim form to the court office for issuing.

The date of issue is obviously important because, once issued, proceedings must be served within a limited period of time (or extra time must be asked for to serve them).[5] Further, in some cases, the date an action was brought can be very significant as far as limitation periods[6] are concerned. PD 7 provides that where the claim form was received in the court office on an earlier date than that on which it was issued by the court, the claim is 'brought' on that earlier date for the purposes of the Limitation Act 1980 and any other relevant statute (PD 7, para 5.1). The date on which the claim form was received by the court will be recorded by a date stamp either on the claim form held on the court file or on the letter that accompanied the claim form when it was received by the court (PD 7, para 5.2).

---

2   See Chapter 14, Part 8 Claims.
3   See r 49 for specialist proceedings and Chapter 2, Sources of Civil Procedure: Structure and Jurisdiction of the Civil Courts, p 18.
4   See Chapter 10 for the special rules for the issue of proceedings for service on a defendant outside the jurisdiction.
5   See below, p 79, for extensions of time for service of the claim form.
6   See Chapter 3, Limitation of Actions.

PD 7 anticipates that in cases issued very close to the time that the limitation period for bringing that action is about to expire, establishing that the claim was brought before the limitation period expired may be crucial in deciding whether the action can proceed. The practice direction therefore warns parties to recognise the importance of establishing the date the claim form was received by the court and make arrangements themselves to record that date (PD 7, para 5.4).

Rule 2.8(5) may be of relevance here in particular cases, because it provides that when a rule, practice direction, judgment or court order specifies a period of time for doing any act at the court office and that period of time ends on a day when the office is closed, the act shall be in time if done on the next day on which the court office is open. Therefore, if the last day for bringing an action falls on a Sunday, the party will still be in time under the Limitation Act if the claim form is received the following Monday, or next day when the court office reopens.

Which court?

Although procedure has been unified for the High Court and the county courts, the courts still retain their distinct existence and, for certain types of action, separate jurisdiction.[7] The new rules reinforce the trend that was started with the High Court and County Courts Jurisdiction Order 1991,[8] namely, reserving the High Court for specialist proceedings and those which are more valuable, serious and complex.

There are restrictions on issuing proceedings in the High Court. Unless the monetary value of a non-personal injury claim is more than £15,000, or an enactment specifies that the claim may be commenced in the High Court; or the case needs to be in one of the specialist High Court lists, the claim should not be started in the High Court (r 16.3(5)). Further, in the case of claims issued in the Royal Courts of Justice, unless the estimated value of the claim is £50,000 or more, or it is the type of case that should be brought in the High Court and is suitable for trial in the Royal Courts of Justice, it likely to be transferred to a county court (PD 29, para 2.2). The threshold of £15,000 means that all actions in the High Court will be treated as multi-track[9] cases.

---

7 See Chapter 2, Sources of Civil Procedure: Structure and Jurisdiction of the Civil Courts, for the detailed rules on the jurisdiction of the courts and the transfer of actions between the courts.

8 SI 1991/724.

9 See Chapter 18, The Multi-Track.

Personal injury claims

Proceedings that include a claim for damages in respect of personal injuries must not be started in the High Court unless the value of the claim is £50,000 or more[10] (PD 7, para 2.2).

Chapter 11 (Statements of Case) should be consulted for the requirements for statements of value on the claim form.

These rules restrict the issuing of proceedings in the High Court, but they are not rules of jurisdiction; so although, in some cases, an action cannot be *started* in the High Court, this does not necessarily mean that it will not be *heard* in the High Court. Also, these rules do not limit the jurisdiction of the county courts, so there is no restriction on an action that is valued over £15,000 being started in a county court. Further, the court has wide powers to transfer proceedings between the High Court and county courts.[11]

Court fees

The claimant is charged a court fee to issue proceedings. Litigants of modest means can apply to the court for an exemption or remission from the court fee and those on State means-tested benefits will continue to be granted an automatic exemption. A scale of fees has been set which rises according to the value of the claim, with a top fee of £500.[12]

The reasoning behind a sliding scale is the likelihood that higher value claims will be defended and resulting hearings will last longer. The intention is that fees will broadly match the cost of the service that is provided; but that amount has been fixed to reflect the average cost of the service provided rather than the actual cost for a particular case. In consequence, issue fees have been increased substantially. One of the reasons for this is the idea that increased fees will act as a deterrent to starting litigation. It also reflects the political intention of the Lord Chancellor's Department to make the court system self-funding and the message to litigants is that they should not expect the taxpayer to pay for, or subsidise, the court services they use.[13] This is a completely novel concept in our legal system and evidence of the government's desire to control the cost of the court system to the public purse. Whether it can withstand challenge under the Human Rights Act 1998 as a bar

---

10 The High Court and County Courts Jurisdiction Order 1991, Art 5.

11 See Chapter 2, Sources of Civil Procedure: Structure and Jurisdiction of the Civil Courts, for provisions as to transfer of proceedings.

12 See the County Court Fees Order 1999 SI 1999/689 and the Supreme Court Fees Order 1999 SI 1999/687 (as amended). Details of court fees are available on the court service website: www.courtservice.gov.uk.

13 See the Lord Chancellor's Consultation Paper on *Fee Levels and Charging Points*, November 1998 available on the Lord Chancellor's Department website: www.lcd.gov. uk/consult/civ-just/civilffr.htm.

to access to the courts and, therefore, a breach of Art 6 of the European Convention on Human Rights (right to a fair trial), remains to be seen.

THE CLAIM FORM[14]

The vast majority of actions must be started using the prescribed claim form number N1 (PD 7, para 3.1). This is very similar in format to the old county court summons form. For those actions using the alternative procedure for claims[15] (for instance, actions about the construction of a document where there is no substantial dispute of fact) a different form, N208, is prescribed (PD 7, para 3.1). For those actions brought under the specialist jurisdictions[16] a practice direction relating to that jurisdiction may specify a practice form which has been approved for those types of proceedings (PD 7, para 3.4).

Particulars of claim

Particulars of claim[17] must be contained on, or served with the claim form (r 7.4(1)(a)). Alternatively, particulars of claim can be served on the defendant within 14 days after service of the claim form (r 7.4(1)(b)). However, if the latter course is taken, the particulars of claim must be served on the defendant no later than the latest date for serving a claim form (r 7.4(2)). The claim form itself must be served within four months after the date of issue (r 7.5) (or six months where the claim form is to be served out of the jurisdiction (r 7.5(3)).[18] Therefore, if service of the claim form is delayed until the end of that four month period, the particulars of claim must also be served before the end of that four month period, so the additional 14 days does not run after the end of the four month period for issue.

As for the contents of the particulars of claim, see Chapter 11, Statements of case.

The possibility of serving a claim form giving a brief outline of the claim, followed by particulars of claim, which supply the detail, at a later date effectively reproduces in the CPR's the 'generally' versus 'specially' endorsed writ procedure formerly available under the old rules. The Rules Committee gave lengthy consideration as to whether this distinction should be retained.

---

14 For the detailed content of a claim form and other statements of case, see Chapter 11.
15 See Chapter 14, Part 8 Claims.
16 See Part 49, referred to in Chapter 2, Sources of Civil Procedure: Structure and Jurisdiction of the Civil Courts.
17 For the detailed content of particulars of claim and other statements of case, see Chapter 11, Statements of Case
18 See Chapter 10, Service out of the Jurisdiction.

The concern was that this procedure ran contrary to two fundamental principles of the civil justice reforms, namely, that there should be a unified procedure for claims, and that a claimant should be ready to proceed with a case when he starts an action. It was also feared that it could be used as a delaying tactic. However, this procedure was allowed to continue for the reason that it enables claims to be commenced in emergency circumstances when there is not enough time to prepare the full claim form.[19]

If the particulars of claim are not included in or have not been served with the claim form, the claim form must include a statement that particulars of claim will follow (r 16.2(2)).

If the particulars of claim are contained in or served with the claim form, a copy will be filed at the court on issue. If the claimant serves particulars of claim separately from the claim form he must, within seven days of service on the defendant, file a copy of the particulars together with a certificate of service (r 7.4(3)). The certificate of service must state that the particulars of claim have not been returned undelivered and specify the date of service. Which date to specify differs according to the method of service used, so, for instance, if postal service is used, the date of posting must be specified (r 6.10).[20]

Statements of truth

The claim form must be verified by a statement of truth.[21] If the particulars of claim are not included in the claim form, they must also contain a statement of truth (PD 7, para 7.1).

The Human Rights Act 1998

If a claimant is seeking a remedy under the Human Rights Act 1998 he must state that in his statement of case. The prescribed forms for starting a claim now include a box which the claimant must tick indicating whether or not his claim does or will include any issues under the Human Rights Act 1988. Further details of any such claim must be provided in the claimant's statement of case.[22]

---

19 See the Consultation Paper on the proposed new procedures for the specialist jurisdictions of the High Court (www.lcd.gov.uk/consult/civ-just/accjus1.htm).
20 See Chapter 9, Service of Documents, p 109, for detailed consideration of a certificate of service.
21 See Chapter 11, Statements of Case, p 128, for details.
22 See Chapter 37, The Human Rights Act 1988.

Information on funding arrangements[23]

If the claimant has entered into a funding arrangement, on issuing proceedings the claimant is required to file a copy of Form N251 at court along with his claim form. Form N251 requires the claimant to give specified details about the funding arrangement.[24]

FIXED DATE CLAIMS

Rule 7.9 provides for a Practice Direction to set out the circumstances when the court will give a fixed date for a hearing when it issues a claim. The Practice Direction supplementing this rule sets out this special procedure for Consumer Credit Act claims.[25] This reproduces the procedure for such actions established under the old rules and is an example of a specialised action which needs a modified procedure from that provided by the standard claim form procedure. Similarly, PD 7D provides that in cases brought by the Inland Revenue to recover taxes or NIC, the court will fix a hearing on the filing of a defence rather than allocate to track.[26]

The same rule also refers to a practice direction listing claims that will have their own specific claim form and modified procedure. There are already practice directions for specialised proceedings as defined under Part 49 which specify the content of the claim form for the actions to which they relate, but the rule also lays the foundation for further variations in the claim form for actions outside of these specialised proceedings which need a modified procedure.

PRODUCTION CENTRE FOR CLAIMS

A practice which was introduced under the old rules carries on under the new rules, namely, the existence of a Production Centre for claims (r 7.10). This was formerly known as the Summons Production Centre and is based at Northampton County Court. This is a court service for the bulk issue of claim forms. The Centre benefits from a computerised system which enables users to supply the necessary claim forms electronically.

It is only available for certain county court proceedings where the claim is for a specified sum of money of less than £100,000. A party must seek permission before issuing a claim through the Production Centre. Once

---

23 See Chapter 38, Funding Litigation.
24 *Ibid*, for details.
25 PD 7B.
26 See Chapter 15, Judicial Case Management: Allocation.

permission is granted, the party will become a 'Centre user' (PD 7C). Such a service is used by large companies for collecting debts, often from defaulting consumers. Since large numbers of claim forms need to be processed, they are diverted to this special centre rather than the usual court office and the claimant is given a favourable rate for the cost of processing each claim. Once a claim becomes defended, it will be transferred out of the Production Centre to an appropriate county court if the claimant indicates that he wishes to proceed with the matter (PD 7C, para 5.2(4)).

NOTICE OF ISSUE

When the claimant sends the claim form to the court for issue, the court will send a notice of issue, in one of three prescribed forms, to the claimant notifying the claimant that the claim has been issued.[27] The notice, either in Form N205A (notice of issue of claim for a specified amount of money), N205B (notice of issue of claim for an unspecified amount of money) or N205C (notice of issue of a non-money claim) will specify the date when the claim was issued and, if served by the court,[28] the date when it was posted, and give the deemed date of service. The forms relating to money claims (N205A and N205B) also include a section for the claimant to complete and return to court to enter judgment if the defendant does not respond[29] within the specified time.[30]

FORMS FOR THE DEFENDANT

When particulars of claim are served on the defendant, whether with or on the claim form or separately, they must be accompanied by three forms:

- a form for defending the claim (and making a counterclaim);
- a form for admitting the claim; and
- a form for acknowledging service.

This is known as a 'Response Pack' (N9) (r 7.8(1)).

The defendant does not have to respond to proceedings at all until particulars of claim are served on him. However, service of the

---

27 See Chapter 23, Striking Out, p 268, for the circumstances when the claim form can be referred to the judge after issue.
28 See Chapter 9 on options for service.
29 See Chapter 8, Responding to an Action, for the procedure for responding to a claim.
30 See Chapter 21 on judgment in default.

acknowledgment of service gives the defendant a further period in which to file his defence.[31]

VALIDITY OF THE CLAIM FORM

The rules provide that once a claim form has been issued, it *must* be served on the defendant (r 7.5(1)). This is in keeping with the general principles of the rules that once a party decides to start proceedings, he should pursue them with due diligence. In any event, as a general rule, the claim form must be served within four months after the date of issue (r 7.5(2)). The period of service is six months where the claim form is to be served out of the jurisdiction (r 7.5(3)).

Extension of time for serving a claim form

If a claimant is unable to serve a claim form within four months of the date of issue, he can apply for an order extending the period within which the claim form may be served (r 7.6).

Period within which application for an extension should be made

In the first instance, the claimant should apply for an order extending the period within which the claim form may be served before the expiry of the initial four month period of validity of the claim form (r 7.6(2)(a)). If an order is granted extending the time within which the claim form may be served, but the claimant requires a further period of time to serve the claim form, he should apply for a further extension of time before the expiry of the period granted by the original extension (r 7.6(2)(b)).

Applications for an extension outside the specified period

If the claimant does not apply for an extension of time, or further extension of time, within the time periods specified in r 7.6(2), the circumstances within which the court has power to grant an extension of time for service of the claim form are limited to the following:

- if the court has been unable to serve the claim form; or
- the claimant has taken all reasonable steps to serve the claim form but has been unable to do so; and

---

31 See r 9.1 and Chapter 8, Responding to an Action.

- in either case the claimant has acted promptly in making the application for an extension of time (r 7.6(3)).

The discretion to extend time for service does not apply if none of the criteria set out in r 7.6(3) above are applicable.[32]

Procedure for applying for an extension of time

In all circumstances when an application for an extension of time for service of the claim form is made it should be made in accordance with Part 23[32a] and be supported by evidence (r 7.6(4)(a)).

The evidence should state: all the circumstances relied on, the date of issue of the claim, the expiry date of any order extending time for service and a full explanation as to why the claim has not been served (PD 7, para 8.2).

As the defendant has not at this stage been served with the proceedings, the application can be made without notice (r 7.6(4)(b)). However, if the order is granted and the claim form is served, the defendant can apply to have service of the claim form set aside (r 23.10).[32b] If the claimant anticipates that the defendant will make such an application it may be more cost effective, and in accordance with the overriding objective, to make the application for the extension of time for service *on notice* to the defendant so that only one hearing will be necessary to decide all the relevant matters.

Issuing and serving a claim form when expiry of limitation period is imminent

It may be legitimate to issue and serve a claim form without a full particulars of claim where, for example, a limitation period is looming and the solicitors have only just been instructed by the claimant and there is no time for any appropriate pre-action protocol to be worked through. Such a course may be preferable to issuing the claim form and then applying to the court for extensions of time within which to serve the claim form, and was the course suggested by Lord Woolf in *Jones v Telford and Wrekin Council*,[33] where the claimant was waiting for favourable medical reports and had applied for and been granted three extensions of time to serve proceedings. Lord Woolf favoured this course on the basis that a defendant should be notified of a claim as early as possible in order to take steps to defend it.

---

32 *Vinos v Marks & Spencer plc* [2000] 1 WLR 1311; [2000] 2 All ER 801; *Satwinder Kaur v CTP Ltd* (2000) Lawtel, 11 July, CA.
32a See Chapter 19, Making Applications for Court Orders.
32b *Ibid.*
33 (1999) *The Times*, 29 July.

This is likely to be an increasing trend in the light of the various organisations that now encourage parties to make claims in respect of accidents. In that event, the court may be tempted to stay the proceedings to give the parties an opportunity to operate the pre-action protocol where there was not time before the issue of proceedings.

APPLICATION BY DEFENDANT FOR SERVICE OF THE CLAIM FORM

Rule 7.7 provides that where a claimant issues but does not serve a claim form on the defendant, the defendant can serve a notice on the claimant requiring him to serve the claim form or discontinue the claim. The defendant must give the claimant at least 14 days within which to serve or discontinue. If the claimant fails to comply with the notice, the defendant can apply to the court, which can dismiss the claim or make any other order it thinks just. So, rather than dismiss the claim, the court may decide to give the claimant another chance to comply and make an order in terms that, unless by a certain date the claim form is served, the claimant's action will be struck out.

A number of questions are raised by the existence of this rule. First, what interest does a defendant have in effectively prompting the claimant into pursuing an action against him? Secondly, is this in keeping with the philosophy of the CPR, as it seems to encourage rather than discourage litigation? The answers to these questions may be that in some circumstances, a claimant will start an action against the defendant and publicise the fact so as to cause embarrassment to the defendant without having any intention to pursue the claim at all, presumably because the claim is unmeritorious. This allows the defendant to 'call the claimant's bluff' by demanding that the claimant sue if there is a good claim, but discontinue if there is not. Alternatively, a defendant may wish to get rid of litigation as quickly as possible.

The rule has the potential result that in some cases, a claimant is not given four months within which to serve the claim form on a defendant within the jurisdiction, or six months on a defendant outside of the jurisdiction. The inclusion of the new rule emphasises the premium that the court puts upon the new culture to conduct litigation speedily, but also the intolerance that will be shown to the improper use of litigation, the desirability of notifying a defendant of a claim as soon as possible so that he can take appropriate steps to defend it, as well as the need to try and prepare all relevant information prior to the issue of proceedings, through the medium of pre-action protocols. On the other hand, the existence of this provision creates the potential for abuse by an unscrupulous defendant who may use it to pressurise a claimant into serving proceedings when they are not ready to do so.

CHAPTER 8

RESPONDING TO AN ACTION

INTRODUCTION

Once a claimant has issued proceedings and they have been served on the other parties, those other parties must comply with the procedure for responding to those proceedings or risk judgment being entered against them by default.[1]

There is a special procedure for responding to claims made under Part 8[2] of the CPR and different time limits apply to claims served outside of the jurisdiction.[3] Also, different rules may apply to specialist proceedings.[4] This chapter deals only with the procedure for responding to a claim started under Part 7 of the CPR and served within the jurisdiction.

RESPONSE TO PARTICULARS OF CLAIM

On issuing proceedings,[5] the claimant has the option of either including particulars of claim within or attached to the claim form served on the defendant or of serving particulars of claim separately within 14 days after service of the claim form on the defendant.[6]

If the defendant receives a claim form which states that particulars of claim are to follow, he need not respond to the claim form until particulars of claim have been served on him (r 9.1(2)). If the claimant shows no intention of serving particulars of claim, the defendant could apply for the claimant's action to be struck out, either on the grounds of failure to comply with a rule (being r 7.4(1))[7] under r 3.4(2)(c) or for abuse of process under r 3.4(2)(b). However, the defendant may understandably not wish to make such an application for fear of goading the claimant into making a cross-application for relief from such a sanction, unless the limitation period for the claimant's action has also expired. The court, in the exercise of its case management

---

1 See Chapter 21, Judgment in Default.
2 See Chapter 14, Part 8 Claims.
3 See Chapter 10 for service out of the jurisdiction.
4 See CPR, Part 49 and p 18, Specialist proceedings.
5 See Chapter 7, Starting an Action, for the procedure for starting an action.
6 See r 7.4(1)(a) and Chapter 7, Starting an Action.
7 See Chapter 7, Starting an Action.

powers, may strike out the claimant's action in these circumstances in any event.[8]

When particulars of claim are served on a defendant, they will be accompanied by a response pack (r 7.8).[9] If the defendant does not accept the claim and pay the amount claimed (along with costs) within 14 days after service of the particulars of claim, he must return one of the relevant forms in the response pack, within that period of time, or risk judgment being entered by default (r 10.2). The forms in the response pack are an acknowledgment of service, an admission, or a defence (r 9.2). If the defendant admits only part of the claim, he should file both an admission form and a defence at court (r 9.2(b)).

If a claimant issues and serves a claim form and particulars of claim, and the defendant does not return an admission or defence or counterclaim, but nor does the claimant apply for judgment in default[10] or summary judgment,[11] the claim shall be stayed after six months have expired following the end of the period for filing a defence (r 15.11(1)). Any party may apply for this stay to be lifted (r 15.11(2)).

ACKNOWLEDGMENT OF SERVICE

A defendant has the opportunity to file an acknowledgment of service in order to give him more time to file a defence, or if he disputes that the court has jurisdiction to hear the claim.[12] If the defendant files an acknowledgment of service, he then has a further 14 days after the time limit for acknowledgment has expired within which to file his defence. Filing an acknowledgement of service effectively gives the defendant 28 rather than 14 days after service of particulars of claim within which to file a defence.

Acknowledgment of service form

In order to acknowledge service, the defendant must file Form N9, the prescribed acknowledgment of service form, at court (PD 10, para 2). On receipt of this form the court will send Form N10 to the claimant notifying him, or his legal representative, that the defendant has acknowledged service (r 10.4).

---

8   See Chapter 5, Judicial Case Management: The Overriding Objective, for the court's powers to make an order of its own initiative.
9   See Chapter 7, Starting an action.
10 See Chapter 21, Judgment in Default.
11 See Chapter 22, Summary Judgment.
12 See Chapter 10, Service out of the Jurisdiction.

The defendant must set out his name in full in the acknowledgment of service form. Where the claimant has incorrectly set out the defendant's name in the claim form, the defendant should set it out correctly in the acknowledgment of service form followed by the words 'described as' and the incorrect name used by the claimant in the claim form (PD 10, paras 5.1, 5.2). The court will then notify the claimant in Form N10 of the defendant's correct name as stated in the acknowledgment of service form.

The defendant must indicate on Form N9 whether he intends to defend all or part of the claim or whether he intends to contest the court's jurisdiction.

Signing the acknowledgment of service form

Form N9 must be signed by the defendant or his legal representative on his behalf (PD 10, para 4.1).

If the defendant is a company or other corporation the acknowledgement of service may be signed by the legal representative or by a person holding a senior position in the company, such as a director or chief executive. The person signing on behalf of the company must state what position he holds in the company (PD 10, paras 4.2, 4.3).

If the defendant is a partnership, the acknowledgment of service may be signed by the legal representative or any of the partners or a person having control or management of the partnership business (PD 10, para 4.4). The person signing on behalf of the partnership must sign in their own name and not that of the partnership (CPR Sched 1, RSC Ord 81 r 4).

If the defendant is a child or a patient, the acknowledgment of service must be signed by their litigation friend or legal representative unless the court orders otherwise (PD 10, para 4.5).

Address for service

When acknowledging service, the defendant must include his address for service within the jurisdiction (r 10.5).[13] If the defendant has a legal representative acting on his behalf, he must give the legal representative's business address as the address for service (PD 10, para 3.2).

Multiple defendants

If there is more than one defendant, each defendant must file an acknowledgment of service form. However, if the same legal representative is

---

13   See r 6.5 and Chapter 9, Service of Documents, p 102.

acting for all the defendants, the legal representative may acknowledge service for all the defendants through one acknowledgment of service form (PD 10, para 5.3).

Amending or withdrawing acknowledgment of service

Once filed, an acknowledgment of service may be amended or withdrawn only with permission of the court. The application for permission to amend or withdraw must be made in accordance with Part 23[14] and supported by evidence (PD 10, paras 5.4, 5.5).

Time limits for filing an acknowledgment of service

If a defendant chooses to acknowledge service, he must do so by filing Form N9 at court within 14 days after service of particulars of claim on him. If particulars of claim are contained in or served with the claim form, he must acknowledge service within 14 days after service of the claim form. If particulars of claim are served separately from the claim form, the defendant must acknowledge service within 14 days after service of the particulars of claim (r 10.3).

ADMISSIONS

If a party makes a written admission as to the truth of the whole or part of another party's case, the other party may apply for judgment on that admission (r 14.3(1)).[15] Whether judgment will be entered for the whole or part of a party's case depends on the extent of the admission that appears to the court to have been made (r 14.3(2)). The written admission does not have to be contained within a statement of case, but could be contained in a letter or other document (r 14.1(1) and (2)). Oral admissions may be relied upon as evidence to prove liability in a case, but cannot be relied upon to enter judgment without trial under the procedure set out in Part 14.

In some cases, a defendant will have no grounds to deny liability for a claim. In those circumstances, the cheapest option for a defendant is usually to accept liability before proceedings are issued and negotiate terms of settlement and if proceedings are issued, to admit liability and end the action as soon as possible.

---

14 See Chapter 19 on making applications to court.
15 See Chapter 24, Offers to Settle and Payments into Court, p 292, for the protection given to 'without prejudice' communications.

In many cases relating to the non-payment of a debt, a defendant has no defence to the claim, but is unable or unwilling to pay. The claimant may have to use proceedings to enforce payment of the debt. In those circumstances, the defendant may admit liability but ask for time to pay.

ADMISSIONS IN MONEY CLAIMS

If a claimant brings a claim where the *only* remedy sought is the payment of money and the defendant makes an admission contained in one of the specified practice forms, whether as to the whole or part of the amount claimed, the claimant has the right to enter judgment against the defendant, (apart from in some types of money claim where either party is a child or patient) (r 14.1(3) and (4)).[16]

Time limits for making an admission

The defendant has 14 days after service of particulars of claim within which to return an admission (r 14.2(1)).[17] However, the defendant will still be able to return an admission after this period of time so long as the claimant has not entered judgment in default[18] and if he does so, he will be treated as having complied with the time limits laid down in r 14.2(1) (r 14.2(3) and (4)). This rule is presumably subject to r 15.11 imposing an automatic stay on proceedings after six months' inactivity,[18a] so a defendant would also have to apply for the stay to be lifted in order to return an admission out of time in those circumstances. However, whether a party is required to obtain permission to admit a claim is unlikely to be an issue between the parties.

Amending or withdrawing an admission

If, having made an admission, a party wishes to amend the extent of the admission or withdraw it altogether he must apply to the court for permission to do so (r 14.1(5)). The application should be made in accordance with Part 23.[19] The court may grant permission subject to a condition,[20] for instance, the payment of a sum of money into court.

---

16 See Chapter 26, Special Rules for Children and Patients.
17 See below for circumstances when the admission form should be returned to court or to the claimant.
18 See Chapter 21, Judgment in Default.
18a See above, p 83, Response to particulars of claim.
19 See Chapter 19, Making Applications for Court Orders.
20 See Chapter 5, Judicial Case Management: The Overriding Objective, p 58.

Defendant pays whole of specified money claim

If the claimant's only remedy is the payment of a specified sum of money and the defendant is prepared to pay the whole sum claimed (including interest and fixed costs as specified on the claim form), he should take or send the money to the claimant at the address given on the claim form within 14 days. If a defendant has no defence to the claim and accepts the amount owed, the advantage of paying the whole sum within 14 days is that the defendant can avoid a county court judgment being entered against him, with its attendant consequences in terms of its effect on his credit rating.

Defendant seeking time to pay

If the claimant's only remedy is the payment of a sum of money and the defendant admits liability, instead of paying the amount claimed immediately to the claimant, he can make a request for time to pay. The procedure varies according to the nature of the money claim and the extent of the admission.

If the defendant requests time to pay, he should complete either Form N9A (claim for a specified amount of money) or N9C (claim for an unspecified amount of money) which require the defendant to give information about his income and expenses and to either propose a date by which the sum admitted will be paid, or to propose a sum to be paid monthly (r 14.9(2)). The defendant should give as much detail about his means as requested either within Form N9A or N9C or provide the same details in writing (PD 14, para 2.2) The defendant must also give brief reasons why the whole sum cannot be paid immediately.

ADMISSION OF WHOLE OF CLAIM FOR A SPECIFIED AMOUNT OF MONEY

If the claimant's only remedy is a specified amount of money and the defendant has admitted liability for the whole sum and not requested time to pay, the claimant can request that judgment be entered against the defendant by filing Form N205A and specifying either that payment be made immediately, a date by which the whole sum is to be paid, or the times and rate of payment by instalments (r 14.4(4)). On receipt of Form N205A, the court will enter judgment for the claimant to be paid in the manner requested by the claimant (r 14.4(5) and (6)).

If the claimant's only remedy is a specified amount of money and the defendant admits liability for the whole sum, but requests time to pay, the defendant should return the prescribed Form N9A to the claimant at the address on the claim form within 14 days of service of the claim form (rr 14.4, 14.9(2) and PD 14, para 3.1).[21]

If the defendant sends Form 9A to the claimant on which he has admitted liability and requested time to pay, the claimant should return Form N225 (along with Form N9A) to the court indicating whether he accepts the defendant's proposal as to payment or not.

If the claimant returns Form N225 indicating that he accepts the defendant's proposal as to payment, the court will enter judgment for the claimant with payment to be made at the time and rate specified in the defendant's proposal (r 14.9(4)–(6)).

If the claimant rejects the proposal, he should indicate on Form N225 how he wants the defendant to pay and the reasons for rejecting the defendant's proposals for payment. On receipt of Form N225, the court will enter judgment for the claimant, but with an order that the time and rate of payment will be decided by the court (r 14.10).[22]

Claimant's entitlement to interest

Where a claimant is claiming a specified amount of money if judgment is entered following the defendant's admission, it will include an amount for interest up to the date of judgment so long as certain conditions are met. These are that the claimant must have given the requisite details about interest in his particulars of claim as required by r 16.4;[23] the request for judgment includes a calculation of interest from the date of issue of the claim form to the date judgment is requested; and (if interest is claimed under s 35A of the Supreme Court Act 1981 or s 69 of the County Courts Act 1984) the rate claimed is no higher than that which was available under those provisions when the claim form was issued (r 14.14(1)).

If these conditions are not met, judgment shall be for an amount of interest to be decided by the court (r 14.14(2)). On entering judgment, the court will give any directions it considers appropriate for deciding the amount of the interest; this can include allocating the case to a track (r 14.8). However, the court is likely to order that the amount be decided at a disposal hearing (PD 26, para 12.6).[24]

---

21 See above, p 83, Response to particulars of claim, for time limits.
22 See below, p 92, Court determination of rate of payment.
23 See Chapter 11, Statements of case.
24 See below, p 94, Disposal hearings.

ADMISSION OF PART OF CLAIM FOR A SPECIFIED AMOUNT OF MONEY

If the claimant's only remedy is a specified sum of money and the defendant admits liability for part of the sum claimed, he should complete Form N9A and file it at court within 14 days of service of the particulars of claim indicating the amount he admits he is liable for (PD 14, para 3.2).[25] The defendant may also file a defence[26] as to the rest of the claim (PD 14, para 3.3).

On receipt of the part admission, the court will serve Form N225A on the claimant and the claimant must file at court, and serve a completed copy of Form N225A on the defendant, within 14 days after it is served on him, indicating whether:

- he accepts the amount admitted in satisfaction of the claim (and the defendant's proposals for payment, if any);
- he does not accept the amount admitted by the defendant and wishes the proceedings to continue; or
- if the defendant has requested time to pay, he accepts the amount admitted in satisfaction of the claim but not the defendant's proposals as to payment (r 14.5(3) and (4)).

If the claimant accepts the defendant's part admission of liability in satisfaction of his claim he can obtain judgment against the defendant by filing a request in Form N225A. If the defendant has not asked for time to pay, the claimant can indicate whether payment is to be made immediately, within a certain time, or specify the time and rate for payment by instalments (r 14.5(7). Judgment will then be entered for the claimant for the amount admitted in the manner requested by the claimant and including an order for payment of fixed costs as stated on the claim form (r 14.5(9)).

If the claimant accepts the amount admitted in satisfaction of the claim, but not the defendant's proposals as to payment, the claimant should indicate on Form N225A how he wants the defendant to pay and the reasons for rejecting the defendant's proposals for payment. Judgment will be entered for the claimant but the time and rate of payment will then be decided by the court (r 14.5(6)).[27]

If the claimant does not accept the defendant's part admission of the claim and wishes proceedings to continue, they will be treated like any other defended action and allocated in accordance with Part 26.[28]

---

25 See above, p 83, Response to particulars of claim, for time limits.
26 See below, p 95, Defence.
27 See below, p 94, Disposal hearings.
28 See Chapter 15, Judicial Case Management: Allocation.

If the claimant does not file the notice within 14 days after it is served on him, the claim will be stayed until he does serve the notice (r 14.5(5)).

ADMISSION OF WHOLE CLAIM FOR AN UNSPECIFIED AMOUNT OF MONEY

If the claimant's only remedy is an unspecified amount of money and the defendant admits liability for the claim by filing an admission in Form N9C, the court will serve a copy of Form N9C on the claimant, who can obtain judgment by filing Form N226.

On receipt of Form N226, the court will enter judgment for an amount to be decided by the court and costs (r 14.6). On entering judgment, the court will give any directions it considers appropriate for deciding the amount of the judgment; this can include allocating the case to a track (r 14.8). However, the court is likely to order that the amount be decided at a disposal hearing (PD 26, para 12.6).[29]

If the claimant does not request judgment within 14 days after service of the admission on him, his claim will be stayed until he files the request for judgment (r 14.6(7)).

ADMISSION OF LIABILITY FOR AN UNSPECIFIED AMOUNT OF MONEY, WITH OFFER OF SUM IN SATISFACTION

If the claimant's only remedy is an unspecified amount of money and the defendant admits liability and offers a sum in satisfaction of the claim by filing an admission in Form N9C, the court will serve a copy of Form N9C on the claimant and the claimant will be required to indicate by returning Form N226 whether or not he accepts the amount in satisfaction of the claim (r 14.7(1)–(3)).

If the claimant accepts the defendant's offer in satisfaction of the claim, he can enter judgment against the defendant by filing a request in Form N226. If the defendant has not asked for time to pay, the claimant can indicate whether payment is to be made immediately, within a certain time or specify the time and rate for payment by instalments (r 14.7(5) and (6)). Judgment will then be entered for the claimant for the amount admitted in the manner requested by the claimant and with an order for payment of fixed costs as stated on the claim form (r 14.7(7) and (8)).

---

29 See below, p 94, Disposal hearings.

If the claimant indicates on Form N226 that he does not accept the amount offered by the defendant in satisfaction of the claim, he may obtain judgment by filing a request on that form. The court will enter judgment for an amount to be decided by the court and costs (r 14.7(9) and (10)). On entering judgment, the court will give any directions it considers appropriate for deciding the amount of the judgment; this can include allocating the case to a track (r 14.8). However, the court is likely to order that the amount be decided at a disposal hearing (PD 26, para 12.6).[30]

If the claimant accepts the amount admitted in satisfaction of the claim, but not the defendant's proposals as to payment, the claimant should indicate on Form N226 how he wants the defendant to pay and the reasons for rejecting the defendant's proposals for payment. Judgment will be entered for the claimant, but the time and rate of payment will then be decided by the court (r 14.7(9) and (10)).[31]

If the claimant does not file Form N226 within 14 days after it has been served on him, the claim will be stayed until he files the notice (r 14.7(4)).

COURT DETERMINATION OF RATE OF PAYMENT

In those cases where the defendant has admitted liability for a money claim, but has requested time to pay and the claimant has indicated when returning the relevant practice form that he accepts the amount admitted by the defendant but does not accept the defendant's proposals as to the time and rate of payment, the court will fix the time and rate of payment (rr 14.9 and 14.10).

The time and rate of payment may be decided either by:

- a court officer; or
- a judge.

A court officer may determine the rate of payment where the only claim is for a specified amount of money and the amount outstanding (including costs) is not more than £50,000 (r 14.11(1) and PD 14, para 5.2(2)). The court officer has no power to hold a hearing in order to determine this amount and will determine the time and rate of payment by considering the information provided by the claimant and defendant in writing (r 14.11(2)).

A judge can determine the amount either with or without a hearing (r 14.12(1)). If the judge decides to hold a hearing, he must give each party at least seven days' notice of the hearing (r 14.12(3)).

---

30 See below, p 94, Disposal hearings.
31 See below.

The proceedings will be transferred automatically to the defendant's home court[32] if the following conditions are satisfied:

- the only claim is for a specified amount of money;
- the defendant is an individual;
- the claim has not been transferred to another defendant's home court, for example, under automatic transfer provisions when a defence is filed;[33]
- the claim was not started in the defendant's home court; and
- the claim was not started in a specialist list.[34]

When deciding on the time and rate of payment, the court will take into account the information provided by the defendant as to his means[35] and the claimant's objections to the defendant's proposals set out in the relevant practice form (PD 14, para 5.1). If the defendant has shown by the completion of a statement of means that he would be financially unable to make anything other than a small instalment payment, and the claimant has been unable to present any evidence to contradict the defendant's statement of means, the court officer or judge is unlikely to order that a greater sum should be paid instead. This will be the case even if this means that it will take the defendant a number of years to repay the amount admitted.

Challenging court's determination of time and rate of payment

Where a court officer has determined the time and rate of payment, or a judge has made the determination without a hearing, either party may apply for the decision to be redetermined by a judge (r 14.13(1)).

If the determination was made by a court officer, the redetermination may be made by the judge without a hearing, unless the party applying for the redetermination requests a hearing (PD 14, para 5.4). However, if the determination was made by a judge, the redetermination must be made at a hearing unless the parties otherwise agree (PD 14, para 5.5).

The party wishing to apply for a redetermination must do so within 14 days of service on him of the original order as to the time and rate of payment (r 14.13(2)). The application must be made under Part 23.[36]

---

32 See Chapter 15, Judicial Case Management: Allocation, p 154, for definition of defendant's home court.

33 See Chapter 15, Judicial Case Management: Allocation, p 153.

34 See Part 49 and p 18, Specialist proceedings.

35 See above, p 88, Defendant seeking time to pay.

36 See Chapter 19, Applications for Court Orders.

If an application for a redetermination is made, in certain circumstances the proceedings will be transferred to the defendant's home court[37] if the redetermination is to be by way of a hearing (r 14.13(3)).

Varying the rate of payment

If the defendant's circumstances change such that he can no longer afford to make payments at the rate determined or redetermined by the court, or if the claimant has evidence that the defendant's circumstances have changed and he can afford to make increased payments, either party can make an application under Part 23 to vary the time and rate of payment (PD 14, paras 6.1, 6.2).

DISPOSAL HEARINGS

If the claimant's claim is for an unspecified sum of money and judgment has been entered following the defendant's admission of liability, for an amount of money and/or interest to be decided by the court plus costs, the court will give directions as to how that amount will be determined. This will include the circumstances where the court has entered judgment for an amount of interest to be decided by the court (r 14.8).[38]

Where judgment is entered for an amount to be decided by the court following the defendant's admission, the case will not have been allocated to a case management track. In those circumstances, where liability is obviously not in issue, it will not usually be appropriate for the court to allocate the case to a track and the court will usually direct that a disposal hearing be listed instead (PD 26, para 12.3).

At the disposal hearing, the court will either decide the amount the claimant is entitled to on the judgment, or give directions for the matter to be decided and allocate the claim to a track. Evidence relied on at a disposal hearing should be in the form of a witness statement or statement of case and/or application notice if verified by a statement of truth (r 32.6). However, the court will not exercise its power to decide the amount there and then unless any written evidence the claimant is relying upon has been served on the defendant at least three days before the disposal hearing (PD 26, para 12.8(5)).

---

37 See above, p 92, Court determination of rate of payment, for the circumstances for transfer.

38 See above, p 89, Claimant's entitlement to interest.

Under PD 26, para 12.3, the court is likely to allocate the case to a track for the amount to be decided by the court, rather than determine the amount at a disposal hearing if:

- it is appropriate to allocate the case to the small claims track. A small claims track hearing, rather than a disposal hearing will be appropriate for those claims with a financial value within the small claims track. In these circumstances the court is likely to allocate the case to the small claims track and treat the disposal hearing as the final hearing under the small claims track. The hearing will be informal and subject to the 'no costs' rule;[39] or

- the amount payable appears to be genuinely disputed on substantial grounds. In these circumstances it will be appropriate to deal with the case like any other disputed matter. The court can make various orders including directing allocation questionnaires to be filed and fixing a date for a hearing, specifying what level of judge the hearing should take place before and the nature of the hearing (PD 26, para 12.2).

Jurisdiction of Masters and district judges

The Master and district judge have jurisdiction to determine the amount to be paid when judgment is entered following an admission, irrespective of the financial value of the claim and irrespective of whether the matter is dealt with at a disposal hearing or at a hearing following allocation to a track (PD 26, para 12.10).

Costs of the disposal hearing

The court has a discretion as to the costs of the disposal hearing. The court can also order a summary assessment of those costs. The usual order will be for the defendant to pay the claimant's costs of the disposal hearing, but the court can make other orders. However, if the claim has been allocated to the small claims track, the 'no costs rule' will apply (PD 26, para 12.9).

DEFENCE

In order to defend all or part of a claim, a defendant must file a defence (r 15.2).[40] A different procedure applies where the claimant starts an action

---

39   See Chapter 16, The Small Claims Track, p 184.
40   See Chapter 11, Statements of Case, for rules as to the contents of the defence.

under Part 8[41] and in some cases relating to specialist proceedings,[42] and this chapter is only concerned with the procedure where a claim not falling within the definition of specialist proceedings is started under Part 7.

The defence may deny liability for the claimant's claim[43] but it may also include a claim for a set off or counterclaim which can, in some cases, exceed the amount of the claimant's claim.[44] If the defendant counterclaims against the claimant, the defence and counterclaim should be contained within the same document, with the counterclaim following on from the defence (PD 15, para 3.1).

The defendant can use either form N9B (defence to a specified amount) or N9D (defence to an unspecified amount or non-money claim) contained in the response pack served on the defendant with the particulars of claim, for the purposes of a defence (PD 15, para 1.3).

The defendant's defence, like all other statements of case, should be verified by a statement of truth.[45]

So long as the defendant files and serves a document which purports to be a defence within the requisite time limits, he will avoid judgment being entered against him in default. However, if justified, the claimant can apply for the defence to be struck out under Part 3.4[46] and for judgment to be entered or for summary judgment under Part 24.[47] The court can also strike out a defence of its own initiative.[48]

Time limits for filing a defence

In most cases, a defendant must file a defence at court either:

- 14 days after service of the particulars of claim; or
- if the defendant files an acknowledgment of service,[49] 28 days after service of the particulars of claim (r 15.4).

These time limits do not apply if the claim form is served out of the jurisdiction,[50] if the defendant makes an application disputing the court's

---

41 See Chapter 14, Part 8 Claims.
42 See Part 49 and p 18, Specialist proceedings.
43 The defence cannot simply be a bare denial (see Chapter 11, Statements of Case, for rules as to the contents of the defence).
44 See Chapter 12, Part 20 Claims.
45 See Chapter 11, Statements of Case, p 128, for details.
46 See Chapter 23, Striking Out.
47 See Chapter 22, Summary Judgment.
48 See Chapter 23, Striking Out, p 268.
49 See above, p 84, Acknowledgment of service.
50 See Chapter 10, Service Outside the Jurisdiction.

jurisdiction,[51] if the claimant applies for summary judgment before the defendant files a defence,[52] and if the claim form is served on a agent of a principal who is overseas.[53]

Parties agreeing to extend time limit for service of the defence

The time limit can also be extended by up to 28 days if the claimant and defendant so agree. If such an agreement is made, the defendant must notify the court in writing (r 15.5).

Service of the defence

A copy of the defence must be served[54] on every other party (r 15.6).

Response to a defence

A claimant can file a reply to the defence if there are any matters raised by the defence which call for a reply.[55] If the claimant wishes to file a reply, he must do so when he files his allocation questionnaire[56] and he must serve a copy on all the other parties at the same time as he files it (r 15.8).

If the defendant has made a counterclaim against the claimant, this will be treated as a claim in its own right and the claimant must file a defence to the claim, or risk judgment being entered in default (r 12.3(2)).[57] If the claimant serves a reply and defence to counterclaim, in most cases, these should be contained in the same document with the counterclaim following on from the reply (PD 15, para 3.2).

However, no party may file any further statement of case after a reply without the permission of the court (r 15.9).

---

51   *Ibid.*
52   See Chapter 22, Summary Judgment.
53   See Chapter 9, Service of Documents, p 106.
54   See Chapter 9 for rules as to Service.
55   See Chapter 11, Statements of Case, for the content of a reply.
56   See Chapter 15, Judicial Case Management: Allocation.
57   See Chapter 21, Judgment in Default.

Defendant's defence is that money claimed has been paid

It is sometimes the case that a defendant is served with proceedings claiming a specified amount of money and his defence is that he has paid the sum claimed to the claimant.

If the defendant states this in his defence, the court will send Form N236 to the claimant on which he must indicate whether he wishes the proceedings to continue (r 15.10(1)). The claimant must file at court and serve a copy on the defendant of his response in Form N236 (r 15.10(2)).

If the claimant disputes that the defendant has paid the amount claimed, he should indicate in his response that he wishes the proceedings to continue. The court will then follow the procedure for allocation under Part 26.[58]

If the claimant admits that the defendant has paid the amount claimed, he should then take steps to discontinue the proceedings. If a claimant discontinues, he will usually be liable to pay the defendant's costs of the action.[59]

If the claimant fails to respond to the court's notice within 28 days after service on him, his claim shall be stayed (r 15.10(3)). Either party can apply for the stay to be lifted (r 15.10(4)). The defendant may apply to lift the stay if he is satisfied that he paid the sum claimed by the claimant before proceedings were started and he wishes the claimant to discontinue the action and pay his costs incurred in responding to it.

---

58 See Chapter 15, Judicial Case Management: Allocation.
59 See Chapter 34, Discontinuance.

CHAPTER 9

SERVICE OF DOCUMENTS[1]

INTRODUCTION

Under the old rules, there were differences in the methods of service permissible for service of originating process (the collective name for the documents that could be used to start proceedings) and those permissible for all other types of document. The rules restricted the methods available for originating process but allowed a greater variety of methods for other documents such as pleadings, including such means as document exchange and fax. Further, there were differences in practice between the two courts in that the Rules of the Supreme Court made no provision for proceedings issued in the High Court to be served by the court, whereas in the county court, service of proceedings issued by the court was the usual mode.

Lord Woolf recommended that there be no restrictions on the methods of service that could be used even for service of originating process. He believed that, so long as the method of service allowed a party to ascertain the contents of the document served, and the court was satisfied that this had occurred or was likely to have done so, the means by which this came about would be irrelevant. However, he also acknowledged that the process of service of documents relating to court proceedings was of fundamental importance, since it is the means by which parties are notified of claims against them and put in a position to respond. Accordingly, before the court can act on the assumption that a party has been served, it must be satisfied that the method of service used is likely to have achieved its aim and he noted that historically, rules of court have restricted the permissible methods of service of originating process. For these reasons, he accepted that if a more unusual method was used, a party would have a greater task in satisfying the court that service had been effective.[2]

The CPR have now unified the rules for service of the claim form and all other documents. There are some additional rules for service of the claim form, but the main body of the rules on service are the same whichever document is being served. Despite Lord Woolf's recommendations, and perhaps because of his note of caution, the new rules have not adopted a *laissez faire* approach to service and, in fact, there are still a limited number of prescribed methods of service (although the court does have the power to

---

1   See Chapter 10 for the rules on service out of the jurisdiction.
2   See *Access to Justice*, Final Report, Chapter 12, pp 120–23, paras 20–30 (www.lcd.gov.uk/civil/finalfr.htm).

sanction other methods not provided for by the rules). Further, even though there are now more ways to effect service of the claim form, allowing for service using modern means of communication such as email, the standard method is likely to be ordinary, pre-paid, first class post. There are also restrictions on the circumstances when a party can employ a method such as fax or email. Also, now, both courts will effect service of documents such as the claim form, although a party can instead elect to effect service himself.

The rules on service of documents can be found in Part 6 and its accompanying Practice Direction. These rules apply to service of all documents unless any other enactment, a rule in another Part, or a practice direction makes different provision or the court orders otherwise (r 6.1).

Who is to serve?

The general rule is that the court will effect service of a document that it has issued or prepared (r 6.3(1)). The court will always issue the claim form so, in general, the court will serve it. The party on whose behalf the document is to be served can notify the court that he wishes to serve it himself, but unless he does so the court will effect service (r 6.3(1)(b)). This unifies the position between the High Court and county courts and will obviously assist litigants in person. It will also reduce the incidence of actions where proceedings are issued but not served because, unless the party notifies the court otherwise, the court will serve proceedings as a matter of course.[3]

The service of the claim form can be distinguished from the service of other types of documents between the parties. Thus, although the general rule is that the court will effect service, this is a general rule that applies only to documents the court issues or prepares and it will not apply if a rule or practice direction provides that a party must serve the document in question (r 6.3(1)(a) and (c)).

Where a party prepares a document that is to be served by the court, the party must file a copy for the court, and for each party to be served (r 6.3(3)).

Where the court effects service, the court decides which of the methods of service provided by the rules to employ (r 6.3(2)). However, that method will normally be first class post (PD 6, para 8.1). First class post is generally thought to be cheap and reliable. However, where the court attempts to serve the document and is unsuccessful, the court must send a notice of non-service to the party who requested service, stating which method of service was attempted (r 6.11).

It is expected that if the court is unable to effect service by first class post, it will notify the party requesting service and leave it to that party to attempt

---

3   See Chapter 7, Starting an Action, for time limits for serving a claim form after issue.

service rather than go on and use another permitted method. Moreover, when a party receives a notice of non-service from the court, he should take steps to effect service himself as the court is under no further duty to effect service (PD 6, para 8.2). The new rules do not permit personal service by the court bailiff, a method formerly available in the county court when postal service had failed.[4]

METHODS OF SERVICE

For all documents (not just the claim form), the following are the available methods of service:

- personal service;
- first class post;
- leaving the document at an office, business or residential address;
- through a document exchange system;
- by fax or other means of electronic communication; or
- for a company, by any method permitted under Part 6 as well as by a method permitted by the Companies Act 1985 (r 6.2).

In addition, there are special rules about service of the claim form which include the provision of additional methods of service. These are:

- service of the claim form by a contractually agreed method (r 6.15); and
- service of the claim form on an agent of a principal who is overseas (r 6.16).

Personal service

Historically, personal service was the main method of service in the High Court until 1979. The rules were then changed to include service by post, which rapidly became the standard method. It was treated as enough if the person to be served had the documents in his possession long enough to ascertain what they were even if they were then handed back to the person effecting service (see *Nottingham Building Society v Peter Bennett and Co*).[5]

Personal service may be favoured when there is not enough time to serve proceedings by any other means, for example, when a claim form is served on the last day of validity of the claim form[5a] and the last day before the limitation period[6] for that particular cause of action expires. Other reasons

---

4   Under CCR Ord 7 r 10(4).
5   (1997) *The Times*, 26 February.
5a   See Chapter 7, Starting an Action, p 79.
6   See Chapter 3, Limitation of Actions.

may be where the defendant is thought to be evading service or where the claimant wants publicity for the starting of the action and the defendant can, for instance, be filmed being served with proceedings.

Personal service on an individual involves leaving the document with that individual (r 6.4(3)). Personal service on a partnership, where partners are being sued in the name of the firm, involves leaving the document either with one of the partners or on a person who, at the time of service, has control or management of the partnership business at its principal place of business (r 6.4(5)). The practice direction supplementing Part 6 provides for a notice of service on a partner, which is to be in Form N218, to be given to the person who is served stating whether they are served as a partner or as a person having control or management of the partnership business or both (PD 6, para 4.2).

Personal service on a company or other corporation involves leaving the document with a person holding a senior person within it (r 6.4(4)). A 'senior person' in a registered company or corporation is a director, treasurer, secretary, chief executive, manager or other officer of the company or corporation. In respect of a corporation which is not a registered company, in addition to the above, a 'senior person' also includes the mayor, chairman, president, town clerk or similar officer of the corporation (PD 6, para 6.2).

Personal service is allowed in all types of proceedings covered by the new rules. However, if a solicitor is authorised to accept service on behalf of a party and he has notified the person serving the document that he is so authorised, the document must be served on the solicitor rather than the party personally unless personal service is required by an enactment, rule, practice direction or court order (r 6.4(2)).

Address for service

Unless proceedings fall under Section III of Part 6 (service out of the jurisdiction)[7] a document must be served within the jurisdiction. It is to be noted that the CPR do not specify that the *person* to be served must be within the jurisdiction at the time of service, only that the *document* must be served within the jurisdiction.

The CPR provide that a party must give an address for service within the jurisdiction (r 6.5(2)). Where a party who resides or carries on business within the jurisdiction does not give his solicitor as his address for service, he must give his residence or place of business as his address for service (r 6.5(3)). However, where no solicitor is acting for the party to be served and the party has not given an address for service, the rules contain a table that specifies

7   See Chapter 10 for service out of the jurisdiction.

where the document to be served must be sent (r 6.5(6)). In general terms, in the case of an individual, the document must be sent to the party's usual or last known residence. In the case of a proprietor of a business or a partnership, the document must be sent to the party's usual or last known place of residence or business. In the case of a company, the document must be sent to a principal office or place where the company carries on its business or activities and which has a real connection to the claim.[8]

In the case of service of the claim form, if a defendant is acting through a solicitor, the claimant can serve the claim form on the defendant's solicitor only if the solicitor is authorised to accept service on the defendant's behalf (r 6.13(2)).

Where the claimant wishes the court to serve the claim form, it must include the defendant's address for service on the claim form (r 6.13(1)). What the defendant's address is for service should be determined in accordance with the above rules.

If a party or the party's legal representative change their address for service, they are under an obligation to give notice in writing of the change immediately to the court and every other party (PD 6, para 7).

In the case of children and patients, there are special rules about who documents must be served on.[9]

First class post and leaving the document at the party's address

When the court effects service, although it can use any method of service specified by the rules, it will usually employ first class post (PD 6, para 8.1). The court will post the document to the address for service provided by the party in accordance with the rules set out above.

Alternatively, when the party effects service, it can post the document by first class post or simply leave the document at the relevant address. Unlike the old rules, there is no requirement that the document be inserted through a letterbox when it is left at the address for service. Although *prima facie* this would allow the use of any method to leave the document at the address, for example, under the door, or through a window, such methods would not necessarily be in the interests of the party serving the document. This is because in such circumstances, if there is any dispute about non-receipt, use of a more unconventional method of leaving the document at the address, which runs the risk of being overlooked by the party being served, may work against the party trying to prove service.

---

8   See the table set out at r 6.5(6).
9   See r 6.6 and Chapter 26, Special Rules for Children and Patients.

Document exchange (DX)

This method of service can only be used if either the party's address for service includes a numbered box at a DX on the writing paper of the party to be served, or his legal representative, where that legal representative is authorised to accept service, sets out the DX box number. This is the only positive requirement imposed upon a party who wishes to utilise DX for service. In fact, in order to avoid service by DX, the party to be served must have indicated in writing that they are unwilling to accept service by DX (PD 6, para 2.1).

Service is effected by leaving the document addressed to the numbered box either at the DX of the party who is to be served or at a DX which sends documents to that party's DX every business day (PD 6, para 2.2).

Service by electronic means

It is now possible to serve the claim form as well as other documents by electronic methods such as fax or email. Certain conditions must be fulfilled before these methods can be used, but there is no requirement that if such a method is used, it is followed up by a hard copy sent by post or DX. Instead it is left to the party who chooses to use this method to consider the wisdom of such a course. The Practice Direction to Part 6 does say, however, that if a hard copy is not sent and the document is proved not to have been received, then the court may take account of the fact that a hard copy was not sent when considering any application arising out of that non-receipt (PD 6, para 3.4). Therefore, if a hard copy is not sent, it will be easier for the potential recipient to prove non-receipt.

Service by facsimile (fax)

In order to serve the claim form, or other document, by fax, the party who is to be served, or his legal representative, must previously have indicated in writing to the party serving that he is willing to accept service by fax and given the fax number to which the document is to be sent (PD 6, para 3.1).

Although there seems to be a positive requirement that the person to be served has agreed to be served by fax, and that is certainly true where a party is acting in person, it is, in fact, not entirely the case where the party is acting by a legal representative. This is because it seems that the mere fact that the legal representative has a fax number on his writing paper will be treated as sufficient written indication of acceptance of service by fax (PD 6, para 3.1(3)(b)). Also, if a fax number is set out on a statement of case or a response to a claim filed with the court, that too will be treated as sufficient written acceptance of service by fax (PD 6, para 3.1(3)(c)). Further, if the party on whom the document is to be served is acting by a legal representative, the fax must be sent to the legal representative's business address (PD 6, para 3.1(2)).

Service by email and other electronic means

In order to use other electronic means for service, such as email, the party serving the document and the party on whom it is served must both be acting by a legal representative. The document must be served at the legal representative's business address, and the legal representative must have previously indicated, in writing, his willingness to accept service by this method and have provided his email address or other electronic identification such as an ISDN or other telephonic link number (PD 6, para 3.3).

Service on a company

A company can be served by any method permitted under Part 6, as well as methods set out in the Companies Act 1985, which in outline are:

- service by leaving a document or posting it to an authorised place under s 725 of the Companies Act 1985;
- service on overseas companies under s 695 of the Companies Act 1985; and
- service of documents on companies incorporated outside the UK and Gibraltar and having a branch in Great Britain under s 694A of the Companies Act 1985.

Service by an alternative method

Where there is good reason to do so, the court can sanction service by a method not provided for by the rules as an alternative to the prescribed methods (r 6.8). Service by an alternative method is the new terminology for what was formerly known as substituted service. Under the old rules, such an application was classically made when it was thought that a party was evading service and that therefore, it would be difficult to effect service on him using standard methods of service. Also, an application was often made following road traffic accidents when the defendant was uninsured or untraceable and the claimant sought to serve proceedings on an insurer or the Motor Insurers Bureau instead (*Gurtner v Circuit*).[10]

---

10 [1968] 2 QB 587.

The application should only be made when the claimant has either tried other prescribed methods of service which have failed, or where the claimant has evidence that the prescribed methods are unlikely to be successful. The application should be made in accordance with Part 23[11] and supported by evidence stating the reason why an order for an alternative method of service is sought and what steps have been taken to serve by other permitted means (r 6.8 and PD 6, para 9.1). Although not expressly required by the CPR, it is also likely that the court will expect the applicant to specify the alternative method of service that should be permitted and explain why that method is likely to succeed in bringing the document to the party's attention. Examples of alternative methods are service at the address of a person with whom it is known the party to be served has contact with, or by putting a notice in a newspaper.

Additional methods of service of the claim form

Service by a contractually agreed method

Often, contractual agreements contain a term specifying how, if it becomes necessary to start proceedings arising from the contract, those proceedings may be served. Under the CPR, if a claim form is issued containing a claim only in respect of that contract, service by the method specified in the contract will be valid (r 6.15). This is subject to the serving party seeking permission to serve proceedings out of the jurisdiction if such permission is necessary.[12]

Service of claim form on agent of principal who is overseas

In certain circumstances, a party can make an application for a claim form to be served on the defendant's agent in the jurisdiction where the principal is overseas and cannot be served out of the jurisdiction. These are that the claimant entered into the contract with the defendant's agent within the jurisdiction, that the defendant's agent resides, carries on or has a place of business within the jurisdiction, and that at the time the application is made either the agent's authority has not been terminated, or he still has business relations with his principal. Also, at the time the contract was entered into and at the time of the application it must be the case that the principal was not residing or carrying on business within the jurisdiction (r 6.16 and PD 6, para 9.2).

---

11 See Chapter 19, Making Applications for Court Orders.
12 Chapter 10 for the rules about service of proceedings out of the jurisdiction.

Service on members of HM Forces and US Air Force

Special rules exist for service of documents in civil proceedings on these parties (PD 6, para 5 and Annex).

Other rules about service

For certain types of action, some of the old RSC and CCR on service have been preserved in the schedules to the CPR. For instance, where a claim form contains a claim for the possession of land, the court may authorise service of proceedings on the defendant to be effected by affixing a copy of the claim form on some conspicuous part of the land. The claimant must apply for permission to effect service in this way.[13]

Service outside the CPR

The CPR set out a number of permissible methods of service, but there is nothing in the rules which expressly prohibits the parties from agreeing between themselves on a mode of service not provided for by the rules. However, there is nothing in the rules which expressly allows them to do so either.

In the case of *Kenneth Allison Ltd (In Liquidation) v AE Limehouse and Co (A Firm)*,[14] it was held, under the old rules, that the party serving the document was entitled to rely on an ad hoc agreement, made between the parties at the time of service, as to the mode of service, even though it was not a method provided for by the rules. In that case, the claimants issued proceedings for negligence against the defendants, a firm of chartered accountants. On the last day of validity of the writ[15] and the last day before the expiry of the limitation period for the action, a process server attended at the defendants' offices where he told the senior partner's personal assistant that he wished to serve a writ. She consulted one of the partners and he authorised her to accept the writ. She then told the process server that she had been so authorised and received the writ from him. Such service did not constitute personal service on the partner as for such service the document had to be handed to or left in the possession of the party to be served.

It was argued by Lord Goff in that case that there is strong force in the argument that there should be mandatory methods of service so that those concerned at court offices, especially those who have to deal with applications

---

13 See r 55.6 and PD 55, para 4.
14 [1991] 4 All ER 500.
15 Now claim form.

for judgment in default, would know, by reference to rules of court, the precise date when proceedings were treated as having been served.[16] However, Lord Bridge of Harwich, who gave the leading judgment, also adopted the view that the rules should be the servants and not the masters of the court, and should not be construed so as to prevent the parties from acting reasonably when particular situations were met, in circumstances where there was no danger that the defendant would be unsure as to when service was effected.[17]

The court is unlikely to have much sympathy with a party who gets into difficulties effecting service if this is due to the party's own incompetence and delay, and ideally a party should use one of the permitted methods of service. However, it is arguable that if a similar situation were to arise under the CPR, the court, in applying the overriding objective[18] to deal with cases justly, would be likely to treat service in such circumstances as valid. Under the ethos of the new rules, the court is unlikely to entertain technical arguments about whether the rules on service have been complied with in a situation where the document and its contents have come to the party's attention and no real prejudice has been suffered.

Deeming service

If a document is personally served on a business day *before* 5 pm, service takes effect as soon as the document is left with the person to be served. A business day for these purposes is any day except Saturday, Sunday or a Bank Holiday (r 6.7(3)). However, if a document is personally served after 5 pm on a business day or on a day which is not treated as a business day, it will be treated as being served on the next business day (r 6.7(2)).

In all other cases, the rules set out when a document which is served using other methods permitted by the rules is deemed to be served. This varies according to the method of service used. So, if a document is served by first class post, it will be deemed to be served the second day after it was posted, while a document will be deemed to be served the day after it was delivered to or left at a permitted address and the day after it was left at the document exchange. If a document is transmitted by fax on a business day before 4 pm, it will be deemed to be served the same day, otherwise it will be deemed to be served on the next business day after the day it was transmitted. For any other electronic method, such as email, the document will be deemed to be served the second day after the day on which it was transmitted (r 6.7).

---

16 [1991] 4 All ER 500, p 513f–g.

17 *Ibid*, p 508f–h.

18 See Chapter 5, Judicial Case Management: The Overriding Objective.

It should be borne in mind that r 2.8 excludes Saturday, Sunday, Bank Holidays, Christmas Day or Good Friday from calculations of time of five days or less.[19] Therefore, when calculating when service is deemed to have taken effect, these days should be excluded from the calculation.

When service is effected on a party's solicitor in accordance with the rules, the deemed date of service is also that set out in the table in r 6.7 and, therefore, depends on the method of service employed.

As with any other deemed date, a deemed date of service can be rebutted by proof of the actual date of service if that becomes significant, for example, if it is alleged that time limits for responding, etc, have not been complied with.

Certificate of service of the claim form

When the court serves the claim form, it will send the claimant a notice of service which will include the date when the claim form is deemed to be served in accordance with the above rules (r 6.14(1)). If the claimant elects to serve the claim form himself, he must file a certificate of service within 7 days of service of the claim form (r 6.14(2)).

The certificate of service is in Form N215. Once filed, it will allow the court to act on the assumption that service has been successfully effected. The certificate of service must include a signed statement that the claim form has not been returned undelivered, and other details depending on which method of service was used. So, for postal service, the certificate must give the date of posting; for personal service, the date when it was personally served. The date of delivery to the document exchange or the date when the claim form was delivered to or left at the permitted place must be given if these methods were used. If service is effected by fax, the date and time of transmission must be given. For other electronic means, the date and time and means used must be given. Further, if the court permits an alternative method of service, the court will specify what information must be included in the certificate of service (r 6.10).

The certificate of service must also give the deemed date of service (r 6.7). Failure to file a certificate of service of the claim form will preclude the claimant from entering judgment in default.[20]

Such a certificate of service is always necessary if the claimant serves the claim form himself, but may also have to be filed in respect of other documents if required by a rule, practice direction or court order (r 6.10). One example of this is that if the claim form is served on the defendant without

---

19 See Chapter 2, Sources of Civil Procedure: Structure and Jurisdiction of the Civil Courts, p 19.
20 See r 6.14(2)(b) and Chapter 21, Judgment in Default.

particulars of claim, the claimant must file a certificate of service within seven days of service of the particulars of claim (r 7.4(3)).

Dispensing with service

If the circumstances justify it, the court can dispense with the requirement for service of a document (r 6.9). A similar power existed under the old rules and an example of when it is likely to be exercised is if a party is in possession of a document during the course of a hearing that can be simply given to the other party there and then. As the other party has actual possession of the document, the court may well dispense with the need for formal service. However, presenting documents at a late stage is liable to give rise to costs and other penalties.

CHAPTER 10

SERVICE OUT OF THE JURISDICTION

INTRODUCTION

The Civil Procedure Rules have hardly made any serious changes to the rules on service out of the jurisdiction. As before, the position very much depends on whether permission is required or not for service and the question of the time to be allowed for responding to this service, bearing in mind the location of the respondent.

'Jurisdiction' is defined by r 2.3 as England and Wales and any part of the territorial waters of the UK next to England and Wales; therefore, service in any other place constitutes service out of the jurisdiction.

PERMISSION OF THE COURT NOT REQUIRED

There are broadly two situations where the permission of the court is not required to serve proceedings out of the jurisdiction:

- where the claim is one which the court has power to determine under the Civil Jurisdiction and Judgments Act 1982 (the 1982 Act) and there are no other pending proceedings between the parties concerning the same claim either in the UK or any other Convention territory, that is, any country which is a signatory to the Brussels or Lugano Conventions. In addition, the defendant must be domiciled in the UK or in any Convention territory, the relevant parts of the 1982 Act must apply or the defendant is a party to an agreement which confers jurisdiction under the 1982 Act (r 6.19(1));

- or, in the alternative, where by any other enactment the court in this jurisdiction has power to determine the dispute even though the defendant to the claim is not within the jurisdiction or the facts giving rise to the claim did not occur within the jurisdiction (r 6.19(2)).

In any event, the claim form must contain a statement of the basis on which the claimant is entitled to serve out of the jurisdiction without the permission of the court (r 6.19(3)). The usual form of words of the statement are:

> I state that the High Court of England and Wales has power under the Civil Jurisdiction and Judgments Act in 1982 to hear this claim and that no proceedings are pending between the parties in Scotland, Northern Ireland or another Convention territory of any contracting state as defined by s 1(3) of the Act (PD 6B, para 1.1).

Similar statements are also provided for in PD 6B, paras 1.2 and 1.3 in respect of service to other jurisdictions provided for by the rules where permission is required.[1]

PERMISSION OF THE COURT REQUIRED

This depends on the nature of the action being taken (r 6.20):

- general grounds – permission is required if the claim is against someone domiciled within the jurisdiction; for an injunction; against someone on whom the claim form has been served and the claimant wishes to serve on any another party;
- interim remedies – where the claim is for an interim remedy as specified by s 25(1) of the 1982 Act;
- contract – where the contract was made within the jurisdiction; by or through an agent trading or residing within the jurisdiction; is governed by English law; or contains a provision that the courts here shall have jurisdiction to deal with any claim arising out of the contract. In addition, permission will also be required where the claim is in respect of a breach of contract committed within the jurisdiction or for a declaration that no contract exists where, if it did exist, it would be a contract in respect of which the English courts would have jurisdiction;
- tort – where damage was sustained within the jurisdiction or damage resulted from an act committed within the jurisdiction;
- enforcement – where a claim is made to reinforce any judgment or award of an arbitrator;
- property – where the claim wholly concerns property within the jurisdiction;
- trusts – where the trust is one that ought to be executed according to English law and the person on whom the claim form is to be served is a trustee; concerning the administration of an estate of someone who died within the jurisdiction; rectification of a will; and various other trust proceedings;
- claims by the Inland Revenue other than against persons domiciled in the UK.
- claims for costs against non-parties;
- any other claims provided for by statute.

---

1   See below.

The application for permission

The application[2] must be supported by written evidence stating the grounds on which the application is made and the relevant provisions of r 6.20, contain confirmation that the claimant believes that the claim has a reasonable chance of success; and the defendant's address or the place where he is likely to be found if his address is not known (r 6.21(1)). A complete set of documents must be provided for each party to be served out of the jurisdiction. These include a copy of the particulars of claim if not already included on the claim form, the claim form, the forms for responding to the claim and any translation that may be required by the courts (PD 6B, para 2.1).

Permission will be dependent on the court here being satisfied that this jurisdiction is the proper place in which to bring the claim (r 6.21(2A)). Where the application is for permission to serve a claim form in Scotland or Northern Ireland and the claim is one that could also be dealt with in those jurisdictions, the court will consider the question of cost and convenience (r 6.21(3)).

TIME LIMITS FOR RESPONDING TO THE CLAIM

When giving permission, the court will specify the periods within which the respondent may answer the claim by filing an acknowledgment of service, admission or defence (r 6.21(4)). The relevant periods for responding to proceedings will depend on the country to which the notice is being sent. Reference should be made to PD 6B, paras 7 and 9.1 as to the requisite number of days by reference to country.

Where permission is not required and the defendant is in Scotland, Northern Ireland or in the European territory of a Contracting State as defined by s 1(3) of the 1982 Act, the relevant period is 21 days from service of the particulars of claim whether contained in the claim form or served later (r 6.22(2)). In the case of any other country which is a Contracting State, the relevant time period is 31 days (r 6.22(3)).

The relevant period for serving a defence where permission is not required is 21 days after service of the particulars of claim or 35 days from service of the particulars of claim where the defendant has filed an acknowledgment of service where the defendant is in Scotland, Northern Ireland or in the European territory of a Contracting State as defined above (r 6.23(2)). In the case of any other country which is a Contracting State, the relevant time period is 31 days after service of the particulars of claim or 45 days after service of the particulars of claim (r 6.23(3)).

---

2   Part 23 – see Chapter 19, Making Applications for Court Orders.

The rules provide for service to be effected by any method permitted by the law of the country in which it is to be served, or as is permitted by a Civil Procedure Convention or through foreign governments, judicial authorities and British consular authorities (r 6.24). There are also special provisions for service of the claim form on a State (r 6.27).

SERVICE OF DOCUMENTS OTHER THAN CLAIM FORM (r 6.30)

Where permission of the court is required for service of a claim form out of the jurisdiction, it is also required to serve any notice of application out of the jurisdiction (r 6.30(2)). Similarly, where permission is not required to serve proceedings out of the jurisdiction, no permission is required to serve a notice of application out of the jurisdiction (r 6.30(3)).

The period for responding to an application notice will depend on the country to which the notice is being sent. Reference should be made to PD 6B, paras 8.1 and 9.1 as to the requisite number of days by reference to country.

PROOF OF SERVICE (r 6.31)

Where the defendant does not turn up in response to a fixed date claim form, the claimant will not be able to proceed unless he is able to provide written evidence showing that the claim form has been properly served.

DISPUTING THE COURT'S JURISDICTION

Where a defendant is served with proceedings out of the jurisdiction and he disputes that the court has jurisdiction to try the claim or believes that the court should not exercise its jurisdiction in the particular circumstances of the case, he should apply to the court for an order declaring that it has no such jurisdiction or that it should not exercise any jurisdiction which it may have (r 11.1). However, before making such an application, the defendant must first file an acknowledgment of service[3] (r 11.2). The CPR specifically provides that filing an acknowledgment of service does not result in the defendant losing any right he may have to dispute the court's jurisdiction (r 11.3).

---

3   See Chapter 8, Responding to an Action, p 84.

Making an application to dispute the court's jurisdiction

The acknowledgement of service forms, (N9 for claims under Part 7[4] and N210 for claims under Part 8[5]) contain a box in which the defendant can indicate that he contests the court's jurisdiction. Having filed an acknowledgment of service indicating that he disputes the court's jurisdiction the defendant should then apply to the court for an order declaring that it has no such jurisdiction or should not exercise any jurisdiction which it should have (rr 11.1(b) and 11.2).

The application, which should be made under Part 23,[6] must be made within the period of time for filing a defence in claims under Part 7[7] and within 14 days from the filing of the acknowledgment of service for claims under Part 8[8] (rr 11.4, 11.10). In both cases the application must be supported by evidence (r 11.4). If the defendant files an acknowledgment of service, but does not make such an application, with the time specified will be treated as having accepted that the court has jurisdiction to try the claim (r 11.5). In such circumstances, if the defendant does in fact wish to contest the court's jurisdiction he should apply for an order for permission to do so out of time.[9]

In the case of claims proceeding under Part 7,[10] if the defendant makes an application to dispute the court's jurisdiction he does not need to file a defence to the claim before the application is heard (r 11.9). This is for the obvious reason that if the court accepts the defendant's application and makes a declaration that the court does not have jurisdiction to hear the claim a defence to the claim is unnecessary.

Orders the court may make

If the court makes an order declaring that the court has no jurisdiction to try the claim or will not exercise its jurisdiction it may make further provision to dispose of the proceedings. This includes powers to make orders such as setting aside the claim form, setting aside service of the claim form, discharging any order made before the claim was commenced[11] or before the claim form was served or staying the proceedings (r 11.6).

---

4   See Chapter 7, Starting an Action.
5   See Chapter 14, Part 8 Claims.
6   See Chapter 19, Making Applications for Court Orders.
7   See Chapter 8, Responding to an Action, for Part 7 claims.
8   See Chapter 14, Part 8 claims.
9   See Chapter 5, Judicial Case Management: The Overriding Objective.
10 See Chapter 8, Responding to an Action.
11 See Chapter 20, Interim Remedies.

If the court does not make a declaration that the court does not have jurisdiction or will not exercise jurisdiction, the defendant must then file a fresh acknowledgment of service in the proceedings within 14 days of the declaration, or such other period as the court may direct, as the original acknowledgment of service will no longer be effective (r 11.7). On filing a fresh acknowledgment of service the defendant will be treated a having accepted that the court has jurisdiction to try the claim (r 11.8).

CHAPTER 11

STATEMENTS OF CASE

INTRODUCTION

The provisions for statements of case are contained in CPR Part 16 and the Practice Direction thereto. 'Statement of case' is the new term for a pleading and includes:

- a claim form;
- particulars of claim where these are not included in a claim form;
- a defence;
- a Part 20 claim;
- a reply to defence; and
- any further information given in relation to them voluntarily or by court order (see definition in r 2.3(1)).

The provisions of Part 16 do not apply to the Part 8 alternative procedure[1] (r 16.1).

The intention is to replace the old stylised form of pleading, often settled by counsel, with a plain English explanation of the position of each of the parties with regard to the action. Thus, a straightforward statement of the claimant's case must be put forward to be met by a proper response from the defendant, bare denials not being acceptable.

General guidance as to the function of statements of case was given by Lord Woolf in *McPhilemy v Times Newspapers Ltd*.[1a] In that case, Lord Woolf criticised the excessive particulars provided by the parties' statements of case asserting instead that '[n]o more than a concise statement of [the] facts is required'.[2] Although he recognised that statements of case are 'critical to identify the issues and the extent of the dispute between the parties',[3] he stated that the need for extensive statements of case should be reduced by the requirement to exchange witness statements and to identify and attach copies of documents which are relied on. He went on to say that he believed that 'excessive particulars can achieve directly the opposite result from that which is intended. They can obscure the issues rather than providing clarification'.[4]

---

1   See Chapter 14, Part 8 Claims.
1a [1999] 3 All ER 775.
2   *Ibid*, p 793b.
3   *Ibid*, p 793a.
4   *Ibid*, p 793c.

Lord Woolf's view was endorsed in the case of *The Royal Brompton Hospital NHS Trust v Hammond and Others*.[5] In that case, Seymour J warned that the requirement for concise pleadings was not meant to convey the message that statements of case were no longer of importance in defining a party's case (which must be done accurately and with care), or that there would be a general licence to depart at will from a pleaded case.

THE CLAIM

The claim form must:

- contain a concise statement of the nature of the claim;
- specify the remedy which the claimant seeks;
- in a money claim, state the value which the claimant places on the claim; and
- contain such other matters as may be set out in a practice direction (r 16.2(1)).

There is no requirement that the claimant make clear, even in the most general terms, the grounds on which he brings his claim, but if no reasonable grounds are disclosed, the claim may be struck out (r 3.4(2)(a)).[6]

In a claim for money, the claim form must also specify the amount of money claimed, or, if the claimant is unable to do so, he must state in the claim form that he expects to recover (r 16.3(2)):

- not more than £5,000;
- more than £5,000 but not more than £15,000; or
- more than £15,000.

Alternatively, the claimant may state that he does not know how much he expects to recover. This is likely to be an unattractive option, as such a statement will almost inevitably lead to the charging of the maximum court fee!

Value of the claim

When calculating how much he expects to recover, the claimant must disregard:

- interest;
- costs;

---

5   The court service website (www.courtservice.gov.uk).
6   See Chapter 23, Striking Out.

- the possibility that the court may make a finding of contributory negligence against him;
- the possibility that the defendant may make a counterclaim or claim a set off; or
- that the defendant may have to pay sums to the Secretary of State for Social Security under the recoupment provisions[7] provided by s 6 of the Social Security (Recovery of Benefits) Act 1997 (r 16.3(6)).

In a claim which does not exceed £5,000 in value for, or which includes a claim for, personal injury, the claimant must also state the amount he expects to recover as general damages for pain, suffering and loss of amenity (r 16.3(3)). This is relevant on allocation of the claim to track should it become defended. If the pain, suffering and loss of amenity element of the claim exceeds £1,000, the claim will not be allocated to the small claims track.

Similarly, in a claim which includes a claim by a tenant of residential premises against his landlord where the tenant is seeking an order that the landlord carry out repairs or other work to the premises, the claimant must state whether the amount of damages he expects to recover for this part of the claim, or any resulting damages claim, exceeds or does not exceed £1,000 (r 16.3(4)). Again, if such a claim or resulting claim is expected to exceed £1,000, it will not be allocated to the small claims track should it become defended.

Where the claim form is issued in the High Court, the claimant must either state that he expects to recover more than £15,000, or else he must show by naming it, an enactment which provides that the claim may be commenced only in the High Court, or otherwise he must state that the claim is one of those on the specialist jurisdiction lists[7a] (r 16.3(5)).

The distinction has now gone, for the purposes of claims brought under the CPR, between 'liquidated' and 'unliquidated' claims. The distinction now is between a claim for 'a specified sum' and a claim for 'an unspecified sum'. The importance of the distinction is in how admissions are dealt with,[8] and also in connection with the new rules for automatic transfer.[9]

It should be borne in mind by defendants that there may be judgment for more than initially claimed (r 16.3(7)) – the old position, that the claim was limited to the amount which the plaintiff had claimed, does not now apply. Furthermore, the court is now expressly empowered to grant any remedy to which the claimant may be entitled whether or not the claimant has sought it

---

7   See Chapter 24, Part 36 offers and payments, p 285, for an explanation of the recoupment provisions.

7a See p 18, Specialist proceedings.

8   See Chapter 8, Responding to an Action.

9   See Chapter 15, Judicial Case Management: Allocation, p 153.

(r 16.2(5)). Claimants may still seek 'such further or other relief as the court deems appropriate' – the previous practice.

A claimant is not bound only to make an unspecified claim in cases where there has previously been an assessment, for example, for personal injuries ('damages not exceeding £x'), but can elect to make a specified claim ('damages in the sum of £x') and claim a default judgment[10] for that sum.

Contents of particulars of claim

(1) Particulars of claim must include:

    (a) a concise statement of the facts on which the claimant relies;

    (b) if the claimant is seeking interest, a statement to that effect and the details set out in paragraph (2);[11]

    (c) if the claimant is seeking aggravated damages or exemplary damages, a statement to that effect and his grounds for claiming them;

    (d) if the claimant is seeking provisional damages,[12] a statement to that effect and his grounds for claiming them; and

    (e) such other matters as may be set out in a practice direction.

Claim for interest

If a claimant wishes to recover interest on his claim he must provide the particulars required by r 16.4(2). If a claim for interest is not made, none will be recoverable.

(2) If the claimant is seeking interest he must:

    (a) state whether he is doing so –

        (i) under the terms of a contract,

        (ii) under an enactment and if so which, or

        (iii) on some other basis and if so what that basis is; and

    (b) if the claim is for a specified amount of money, state –

        (i) the percentage rate at which interest is claimed;

        (ii) the date from which it is claimed;

        (iii) the date to which it is calculated, which must not be later than the date on which the claim form is issued;

        (iv) the total amount of interest claimed to the date of calculation; and

        (v) the daily rate at which interest accrues after that date.

---

10 See Chapter 21, Judgment in Default.

11 See below.

12 See Chapter 25, Provisional Damages.

Interest may be recoverable as of right at a specified rate and from a specified time under the terms of a contract. If a contract does not specify that interest is recoverable following breach, or where the claim is not based on a contract, the claimant may seek interest under s 35A of the Supreme Court Act 1981 for High Court claims or s 69 of the County Courts Act 1984 for county court claims. Whether such statutory interest is recoverable is in the court's discretion, although it is almost invariably awarded. The current rate of interest is 8%.

In the case of personal injuries or death claims the court *must* award interest if the damages exceed £200 unless the court is satisfied that there would be satisfactory reasons not to do so (s 35A(2) of the Supreme Court Act 1981).

If a party falls within the requirements of the Late Payment of Commercial Debts (Interest) Act 1998, which provides for a small business creditor to recover interest on debts arising under a commercial contract from a large business debtor, higher rates of interest may be claimed, currently at the rate of 8% above base rate.

In the case of a claim for a specified amount of money, if the claimant has provided the requisite details regarding any claim for interest, if judgment is entered in default it will include the amount claimed for interest.[13]

Claims in respect of land

Where a claim is made for an *injunction or declaration in respect of or relating to any land or the possession, occupation, use or enjoyment of any land*, the particulars of claim must:

(1) state whether or not the injunction or declaration relates to residential premises, and

(2) identify the land by reference to a plan where necessary (PD 16, para 8.1).

Claims for the possession of goods

Where a claim is brought to enforce a right to recover *possession of goods* the particulars of claim must contain a statement showing the value of the goods (PD 16, para 8.2).

Breach of contract claims

Where a claim is based upon a *written agreement*:

---

13   See Chapter 21, Judgment in Default, p 236.

(1) a copy of the contract or documents constituting the agreement including any general conditions of sale incorporated in the contract should be attached to or served with the particulars of claim and the original(s) should be available at the hearing,

(2) but where the documents constituting the agreement are bulky this Practice Direction is complied with by attaching or serving only the relevant parts of the contract or documents) (PD 16, para 8.3).

Where a claim is based upon an *oral agreement*, the particulars of claim should set out the contractual words used and state by whom, to whom, when and where they were spoken (PD 16, para 8.4).

Where a claim is based upon an *agreement by conduct*, the particulars of claim must specify the conduct relied on and state by whom, when and where the acts constituting the conduct were done (PD 16, para 8.5).

Matters relied on which must be specifically set out in the particulars of claim

There are certain details which must be specifically pleaded if a claimant's claim includes any of the following:

A claimant who wishes to rely on evidence:

(1) under s 11 of the Civil Evidence Act 1968 of a conviction of an offence, or

(2) under s 12 of the above-mentioned Act of a finding or adjudication of adultery or paternity, must include in his particulars of claim a statement to that effect and give the following details:

 (1) the type of conviction, finding or adjudication and its date,

 (2) the Court or Court Martial which made the conviction, finding or adjudication, and

 (3) the issue in the claim to which it relates (PD 16, para 9.1).

The claimant must specifically set out the following matters in his particulars of claim where he wishes to rely on them in support of his claim:

(1) any allegation of fraud,

(2) the fact of any illegality,

(3) details of any misrepresentation,

(4) details of all breaches of trust,

(5) notice or knowledge of a fact,

(6) details of unsoundness or mind or undue influence,

(7) details of wilful default, and

(8) any facts relating to mitigation of loss or damage (PD 16, para 9.2).

Note that in pleading misrepresentation, it is always necessary to allege that the party alleging them has relied on this misrepresentation, and to his detriment, and precedent books should be consulted. There is now a requirement to 'deal with any facts relating to mitigation', meaning the extent to which the claimant has mitigated or endeavoured to mitigate his loss. Curiously, there is no such requirement on a defendant.

Any party may:

(1) refer in his statement of case to any point of law on which his claim is based,

(2) give in his statement of case the name of any Witness whom he proposes to call, and

(3) attach to or serve with the statement of case a copy of any document which he considers is necessary to his claim (including any expert's report to be filed in accordance with Part 35) (PD 16, para 14.3).

Where the claim is in respect of personal injuries, the Practice Direction to Part 16 provides that the particulars must contain:

(1) the claimant's date of birth, and

(2) brief details of the claimant's personal injuries.

The claimant must attach to his particulars of claim a schedule of details of any past and future expenses and losses which he claims.

Where the claimant is relying on the evidence of a medical practitioner, the claimant must attach to or serve with his particulars of claim a report from a medical practitioner about the personal injuries which he alleges in his claim (PD 16, paras 4.1–4.3).

In a provisional damages claim,[14] the claimant must state in his particulars of claim:

(1) that he is seeking an award of provisional damages under either s 32A of the Supreme Court Act 1981 or Section 51 of the County Courts Act 1984,

(2) that there is a chance that at some future time the claimant will develop some serious disease or suffer some serious deterioration in his physical or mental condition, and

(3) specify the disease or type of deterioration in respect of which an application may be made at a future date (PD 16, para 4.4).

Formerly, the medical report was required 'to substantiate the injuries alleged'. Presumably the changed wording is only so as to reduce this wording to basic English, but the new wording seems less stringent than before.

In a fatal accident claim, the claimant must state in his particulars of claim:

(1) that it is brought under the Fatal Accidents Act 1976,

(2) the dependants on whose behalf the claim is made,

(3) the date of birth of each dependant, and

---

14 See Chapter 25, Provisional Damages.

(4) details of the nature of the dependency claim.

A fatal accident claim may include a claim for damages for bereavement.

In a fatal accident claim, the claimant may also bring a claim under the Law Reform (Miscellaneous Provisions) Act 1934 on behalf of the Estate of the deceased (PD 16, paras 5.1–5.3).

(For information on apportionment under the Law Reform (Miscellaneous Provisions) Act 1934 and the Fatal Accidents Act 1976 or between dependants, see Part 37 and the Practice Direction which supplements it.)

In a claim for recovery of land, the particulars of claim must:

(1) Identify the land sought to be recovered.

(2) State whether the claim relates to residential premises.

(3) If the claim relates to residential premises, state whether the rateable value of the premises on every day specified by s 4(2) of the Rent Act 1977 in relation to the premises exceeds the sum so specified or whether the rent for the time being payable in respect of the premises exceeds the sum specified in s 4(4)(b) of the Act.

(4) Where the claim relates to residential premises and is for non-payment of rent, state:

(a) the amount due at the start of the proceedings,

(b) details of all payments which have been missed,

(c) details of any history of late or under payment,

(d) any previous steps taken to recover the arrears of rent with full details of any Court proceedings, and

(e) any relevant information about the defendant's circumstances, in particular whether any payments are made on his behalf directly to the claimant under the Social Security Contributions and Benefits Act 1992.

(5) Give details about the agreement or tenancy, if any, under which the land was held, stating when it determined and the amount of money payable by way of rent or licence fee.

(6) In a case to which s 138 of the County Courts Act 1984 applies (forfeiture for non-payment), state the daily rate at which the rent in arrear is to be calculated.

(7) State the ground on which possession is claimed whether statutory or otherwise, and

(8) In a case where the claimant knows of any person entitled to claim relief against forfeiture as under-lessee (including a mortgagee) under s 146(4) of the Law of Property Act 1925 (or in accordance with s 38 of the Supreme Court Act 1981), give the name and address of that person.

(See also further rules about recovery of land in RSC Ords 88 and 113 (Sched 1 to the CPR) and CCR Ords 6 and 24 (Sched 2 to the CPR) (PD 16, para 6.)

Where the claim is for the delivery of goods let under a hire purchase agreement to a person other than a company or other corporation, the claimant must state in the particulars of claim:

(1) the date of the Agreement,

(2) the parties to the Agreement,

(3) the number or other identification of the Agreement,

(4) where the claimant was not one of the original parties to the Agreement, the means by which the rights and duties of the creditor passed to him,

(5) whether the Agreement is a regulated agreement and if it is not a regulated agreement, the reason why,

(6) the place where the Agreement was signed by the defendant,

(7) the goods claimed,

(8) the total price of the goods,

(9) the paid-up sum,

(10) the unpaid balance of the total price,

(11) whether a Default Notice or a Notice under Section 76(1) or 98(1) of the Consumer Credit Act 1974 has been served on the defendant, and if it has, the date and method of service,

(12) the date when the right to demand delivery of the goods accrued,

(13) the amount (if any) claimed as an alternative to the delivery of goods, and

(14) the amount (if any) claimed in addition to:

    (a) the delivery of the goods, or

    (b) any claim under (13) above, with the grounds of each claim (PD 16, para 7.1).

Where the claim is not for the delivery of goods, the claimant must state in his particulars of claim:

(1) the matters set out in paragraph 8.19(1) to (6) above,

(2) the goods let under the Agreement,

(3) the amount of the total price,

(4) the paid up sum,

(5) the amount (if any) claimed as being due and unpaid in respect of any instalment or instalments of the total price, and

(6) the nature and amount of any other claim and how it arises (PD 16, para 7.2).

Defamation

As before, proceedings for defamation[15] may not be started, nor transferred, to the county court save by agreement in writing between the parties. Practice

---

15 See Chapter 2, Sources of Civil Procedure: Structure and Jurisdiction of the Civil Courts, p 14.

Direction 16, para 8 contains the requirements for the contents of the particulars of claim.

Specialist proceedings

(For definition see Part 49.)[16] The Claim Form N1 cannot always be used, as 'it may be necessary' to follow the relevant Practice Direction and use the practice form approved for issue of the particular specialist proceedings, that is, one of those proceedings listed in Parts 49 and 50. The CPR will apply only to the extent that they are not inconsistent with Rules and Practice Directions which apply to these specialist claims (PD 16, para 1.2).

THE DEFENCE

In response, a 'defence' must:
- (a) State:
    - (i) which parts of the claim the defendant admits
    - (ii) which parts he denies;
    - (iii) which parts he neither admits nor denies, because he does not know whether they are true, but which he wishes the claimant to prove;
- (b) Give the defendant's version of the facts in so far as they differ from those in the statement of claim;
- (c) Say why the defendant disputes the claimant's entitlement to any, or to a particular, remedy or the value of the claim or assessment of damages; and
- (d) Specify any document vital to the defence (r 16.5).

Defence: details

16.5(3) A defendant who –
- (a) fails to deal with an allegation; but
- (b) has set out in his defence the nature of his case in relation to the issue to which that allegation is relevant,

shall be taken to require that allegation to be proved.
- (4) Where the claim includes a money claim, a defendant shall be taken to require that any allegation relating to the amount of money claimed be proved unless he expressly admits the allegation.
- (5) Subject to paragraphs (3) and (4), a defendant who fails to deal with an allegation shall be taken to admit that allegation.

---

16 Chapter 2, Sources of Civil Procedure: Structure and Jurisdiction of the Civil Courts, p 18.

(6) If the defendant disputes the claimant's statement of value under rule 16.3 (*in relation to a claim for personal injuries*) he must:

(a) state why he disputes it; and

(b) if he is able, give his own statement of the value of the claim.

Additionally, by PD 16, para 15.1:

Where the claim is for personal injuries and the claimant has attached a medical report in respect of his alleged injuries, the defendant should:

(1) state in his defence whether he

(a) agrees,

(b) disputes, or

(c) neither agrees nor disputes but has no knowledge of the matters contained in the medical report,

(2) where he disputes any part of the medical report, give in his defence his reasons for doing so, and

(3) where he has obtained his own medical report on which he intends to rely, attach it to his defence.

15.2 Where the claim is for personal injuries and the claimant has included a schedule of past and future expenses and losses, the defendant should include in or attach to his defence a counter-schedule stating:

(1) which of those items he

(a) agrees,

(b) disputes, or

(c) neither agrees nor disputes but has no knowledge of, and

(2) where any items are disputed, supplying alternative figures where appropriate.

For special requirements for defences in defamation cases, see PD 16, para 16.

Note that the requirement to specify a document is mandatory as compared to the discretionary requirement to attach a document to a claim.[17] Damages can be admitted, if desired for the purpose of the action, whichever way it goes, but otherwise a defendant shall not be taken to admit damages unless he does expressly admit them.

A defence which admits liability, but which denies damage, may well be treated by the court as an admission of an unspecified claim and judgment may be entered with damages to be assessed at a disposal hearing. The fact that an issue as to quantum is not raised in a 'defence' or that there has been a default judgment does not necessarily mean that issue cannot be raised at a hearing on quantum.[18]

---

17 See above, p 123.

18 See *Lunnun v Singh and Others* (1999) *The Times*, 19 July, CA.

Statements of value[19] can be disputed, in which case the defendant must say why and, if able, give his own (r 16.6). Representative capacities must be stated in a defence, and if an acknowledgment of service has not been given, an address for service must be supplied (r 16.7 and 16.8).

Defence of set off

Where a defendant contends that he is entitled to money from the claimant and relies on this as a defence to the whole or part of the claimant's claim, he can include this contention in his defence and set off against the claim. A defendant can contend this without making a counterclaim against the claimant under Part 20 (r 16.6). On the other hand, a defendant can also plead the set off as a counterclaim to which the provisions of Part 20[20] would apply and for which a court fee would be payable.

REPLY

A reply is optional. If the claimant does wish to file a reply in response to the defence, he should do so when he files his allocation questionnaire.[21] There are to be no further 'statements of case' after a reply without the permission of the court (r 15.9).

16.7(1) A claimant who does not file a reply to the defence shall not be taken to admit the matters raised in the defence.

(2) A claimant who:

(a) files a reply to a defence, but

(b) fails to deal with a matter raised in the defence,

shall be taken to require that matter to be proved.

It may be that eventually, replies will become less common save in those cases where there is a positive assertion by the defendant which is not covered by the particulars of claim or which the claimant wishes to meet by raising a positive case himself.

STATEMENT OF TRUTH

This is a statement that the party putting forward a document believes it to be true. It should appear on all statements of case. It is usually signed by a party,

19 See above, p 118.
20 See Chapter 12, Part 20 Claims.
21 See Chapter 15, Judicial Case Management: Allocation.

litigation friend or legal representative (r 22.1(6)). PD 22, para 3.11 sets out who should sign the statement in the case of managing agents, trusts, companies, insurers and the Motor Insurers' Bureau, and in-house legal advisers.

If there is no signed statement of truth, then the party cannot rely on the document as evidence of any of the matters set out in it and/or a statement of case not so verified may be struck out (PD 22, para 4). The costs consequences for failing to verify a statement of case are set out at PD 22, para 4.3 and will usually mean that the costs will have to be paid by the party who failed to verify in any event and forthwith. The effect of having the signed statement of truth is to turn the statement of case into evidence that can be used to support an application such as for summary judgment.

The form of statement is:

'I believe [or, as the case may be, 'the claimant believes'] that the facts in this [name of document being verified] are true' (PD 22, para 2).

A false statement amounts to a contempt (r 32.14), so practitioners are advised that only those with direct knowledge of the facts should actually sign the statement of truth, although the form of the statement of truth does allow the signatory to say that 'the claimant believes it to be true'. Practitioners cannot sign a witness statement other than their own. Where a party is legally represented, and the legal representative signs the document, it will be assumed that he did explain to the client beforehand the possible consequences if the statement turns out not to be true (PD 22, para 3.8). Note that the cost of using an affidavit instead of a statement verified under Part 22 can only be recovered if the rule or practice direction requires an affidavit. The net result of this is that affidavits are now much less likely to be used.

SUBSEQUENT AND AMENDED STATEMENTS OF CASE

A subsequent statement of case must not contradict or be inconsistent with an earlier one; for example, a reply to a defence must not bring in a new claim. Where new matters have come to light, the appropriate course may be to seek the court's permission to amend the statement of case.

The previous, rather lax, system in the county court of allowing amendments without leave up to a return day has been tightened up. A statement of case which has not yet been served may always be amended, and no permission is required (r 17.1). But note r 17.2:

(1) If a party has amended his statement of case where permission of the court was not required, the court may disallow the amendment.

(2) A party may apply to the court for an order under paragraph (1) within 14 days of service of a copy of the amended statement of case on him.

If an amendment is required after service, an application must be filed in accordance with Part 23,[22] accompanied by the proposed amendment. The application may be dealt with at a hearing, but not if the court considers a hearing would not be appropriate, or where the parties themselves agree that a hearing is unnecessary, or simply agree the amendment, although this would be subject to scrutiny by the court (r 23.8 and PD 17, para 1.1).

Any party who seeks permission will find that permission is given subject to directions as to amendments made as to any other statements of case, and as to service. A party applying for an amendment will usually be responsible for the costs of and arising from the amendment. If a statement of case is amended, the statement of truth should be re-verified (PD 17, para 1.4). As to amendments made after a limitation period has expired, r 17.4 confirms the previous practice of the court to allow amendments only if there is a new claim arising out of the same facts. An amendment to correct the name of a party after a genuine mistake is allowable, if the court permits, under r 17.4(3).[23]

REQUEST FOR FURTHER INFORMATION

This replaces the previous rules on requests for further and better particulars and interrogatories.

18.1(1) The court may at any time order a party to –

    (a) clarify any matter which is in dispute in the proceedings; or

    (b) give additional information in relation to any such matter, whether or not the matter is contained or referred to in a statement of case.

The court may exercise this power either on its own initiative or on application by a party. Before seeking such an order there should have first been a request in writing to the other side who should be given a reasonable amount of time in which to respond (PD 18, paras 1 and 2).

Although the application must usually be made on notice, in accordance with Part 23 (see Chapter 19, Making Applications) (PD 18, para 5.1), where the respondent does not reply to the request (minimum period 14 days) the application may be made without notice (PD 18, para 5.5). Consideration should carefully be given as to the efficacy of making a request before disclosure and the exchange of witness statements.[24] It is no longer essential to repeat *verbatim* the request for information when supplying it.

---

22 See Chapter 19, Making Applications for Court Orders.
23 See Chapter 13, Adding or Substituting a Party.
24 *Hall v Selvaco* (1996) *The Times*, 27 March, CA.

CHAPTER 12

PART 20 CLAIMS

INTRODUCTION

Any claim, other than a claim by a claimant against a defendant, is called a Part 20 claim (r 20.2(1)). The old reference to third party has gone – in fact, what used to be third party claims are now joined by counterclaims, which has resulted in a somewhat confused situation, for example, the defendant to a counterclaim (that is, the claimant) also becomes known as a Part 20 defendant.

Part 20 claims fall into four categories:

- counterclaims against claimant(s);
- counterclaims against claimant(s) and a non-party;
- claims for contribution or indemnity made between defendants to the claim;
- any other claim made by a defendant against a non-party (r 20.2(1)).

Any person who becomes a defendant to a Part 20 claim may himself bring a similar claim against another (whether or not already a party), and this, too, will be a Part 20 claim.

PROCEDURE RULES APPLYING TO PART 20 CLAIMS

The CPR apply generally to Part 20 claims as if they were claims (r 20.3(1)). However, by r 20.3(2), the following rules do not apply to Part 20 claims:

(a) Rules 7.5 and 7.6 (time within which a claim form may be served);[1]

(b) Rule 16.3(5) (statement of value where claim to be issued in the High Court);[2] and

(c) Part 26 (case management – preliminary stage),[3]

and by r 20.3(3) the following rules do not apply, except where the Part 20 claim is a counterclaim:

(a) Part 12 (default judgment);[4] and

---

1   See Chapter 7, Starting an Action, p 79.
2   See Chapter 11, Statements of Case, p 118.
3   See Chapter 15, Judicial Case Management: Allocation.
4   See Chapter 21, Judgment in Default.

(b) Part 14 (admissions)[5] except Rules 14.1(1) and (2) (which provide that a party may admit in writing the truth of another party's case) and 14.3 (admission by notice in writing – application for judgement).

COUNTERCLAIMS

A counterclaim may be made without permission where:

- it is brought against the claimant or one or more of them; and
- it is filed with the defence.

Thus, leave will be required to commence a counterclaim:

- before or after filing of the counterclaimant's defence;
- where no defence is filed (r 20.4).

Form of counterclaim and the reply

Where a defendant to a claim serves a counterclaim under this Part, the defence and counterclaim should normally form one document with the counterclaim following on from the defence.

Where a claimant serves a reply and a defence to counterclaim, the reply and the defence to counterclaim should normally form one document with the defence to counterclaim following on from the reply (PD 6, paras 6.1 and 6.2).

A blank form for a Part 20 claim is part of the response pack sent out by the court with the claim form to a defendant. Ironically, a response pack, indicating the need to serve and file a defence to the counterclaim, is not provided for the recipient of a Part 20 counterclaim, which may cause problems when it comes to filing a defence and thereby avoiding judgment in default.[6]

A counterclaim is a statement of case and, therefore, subject to the

---

5   See Chapter 8, Responding to an Action, p 86.
6   See below, p 137, and Chapter 21, Judgment in default.
7   See Chapter 11, Statements of Case.
8   See r 20.9 below as to the matters the court will take into account.

requirements of Part 16.[7]

The defendant can make a counterclaim against the claimant in respect of any cause of action whether or not it is connected to the claimant's claim against him. However, if the counterclaim is in respect of a totally unrelated matter, the court is likely to order that it be dealt with separately and not as part of the claimant's action.[8]

PD 20 provides:

4.1 The contents of a Part 20 claim should be verified by a statement of truth.[9] Part 22 requires a statement of case to be verified by a statement of truth.

4.2 The form of the statement of truth should be as follows:

'[I believe][Part 20 claimant]' believes] that the facts stated in this statement of case are true'.

4.3 Attention is drawn to rule 32.14 which sets out the consequences of verifying a statement 'of case containing a false statement without an honest belief in its truth.

Filing and service

The counterclaim is made by filing particulars of the counterclaim and must be served with the defence. A defence to counterclaim must be filed within 14 days of service of the counterclaim. Under r 20.4(3) an acknowledgment of service may not be filed in relation to a counterclaim, which is anomalous, because it may be used for every other form of Part 20 claim, thereby giving the defendant to the Part 20 claim an additional 14 days in which to file a defence.

A counterclaimant may thus be in the position of having to file his allocation questionnaire before he knows how the claimant (defendant to counterclaim) pleads to the counterclaim. However, r 3.1(2) provides:

Except where these Rules provide otherwise, the court may –

(a) extend or shorten the time for compliance with any rule, practice direction or court order (even if an application for extension is made after the time for compliance has expired).

Rule 20.12 provides that where a Part 20 claim form is served on a person who is not already a party (which would include where a counterclaim is served on a person other than the claimant) it must be accompanied by:

(a) a form for defending the claim;

(b) a form for admitting the claim;

(c) a form for acknowledging service; and

(d) a copy of:

---

9   See Chapter 11, Statements of Case, p 128.

(i) every statement of case which has already been served in the proceedings; and

(ii) such other documents as the court may direct.

See also r 20.8:

(1) Where a Part 20 claim may be made without the court's permission, the Part 20 claim form must –

(a) in the case of a counterclaim, be served on every other party when a copy of the defence is served;

(b) in the case of any other Part 20 claim, be served on the person against whom it is made within 14 days after the date on which the party making the Part 20 claim files his defence.

(2) Paragraph (1) does not apply to a claim for contribution or indemnity made in accordance with rule 20.6.[9a]

(3) Where the court gives permission to make a Part 20 claim, it will at the same time give directions as to the service of the Part 20 claim.

PD 20, para 7.1 provides:

7.1 The title of every Part 20 claim should contain:

(1) the full name of each party, and

(2) his status in the proceedings (eg, claimant, defendant, Part 20 claimant, Part 20 defendant), for example:

AB claimant

CD defendant/Part 20 claimant

EF Part 20 defendant.

7.2 Where a defendant makes a counterclaim not only against the claimant but also against a non-party the title should show this as follows:

AB claimant/Part 20 defendant

CD defendant/Part 20 claimant and

XY Part 20 defendant.

7.3 Where there is more than one Part 20 claim, the parties to the first Part 20 claim should be described as 'Part 20 claimant (1st claim)' and 'Part 20 defendant (1st claim)', the parties to the second Part 20 claim should be described as 'Part 20 claimant (2nd claim)' and 'Part 20 defendant (2nd claim)', and so on. For example:

AB claimant and Part 20 defendant (2nd claim)

CD defendant and Part 20 claimant (1st claim)

EF Part 20 defendant (1st claim) and Part 20

claimant (2nd claim)

GH Part 20 defendant (2nd claim).

7.4 Where the full name of a party is lengthy it must appear in the title but

---

thereafter in the statement of case it may be identified by an abbreviation such as initials or a recognised shortened name.

7.5 Where a party to the proceedings has more than one status eg claimant and Part 20 defendant (2nd claim) or Part 20 defendant (1st claim) and Part 20 claimant (2nd claim) the combined status must appear in the title but thereafter it may be convenient to refer to the party by name, eg Mr Smith, or, if paragraph 7.4 applies, by initials or a shortened name.

Counterclaims against non-party

Permission is always required to bring a new party into existing proceedings and thus is required to make this type of Part 20 claim. Permission is not required where the Part 20 claim is issued at the same time as the defence. A defendant who wishes to counterclaim against a person other than the claimant must apply to the court for permission to do so (r 20.5(1)). If the court grants permission, it will also give directions as to the management of the case (r 20.5(3)).

The application must be made under Part 23[10] and can be made without notice. However, if the court grants permission following an application without notice, the joined party can apply for the order to be set aside (r 23.10).

CONTRIBUTION AND INDEMNITY

This type of Part 20 claim may be brought without permission at any time by a defendant who has acknowledged service or filed a defence against a co-defendant to the claim (r 20.6). The claim is made by filing a notice containing a statement of the nature and grounds of the claim for a contribution or indemnity and serving it on the defendant to the Part 20 claim. The Part 20 claim must be served within 14 days of issue. The rules about filing defence and acknowledgment of service are the same as for a claim.

OTHER PART 20 CLAIMS

This is any claim brought by a defendant against any person who is not already a party for contribution or indemnity or some other remedy (r 20.7).

This type of Part 20 claim may be made without permission where it is issued before or at the same time as the defence of the defendant making the

---

10 See Chapter 19, Making Applications for Court Orders.

Part 20 claim and is made by filing a Part 20 claim form (r 20.7(2) and (3)(a)). The Part 20 claim must be served within 14 days after the party making the Part 20 claim files his defence and the rules as to acknowledgment of service and defence apply (r 20.8(1)(b)).

An application for permission to make a Part 20 claim may be made without notice. If permission is given, the judge must at the same time give directions for the filing of defence to the Part 20 claim.

Applications for permission, where counterclaim, or other Part 20 claim is not served with defence

Under PD 20, para 2.1:

2.1 An application for permission to make a Part 20 claim must be supported by evidence stating:

(1) the state which the action has reached;

(2) the nature of the claim to be made by the Part 20 claimant or details of the question or issue which needs to be decided;

(3) a summary of the facts on which the Part 20 claim is based, and

(4) the name and address of the proposed Part 20 defendant.

(For further information regarding evidence see the Practice Direction which supplements Part 32.)[11]

2.2 Where delay has been a factor contributing to the need to apply for permission to make a Part 20 claim an explanation of the delay should be given in evidence.

2.3 Where possible the applicant should provide a timetable of the action to date.

2.4 Rules 20.5(2) and 20.7(5) allow applications to be made to the court without notice unless the court otherwise directs.

Where the court gives permission to make a Part 20 claim later, after a defence has been served, directions will be given as to service (r 20.8).

Permission to make a Part 20 claim involves an application supported by elaborate evidence, and accordingly it is obviously strongly advisable to serve all Part 20 claims with the defence if at all possible, although it should be remembered that permission is always required where the defendant wishes to counterclaim against a person other than the claimant.[12] Applications are normally made without notice. The application is likely to be dismissed if not supported by the mandatory supporting evidence required by PD 20, para 2.

---

11 See Chapter 31, Evidence.

12 See above, p 135.

13 See Chapter 15, Judicial Case Management: Allocation.

CASE MANAGEMENT UNDER PART 20

If a defence to a Part 20 claim is filed, the case will be referred to the procedural judge to consider giving management directions. Note that Part 26 (Allocation)[13] does not apply to Part 20 claims but the judge:

- must, so far as possible, manage the Part 20 claim(s) with the claim; and
- may order that a Part 20 claim be managed separately from the claim (r 20.13).

The court's powers at the case management hearing are contained in PD 20, paras 5.3 and 5.4, which provide:

5.3 At the hearing the court may:

   (1) treat the hearing as a summary judgment hearing;

   (2) order that the Part 20 proceedings be dismissed;

   (3) give directions about the way any claim, question or issue set out in or arising from the Part 20 claim should be dealt with;

   (4) give directions as to the part, if any, the Part 20 defendant will take at the trial of the claim;

   (5) give directions about the extent to which the Part 20 defendant is to be bound by any judgement or decision to be made in the claim.

5.4 The court may make any of the orders in 5.3(1) to (5) either before or after any judgment in the claim has been entered by the claimant against the defendant.

Whenever the court is considering whether to permit a Part 20 claim, dismiss it, or require it to be dealt with separately, it must have regard to the matters set out in r 20.9.

The matters to which the court may have regard include:

(a) the connection between the Part 20 claim and the claim made by the claimant against the defendant;

(b) whether the Part 20 claimant is seeking substantially the same remedy which some other party is claiming from him; and

(c) whether the Part 20 claimant wants the court to decide any question connected with the subject matter of the proceedings:

   (i) not only between existing parties but also between existing parties and a person not already a party; or

   (ii) against an existing party not only in a capacity in which he is already a party but also in some further capacity.

14   See Chapter 21, Judgment in Default.

DEFAULT JUDGMENT IN PART 20 CLAIMS

Note that default judgment[14] can now be obtained in the county court on a counterclaim as well as in the High Court (r 20.3(3)). If the counterclaim is for money, or delivery of goods where the defendant (to the counterclaim) is given the alternative of paying the value of the goods, this can be done administratively. This is completely new for the county court and follows the High Court procedure. It will be particularly important in road traffic accident cases where, traditionally, defences to counterclaims are often overlooked.

For other types of Part 20 claim, except claims for contribution or indemnity between defendants to the claim (where you cannot obtain a default judgment at all), there are special rules where the Part 20 defendant has failed to file an acknowledgment of service or defence. In such cases the Part 20:

- defendant is deemed to admit the Part 20 claim;
- defendant is bound by any judgment in the main proceedings so far as it is relevant to the Part 20 claim;
- claimant may obtain judgment by filing a request in the relevant practice form provided:
  - default judgment has been taken against that Part 20 claimant; and
  - he has satisfied that default judgment; and
  - the remedy he seeks is limited to contribution or indemnity (r 20.11(2) and (3)).

If any of those conditions is not met, the Part 20 claimant may only enter default judgment if he obtains the court's permission.

CHAPTER 13

ADDING OR SUBSTITUTING A PARTY

INTRODUCTION

Any number of claimants or defendants may be joined as parties to a claim (r 19.1). The new rules are similar to the old – an application is required and can be by any party, or intended party, with a hearing, or by consent and must be supported by evidence (see Part 23).[1]

Note r 19.1:

(2) The court may order a person to be added as a new party if –

    (a) it is desirable to add the new party so that the court can resolve all the matters in dispute in the proceedings; or

    (b) there is an issue involving the new party and an existing party which is connected to the matters in dispute in the proceedings, and it is desirable to add the new party so that the court can resolve that issue.

(3) The court may order any person to cease to be a party if it is not desirable for that person to be a party to the proceedings.

(4) The court may order a new party to be substituted for an existing one if –

    (a) the existing party's interest or liability has passed to the new party; and

    (b) it is desirable to substitute the new party so that the court can resolve the matters in dispute in the proceedings.

The court has a very wide discretion as to whether to make the order. As with amendments generally it is likely that the application will be granted if it does not cause injustice to other parties which cannot otherwise be compensated by costs (*Beoco Ltd v Alfa Laval Co Ltd*)[2] and the principles of the overriding objective are upheld. The Practice Direction makes it clear that a party applying for an amendment will usually be responsible for the costs of and arising from the amendment.

CLAIMANTS: ADDING AND SUBSTITUTING

The applicant must file:

- the application;
- proposed amended claim form;

---

1   See Chapter 19, Making Applications for Court Orders.
2   [1994] 4 All ER 464, CA.

- proposed amended particulars of claim;
- written consent of new claimant (r 19.3 and see the Practice Direction thereto).

New defendants

To be served with:

- copy order;
- the amended claim form and amended particulars of claim; and
- the 'response pack' to a claim form (PD 19, para 3.2(3)).

Special provisions about adding or substituting after the end of a period of limitation under the Limitation Act 1980 (r 19.4)

Adding or substituting a party can sometimes cause problems where the limitation period has expired. An order can only be obtained if the limitation period was current when the proceedings were 'started' and the substitution or addition 'is necessary' on the court being satisfied that the party previously named was by mistake for the new correct party, and unless the new party is added or substituted the claim cannot properly be carried on by, or against the original party; or where the original party has died or had a bankruptcy order made against him.

For personal injury claims and fatal accidents, see ss 11 and 12 of the Limitation Act 1980. For circumstances in which a new cause of action may be introduced, see s 35 of the same Act.[3]

The fact that an accrued contractual limitation defence is arguable is no reason for refusing to order the substitution of a party to proceedings, since substitution does nothing to deprive that party of the benefit of that defence: there is no conflict or inconsistency between rr 17.4 and 19.4.[4] Rule 19.5 applies where the application is to substitute a new party for a party who was mistakenly named in the claim form, whereas r 17.4(3) (amendments to statements of case after the end of a relevant limitation period) applies where the intended party was named in the claim form but there was a genuine mistake as to the name of the party and no one was misled. There is no significant conflict between the two rules.[5]

---

3   See Chapter 3, Limitation of Actions, p 32.
4   *International Distillers and Vintners Ltd (t/a Percy Fox and Co) v JF Hillebrand (UK) Ltd and Others* (2000) *The Times*, 25 January, QBD (David Foskett QC).
5   *David Gregson v Channel Four Television Corporation* (2000) *The Times*, 11 August, CA.

CHAPTER 14

PART 8 CLAIMS

INTRODUCTION

Although Lord Woolf recommended the introduction of a single method to start proceedings, not all proceedings are suited to the same procedure. The procedure for bringing an action under Part 7[1] is based on a structure whereby parties in dispute identify facts and issues on which their case is based, follow a series of procedural stages culminating in a trial at which the parties produce evidence, primarily in the form of witnesses to support the facts on which their claim is based, with argument as to the relevant law to apply to those issues.

However, not all claims involve disputes of fact. The facts may be agreed and the dispute may be about the application of a point of law to those agreed facts or the construction of a document relating to those facts. Also, in some instances, the parties may have to apply to the court for approval of a settlement, such as for a child or patient[1a] or to approve the exercise of a power vested in them, for instance as a trustee, for which there may be no opponent.

In those circumstances, the procedure followed when a Part 7 claim form is issued, geared as it is to identifying the factual issues in dispute and preparing for a witness action, would not be appropriate. Therefore, in order to provide an appropriate procedure for those types of claim, the CPR provides an 'alternative procedure for claims' under Part 8.

New proceedings for possession matters come into force on 15 October 2001, details of which appear below at p 146.

PART 8 CLAIMS

There are two broad circumstances when the Part 8 procedure should be used. Unless a rule or practice direction expressly provides that the Part 8 procedure cannot be used for the type of claim in question, these are where:

- the claimant seeks the court's decision on a question which is unlikely to involve a substantial dispute of fact; or

---

1 See Chapter 7, Starting an Action.
1a See Chapter 26, Special Rules about Children and Patients.

- where a rule or practice direction requires its use in relation to a specified type of proceedings (r 8.1(2), (4) and (6)).

Proceedings specifying the use of a Part 8 claim

The Practice Direction to Part 8, which was originally published with the CPR in January 1999, gives examples of where the procedure may be used:

1.4 The types of claim for which the Part 8 procedure may be used include:

(1) a claim by or against a child or patient which has been settled before the commencement of proceedings and the sole purpose of the claim is to obtain the approval of the court to the settlement,

(2) a claim for provisional damages which has been settled before the commencement of proceedings and the sole purpose of the claim is to obtain a consent judgment,

(3) provided there is unlikely to be a substantial dispute of fact, a claim for a summary order for possession against named or unnamed defendants occupying land or premises without the licence or consent of the person claiming possession.

Practice Direction 8B was issued in late March 1999 and sets out a list of all those proceedings where the Part 8 procedure *must* be used. The Practice Direction is divided into three sections, A, B, and C. Section A applies to:

- all claims listed in Table 1 to the Practice Direction;
- claims where an Act provides that an application of claim is to be brought by originating summons; and
- claims or applications that before 26 April 1999 would have been brought by originating summons, but only if such claim or application is not listed in Section C to the Practice Direction,

provided that no other method of bringing the claim after 26 April 1999 is prescribed in a Schedule, rule or practice direction.

The matters listed in Table 1 are all *High Court* matters and include:

- enforcement of charging orders;
- some applications for reciprocal enforcement of judgments;
- some proceedings by and against the Crown;
- mortgage possession actions;
- proceedings under the Landlord and Tenant Acts 1927, 1954 and 1987;
- applications for possession under RSC Ord 113 (squatters).

Section B applies to:

- all claims listed in Table 2 to the Practice Direction;
- in the county court, claims for:

(a) the recovery of possession of land; or

(b) damages for harassment under s 3 of the Protection from Harassment Act 1997;

- claims that before 26 April 1999 would have been brought in the High Court by originating motion, but only if not included in Section C to the Practice Direction;

- in the county court, by originating application or petition,

provided that no other procedure is prescribed in an Act, Schedule, rule or practice direction.

The matters listed in Table 2 include:

- in the *High Court*:
  (a) appeals by case stated under RSC Ord 56 rr 8 and 10;
  (b) various other appeals under RSC Ord 94;
  (c) references to the European Court;

- in the *county court*:
  (a) summary possession proceedings under CCR Ord 24;
  (b) enforcement of charging orders by sale;
  (c) applications under the Landlord and Tenant Acts 1927, 1954, 1985 and 1987, including, importantly, applications for a new tenancy under s 24 of the 1954 Act (although it looks as though the old type of claim form can be used for the latter);
  (d) certain applications under the Consumer Credit Act 1974;
  (e) accelerated possession order applications;
  (f) injunction applications under s 152 of the Housing Act 1996.

Also, some of the rules relating to those specified proceedings provide that certain rules under the Part 8 procedure do not apply to them or modify the rules to suit the particular proceedings, and if that is the case, the modified procedure should be followed (r 8.1(6)(b) and PD 8, para 1.3).

In the case of *Hannigan v Hannigan*,[2] the claimant used the wrong form to commence a Part 8 claim and made a number of other procedural errors and the defendant applied to have the claim struck out on those grounds. The claimant had fully set out the nature of her claim against the defendant and, although the court did not condone sloppy practices, such as failing to follow the correct procedure, it held that it would not be in accordance with the overriding objective to strike out the whole proceedings for a mere procedural failure. However, although in most cases substance will be more important than form when deciding whether proceedings should be struck out, the court

---

2   [2000] 2 FCR 650; (2000) *The Independent*, 23 May; [2000] ILR, 3 July, CA.

did warn that there were plenty of other sanctions that the court would use to punish failures to comply with the rules.

PART 20 CLAIMS

A party to a Part 8 claim may not make a Part 20 claim without first obtaining the court's permission (r 8.7).

Differences between Part 7[3] and Part 8 claims

Note that the practice for possession matters differs from that of other Part 8 claims and this will be dealt with separately below.

High Court

The main differences between the general procedure under Part 7 and the Part 8 (High Court) procedure are under Part 8:

- the claimant must file and serve any evidence on which he wishes to rely with the claim form;
- an acknowledgment of service *must* be filed;
- the defendant must file and serve any evidence on which he wishes to rely when he files and serves his acknowledgment of service;
- the acknowledgment is served by the defendant;
- a defence is not required;
- default judgment is not available;
- the claim is treated as allocated to the multi-track;
- the claimant must file and serve any evidence in reply within 14 days of service of the defendant's evidence;
- the court may require or permit any party or witness to attend to give oral evidence or to be cross-examined.

A defendant may object to the use of the Part 8 procedure and the court has power, whether of its own motion or otherwise, to order that the procedure should cease to apply.

County court

Section B of PD 8B (county court procedure) varies the general Part 8 procedure described above. The 'variant' element of the procedure is that a

---

3   See Chapter 7, Starting an Action.

date for hearing will be fixed on issue, at least 21 days' notice of which will be required to be given. Section B also provides that an acknowledgment of service is *not* required to be served, but it would appear that r 8.4(2) will still apply. This provides that a defendant who has not filed an acknowledgment may attend the hearing, but may not take any part in it without the court's permission.

Otherwise, the Part 8 procedure will apply, which includes the filing of evidence on issue for the claimant, and with the acknowledgment of service for the defendant.

CONTENTS OF THE PART 8 CLAIM FORM

County Court Rules (CCR) Ords 6 and 7 make special provision for the contents of the particulars of claim in certain types of claim and for service of them, and there are also to be found in the CCR further special provisions relating to the venue for bringing proceedings and for periods of notice for hearings. Paragraphs B2 and B3 of the Practice Direction make it clear that such special provisions continue to apply in precedence to the general provisions of PD 8B.

Section C applies to certain appeals in the High Court.

The procedure

The Part 8 claim form should be in Form N208 and *must* state:
- that Part 8 applies to the proceedings; and
- either the question which the claimant wants the court to decide, or the remedy which the claimant is seeking, with the legal basis for it.

Also, the Part 8 claim form *must* state such of the following as are applicable:
- any enactment under which the claim is being made;
- any representative capacity the claimant is claiming under;
- any representative capacity the defendant is being sued under (r 8.2 and PD 8, para 2.2).

The Part 8 claim form must also comply with the requirements of any practice direction under which the claim is brought and which permits or requires the use of the Part 8 procedure (PD 8, para 2.2).

The Part 8 claim form must be verified by a statement of truth[4] (r 22.1).

Possession matters

Claimants must use the not very user-friendly pre-26 April forms (N5, N119, N120 – see Part 4 (Forms) and PD 8B, para B8(2)). There is no change in the information that must be included in particulars of claim (see CCR Ord 6 rr 3 and 5, which are retained in CPR Sched 2) notwithstanding PD 16, paras 6 and 7, which appear to be redundant. As before, on issue, the court fixes a date for the hearing (PD 8B, para B9) and, except in cases where other rules provide for a shorter period, 21 days' notice of the hearing must be given. At the hearing, the court may hear the case or give directions.

CHANGES TO LANDLORD AND TENANT PROCEDURE

General

A new Part 55 and Part 56 have been drawn up to deal with, respectively, possession proceedings and applications under the Landlord and Tenant Acts and related proceedings. They are not due to be implemented before 15 October 2001, but they will effectively take such proceedings out of Part 8 and provide their own procedure, although it is not anticipated that it will be much different from that at present.

Part 55 must be used where the claim is brought by a landlord, lender or licensor (r 55.2) and in a claim against trespassers (Particulars of Claim Form N121 – see Chapter 22, Summary Judgment). Proceedings must be started in the county court for the district where the property is situated (r 55.3(1)), but proceedings can be started in the High Court if there are exceptional circumstances (r 55.3(2)) such as complicated issues of fact, points of law of general importance, claims against trespassers which require immediate determination etc.

Procedure

Possession proceedings will have their own single claim form (N5) to which an acknowledgment of service will not be necessary (r 55.7(1)). Particulars of claim are either in Form N119 (rented) or N120 (mortgage). Except in accelerated possession cases (see below) a defence will not be mandatory nor

---

4   See Chapter 11, Statements of Case, p 128.

will it stop a defendant from being heard at trial but the court may take it into account when considering costs (r 55.7(3)) – cf present procedure set out above. However, when served with the claim from, the defendant will receive a set of notes (N7 – rented, N11M – mortgage).

Return date hearing

For standard possession proceedings, any return date will not be less than 28 days from issue, and the standard period between issue and hearing date will be 8 weeks.

If the claim is not allocated to fast or multi-track (see below), the court can consider evidence in writing unless it otherwise orders (r 55.8(3)). All witness statements must be filed and served at least 2 days before the hearing (r 55.8(4)) unless the claim is against trespassers in which case they should have filed and served with the claim form (r 55.8(5)).

When the claim is 'genuinely disputed on grounds which appear to be substantial', the court may deal with the question of allocation and/or directions (r 55.8(2)). When considering which track to allocate matters to, the court will not only consider the matters required by r 26.8 (see Chapter 15, Judicial Case Management: The Overriding Objective) but also the amount of any arrears, the importance of retaining the property to the defendant and the importance of vacant possession to the claimant (r 55.9(1)). The case cannot be allocated to the small claims track without the consent of the parties (r 55.9(2)).

Accelerated possession claims

In accelerated possession cases (Claim Form N5B) (which, if unopposed, will usually be dealt with by the judge on paper only) if the defendant wishes to oppose the claim or seek a postponement of possession, they will need to file a defence (N11B) within 14 days of service of the claim form (r 55.14). If the defendant does not file a defence and there is no request by a landlord for the judge to consider the matter within three months after service, the claim will be stayed (r 55.15(4)).

On considering the claim, the judge may either grant the order without a hearing, fix a hearing date if not satisfied, or strike the claim out if no reasonable grounds are shown (r 55.16).

The claimant may indicate in their claim form that they are content for the court to deal with any request by the defendant for a postponement (of up to 42 days) of the possession order without a hearing (PD 55, para 8.2). In any event, if the judge is satisfied that an order for possession should be made, he must order it to take effect in 14 days, but if there has been a request for postponement by the tenant, where the landlord has not consented to the application being dealt with without a hearing, a hearing of that request must be fixed to take place before the date on which possession is to be given up (r 55.18).

The court has power to set aside or vary the order on application within 14 days of service or order, or on its own initiative (r 55.19).

Part 56

This new part replaces RSC Ord 97 and CCR Ord 43, as to applications under the Landlord and Tenant Acts 1927, 1954, 1985 and 1987; CCR Ord 49 r 1 as to those under the Leasehold Reform Act 1967; and CCR Ord 49 r 9 as to those under the Leasehold Reform, Housing and Urban Development Act 1993. Certain other landlord and tenant provisions are also covered. No forms are intended to be prescribed for proceedings under Part 56. By and large, it appears that the Part 8 procedure and the claim form are to be used.

ISSUE OF A PART 8 CLAIM FORM

Part 8 proceedings are started when the Part 8 claim form is issued by the court. The same rules on issue and service of a claim form under Part 7[5] apply to a Part 8 claim form (PD 8, para 2.1). Therefore, the Part 8 claim form must be served on the defendant (if any) within four months of it being issued, or within six months if it is served out of the jurisdiction.[5a]

Additional information about a funding arrangement[6]

If a party has entered into a funding arrangement, such as a conditional fee agreement which provides for a success fee, he is required to give his opponent certain information about the funding arrangement. On issuing the Part 8 claim form, the claimant must file at court and serve on the other parties a notice containing information about the arrangement as specified in Form N251 (PD 44, Section 19, paras 19.1–19.2). If the defendant has entered into a funding arrangement, he must file the notice in Form N251 when he files his acknowledgment of service.

In all other circumstances, for instance, if the funding arrangement is entered into after the claimant starts proceedings or after the defendant files his acknowledgment of service at court, a party must file and serve notice of the funding arrangement within seven days of entering into it (PD 44, s 19, para 19.2(4)).

---

5   See Chapter 7, Starting an Action.
5a See Chapter 10, Service out of the Jurisdiction.
6   See Chapter 38, Funding Litigation.

RESPONDING TO A PART 8 CLAIM FORM

Time and method for responding

In the High Court, if a defendant is served[7] with a Part 8 claim form, he must file and serve an acknowledgment of service on every other party, not more than 14 days after service of the Part 8 claim form on him (r 8.3(1)). The acknowledgment of service should be in Form N210, but an informal document, such as a letter, will also be acceptable (PD 8, para 3.2). An acknowledgment of service is not required in the county court and the following provisions relating to it do not apply. It should be noted that the defendant does not file or serve a defence to the Part 8 claim (r 8.9(a)).

Different time periods for acknowledging service apply where the claim form is served out of the jurisdiction[8] and where it is served on an agent of a principal who is overseas (r 8.3(3)(a)).[9]

Contents of the acknowledgment of service form

The defendant must indicate in the acknowledgment of service form whether he contests the claim.

Also, if he seeks a different remedy to that set out in the claim form, he must state what that remedy is (r 8.3(2)).

The acknowledgment of service form must be signed by the defendant or his legal representative and include the defendant's address for service (rr 8.3(3)(b) and 10.5).

Disputing the court's jurisdiction[10]

If the defendant disputes the jurisdiction of the court to hear the claim, he must acknowledge service, indicating that he disputes the court's jurisdiction and make an application to this effect within 14 days after filing the acknowledgment of service (r 8.3(4)).

Consequences of failure to respond to Part 8 claim form

If a defendant fails to file an acknowledgment of service to the Part 8 claim form within the time period specified, although the defendant may attend the

---

7   See Chapter 9, Service of Documents.
8   See Chapter 10, Service out of the Jurisdiction.
9   See Chapter 9, Service of Documents.
10 See Chapter 10, Service out of the Jurisdiction, p 114.

subsequent hearing of the claim, he may not take part in it, unless the court gives permission for him to do so (r 8.4).

Default judgment or judgment on an admission not applicable to Part 8 claims

Judgment in default[11] under Part 12 is not available for proceedings commenced under Part 8 (r 8.1(5)). Nor can the claimant obtain judgment by request on an admission (r 8.9(b)).[12]

DIRECTIONS IN PART 8 PROCEEDINGS

The court may give directions immediately a Part 8 claim form is issued, either on the application of a party or of its own initiative. This may include fixing a hearing date where there is no dispute, such as claims for the approval of child or patient settlements, or in claims where there is a dispute but a date for a hearing could be conveniently given, such as claims for mortgage possession or the appointment of a trustee (PD 8, para 4.1).

Where the court does not fix a hearing date when the Part 8 claim form is issued, it will give directions for the disposal of the claim as soon as practicable after the defendant has acknowledged service, or if the defendant fails to acknowledge service, after the time period for doing so has expired (PD 8, para 4.2).

Certain applications under Part 8 may not require a hearing, being dealt with on paper instead, such as a consent application under s 38 of the Landlord and Tenant Act 1954 (PD 8, para 4.3).

However, in more complicated cases, the court may convene a directions hearing before giving directions (PD 8, para 4.4).

Defended Part 8 claim

If the defendant files an acknowledgment of service to a Part 8 claim and any written evidence, the court will give directions as to the future management of the case (r 8.8(2)).

---

11 See Chapter 21, Judgment in Default.
12 See Chapter 8, Responding to an Action.

Allocation to a track

However, all Part 8 claims shall be treated as allocated to the multi-track so the court does not have to apply Part 26 and decide which track to allocate it to (r 8.9(c)).

FILING AND SERVICE OF EVIDENCE

The claimant *must* file, and serve copies on every other party, of any written evidence on which he intends to rely, at the same time as filing and serving the claim form (r 8.5(1) and (2)).

The defendant *must* file, and serve copies on every other party, of any written evidence on which he intends to rely, when he files and serves his acknowledgment of service (r 8.5(3) and (4)).

If the defendant relies on written evidence, the claimant may, within 14 days of service of the evidence on him, file and serve on every other party, further written evidence in reply (r 8.5(5) and (6)).

If a party fails to file and serve copies of the written evidence in accordance with the rules, he may not rely on it at the hearing, unless the court gives permission (r 8.6(1)). However, the parties can agree in writing to grant each other extra time to file evidence: in the case of a defendant, up to a maximum of 14 days after he files his acknowledgment of service, so long as the written agreement to this effect is filed at court by the defendant at the same time as the acknowledgment of service. In the case of a claimant, the parties can agree to extend the time for the claimant to file evidence in reply to the defendant's evidence up to a maximum of 14 days after the defendant files his acknowledgment of service (PD 8, para 5.6).

If the other party will not agree, a party may apply to the court under Part 23[13] for an extension of time to serve and file evidence or for permission to serve and file additional evidence (PD 8, para 5.5). If a party needs extra time to serve evidence, he should apply for it before the original time limit fixed by the rules expires, as the court is more likely to grant the extra time at that stage than if the application is made only after that time.

If it is deemed necessary for a party to give oral evidence at the hearing, the court will give directions requiring the attendance at the hearing of the witness who has given written evidence so that they are available for cross-examination (r 8.6(2) and (3)).

---

13 See Chapter 19, Making Applications.

Form of written evidence

Written evidence will normally be in the form of a witness statement or affidavit (PD 8, para 5.2). The claimant may rely on the matters set out in his claim form as evidence if the claim form is verified by a statement of truth (r 8.5(7)).[14]

ISSUE OF CLAIM FORM WITHOUT NAMING DEFENDANTS

There are some circumstances when the court may give permission for a claim form to be issued under Part 8 without naming a defendant. Those circumstances will be prescribed in a practice direction. An application for permission should be made by application notice, under Part 23, before the claim form is issued. The application need not be served on any other person and must be accompanied by a copy of the claim form the applicant proposes to issue. If the court gives permission, it will give directions for the future management of the claim (r 8.2A).

INAPPROPRIATE USE OF PART 8 PROCEDURE

If a claimant issues a Part 8 claim form and a court officer believes that the Part 8 procedure is inappropriate for the claimant's claim, he may refer the matter to the judge for the judge to consider the point (PD 8, para 1.5). If the judge decides that the Part 8 procedure is inappropriate for the claim, he may order that the claim continue as if the claimant had not used the Part 8 procedure. The court will then allocate the claim to a track and give appropriate directions for the further conduct of the matter (PD 8, para 1.6).

If proceedings are brought using the Part 8 procedure, but it subsequently becomes apparent that such procedure is not appropriate, and the Part 7 procedure, or some other procedure, should have been used instead, rather than treat the proceedings as a nullity, the court can order that the claim continue as if the claimant had not used the Part 8 procedure (r 8.1(3)).

If the defendant does not believe that the Part 8 procedure is appropriate, because either there is a substantial dispute of fact or because its use is not authorised by any rule or practice direction, he must state his reasons in writing for this belief when he files his acknowledgment of service. If the statement setting out the reasons includes matters of evidence, it should be verified by a statement of truth (r 8.8(1) and PD 8, para 3.6).

---

14 See Chapter 11, Statements of Case.

CHAPTER 15

JUDICIAL CASE MANAGEMENT: ALLOCATION

INTRODUCTION

Part 26 deals with case management for what is described as the 'preliminary stage'. The preliminary stage involves such matters as automatic transfer and allocation to a track. The next stage of case management will begin if a case proceeds to be allocated to a track. If this stage is reached, the nature and extent of the case management carried out by the court will depend on the track to which the case is allocated.[1]

AUTOMATIC TRANSFER

A claimant is free to start proceedings in a court[2] located in any part of the jurisdiction of England and Wales. However, under r 26.2, if the defendant files a defence, the proceedings will be automatically transferred to the defendant's home court if the following circumstances all apply:

- the claim is for a specified amount of money;
- the claim was commenced in a court which is not the defendant's home court;
- the claim has not been transferred to another defendant's home court under r 13.4[3] or r 14.12;[4]
- the defendant is an individual; and
- the claim was not commenced in a specialist list.[5]

Note that for there to be automatic transfer, the defendant must be an 'individual'. While this clearly excludes companies and multiple partnerships, what is not so clear is whether a defendant who uses a trade name, for example, 'James Smith trading as Smith and Co', should also be treated as an 'individual' for these purposes.

Where the claim was issued out of the Production Centre at Northampton, it will not be automatically transferred on the filing of a defence unless the claimant states that he wants the case to continue.[6]

---

1   See Chapters 16, 17 and 18 on the small claims, fast and multi-track.
2   But see Chapter 2 on the jurisdiction of the county courts and High Court.
3   See Chapter 21, Judgment in Default, p 244.
4   See Chapter 8, Responding to an Action, p 93.
5   As defined in Part 49, see p 18.
6   PD 7C, see Chapter 7, Starting an Action, p 77.

The defendant's home court

Depending on whether the case is proceeding in the High Court or a county court, the defendant's home court is defined as either the county court for the district in which the defendant resides or carries on business, or the district registry for the district in which the defendant resides or carries on business, or if there is no district registry, the Royal Courts of Justice (r 2.3). It should be noted that the reference is to the home court of the defendant personally and does not include the defendant's solicitor's home court – that provision was recently removed (2 October 2000), as the solicitor's address was often some distance from that of the client.

Where there are two or more defendants to a claim who have different home courts, the proceedings will be transferred to the home court of the defendant who files a defence first, so long as the above circumstances also apply (r 26.2(5)).

If a defendant files a defence to a claim on the basis that the money claimed has been paid or, if the defendant admits part of a claim for a specified amount of money, the claimant will be asked to notify the court whether he wishes to proceed with the action (see rr 14.5 and 15.10). If the claimant notifies the court that he does wish to proceed, and the above circumstances apply, the proceedings will be transferred to the defendant's home court on receipt of the claimant's notification (r 26.2(4)).

ALLOCATION

If a claim is defended, the court will allocate the claim to one of the three case management tracks. It is expressly provided that in exercising its powers of case management to allocate a case to a track, the court will expect to do so as far as possible in co-operation with the parties in order to deal with cases justly in accordance with the overriding objective (PD 26, para 4.1).

The three case management tracks are the small claims track, fast track and multi-track. Which track a case should be allocated to will depend on a number of factors such as the amount claimed, the length of any trial, the complexity of the case and the type of remedy sought. The level of case management involved for each track increases with the least being applied to cases allocated to the small claims track and the most to those cases on the multi-track.[7]

7   See Chapters 16, 17 and 18 on the small claims, fast and multi-track for more details.

THE ALLOCATION QUESTIONNAIRE

In order to assist the court in its decision as to which track a claim should be allocated to, both parties must return an allocation questionnaire. Form N150 is the prescribed form for the allocation questionnaire (PD 26, para 2.1(1)).

Timing for court service of allocation questionnaire

The court will serve an allocation questionnaire on each party when a defence is filed (r 26.3(1)).

Where there are two or more defendants and at least one of them files a defence, the court will serve the allocation questionnaire either when all the defendants have filed a defence or when the period for the filing of the last defence has expired,[8] whichever is the sooner (r 26.3(2)).

When a defence is filed and the circumstances are such that proceedings will be automatically transferred to the defendant's home court,[9] the court in which proceedings were commenced will serve an allocation questionnaire before the proceedings are transferred (r 26.3(3)).

However, if the defendant admits part of the claimant's claim,[10] or the defendant's defence is that money claimed has been paid, and the circumstances are such that the proceedings will *not* be transferred to the defendant's home court,[11] an allocation questionnaire will not be served until the claimant notifies the court whether he wishes to proceed with the claim (r 26.3(4)). However if a part admission is made, or the defence is that money claimed has been paid, but the circumstances are such that proceedings *will* be automatically transferred to the defendant's home court, it would seem that r 26.3(3) above will apply, and the court will serve an allocation questionnaire on the parties *before* transferring the proceedings and *before* the claimant has notified the court that he wishes to proceed with the claim.

If a defence is filed, the claimant can apply to the court for the allocation questionnaire to be served earlier than it would do under the above rules (r 26.3(5)).

---

8   See Chapter 8, Responding to an Action, p 96.
9   See above, p 154.
10 See Chapter 8, Responding to an Action, p 90.
11 See above, p 154.

Contents of the allocation questionnaire

The allocation questionnaire is designed to provide the court with enough information about the case so that it can decide which track to allocate it to and which case management directions to order without requiring the parties to provide further information or hold a hearing to decide. The expectation is that the information provided by the parties in the allocation questionnaire will be sufficient for most cases (PD 26, para 4.1).

The allocation questionnaire consists of 8 sections designed to provide the court with enough information to allocate the claim to a track. The information that a party must provide is as follows:

- whether a party would like a stay of proceedings in order to attempt to settle the case by ADR or other means;[12]

- which track the party considers is most suitable for the case. The court will take the views of the parties into account, but ultimately this decision is for the court to make. If a party believes that the case should be allocated to a track which is not the normal track for a case,[13] he should give reasons for his belief, for example, if a case within the financial limits of the small claims track arises out of a complex matter such that it would not be suitable to be heard on the small claims track;

- whether the party has complied with any applicable pre-action protocol[14] and if not, why not, and if no pre-action protocol applies to the claim whether the party has exchanged information and documents in order to assist in settling the claim;

- whether the party intends to make any applications, for example, for summary judgment or permission to join another party. If the party indicates that he is likely to make such an application, the court is unlikely to allocate the case until the application is heard;[15]

- the identity of the party's witnesses of fact and the facts they will give evidence of. If a party intends to rely on a number of witnesses to a number of different issues this may indicate that any trial would be likely to last longer than one day making the case unsuitable for the small claims or fast track;

- whether a party would like permission to use expert evidence at trial, and if so whether that should be oral or written evidence, if oral the reason why such evidence is necessary and whether the party considers the case suitable for a single joint expert;[16]

---

12 See below, p 161.
13 See below, p 163, for the normal scope of each track.
14 See Chapter 4, Pre-Action Protocols.
15 See below, p 159.
16 See Chapter 30, Experts and Assessors.

- a figure for the amount of the claim in dispute;
- whether the party would like the case heard at a court in a particular location. A party may, for instance, request that the case is heard at a local court if that would be convenient for his witnesses;
- an estimate of the length of the trial and trial dates to avoid;
- an estimate of costs incurred to date and to be incurred;[17]
- a copy of suggested directions and an indication whether they are agreed;
- other information, which may assist the court to manage the claim.[18]

Co-operation in completing the allocation questionnaire

In keeping with the obligation of the parties to help the court further the overriding objective,[19] there is an onus on the parties to consult one another and co-operate in completing their allocation questionnaires and providing the court with the necessary information so that it can decide which track to allocate a case to and which case management directions are necessary. In this way, the parties should try to agree the case management directions which they will invite the court to make (PD 26, para 2.3(1) and (2)). However, being involved in consultation with the other party about case management directions would not justify delay in filing the allocation questionnaire (PD 26, para 2.3(3)).

Note that the parties are not obliged by any rule or practice direction to serve the allocation questionnaires on each other, nor do the courts always supply copies of the completed ones to the parties.

Additional information

If the allocation questionnaire does not provide the court with enough information to allocate a claim to a track, the court will order a party to provide further information about his case within 14 days of the order (r 26.5(3) and PD 26, para 4.2(2)). The court will serve the order seeking further information in Form N156. Such further information may also be sought if the court is deciding whether it is necessary to hold an allocation hearing before allocating proceedings to a track (r 26.5(3)).

A party can also provide the court with additional information outside of that which must be provided in the allocation questionnaire if he believes it may affect the court's decision about allocation to a track or case management

---

17 See below, p 161.
18 See below.
19 See r 1.3 and Chapter 5, Judicial Case Management: The Overriding Objective.

(PD 26, para 2.2(1)). Examples of additional information which would help the court are given in the Practice Direction. These are listed as:

- a party's intention to apply for summary judgment or some other order than may dispose of the case or reduce the amount in dispute or the number of issues remaining to be decided;
- a party's intention to issue a Part 20 claim or to add another party;
- the steps the parties have taken in the preparation of evidence (in particular, expert evidence), the steps they intend to take and whether those steps are to be taken in co-operation with any other party;
- the directions the party believes will be appropriate to be given for the management of the case;
- any particular facts that may affect the timetable the court will set; and
- any facts which may make it desirable for the court to fix an allocation hearing or a hearing at which case management directions will be given (PD 26, para 2.2(3)(a)–(f)).

If a party believes there is additional information that should be provided to the court, he should either get the agreement of the other party that the information is correct and should be put before the court, or at least deliver a copy of the additional information to the other party. Unless this is done, and confirmed in the document containing the additional information, as a general rule, the court will not take the information into account (PD 26, para 2.2(2)).

Allocation hearings

If it is necessary to do so, the court will order an allocation hearing of its own initiative before allocating a claim to a track (r 26.5(4) and PD 26, para 6.1). The circumstances when the court is likely to hold an allocation hearing are if, for example, one of the parties has failed to file an allocation questionnaire or failed to provide further information after being ordered to do so by the court, or if the parties have requested the case be allocated to different tracks and it is not clear which track is the most appropriate.

If the court decides to hold an allocation hearing, it will serve notice of the hearing in Form N153 at least seven days before the hearing is to take place. Form N153 will give a brief explanation of the reason for ordering the hearing (PD 26, para 6.2).

With the advent of active judicial case management and the duty of the parties to assist the court in dealing justly with cases in accordance with the overriding objective, the legal representative attending any allocation hearing ought to be the person responsible for the case. If this is not possible, the person attending must in any event be familiar with the case and be able to provide the court with the information it is likely to need in order to decide which track to allocate the case to and which case management directions to make. The person attending must also have sufficient authority to deal with any issues that are likely to arise (PD 26, para 6.5).

If the court orders an allocation hearing because a party has failed to file an allocation questionnaire or failed to provide extra information which the court has ordered, the court is likely to order the party in default to pay the costs on the indemnity basis of any other party who has attended the hearing, summarily assess those costs and order them to be paid forthwith or within a stated period. The court is also likely to order that if the party in default does not pay those costs within the time stated, his statement of case will be struck out. If the party in default does not attend the hearing or carry out the necessary steps, the court is likely to order that unless those steps are carried out within the time specified, his statement of claim will be struck out (PD 26, para 6.6). These are specified as the usual sanctions for failure to comply with the allocation procedure, but the court has the power to order otherwise (PD 26, para 6.6(1)).

Applications made before allocation

In some cases, a court hearing will take place before the claim is allocated to a track, for instance, where a party makes an application for an interim injunction[20] or summary judgment.[21] In those circumstances, the court can treat the hearing as an allocation hearing, allocate the case to a track and give case management directions (PD 26, para 2.4(1)). The court does not have to notify the parties that it proposes to treat the hearing as an allocation hearing (PD 26, para 6.3). Alternatively, if the application is made before the parties have filed allocation questionnaires, the court can fix a date for allocation questionnaires to be filed and give other directions (PD 26, para 2.4(2)).

A party who intends to make the type of application which may result in the early termination of a case, such as an application to strike out a statement of case, or part of a statement of case or an application for summary judgment, should make the application before or when filing his allocation questionnaire (PD 26, para 5.3(1)). If a party makes an application for such an order before the case has been allocated to a track, the court will not normally allocate the case before the hearing of the application (PD 26, para 5.3(2)).

If a party indicates in his allocation questionnaire that he intends to make the type of application referred to above which may result in the early termination of a case, but he has not yet made the application, the judge will usually direct that an allocation hearing is listed (PD 26, para 5.3(3)); the

---

20   See Chapter 20, Interim Remedies.
21   See Chapter 22, Summary Judgment.

intention being that the application is heard at the allocation hearing, so long as the application has been issued and served giving the other party the requisite notice (PD 26, para 5.3(4)).

Where the court proposes to make such an order of its own initiative, it will not allocate the claim to a track, but instead will either:

- fix a hearing, giving the parties at least 14 days notice of the date of the hearing and of the issues which it is proposed that the court will decide; or

- make an order directing a party to take the steps described in the order within a stated time and specifying the consequence of not taking those steps, for example, an order for a party to file a properly formulated statement of case within a specified time, otherwise the claim or defence will be struck out (PD 26, para 5.4).

Where the court decides, at a hearing in which a party is applying for the early termination of a case, or the court has ordered such a hearing of its own initiative, that the claim should continue, it will either treat the hearing as an allocation hearing, allocate the claim and give case management directions or give other appropriate directions (PD 26, para 5.5).

Filing the allocation questionnaire

The court serving the allocation questionnaire will specify a date by which the completed allocation questionnaire must be filed. The court will serve Form N152 on the parties which contains a notice that a defence or counterclaim has been filed and which specifies a date by which, and the court to which, completed allocation questionnaires must be filed. This date must be at least 14 days after the date when the allocation questionnaire is deemed to be served on the party in question (r 26.3(6)).[22]

Failure to file an allocation questionnaire

If no party files an allocation questionnaire within the time specified by the court, the file will be referred to the judge for directions (PD 26, para 2.5(1)(a)). Under r 26.5(5), the judge can make any order he considers appropriate, but the usual order he will make in those circumstances is for the claim and any counterclaim to be struck out unless an allocation questionnaire is filed within three days from service of that order (PD 26, para 2.5(1)(b)).

Where one party files an allocation questionnaire, but another party does not, the court may allocate the claim to a track if it considers it has enough information to do so, or list an allocation hearing and order all or any party to

---

22 See Chapter 9, Service of Documents, for deemed dates of service (r 6.7).

attend (PD 26, para 2.5(2)). It is likely that if it is necessary for the court to hold an allocation hearing in these circumstances, it will order the party in default to pay the costs of the hearing.

Costs estimate

For claims outside the limits of the small claims track,[23] a costs estimate must be filed at court and served on all other parties when the allocation questionnaire is filed (para 6 of the Costs Practice Direction supplementing Parts 43 to 48). The solicitor acting for a party must also deliver a copy of the costs estimate to his client no later than the time when he files it at court.

Precedent H in the Schedule to the Costs Practice Direction should be used (PD 26, para 2.1(2)(b)) and a legal representative should not be deceived into thinking that it is enough to simply provide the two figures for current and estimated costs as suggested by the allocation questionnaire itself. The costs estimate should give an itemised breakdown showing separately the amounts for profit costs, disbursements and VAT incurred and to be incurred which the party expects to recover from the other party if successful. Only base costs need to be shown, and not the amounts of any additional liability[24] if a funding arrangement[25] has been entered into (PD 26, para 2.1(2)(c)). The court may have regard to the estimates when dealing with any final order for costs (PD 43, Section 6), so care should be taken not to over or underestimate.

Stay to allow for settlement

In accordance with the overriding objective, part of the court's case management function involves encouraging the parties to use ADR if appropriate and helping the parties to settle the case.[26]

In accordance with this objective, the allocation questionnaire contains a section asking the parties whether they would like the proceedings to be stayed in order to give them an opportunity to settle the case by ADR or other means (r 26.4(1)).

Length of stay

If all the parties request a stay, or if the court considers of its own initiative that such a stay would be appropriate, the court will order that the

---

23 See below, p 165.
24 See Chapter 38, Funding Litigation.
25 See Chapter 38, Funding Litigation.
26 See r 1.4(2)(e) and (f) and Chapter 5, Judicial Case Management: The Overriding Objective.

proceedings be stayed, in the first instance, for one month to give time for a settlement to be reached (r 26.4(2)).

The court has the power to extend the stay for a further period or until a specified date (r 26.4(3)). It is likely to do this if, for instance, the parties ask for extra time to reach a settlement. The procedure to apply to extend the stay is contained in PD 26, para 3.1. This provides that one of the parties, or his solicitor, should send a letter to the court confirming that all the parties have agreed to apply for an extension of the stay and explaining what steps are being taken to settle the dispute and identifying any mediator or expert assisting to bring about a settlement. The court will generally extend the stay for a maximum period of four weeks unless the parties give good reasons to justify a longer period of time. There is no limit on the number of extensions of time the court may grant.

There is provision for a party to apply for the stay to be lifted (PD 26, para 3.3). This may be appropriate if a party believes that there is no prospect of a settlement being reached and resolution of the dispute is simply being delayed whilst proceedings are stayed.

If the claimant alone requests a stay, the court may be disposed to grant it. However, if the defendant alone requests a stay, the court may be more circumspect, especially if it is thought that the request is merely a delaying tactic.

Notification of settlement

If a settlement is reached during the period of the stay, the claimant must notify the court accordingly (r 26.4(4)).

If the whole of the proceedings are settled during a stay and a party takes one of the following steps:

- applies to the court for a consent order to give effect to the settlement; or
- applies for approval of a settlement where one of the parties is under a disability;[26a] or
- gives notice of acceptance of money paid into court in satisfaction of the claim or applies for money in court to be paid out,

it will be treated as an application for the stay to be lifted (PD 26, para 3.4).

If the claimant does not notify the court that a settlement has been reached, once the period of the stay has expired, the court will give case management directions for the next stage of the case (r 26.5). Rule 26.5 provides that if the court has stayed proceedings under r 26.4, it will allocate the claim to a track at the end of the period of the stay (r 26.5(2)). However, it would appear that the court will only allocate the claim to a track if that is appropriate and before

26a See Chapter 26, Special Rules for Children and Patients.

doing so the court may require a party to provide further information or decide to hold an allocation hearing (PD 26, para 3.2). Many courts have now adopted the practice of sending out 'unless' orders in the absence of any feedback after the expiry of the period of stay, with striking out of the claim and defence in default of any further response.

ALLOCATION TO A TRACK

In most cases, once every defendant to an action has filed an allocation questionnaire, or when the period for filing the allocation questionnaire has expired (whichever is sooner), the court will allocate a claim to one of the three tracks (r 26.5(1)).

A case will not be allocated at this stage if:

- proceedings have been stayed under r 26.4 (r 26.5(1));[27] or
- the court has dispensed with the need for allocation questionnaires (r 26.5(1));[28] or
- the court has ordered the party under r 26.5(3) to provide further information about his case; or
- the court has ordered an allocation hearing under r 26.5(4).

SCOPE OF EACH TRACK

Financial value of the claim

The scope of each track is primarily limited by the financial value of the claim. It is for the court to assess the financial value of a claim (PD 26, para 7.3(1)). In most cases, the court will simply accept the claimant's valuation of the claim as set out in his statement of case. However, if the court believes that the amount the claimant is seeking exceeds what he may reasonably expect to recover, it may order the claimant to provide further information to justify the amount claimed (r 26.5(3) and PD 26, para 7.3(2)).

The financial value of a claim, for the purposes of considering which track it should be allocated to, does *not* include:

- any amount not in dispute;
- any claim for interest;
- costs; and
- any contributory negligence (r 26.8(2)).

---

27 See above, p 161, Stay to allow for settlement.
28 Eg, if a summary judgment hearing is held before allocation.

Any amount not in dispute

General guidance is given in the Practice Direction to Part 26 as to how the court will decide whether an amount is in dispute between the parties. The general principles the court will take into account are stated as follows:

- any amount for which the defendant does not admit liability is in dispute;
- any sum in respect of an *item* forming part of the claim for which judgment has been entered (for example, summary judgment) is not in dispute;
- any specific sum claimed as a *distinct item* and which the defendant admits he is liable to pay is not in dispute;
- any sum offered by the defendant which has been accepted by the claimant in satisfaction of any *item* which forms a *distinct* part of the claim is not in dispute (PD 26, para 7.4).

This list of principles the court will apply when deciding whether an amount is in dispute, with its reference to 'items' forming 'a distinct part of the claim' suggests that a technical distinction is made between the situation where a defendant is prepared to admit to a particular part of a claim, the value of which can be separately itemised, and where a defendant is prepared to admit in general terms that a smaller sum is owed than has been claimed. Following such a definition, only those sums which fall into the former category would be treated as not being in dispute, if admitted to by the defendant, for the purposes of valuation of a claim.

These general principles which the court will apply when determining the valuation of a claim have particular significance for the small claims track. This is because many defendants to, for example, a debt action, where they acknowledge that the claimant is likely to be successful but dispute the amount claimed, will try to bring the claim into the small claims track limit so as to avoid paying the claimant's legal costs.[29] Under the above general principles, the defendant would not be able to do this simply by admitting part of the amount owed, so that the balance outstanding is £5,000 or less,[30] unless the amount admitted is also a distinct item of the claim. Similarly, a party who deliberately exaggerates his claim to take it out of the small claims track is likely to face a costs sanction.[31]

It should be noted, however, that if a claim is allocated to the small claims track, because it is brought within the financial limit of that track following the admission to part of the claim by the defendant, before allocation the claimant

---

29 See Chapter 16, p 184, for the rules about the recovery of costs for cases allocated to the small claims track.

30 See below, p 165, for the financial limit of the small claims track.

31 *Afzal v Ford Motor Co Ltd* [1994] 4 All ER 720, CA.

can apply for judgment with costs on the amount of the claim that has been admitted.[32]

THE SMALL CLAIMS TRACK[33]

Financial value

The small claims is the normal track for any claim which has a financial value of not more than £5,000 (r 26.6(3)). The court has a discretion to keep a matter within the small claims track even where the counterclaim[34] or Part 20 claim exceeds the financial limit.

Special rules for personal injury claims and repairing orders

However, the financial value of a claim is calculated in a different way for personal injury claims[35] and those claims where a tenant of residential premises is seeking an order for repair against his landlord. This was introduced to avoid a tenant being refused public funding for the case, where appropriate, on the basis that the case was merely on the small claims track, bearing in mind the principle of equality between the parties as contained in the overriding objective.

A personal injuries action will only be allocated to the small claims track where the damages claimed for pain, suffering and loss of amenity are less than £1,000 *and* the financial value of the claim is not more than £5,000 (rr 26.6(1)(a) and 26.6(2)). Therefore, if the damages claimed for pain, suffering and loss of amenity exceed £1,000, the claim will not be allocated to the small claims track even if the financial element of the claim is less than £5,000.

Order for repair of residential premises

Where a tenant brings a claim in which he seeks an order requiring the landlord to carry out repairs or other works to the premises, the claim will only be allocated to the small claims track if the costs of the repairs or other work to the premises is estimated not to exceed £1,000 *and* the financial value of any other claim for damages does not exceed £1,000 (r 26.6(1)(b)). Again, both conditions must be met in order for such a case to be allocated to the small claims track.

---

32 See rr 14.3 and 15.1(3) of the Costs Practice Direction supplementing Parts 43–48.
33 See Chapter 16, The Small Claims Track.
34 *Berridge v Bayliss* (1999) Lawtel, 23 November, CA (unreported elsewhere).
35 For a definition of personal injuries claim, see r 2.3.

Features of the small claims track

The small claims track is meant for straightforward claims which do not require substantial preparation and are suitable for a relatively informal hearing. The small claims track procedure is intended to be accessible to litigants in person. In accordance with the principle of proportionality,[36] as the value of the claims is not more than £5,000, it is intended that claims allocated to the small claims track will not incur substantial legal costs and the 'no costs' rule is a deterrent to parties obtaining legal representation to bring their action.

Paragraph 8.1(c) of PD 26 lists the types of case suitable for the small claims track as consumer disputes, accident claims,[37] disputes about the ownership of goods and most disputes between a landlord and tenant other than those for possession.[38] It is also specifically provided that a case involving a disputed allegation of dishonesty will not be suitable for allocation to the small claims track (PD 26, para 8.1(d)).

If both parties consent, a claim which is normally outside the small claims track limit can be allocated to that track. However, the court does not have to allocate such a claim to the small claims track if it is not satisfied that it is suitable for hearing on that track (PD 26, para 8.1(2)).

THE FAST TRACK[39]

Financial value

The fast track is the normal track for any claim which has a financial value of more than £5,000 but not more than £15,000 (r 26.6(4)). However, this general rule is subject to further requirements, namely that the fast track will only be the normal track for claims with a financial value of not more than £15,000 if it is also likely that:

- the trial of the action will not last for more than one day; and
- oral expert evidence at trial will be limited to one expert in any expert field per party and limited to two fields of expertise (r 26.6(5)).

---

36 See the overriding objective, Chapter 5.
37 But see the special rules for personal injury actions on the small claims track, above, p 165.
38 But see the special rules for cases of disrepair of residential tenancies, above, p 165.
39 See Chapter 17, The Fast Track.

Features of the fast track

Although claims allocated to the fast track are heard at a formal trial, the procedure is more limited than cases heard on the multi-track. In most instances, the trial is set down for one day, a trial timetable will usually be set in which evidence and cross-examination will be controlled, disclosure of documents will be limited and expert evidence will be presented by way of written report.

Although it is a key feature of a fast track trial that it will last no longer than one day, the mere *possibility* that a trial *may* last longer than one day is not a conclusive reason for the court to allocate a case to the multi-track instead (PD 26, para 9.1(3)(c)). However, where it is clear that the case *will* last longer than a day the fast track will not be appropriate because of the limits on advocates' fees and the provision that the part-heard case will normally be heard the next day.[40]

Where a case involves a counterclaim or other Part 20 claim that will be heard with the main action and, as a result, the trial will last for more than one day, the court cannot allocate the case to the fast track (PD 26, para 9.1(3)(e)).

THE MULTI-TRACK[41]

Financial value

The multi-track is the normal track for any claim which has a financial value of more than £15,000 (r 26.6(6)).

Features of the multi-track

The multi-track is suitable for complex cases or cases of high value which are likely to involve the most pre-trial preparation and case management directions. The multi-track allows the court the discretion to decide how much case management a case requires. Some cases with a financial limit above the fast track limit may be relatively straightforward and if the parties will not consent to the case being allocated to the fast track, the court has the discretion to tailor the case management directions on the multi-track so that, in effect, the directions ordered are the same as those for a fast track case.

---

40 See Chapter 17, The Fast Track.
41 See Chapter 18, The Multi-Track.

CIVIL TRIAL CENTRES AND FEEDER COURTS

Certain courts have been designated Civil Trial Centres. Courts which are not Civil Trial Centres will be 'feeder courts'. The case management of a claim allocated to the multi-track, apart from claims involving possession of land in the county court where the defendant has filed a defence and cases dealt with at the Royal Courts of Justice, will be dealt with at a Civil Trial Centre (PD 26, paras 10.1, 10.2(1)).

A claim involving specialist proceedings[42] as defined in Part 49 will be allocated to the multi-track whatever its value and the case management of such a case must be dealt with at a Civil Trial Centre (PD 26, para 10.2(2)).

Where a judge at a feeder court decides, on the basis of the allocation questionnaires and any other documents filed by the parties, that a claim should be dealt with on the multi-track, he will normally allocate the claim to the multi-track, give case management directions and transfer the claim to a Civil Trial Centre (PD 26, para 10.2(5)). In some areas, however, such as Greater London, following guidance from the designated civil judge, the feeder court will transfer the case to the Trial Centre at central London without first giving directions. If the judge at the feeder court decides that an allocation hearing or some pre-allocation hearing is to take place, the hearing will take place at the feeder court (PD 26, para 10.2(6)). If the case proceeds and is allocated to the multi-track, it will then be transferred to a Civil Trial Centre (PD 26, para 10.2(7)). The judge at the feeder court can, however, transfer the case to a Civil Trial Centre for the decision on allocation to be made (PD 26, para 10.2(8)).

If a case allocated to the multi-track is likely to need more than one case management conference, and the Civil Trial Centre is inconveniently located for the parties or their legal representatives, a judge sitting at a feeder court may, with the permission of the designated civil judge, decide that case management should take place at the feeder court for the time being (PD 26, para 10.2(10)).

A designated civil judge may transfer claims from feeder courts to a Civil Trial Centre notwithstanding the track a claim has been allocated to. He may also allow a feeder court to keep for trial a claim, or category of claims, usually allocated to the multi-track. Whether such permission is granted will depend on the ability of the feeder court in relation to the Civil Trial Centre to provide suitable and effective trial within an appropriate trial period (PD 26, para 10.2(11)).

---

42 See Chapter 2, Sources of Civil Procedure: Structure and Jurisdiction of the Courts, p 18.

GENERAL RULES FOR ALLOCATION

It would seem that in most cases, the court will allocate a claim to a track according to whether its financial value falls within the scope of a track (as set out above). In any event, a court cannot allocate a claim to a track if its financial value exceeds the normal limit of that track, unless all the parties consent to the allocation of the claim to that track (r 26.7(3)).

Factors relevant to allocation

However, not all claims have a financial value and it would not be appropriate to allocate some claims, having a financial value falling within the normal scope of a track, to the normal track. Therefore, the rules provide a list of matters the court must have regard to when deciding which track to allocate a case to. These are:

- the financial value, if any of the claim;[43]
- the nature of the remedy sought;
- the likely complexity of the facts, law or evidence;
- the number of parties or likely parties;
- the value of any counterclaim or other Part 20 claim and the complexity of any matters relating to it;
- the amount of oral evidence which may be required;
- the importance of the claim to persons who are not parties to the proceedings;
- the views expressed by the parties; and
- the circumstances of the parties (r 26.8(1)(a)–(i)).

Therefore, for a claim with no financial value, the court will decide which track would be most suitable for it by considering the other non-financial considerations set out above (r 26.7(2)). This is particularly true of residential possession cases which, as Part 8 proceedings, would normally be allocated to multi-track but where the reality is that, depending on the size and complexity of the case, they might be more suitable for the fast or even the small claims track.

---

43 See above, p 163.

The value of any counterclaim or other Part 20 claim

Where there is more than one money claim, for instance, where the defendant counterclaims, in order to assess the financial value of the claim the court will not usually simply aggregate the amount of the claim and counterclaim and will instead regard the largest claim as determining the financial value of the action (PD 26, para 7.7), although they are not bound to.[44]

Multiple claimants

Where two or more claimants start an action against the same defendant using the same claim form, but each claimant has a claim against the defendant separate from the other claimants, the court will consider the claim of each claimant separately when it assesses the financial value of the claim (r 26.8(3)).

The parties' views as to allocation

The parties' views will be treated as an important factor by the court when making its decision, but those views cannot prevent the court from allocating the case to the track it considers most appropriate even if all the parties have agreed on a different track (PD 26, para 7.5).

NOTICE OF ALLOCATION

When the court allocates a claim to a track, it will serve a notice of allocation on each party along with a copy of the allocation questionnaires and any additional information[45] filed by the other parties to the action (r 26.9).

Where the court allocates a case to the fast track, it will send a notice of allocation in Form N154, Form N155 if the case is allocated to the multi-track, and one of Forms N157–160 if the case is allocated to the small claims track (PD 26, para 4.2). The practice directions dealing with the different tracks give details about case management directions which will be made at the allocation stage for each track.[46]

The court will generally give brief reasons for its allocation decision in the notice of allocation unless all the allocation questionnaires have expressed the wish for the claim to be allocated to the track to which the court has allocated it (PD 26, para 4.2(4)).

---

44 *Berridge v Bayliss* (1999) Lawtel, 23 November, CA (unreported elsewhere).
45 See above, p 157 (r 26.5(3)).
46 See Chapters 16, 17 and 18 on the small claims, fast and multi-track for more details.

RE-ALLOCATION

Once the court has allocated a claim to a track, it is not precluded from re-allocating the claim to a different track (r 26.10). This may be appropriate if there has been a change in the circumstances since the case was allocated to a track. The court may re-allocate the case on application by a party or of its own initiative (PD 26, para 11.2).

If the court allocates a claim to a track without an allocation hearing, a party who is dissatisfied with the track the claim has been allocated to should apply to the court to re-allocate the claim. It is presumed that such an application should be made in accordance with Part 23.[47] However, if allocation was made at a hearing at which a party was present, or represented, or of which he had due notice, the dissatisfied party must appeal against the order for allocation (PD 26, para 11.1).

JURY TRIAL

High Court

Where a claim brought in the Queen's Bench Division of the High Court involves an issue against a party of fraud, libel, slander, malicious prosecution or false imprisonment, an application can be made for trial with a jury. If the court is satisfied that such an allegation is in issue, the party has the right to have the action tried with a jury unless the court is of the opinion that the trial requires any prolonged examination of documents or accounts or any scientific or local investigation which cannot conveniently be made with a jury.[48]

County courts

Similar provisions apply to cases proceeding in the county courts except that actions for libel and slander may not be brought or heard in a county court.[49]

---

47 See Chapter 19, Making Applications for Court Orders.
48 Supreme Court Act 1981, s 69.
49 County Courts Act 1984, s 66.

CHAPTER 16

THE SMALL CLAIMS TRACK

INTRODUCTION

In talking about the small claims track, Lord Woolf said:

> I see the small claims scheme as the primary way of increasing access to justice for ordinary people. It is expressly intended for litigants in person ... I believe that the interventionist approach of the small claims scheme provides the most effective protection for litigants who do not have the resources to pay for legal advice and representation and who are not eligible for legal aid.[1]

In the light of this, Lord Woolf recommended an increase in the jurisdiction of the small claims court from £1,000 to £3,000, but in fact it was subsequently increased to £5,000.

SCOPE OF THE SMALL CLAIMS TRACK

The small claims track is the normal track for claims with a financial value of not more than £5,000, subject to the special rules for personal injury and housing disrepair claims (r 26.6).[2] However, just because a claim falls within the financial limit of the small claims track does not mean that a claim will be allocated to this track if, for instance, the complexity of the law or issues involved would make it unsuitable for hearing on the small claims track with its relative informality and limited procedural framework.[3]

The decision as to the value of the claim is that of the court (r 26.7). Any dispute will be resolved by the court prior to allocation, as it will affect the allocation of the case to track. The intentional overstatement of the amount involved to avoid the claim being referred to the small claims track is a clear abuse of process and may lead to sanctions under Part 3 (the court's case management powers)[3a] (*Afzal v Ford Motor Co Ltd*).[4]

The financial value for tracking purposes is that of the claim, not the counterclaim. A judge has discretion to keep a matter within the small claims

---

1   See *Access to Justice*, Interim Report, Chapter 15, paras 3 and 4 (www.lcd.gov.uk/civil/interfr.htm).
2   See Chapter 15, Judicial Case Management: Allocation, p 165.
3   *Ibid*, p 169.
3a See Chapter 5, Judicial Case Management: The Overriding Objective.
4   [1994] 4 All ER 720, CA.

track even if the counterclaim exceeds the limit (*Berridge (Paul) (t/a EAB Builders) v RM Bayliss*[5]).

A claim against a landlord of residential premises which includes a remedy for harassment or unlawful eviction cannot be allocated to the small claims track whatever the financial value of the claim (r 26.7(4)). This is to enable public funding to be available to the claimant if appropriate.

Under PD 26, para 12, the court now has power to allocate proceedings to decide the amount payable under a judgment (now known as a 'disposal hearing') to the small claims track if the financial value of the claim is such that the claim would, if defended, have been allocated to that track. Rule 27.14 below, limiting the court's power to award costs, will then apply.

REMEDIES AVAILABLE IN SMALL CLAIMS ACTIONS

The court has the power to grant any final remedy in small claims actions which it could grant if proceedings were on the fast track or the multi-track (r 27.3). Therefore, the fact that a claimant is seeking a remedy such as an injunction or specific performance would not preclude the action from being allocated to the small claims track if the value and/or complexity are such that it is suitable for hearing on that track.[6]

FEATURES OF THE SMALL CLAIMS TRACK

In summary, the hallmarks of the small claims track are:
- certain parts of the CPR do not apply; for example, Part 36 offers and payments;
- standard directions are usually given;
- trials are usually heard by the district judge in an informal setting in which the strict rules of evidence do not apply;
- the district judge can decide on an appropriate procedure for the trial and the judge's role is usually interventionist;
- The 'no costs rule' applies.

---

5   (1999) Lawtel, 23 November, CA (unreported elsewhere).
6   See Chapter 15, Case Management: Allocation, for the court's decision on allocation.

Parts of the CPR which do not apply to small claims

In recognition of the fact that the small claims track is meant to provide a more informal forum in which to decide a dispute, in proportion to the amount at stake and complexity of the dispute, a number of parts of the CPR, or certain rules within a part, do not apply to the small claims track once the case has been allocated to that track. Also, because legal costs are not usually awarded for small claims cases, certain parts of the CPR, such as Part 36 offers to settle and payments in,[7] are not applicable.

The following *parts*, therefore, are completely excluded:

- Part 18 (further information);
- Part 31 (disclosure and inspection);
- Part 33 (miscellaneous rules about evidence); and
- Part 36 (offers to settle and payments into court) (r 27.2(1)).

The following parts are excluded *except* for the rules indicated:

- Part 25 (interim remedies) except for interim injunctions;
- Part 32 (evidence) except r 32.1 (power of court to control evidence);
- Part 35 (experts and assessors) except rr 35.1 (duty to restrict expert evidence), 35.3 (experts – overriding duty to the court), 35.7 (court's power to direct that evidence is to be given by a single joint expert) and 35.8 (instructions to a single joint expert); and
- Part 39 (hearings) except r 39.2 (general rule – hearing to be in public) (r 27.2(1)).

Directions on the small claims track

If a defence is filed and the case is allocated[8] to the small claims track, in most cases the court will then give directions for the further conduct of the action. Having made directions, the court can then add to them, vary them or revoke them if it is necessary to do so (r 27.7).

Standard directions

For most actions allocated to the small claims track, the court will give standard directions and fix a date for the final hearing. If a case is suitable for standard directions, these will consist of:

---

7   See Chapter 24, Offers to Settle and Payments into Court.
8   See Chapter 15, Judicial Case Management: Allocation.

- a direction for each party to file at court, and serve on every other party, copies of all documents (including any expert's report) on which he intends to rely at least 14 days before the date of the hearing;
- a date for the hearing and the time allowed for the hearing;
- a warning that the court must be informed immediately if the case is settled by agreement before the hearing date; and
- any other standard direction set out in the relevant practice direction (r 27.4(1)).

The Practice Direction to r 27 sets out a variety of standard directions for different types of action such as road accidents, building disputes and contract claims, landlord and tenant, disputes about the return of deposits, and ruined holiday and wedding claims. The practice directions for such claims contain the standard directions and additional directions which are likely to be necessary depending on the nature of the dispute. The practice direction should be consulted for the details, but the directions cover such additional matters as the provision of photographs and plans and witness statements.

Special directions

If standard directions are unsuitable for a case, the court will give special directions and fix a date for a hearing. Special directions are directions instead of or in addition to standard directions (r 27.4(1)(b)). Examples of special directions are: a direction that the hearing will take place at a venue other than the court, for instance, at one of the parties' business premises; or a direction that expert evidence is necessary and should be obtained by way of a single joint expert (see PD 27, Form F).

In some cases, the court will give special directions and direct that the court will consider what further directions are to be given no later than 28 days after the date special directions were given (r 27.4(1)(c)).

Expert evidence

If the court does not make a direction permitting expert evidence, none will be admissible at the hearing, whether written or oral (r 27.5). This is in keeping with the general rule as to the admissibility of expert evidence for all types of hearing.[9] However, in most cases, expert evidence will be admissible and it will be noted that part of the standard directions includes filing and serving copies of the expert evidence on which a party intends to rely.

9   See Chapter 30, Experts and Assessors.

Although expert evidence is permitted on the small claims track, not all the rules in Part 35 apply to the small claims track.[10] This allows expert evidence to be presented in a more informal way, as there is no requirement to present it in the form of a written report as detailed in the Practice Direction to Part 35. In most claims heard on the small claims track, it will not be proportionate to rely on oral expert evidence and if a party wishes to rely on such evidence, he will have to make an application for permission to do so. The court can award up to a maximum of £200 to a party for the cost of obtaining expert evidence.[11]

Preliminary hearings

In some cases, rather than give directions for the further conduct of the action, the court will fix a date for a preliminary hearing instead. The court has the power to order a preliminary hearing in the following circumstances:

- where the court considers that special directions are needed to ensure a fair hearing, but it appears necessary for a party to attend at court to ensure that he understands what he must do to comply with the special directions. This is likely only to apply where the party is a litigant in person. If, for instance, a litigant in person brings a case and the court considers that expert evidence is necessary to decide the case, but the litigant in person has not provided for any, the court may decide to hold a preliminary hearing so that this can be explained to the party and for directions for a single joint expert to be instructed given; or

- to enable the court to dispose of the claim on the basis that one or other of the parties has no real prospect of success at a final hearing;[12] or

- to enable the court to strike out a statement of case or part of one on the basis that it discloses no reasonable grounds to bring or defend the claim (r 27.6(1)).[13]

The court *must* consider the desirability of limiting the expense for the parties involved in attending court when deciding whether to hold a preliminary hearing (r 27.6(2)). This will obviously be an important factor for a case allocated to the small claims track where the amount involved will usually be no more than £5,000 and as legal costs are not usually recoverable.

---

10 See above, p 175.
11 See below, p 184, Costs on the small claims track.
12 See Chapter 22, Summary Judgment.
13 See Chapter 23, Striking Out.

Preliminary hearing to be final hearing

The court can treat the preliminary hearing as a final hearing if all the parties agree (r 27.6(4)) and if there is time.

If a party indicates on their allocation questionnaire[14] that they intend to apply for summary judgment and/or an order to strike out the other party's statement of case, the court may well order that this matter be decided at a preliminary hearing and if the parties agree to this, the preliminary hearing can be treated as the final hearing.

Notice of the preliminary hearing

The court will give the parties at least 14 days' notice of the date of the preliminary hearing (r 27.6(3)).

Directions following a preliminary hearing

If the case is not concluded at the preliminary hearing, at or after the preliminary hearing, the court will give directions for the further conduct of the case. This will include a direction fixing the date of the final hearing (if this has not already been fixed) and informing the parties of the time allowed for the hearing as well as any other appropriate directions, such as the filing and serving of documents (r 27.6(5)).

THE SMALL CLAIMS HEARING

Notice of the final hearing

The court will give the parties at least 21 days' notice of the date fixed for the final hearing, unless the parties agree to accept less notice than this. The notice will also inform the parties of the time allowed for the final hearing (r 27.4(2)).

Hearing before the district judge

In most cases a small claims trial will be heard by the district judge; however, it may be heard by a circuit judge (PD 27, para 1). In most county courts, a small claims trial takes place in the district judge's room in an informal setting (PD 27, para 4.2). The district judge sits behind a desk at the head of a table

---

14 See Chapter 15, Judicial Case Management: Allocation.

whilst the parties sit at tables arranged at each side. The whole proceedings are conducted from a sitting down position. However, the hearing may take place in a court room or in any other appropriate venue, such as the home or business premises of a party (PD 27, para 4.1(3)).

In accordance with the general rule and Art 6 of the Human Rights Act 1998 and the European Convention for Human Rights, a small claims hearing should be held in public unless the interests of justice demand that it should be heard in private (r 39.2(1) and PD 27, para 4.1(1)). There are certain types of claim where privacy is important and for those cases, the general rule is that the hearing will be in private,[15] for example, mortgagee possession actions (PD 27, para 4.1(2)). The court may also decide to hold the hearing in private if both parties agree to it (PD 27, para 4.1(2)).

In practice, small claims hearings held in public are not attended by many members of the public because they normally take place in the district judge's room, which is not usually readily accessible to the public. In those courts where the district judge's room is inaccessible, there is often a notice inviting those who wish to observe the proceedings to inform the court usher so that arrangements for access can be made. However, r 39.2(2) provides that the court does not have to make special arrangements to accommodate members of the public at a hearing. Notwithstanding the absence of a duty to accommodate, PD 39, para 1.10 gives the judge the power to adjourn proceedings to a larger room or court if it is not practicable to accommodate members of the public who want to observe the proceedings.

Form of the hearing

The judge holding the small claims hearing has discretion to adopt any method of proceeding that he considers to be fair (r 27.8(1)).

However, this is within the context of the following rules that:

- the hearing will be informal;
- the strict rules of evidence do not apply;
- the court does not need to take evidence on oath;
- the court may limit cross-examination; and
- the court must give reasons for its decision (r 27.8(2)–(6)).

In practice, it is often the case that district judges adopt a varying approach depending on whether the parties are legally represented or not. If both parties are legally represented, the district judge can be expected to conduct the hearing more formally and rely on the legal representatives to protect their client's interests. However, where one or both parties are acting in person, the

---

15 See r 39.2(3); Chapter 32, Hearings and Judgment.

district judge can be expected to be much more interventionist. Lord Woolf described the district judge's role in these circumstances as 'not only that of an adjudicator. It is a key safeguard of the rights of both parties. In most cases, the judge is effectively a substitute for legal representation ... He must also hold the ring and ensure that each party has a fair chance to present his own case and to challenge that of his opponent'.[16]

Limiting cross-examination

Practice Direction 27 refers to the court's power to limit cross-examination. This includes the power of the judge to:

- ask questions of any witness himself before allowing any other person to do so;
- ask questions of all or any of the witnesses himself before allowing any other person to ask questions of any witnesses;
- refuse to allow cross-examination of any witness until all the witnesses have given evidence-in-chief;
- limit the cross-examination of a witness to a fixed time and/or to a particular subject or issue (PD 27, para 4.3).

Reasons for the decision

Most small claims trials are tape recorded by the district judge. If the hearing is tape recorded, the district judge will usually also tape record his judgment and the reasons for it (PD 27, paras 5.1, 5.4). A party to the proceedings can obtain a transcript of the recording on payment of the transcriber's charges (PD 27, para 5.1).

If the judge does not tape record the hearing and his judgment, he will make a written note of the central points of the oral evidence and the central reasons for his judgment. A party to the proceedings will then be entitled to obtain a copy (PD 27, paras 5.3, 5.4, 5.7).

The reasons for the judge's decision can be given as briefly and simply as the nature of the case allows (PD 27, para 5.5). The judge will normally give his reasons orally at the hearing, but he can decide to send them at a later stage to the parties in writing or fix a hearing in order to give his reasons (PD 27, para 5.5).

---

16 See Interim Report, Chapter 16, para 26. (*Ibid*.)

Representation at a small claims hearing

Small claims proceedings are designed so that litigants in person can act for themselves. In accordance with the Lay Representatives (Right of Audience) Order 1999,[17] a party to a small claims action may present his own case at the hearing or a lawyer or lay representative may present it for him (PD 27, para 3.2(1)). A lay representative is defined as a person other than a barrister, solicitor or a legal executive employed by a solicitor (PD 27, para 3.1). A party may, therefore, have any person present his case at a small claims hearing. A lay representative cannot exercise a right of audience in the following circumstances:

- if his client does not attend the hearing;
- at any stage after judgment; or
- on any appeal against a decision of the district judge in the proceedings (Lay Representatives (Right of Audience) Order 1999 and PD 27, para 3.2(2)).

However, these exceptions are not absolute as PD 27, para 3.2(3), referring to the court's general discretion to hear anybody, states that the court may hear a lay representative even in the circumstances excluded by the order.

A party in any proceedings may choose to have assistance from a so called McKenzie[18] friend. Such a person does not act for the litigant, but provides assistance during the conduct of the proceedings and will usually sit beside the litigant at the trial, take notes and advise *sotto voce* on the conduct of the case. In the light of the fact that a party can have a lay representative act for him at a small claims hearing, the use of a McKenzie friend will be less common than in other hearings where lay representatives have no right of audience.

However, this does not preclude a party from using a McKenzie friend in a small claims hearing. The Court of Appeal reviewed the status of, and entitlement of the litigant to, a McKenzie friend in the case of *R v Bow County Court ex p Pelling*.[19] The court held in that case that, as regards hearings in public, a litigant in person should be allowed the assistance of a McKenzie friend unless the judge is satisfied, in accordance with the overriding objective, that fairness and the interests of justice are such that the litigant should not have such assistance. This principle would apply to small claims hearings (and other hearings) in the judge's chambers which are held in public. However, for hearings held in private, the nature of the proceedings which make it desirable for them to be heard in private may mean that it is

---

17 SI 1999/1225.

18 The name derives from the case of *McKenzie v McKenzie* [1971] P33.

19 [1999] 1 WLR 1807; [1999] 4 All ER 751, also available on the Court Service website, Case No 1999/0478 at www.courtservice.gov.uk/judgments/judg_frame.htm.

inappropriate for a McKenzie friend to assist, and the court will have discretion to exclude a McKenzie friend from such proceedings. Moreover, the court held that the McKenzie friend has no right to provide the assistance and cannot therefore complain about being excluded, the right to assistance being that of the litigant in person.

Any officer or employee may represent a company at a small claims hearing (PD 27, para 3.1.4).

NON-ATTENDANCE OF PARTIES AT SMALL CLAIMS HEARING

Party electing not to attend final hearing

A party can elect not to attend the hearing and ask the court to decide the claim in his absence instead. In those circumstances, the court will take that party's statement of case and any other filed documents into account when it decides the case at the final hearing, so long as that party has made such a request and notified the court that he will not attend the hearing at least seven days before the date of the hearing (r 27.9(1)). On reaching a decision in a case decided where a party has given such notice, the judge will send a note of the reasons for his judgment to both parties (PD 27, para 5.6).

However, if a party, for good reason, cannot attend the date fixed for the hearing, he can apply to the court to adjourn the date fixed for the hearing, rather than ask for it to be decided in his absence.

Claimant failing to attend final hearing

If a claimant fails to notify the court that he will not attend in accordance with r 27.9(1) (referred to above), and fails to attend the hearing, the court may strike out the claimant's claim (r 27.9(2)).

Defendant failing to attend final hearing

If the defendant fails to notify the court that he will not attend in accordance with r 27.9(1) (referred to above) and fails to attend the hearing, and the claimant does attend or gives the notice in r 27.9(1), the court has the power to decide the claim on the basis of the evidence of the claimant alone (r 27.9(3)).

Both parties fail to attend final hearing

If both parties fail to notify the court that they will not attend in accordance with r 27.9(1) (referred to above) and neither party attends the hearing, the court can strike out the claim and any defence and counterclaim (r 27.9(4)).

Setting judgment aside and re-hearing

Where a judgment is given following a small claims hearing in which one of the parties did not attend or give the notice in r 27.9(1), on the application of that party the court has the power to set the judgment aside and order a re-hearing so long as certain conditions are met (r 27.11(1)). These are if the applicant can satisfy the court that:

- he had good reason for not attending or being represented at the hearing or giving notice under r 27.9(1); and
- he has a reasonable prospect of success at a hearing (r 27.11(3)).

Moreover, the party must make the application not more than 14 days after the day on which the judgment was served on him (r 27.11(2)).

If the court grants the application and sets aside the judgment, it must fix a date for a new hearing of the claim. The judge may order that the hearing take place immediately after the hearing of the application to set the judgment aside and that it be heard by the same judge who set the judgment aside (r 27.11(4)).

The rules giving the court the power to set aside judgment do not apply where the court has dealt with the claim without a hearing (r 27.11(5)). In those circumstances, the correct procedure for a party who wishes to challenge the judgment is for him to make an appeal in accordance with Part 52.

DISPOSING OF A SMALL CLAIM WITHOUT A HEARING

The court has the power, but only if all the parties agree, to dispose of the claim without a hearing (r 27.10).

Once a claim has been allocated to the small claims track, if the court deems it suitable for disposal without a hearing, it will notify the parties of this proposal and invite them to notify the court by a specified date whether they agree to it (r 27.4(1)(e)).

If the parties agree to disposal of the claim without a hearing, the court will decide the case on the parties' statements of case and other relevant documents. Once the judge has decided the matter, he will send a written note of his judgment and reasons for it to both parties (PD 27, para 5.6).

Although active case management includes 'dealing with the case without the parties needing to attend at court',[20] the judge cannot insist that the final hearing be dealt with in the absence of the parties, even if he believes it would be a suitable case for disposal in this way. Moreover, it is likely that most litigants would not agree to disposal of the case without a hearing.

COSTS ON THE SMALL CLAIMS TRACK

One of the most important features of the small claims track is the so called 'no costs rule'. This rule is an exception to the indemnity principle of our civil litigation system and provides that a party will not be able to recover the legal costs of a small claims case from their opponent (apart from certain limited costs) even in the event of success. The small claims track is designed to provide a simpler, quicker and more informal procedure for bringing and defending a claim so that a litigant in person can deal with the matter himself, and therefore the policy behind the no costs rule is to discourage the instruction of legal representatives, whose use is felt to be disproportionate to the matter being litigated. However, it should be noted that there is no express restriction on legal representation for small claims. Moreover, the restriction on recovering legal costs applies to the fees of a lay representative acting for a party as well as to lawyers' costs (r 27.14(4)).

Costs in the discretion of the court

Rule 44.3, which provides that costs are in the discretion of the court, applies to small claims as it does to proceedings on any other track and, although provision is made for certain limited costs to be awarded on the small claims track, whether a party is awarded those costs depends on whether the court is prepared to exercise its discretion to order costs.

Costs of issuing proceedings

The restriction on recovering costs from an opponent does not apply to the fixed solicitor's costs attributable to issuing a claim payable under Part 45[20a] and therefore the claimant can usually recover these if the claim is successful (r 27.14(2)(a)).

---

20 See r 1.4(2)(j) and Chapter 5, Judicial Case Management: The Overriding Objective
20a See Chapter 33, Costs, p 399.

Proceedings for an injunction or specific performance

If a party is successful in bringing an action for an injunction or specific performance on the small claims track, the court may order the opponent to pay a sum not exceeding £260 for legal advice and assistance involved in bringing such an action (r 27.14(2)(b) and PD 27, para 7.2).

Costs of an appeal

A successful party can also apply for the costs of an appeal from a decision on the small claims track. Those costs will be summarily assessed (r 27.14(2)(c)).[21]

Unreasonable behaviour

If a party is held to have behaved unreasonably, the court may order them to pay costs to their opponent. The costs will be assessed summarily (r 27.14(2)(d)). It is rare for the judge to order that a party has behaved unreasonably, but an example might be where a party has unnecessarily caused a late adjournment of the hearing, unreasonably refused to negotiate, or failed to turn up at the hearing.

In *Taylor v Ashworth*,[22] a last minute decision by a defendant not to proceed with his defence was held to be unreasonable behaviour, as was the overstatement of the amount of damages claimed and the raising of a speculative and unsupportable defence in *Afzal v Ford Motor Co Ltd*.[23]

Other fees and expenses

The court also has a discretion to order a party to pay any court fees paid by their opponent (r 27.14(3)(a)). This may include such fees as the court issue fee and the allocation fee.[24]

Party and witness expenses

The court also has a discretion to order one party to pay another party's or their witnesses' reasonable travel and accommodation expenses in attending the hearing (r 27.14(3)(b)).

---

21 See Chapter 33, Costs.
22 (1978) 129 NLJ 737, CA.
23 [1994] 4 All ER 720, CA.
24 See Chapter 15, Case Management: Allocation.

Party and witnesses' loss of earnings

Alternatively, the court can order one party to pay a sum up to a maximum of £50 per day for another party's, or their witnesses' loss of earnings in attending the hearing (r 27.14(3)(c) and PD 27, para 7.3). The judge may apportion the amount ordered in relation to the length of the hearing. The principle of 'proportionality' would appear to support this.

Experts' fees

The court also has a discretion to order one party to pay the costs of the other party's expert fees up to a maximum of £200 (r 27.14(3)(d) and PD 27, para 7.3). The standard form of directions sent out by the court does not contain a note as to the limit on experts' fees. If the maximum is exceeded, it may not be recoverable. Some courts are making this clear in their directions.

Lay representatives' fees

Although reference to these is made in r 27.14(4), there is no guidance as to what sums should be allowed.

Pre-allocation costs

If a claimant brings an action for an amount exceeding the financial scope of the small claims track,[25] but the defendant makes a part admission[26] which reduces the value of the claim such that it comes within the scope of the small claims track, the claimant can, before allocation, apply for judgment with costs on the part admission, and the court has a discretion to allow costs in respect of the proceedings down to the date judgment is entered (PD 44, para 5.1(3)). This rule therefore allows a claimant to recover the costs for the part of the claim which exceeds the small claims limit.

The limitation on costs recoverable in small claims matters applies both before and after the matter is allocated to the small claims track unless the court or a practice direction provides otherwise (r 44.9(2)). But note r 44.11(1): 'Any costs orders made before a claim is allocated will not be affected by allocation.'

---

25 See Chapter 15, Judicial Case Management: Allocation.
26 *Ibid*; Chapter 8, Responding to an Action.

Costs in cases allocated to the small claims track by agreement

If a case is outside the financial limits of the small claims track but the parties agree to the case being heard on the small claims track, the case will be treated, for the purposes of costs, as if it had been allocated to the fast track. However, the trial costs shall be in the discretion of the judge and shall not in any event exceed the fixed trial costs[27] provided for fast track trials (r 27.14(5)).

Claims re-allocated to another track

If a claim, having originally been allocated to the small claims track, is re-allocated to another track, the 'no costs' rule will cease to apply to the claim from the date of re-allocation, but this will not include any costs incurred before that date. The costs rules for either the fast track or multi-track will then apply to the proceedings instead, depending on which track the case was subsequently allocated to (r 27.15).

APPEALS AGAINST JUDGMENT IN SMALL CLAIM

The rules of appeals in Part 52[28] apply to appeals from judgments in cases heard on the small claims track in the same way as for hearings on the fast track and multi-track. The previous ground of 'serious irregularity' has now gone and permission to appeal must be obtained. An appeal from a district judge's decision is made to the circuit judge. An appeal from a circuit judge's decision is made to a High Court judge.[29] The requirements on appeal from a small claims case are less onerous than those for other appeals (see PD 52, para 5.5).

---

27 See Chapter 17, The Fast Track and Chapter 33, Costs.
28 See Chapter 35, Appeals.
29 *Ibid*, for more details.

THE FAST TRACK

INTRODUCTION

Fast track cases are a new innovation designed to provided expeditious and economic justice in cases between £5,000 and £15,000 where the trial will not last longer than a day. They feature limited experts' evidence and a guaranteed and virtually immovable trial date within 30 weeks of allocation.

The rules and practice directions make it clear that adherence to the timetable and the preservation of the set trial date are an essential feature of the fast track and that failure to comply with the requirements of the court by specified dates will result in sanctions being imposed unless an extension has been previously granted by way of a prospective application. Sanctions may include striking out, debarring evidence, and various costs orders. The judge can lay down a strict timetable for the hearing itself, which is also expected to be adhered to. As there are fixed costs for the hearing, any adjournment from one day to another means that there will be no extra costs for any subsequent day. Advocates should bear this in mind.

District judges and circuit judges have concurrent jurisdiction in the fast track, with the likelihood that district judges will eventually have sole jurisdiction.

The rate of settlement in fast track trials has proved to be very high, influenced no doubt by the relatively short period for preparation and the application of proportionality to costs. The original proposals were for fixed costs for the whole of the preparation and trial of fast track matters and considerable research was carried out to see if this was feasible. The limitation of fixed costs to the trial itself is a compromise and is probably a short term measure prior to the introduction of fixed costs for the whole of the proceedings.

ALLOCATION

Rule 26.6(5) and (6) provides –

    (5) Subject to paragraph (6), the fast track is the normal track for any claim –

        (a) for which the small claims track is not the normal track;[1] and

        (b) which has a financial value of not more than £15,000.

---

1   See Chapter 16, The Small Claims Track.

(6) The fast track is the normal track for the claims referred to in paragraph (5) only if the court considers that –

(a) the trial is likely to last for no longer than one day; and

(b) oral expert evidence at trial (where allowed) will be limited to –

(i) one expert per party in relation to any expert field; and

(ii) expert evidence in two expert fields.

The claim will *not* be allocated to this track if the court considers that the trial is likely to last longer than five hours (PD 26, para 9.1(3)(a)), taking account of the likely case management directions (see below), the court's powers to control evidence and limit cross-examination (see below) (PD 26, para 9.1(3)(b)) and whether any Part 20 claim is involved[2] as the time for this will be included in the estimate (PD 26, para 9.1(3)(e)). The *mere possibility* that the trial may last longer than five hours or the fact that there is to be a split trial will not prevent allocation to this track (PD 26, para 9.1(3)(c) and (d)). However, if a case is *likely* to last more than one day, then the judge will consider allocating it to the multi-track even though it is within the financial value for the fast track limit.

DIRECTIONS (r 28.2(1))

Once a defence has been filed and the matter allocated to the fast track, the district judge will scrutinise the papers to consider the following:

- whether further details of the claim or defence are necessary;
- whether the matter can be disposed of summarily[3] (where the test will be whether the claimant has a case which has a real prospect of being successful);
- whether a preliminary hearing is necessary (at least three days' notice) (PD 28, paras 3.10(1), 3.10(2));
- the question of venue.

The judge will take account of steps already taken by the parties and their compliance or non-compliance with any relevant pre-action protocol[4] (PD 28, para 3.2; r 28.2(1)).

In addition, the district judge will be responsible for:

- setting a timetable for the preparation and hearing of the case (see below, Listing questionnaire). The timetable can include strict limits on amounts of time for evidence, cross-examination and speeches;

2   See Chapter 12, Part 20 Claims.
3   See Chapter 22, Summary Judgment.
4   See Chapter 4, Pre-Action Protocols.

- determining interlocutory applications;
- exercising discipline for failure to comply with procedural directions.

'Typical' standard timetable (PD 28, para 3.12)

This will start from the date of service of the order for directions and provide for:

- disclosure[5] – four weeks (r 28.3);
- exchange of witness statements – 10 weeks (r 32.4, PD 28, para 3.9(3));
- exchange of experts' reports – 14 weeks;
- dispatch of a listing questionnaire by the court (see below) – 20 weeks;
- return of questionnaire by parties (r 28.5(1), PD 26, para 9.2(1)) – 22 weeks;
- trial listed 30 weeks maximum from the start date (r 28.2(3) and (4)), with notification of the trial 'window' on allocation of not more than three weeks;
- trial date fixed not less than three weeks from notice to parties (r 28.6(2)) unless the parties have agreed to accept shorter notice or, exceptionally, the court has ordered that shorter notice be given (PD 28, para 7.1(2)).

This is only a timetable based on the maximum period of 30 weeks between allocation and trial. In practice, the timetable may be based over a shorter period.

The parties must strive to co-operate with each other (PD 28, para 2.2) and may agree directions provided they comply with PD 28, paras 3.6 and 3.7 (PD 28, para 3.5) which broadly mirror the 'typical' timetable above.

Any party may apply either for an order compelling another to comply with a direction or for a sanction to be imposed or for both (PD 28, para 5.1). The application must be made without delay, but the other party should first be given a warning (PD 28, para 5.2).

The listing questionnaire (r 28.5)

28.5(1) The court will send the parties a listing questionnaire for completion and return by the date specified in the notice of allocation unless it considers that the claim can be listed for trial without the need for a listing questionnaire.

(2) The date specified for filing a listing questionnaire will not be more than 8 weeks before the trial date or the beginning of the trial period.

---

5   See Chapter 29, Disclosure.

A fee of £200 is payable by the claimant on filing the listing questionnaire. The fee is £400 in the High Court, although it is highly unlikely, given the final limits of the track, that a fast track matter will be dealt with by the High Court.

The listing questionnaire requires the parties to provide the following information (PD 28, para 6.1(4)):

Directions

Whether:

- the party has complied with previous directions; and
- if not why, and to what extent further directions are required; and
- if so which and why.

Experts

Whether:

- the court has already given permission for the use of written expert evidence and if so for which experts and in which fields;
- reports have been agreed;
- the experts have met;
- the court has already given permission for the use of oral expert evidence and if so for which experts and in which fields;
- such permission is sought, and if so for which experts and in which fields;
- there are dates *within the trial window* when the experts are not available.

Other witnesses

- How many?
- names and addresses;
- availability details *within the trial window*;
- whether:
  - (a) any statements are agreed
  - (b) special facilities or an interpreter are required and if so what.

Legal representation

Whether, and if so by whom, the party is to be represented, together with availability details.

Other matters

The estimated:

- length of the case; and
- number of pages of evidence in the trial bundle.

If neither party returns the listing questionnaire within 14 days of service, then, according to PD 28, para 6.5(1), the court may make an order requiring return of the questionnaire within three days in default of which the claim will be struck out. If only one party returns the listing questionnaire, then PD 28, para 6.5(2) provides that the judge shall usually give listing directions or fix a listing hearing. If a listing hearing is directed, the court will fix a date which is as early as possible, giving the parties at least three days' notice (PD 28, para 6.3).

The court may give directions as to the issues on which evidence is to be given, the nature of the evidence it requires on those issues and the way in which it is to be placed before the court, and may thereby exclude evidence which would otherwise be admissible (r 32.1). A direction giving permission to use expert evidence will say whether it is to be by report or oral, and will name the experts whose evidence is permitted (PD 28, para 7.2(4)). Permission may be made conditional on the experts discussing their differences and filing a report on the discussion.

Interlocutory hearings

These will, where possible, be avoided, but hearings will be needed in these cases:

- where the court proposes to appoint an assessor (PD 28, para 3.11); (not so, where proposal is for a single joint expert[6]);
- where a party is dissatisfied with directions (PD 28, para 4.3);
- usually, on an application to enforce compliance (PD 28, para 5.1). Indeed, the court will not hesitate from imposing such sanctions as are appropriate for non-compliance for directions within the time constraints of the timetable, a position already strongly supported by the Court of Appeal since the inception of the new rules.

The importance of keeping the trial date

It is essential to note the following:

PD 28, para 5.4

(1) The court will not allow a failure to comply with directions to lead to the postponement of the trial unless the circumstances of the case are exceptional.

(2) If it is practicable to do so the court will exercise its powers in a manner that enables the case to come on for trial on the date or within the period previously set.

(3) In particular the court will assess what steps each party should take to prepare the case for trial, direct that those steps are taken in the shortest

---

6   See Chapter 30, Experts and Assessors.

possible time and impose a sanction for non-compliance. Such a sanction may, for example, deprive a party of the right to raise or contest an issue or to rely on evidence to which the direction relates.

(4) Where it appears that one or more issues are or can be made ready for trial at the time fixed while others cannot, the court may direct that the trial will proceed on the issues which are or will then be ready, and order that no costs will be allowed for any later trial of the remaining issues or that those costs will be paid by the party in default.

(5) Where the court has no option but to postpone the trial it will do so for the shortest possible time and will give directions for the taking of the necessary steps in the meantime as rapidly as possible.

(6) Litigants and lawyers must be in no doubt that the court will regard the postponement of a trial as an order of last resort. The court may exercise its power to require a party as well as his legal representative to attend court at a hearing where such an order is to be sought.

An agreement between the parties to adjourn the trial date is not likely by itself to be enough to secure an adjournment. Indeed, it is clear that the circumstances would have to be truly exceptional in order to justify moving the trial date.

TRIAL

The trial will normally take place at the court where the case is being managed, but it may be at another court if appropriate having regard to the needs of the parties and the availability of court resources. It may be held away from court if need be (PD 28, para 8.1, r 2.7).

Preparation is two sided:

- all judges must properly have digested the papers *before trial* (PD 28, para 8.2);

- the trial bundle must be so put together as to assist such preparation (PD 28, para 7.2(2)(c)) and see PD 39, para 3);

- the parties should attend all hearings with updated costs details, both of costs expended and those likely to be expended. As there is now a requirement for costs estimates to be provided, it is important that those estimates are realistic as the parties may be held to them in any future assessment of costs.[7]

The court may set a timetable for the trial and will confirm or vary the time estimate for the trial (r 28.6(1)(b); PD 28, para 7.2(2)(b)). No 'typical' timetable is suggested by the rules or practice directions, but a possible trial timetable for a one-day fast track case may look something like this:

(NB: a court day should normally be regarded as five hours (see PD 26, para 9.1(1)(3)(a).)

---

7   See Chapter 33, Costs.

Judge's reading time	30 minutes
Opening (may be dispensed with – PD 28, para 8.2)	10 minutes
Cross-examination and re-examination of claimant's witness(s)	90 minutes
Cross-examination and re-examination of defendants' witness(s)	90 minutes
Defendant's submissions	15 minutes
Claimant's submissions	15 minutes
Judge's 'thinking time' and judgment	30 minutes
Summary assessment of costs and consequential orders	20 minutes
Total:	5 hours

If the case has to go over from one day it should, if possible, be heard the next day (PD 28, para 8.6).

As can be seen from the above, evidence-in-chief is not included because it is expected to be provided by witness statement (r 32.5(2)) and cross-examination can be curtailed (r 32.1(3)). The strict timetabling of the trial and the lack of refresher fee (see below) or additional costs make it clear that it is incumbent on the parties or their legal representatives to ensure that the timetable is kept to by proper preparation prior to trial taking into account the imposed constraints. The judge is likely to cut off a party if their time is being exceeded, and he will be watching for deliberate prevarication.

Listing

Fast track cases are likely to be 'block listed' among a number of judges and courts, therefore last minute changes of venue are possible. No other business will normally be listed before a one day trial and since there will be no margin for delay, the court will require a prompt start. The new regime encourages parties to negotiate long before trial and those who leave it until the last moment should arrive at court with plenty of time to spare before the start.

Costs

The costs of fast track proceedings will usually be summarily assessed[8] at the conclusion of the trial (PD 28, para 8.5). Thus, the parties will have been required to exchange costs details on the suggested form[9] at least 24 hours before the hearing. There are fixed costs for the advocate on the trial varying between £350 and £750 depending on the amount awarded in relation to the

---

8   See Chapter 33, Costs.
9   *Ibid*.

claimant and the amount claimed in relation to defendant, but this is not dependent on the length of the trial (r 46.2).[10]

Amount recovered (claimant) or claimed (defendant)	Fee
Up to £3,000	£350
£3,000–10,000	£500
£10,000+	£750

A legal representative attending with counsel will be allowed £250 if his attendance was considered necessary (r 46.3). However, should the case last longer than a day, no refresher is available – a clear incentive to finish within the time estimated.

When the rules for fast track were introduced, the provisions as to Conditional Fee Agreements[11] had not yet been brought into effect, including as they do the question of disputes over the success fee. The added factor of a challenged success fee is likely to breach the timetabling arrangements as set out above and may make it necessary for an adjournment or reference of the argument to a detailed assessment,[12] which is somewhat against the spirit of the fast track hearing.

---

10   See Chapter 33, Costs.
11   See *ibid* and Chapter 38, Funding Litigation.
12   See Chapter 33, Costs.

CHAPTER 18

THE MULTI-TRACK

INTRODUCTION

This is the track for cases over £15,000 and those not otherwise allocated to small claims or fast track (r 26.6(6)). It features customised case management by court, case management conferences, pre-trial review by trial judge and the early fixing of the trial window.

Note PD 29, para 3.2:

The hallmarks of the multi-track are:

(1) the ability of the court to deal with cases of widely differing values and complexity, and

(2) the flexibility given to the court in the way it will manage a case in a way appropriate to its particular needs.

VENUE

Where the case is one commenced in the Royal Courts of Justice over which it has jurisdiction[1] then case management will usually be carried out there (PD 29, para 3.1(1)). The case could be transferred to a county court.[2] Civil Trial Centres[3] are regionally situated and are supplemented by 'feeder', usually smaller, local county courts who usually transfer multi-track cases to the centres. The centres are presided over by designated civil judges who give guidance to the courts within their responsibility as to the application of the CPR and oversee their operation.

A 'feeder' county court normally gives any directions appropriate upon allocation and then transfers the case to a Civil Trial Centre. However, depending on the instructions of the designated civil judge, it may instead transfer to such a centre after allocation to deal with directions or, with the consent of the designated civil judge for the centre, retain the case for the time being for further management if it seems that there will be more than one case management conference and the parties' representatives are an inconvenient distance from the court (PD 26, para 10.2).

---

1 See Chapter 2, Sources of Civil Procedure: Structure and Jurisdiction of the Civil Courts.
2 See Part 30 and PD 29, paras 2.3 and 2.4 and *ibid*.
3 See Chapter 15, Judicial Case Management: Allocation, p 168.

STEPS ON ALLOCATION

The procedural judge, on allocation, may do any or all of the following:

- issue written directions (r 29.2(1)(a));
- set a timetable to fix, as appropriate:
  - (a) a case management conference (CMC);
  - (b) a pre-trial review (PTR) (r 29.2(1)(b) (PD 29, para 4.5);
  - (c) a date for the filing of a completed listing questionnaire (r 29.2(3)(b))
- set a trial date or a window for trial as soon as practicable (r 29.2(2) and (3)(a)).

Directions

Directions, given at or without a hearing, will be tailored to the needs of the case and the steps already taken by the parties. The court will have regard to their compliance or non-compliance with any relevant pre-action protocol[4] (PD 29, para 4.2). Its concern will be to ensure that the issues are identified and that the necessary evidence is prepared and disclosed (PD 29, para 4.3)

The court will expect the parties to co-operate in the giving of directions and may approve agreed directions which they submit (PD 29, para 4.6). See PD 29, paras 4.7 and 4.8 for guidance on the agreed directions which may be approved.

The directions will deal with disclosure of documents,[5] service of witness statements and expert evidence and may regulate amendments of statements of case[6] and the provision of further information. They should form a timetable for the steps to be taken through to the trial and make provision for the trial date or trial period (if not already fixed). In the absence of indications to the contrary, the court's general approach will be to direct (PD 29, para 4.10):

- filing and service of any further information need to clarify a party's case;
- standard disclosure;[7]
- simultaneous exchange of witness statements;
- the instruction of a single joint expert on any appropriate issue; otherwise, simultaneous exchange of experts' reports (unless it is appropriate for reports on the amount of damages to be disclosed subsequently to those on liability); the court will not however (save by agreement) require

---

4   See Chapter 4, Pre-Action Protocols.
5   See Chapter 29, Disclosure of Documents.
6   See Chapter 11, Statements of Case.
7   See Chapter 29, Disclosure of Documents.

instruction of a single expert nor appoint an assessor without fixing a case management conference;[8]

- discussion between experts and a statement thereon, if they are not agreed;
- a case management conference after the time for compliance; and
- the fixing of a trial period.

Parties are advised to consider agreeing directions, although these will be subject to the scrutiny of the court.

Case management conference (CMC) (PD 29, para 5)

The purpose of the CMC is to set the agenda for the case at the earliest possible stage to ensure that the procedures followed and costs incurred are proportionate to the case. The court will fix a CMC if it appears that it cannot properly give directions on it own initiative and no agreed directions have been filed which it can approve. It will be listed as promptly as possible and at least three days' notice will be given.

At the CMC, the following matters are likely to be dealt with:

- directions on the future conduct of the case, including issues such as disclosure;[9]
- establishing the likely time scale of the case – this may include setting dates for the milestone events, for example, a listing hearing, any further CMC, the return of the listing questionnaire, or any pre-trial review;
- setting the trial date or trial window (if this has not already been done);
- agreeing a case summary[10] (PD 29, para 5.7);
- exploring with the parties:
  - (a) the scope for settlement at this stage or the possibility of disposing of any particular issues;
  - (b) the extent to which experts will be needed, including the scope for using a single or joint expert and the need for oral evidence;
  - (c) the extent to which non-experts will be needed, and the need for oral evidence;
  - (d) whether there should be a split trial or trial of a preliminary issue (in which case any directions would need to indicate to which aspect of the case they referred) (PD 29, para 5.3(7)); and whether the case should be tried by a High Court judge or a specialist judge (PD 29, para 5.9).

---

8   See Chapter 30, Experts and Assessors.
9   See Chapter 29, Disclosure of Documents.
10 See below, p 200.

If a party intends to apply for a particular direction which may be opposed, he should serve notice and, if the time allowed for the hearing may thus be insufficient, warn the court accordingly (PD 29, para 5.8).

If a party has legal representation, a representative familiar with the case and with sufficient authority to deal with any issues which may arise must attend (r 29.3(2)). That must be someone personally involved with the conduct of the case, able to deal with fixing the timetable, identification of issues and matters of evidence (PD 29, para 5.2(2)). A wasted costs order will usually be made if the inadequacy of the person attending or his instructions leads to an adjournment (PD 29, para 5.3).[11]

Parties must ensure that all relevant documents (including witness statements and experts' reports) are available to the judge and that all of them know what directions each of them seeks (PD 29, para 5.6). They should consider whether parties personally should attend and whether it would be useful to provide a *case summary* (prepared by the claimant and agreed with the other parties if possible) setting out in 500 words a brief chronology, facts agreed and in dispute and evidence needed (PD 29, para 5.7).

Time for compliance

The time by which something is directed to be done may be varied by written agreement (r 2.11) but this does not apply to (r 29.5), that is:

- the date fixed for a case management conference or pre-trial review;
- the date for return of the listing questionnaire;
- the trial date or trial period; or
- any date the variation of which would make it necessary to vary any of the above.

Preserving the trial date

As with the fast track it is important that, as far as possible, the trial date is maintained. Note PD 29, para 7.4:

1   The court will not allow a failure to comply with directions to lead to the postponement of the trial unless the circumstances are exceptional.

2   If it is practical to do so the court will exercise its powers in a manner that enables the case to come on for trial on the date or within the period previously set.

3   In particular the court will assess what steps each party should take to prepare the case for trial, direct that those steps are taken in the shortest possible time and impose a sanction for non-compliance. Such a sanction

---

11 See also Chapter 33, Costs.

may, for example, deprive a party of the right to raise or contest an issue or to rely on evidence to which the direction relates.

4   Where it appears that one or more issues are or can be made ready for trial at the time fixed while others cannot, the court may direct that the trial will proceed on the issues which are then ready, and direct that no costs will be allowed for any later trial of the remaining issues or that those costs will be paid by the party in default.

5   Where the court has no option but to postpone the trial it will do so for the shortest possible time and will give directions for the taking of the necessary steps in the meantime as rapidly as possible.

6   Litigants and lawyers must be in no doubt that the court will regard the postponement of a trial as an order of last resort. Where it appears inevitable the court may exercise its power to require a party as well as his legal representative to attend court at the hearing where such an order is to be sought.

7   The court will not postpone any other hearing without a very good reason, and for that purpose the failure of a party to comply on time with directions previously given will not be treated as a good reason.

Listing questionnaire

In practice, listing questionnaires are used only in cases in which the timetable is thought likely to give rise to difficulty. In most cases, the direction given will frequently be 'That there be no listing questionnaires, save where required by the Listing Office, in which case the completed questionnaire must be filed within 10 days after receipt by the party required to complete it, or within such other period as the court may direct'.

Where the court considers them necessary, in accordance with the procedural judge's directions, it will send a listing questionnaire to the parties (r 29.6(1)) no later than two weeks before they are to be returned (PD 29, para 8.1(4)), which will be no later than eight weeks before the trial date or trial period (PD 29, para 8.1(3)).The parties are encouraged to exchange copies of their questionnaires before filing them, to avoid the court being given conflicting or incomplete information (PD 29, para 8.1(5)).

The listing questionnaire will help the court in deciding whether to fix a PTR[12] (r 29.7). Where such a hearing has already been fixed, it will inform as to whether that hearing is still required. The form of questionnaire is the same as for fast track.[13] Thus, the listing questionnaire will ask for confirmation that:

---

12   See below, p 202.
13   See Chapter 17, The Fast Track.

- directions with regard to disclosure[14] have been complied with;
- witness statements and expert reports have been exchanged;
- any other directions have been complied with. If directions have not been complied with, the parties will be required to give reasons why:

  (a) confirmation of the remaining issues outstanding to be tried;

  (b) an estimate of the length of trial;

  (c) details of:

  - witnesses who will be attending to give evidence;
  - any special needs of anyone involved with the trial;
  - any other information which the court should know at this stage.

On the basis of the information provided, the court will:

- fix a pre-trial review[15] (giving at least seven days' notice);
- cancel a previously fixed pre-trial review (r 29.7);
- give listing directions;
- fix or confirm the trial date; and/or
- give any directions for the trial itself (including a trial timetable) which it considers appropriate (r 29.8, PD 29, para 8.2).

Where no party files a questionnaire, the court will normally order that if none is filed within three days, the claim and any counterclaim be struck out (PD 29, para 8.3(1). Otherwise, if a party fails to file his questionnaire, the court will fix a listing hearing on a date which is as early as possible (PD 29, para 8.3(2)), giving the parties at least three days' notice (PD 29, para 8.4). It will then normally fix or confirm the trial date and make other orders about steps to be taken to prepare the case for trial whether or not the defaulting party attends (PD 29, para 8.3(2)).

Pre-trial review (r 29.7)

This may be held by the eventual trial judge about 8–10 weeks (variable) before the trial itself in order to:

- resolve any discrepancies between the listing questionnaires;
- check that directions have been complied with;
- finalise the statement of issues to be tried. At the CMC[16] the court will already have endeavoured to narrow the issues to those relevant to be tried (see r 1.4);[17]

---

14 See Chapter 29, Disclosure of Documents.
15 See below.
16 See above, p 199.
17 See r 1.4 and Chapter 5, Judicial Case Management: The Overriding Objective.

- confirm the hearing date;
- set the parameters for the trial including:
  - (a) to confirm which documents and case summaries[18] need to be produced for the trial;
  - (b) where appropriate, to fix the date by which any trial bundles[19] should be lodged (usually seven days before the trial);
  - (c) its length and budget.

The court will give at least seven days' notice of its intention to hold a PTR (r 29.7). It is advisable that the eventual advocates should attend together with their lay clients or persons authorised on their behalf as they may need to take instructions, including on the question of settlement. The dates for the case management conference, pre-trial review and the trial date will not be capable of alteration without leave of the court.[20] Sanctions for failure to comply with directions, orders or timetables will apply as with fast track[21] (see PD 29, para 7 and Chapter 17, Fast Track).

Listing directions

The court may give directions as follows:
- as to the issues on which evidence is to be given, the nature of the evidence it requires on those issues and the way in which it is to be placed before the court, and may thereby exclude evidence which would otherwise be admissible (r 32.1);
- a direction giving permission to use expert evidence will say whether it is to be by report or oral and will name the experts whose evidence is permitted (PD 29, para 9.2(4));
- setting a timetable for the trial and will confirm or vary trial date or week, the time estimate for the trial and the place of trial (r 29.8(c)(i), 29 PD 9.1);
- for the preparation of a trial bundle[22] (PD 29, para 9.2(2)(c)).

The parties should seek to agree the directions and file the proposed order (which will not bind the court) (PD 29, para 9.2(1)), making provision for the matters referred to above and any other matter needed to prepare for the trial (PD 29, para 9.2(2)).

At the moment, it is common for appeals against interlocutory decisions in multi-track cases concerning case management directions to go to the designated circuit judge.

18 See above.
19 See Chapter 32, Hearings and Judgment.
20 See above, p 200.
21 See Chapter 17, The Fast Track.
22 See Chapter 32, Hearings and Judgment.

THE TRIAL

Trial windows given in multi-track cases, instead of a fixture, are curiously for a period of just one week only, rather than the possible three week period which applies in fast track cases (r 29.8(c)(ii)).

Note PD 29, para 10:

10.1   The trial will normally take place at the court where the case is being managed but it may be at another court if it is appropriate having regard to the needs of the parties and the availability of court resources.

10.2   The judge will generally have read the papers in the trial bundle and may dispense with an opening address.

10.3   The judge may confirm or vary any timetable given previously, or if none has been given set his own.

10.4   Attention is drawn to the provisions in Part 32[23] and the following parts of the Rules about evidence, and in particular:

(1) to rule 32.1 (court's power to control evidence and to restrict cross-examination), and

(2) to rule 32.5(2) statements and reports to stand as evidence in chief.

10.5   In an appropriate case the judge may summarily assess costs in accordance with rule 44.7. Attention is drawn to the practice directions about costs and the steps the parties are required to take.[24]

10.6   Once the trial of a multi-track claim has begun, the judge will normally sit on consecutive court days until it has been concluded.

Costs

There are no limits on costs on multi-track matters, once they have been allocated to that track, as there are in small claims and fast track cases. However, they are still subject to full scrutiny by the court in the light of the overriding objective and the principle of proportionality.

They will either be assessed summarily or by way of detailed assessment and issues such as misconduct with regard to the proceedings can be raised.[25]

---

23 See Chapter 31, Evidence.
24 See Chapter 33, Costs.
25 *Ibid.*

CHAPTER 19

MAKING APPLICATIONS FOR COURT ORDERS

INTRODUCTION

During the course of proceedings, and even before proceedings are begun, there are many instances when a party may wish to apply for a court order, over and above the usual directions made for the management of the progress of the case from commencement to trial. For instance, an application may be made for an interim remedy such as an interim payment,[1] or it may be made for final relief such as judgment in default[2] or summary judgment.[3]

An application might also be made against a dilatory opponent to force them to proceed with or defend the action by asking the court to order that, unless the respondent take the next step in the proceedings, the action be struck out or judgment be entered against them. Yet still it may be necessary to apply for an interim remedy before an action has even started, by way of, for instance, an interim injunction[4] to preserve the status quo until the court can determine disputed rights.

Under the old rules, parties were free to make as many applications for court orders in the course of the progress of the case to trial as they wished (subject, of course, to the natural deterrent of a costs order if the application was likely to be unsuccessful). Lord Woolf believed that one of the evils to beset our civil justice system was the culture, particularly amongst the legal profession, of making successive applications for court orders for purely tactical reasons in order to run up costs and wear an opponent down.[5] A classic example was the use of oppressive requests for further and better particulars of pleadings, which were not motivated by a genuine need for clarification of an opponent's case, but in order to cause inconvenience and cost to a party in the process of replying to them.

Now, under the CPR, the court, with its new powers of active case management,[6] will have more control over the making of applications. On the one hand there will be less opportunity to make applications for court orders, because court imposed timetables will truncate the time between starting an action and trial. On the other hand, procedural judges will be actively

---

1   See Chapter 20, Interim Remedies.
2   See Chapter 21, Judgment in Default.
3   See Chapter 22, Summary Judgment.
4   See Chapter 20, Interim Remedies.
5   See *Access to Justice*, Interim Report, Chapter 5, para 41 (www.lcd.gov.uk/civil/interfr.htm).
6   See Chapter 5, Judicial Case Management: The Overriding Objective.

considering not just the merits of an application but also whether the cost and time involved in pursuing it is proportionate to the value of the case.

SIMPLIFYING PROCEDURE

Lord Woolf identified one of his five overall objectives for the drafting of the CPR as being:

> to provide procedures which apply to the broadest possible range of cases and to reduce the number of instances in which a separate regime is provided for a special type of case.[7]

One aspect of this was the introduction in the CPR of Part 23, which sets out the requirements for making applications. So, rather than separately set out in each rule, under which applications could be made, requirements as to parties, forms, time limits, notice, court's powers, etc, Part 23 contains all these matters and applies to all interim applications.

However, despite the intention to have one procedure for all applications for court orders, there are in fact still variations in procedure for different applications. It is therefore also necessary to examine the separate rules for the particular application in question to see if there are any additional or different procedural requirements to those set out in Part 23. Furthermore, some specialist divisions[8] such as the Chancery Division and Commercial Court have their own detailed practice directions which must be followed and which specify more detailed requirements than any in Part 23.

Thus, again, it can be seen that attempts at simplification and unification come up against an insurmountable problem: different processes require different procedures. So, it would be misleading to say that there is now a single procedure for all applications. The most that can be said is that now there is a single form for all applications and that, although there are some rules common to all applications, these are subject to variations to fit different types of application, different types of proceeding and different circumstances.

WHERE TO MAKE AN APPLICATION

The general rule is that the application must be made to the court where the claim was started (r 23.2(1)). So, if proceedings were started in a county court, the application must be made to that court. However, this general rule will not be appropriate in all circumstances. If proceedings were started in one court

---

7   See *Access to Justice*, Final Report, Chapter 20, p 272, para 2 (www.lcd.gov.uk/ civil/finalfr.htm).
8   See Part 49 and p 18.

but then transferred to another, the application must be made to the court to which the claim was transferred (r 23.2(2)). If the parties have been notified of a fixed date for trial, an application must be made to the court where the trial is to take place (r 23.2(3)).

If an application is made before a claim has started, it must be made to the court where it is likely that the claim to which the application relates will be started unless there is good reason to make the application to a different court (r 23.2(4)). This may be the case where a claim is started in a county court, but a certain type of interim relief is only available from the High Court. For instance, the county courts have no general jurisdiction to grant freezing injunctions or search orders (County Courts Remedies Regulations 1991).[9] Therefore, if proceedings are begun in the county court, but the applicant wishes to apply for a freezing injunction, that application should be made to the High Court. The proceedings will then be transferred back to the county court once that application has been dealt with.

Finally, if an application is made after proceedings to enforce judgment have begun, it must be made to any court which is dealing with the enforcement of the judgment unless any rule or practice direction provides otherwise (r 23.2(5)).

Although, generally, most interim applications will be dealt with by a master or district judge, they may refer any matter to a judge which they think should be decided by a judge. This may be the case if the application is particularly substantial or raises matters of public importance. The judge may either deal with the matter or refer it back to the master or district judge (PD 23, para 1). Also, apart from in limited circumstances, a master or district judge does not have the jurisdiction to grant an injunction[10] and this must be dealt with by a judge (PD 25, para 1.2, 1.3).

PROCEDURAL REQUIREMENTS

General rules

The title to Part 23 is 'General Rules about Applications for Court Orders'. It sets out the general rules for making applications, but also the circumstances when the general rules are or can be modified or not followed. (However, as was stated above, it may not be enough simply to follow the requirements of Part 23, and reference should also be made to the rule or practice direction (if any) dealing with the application in question, as well as any relevant specialist

---

9   See Chapter 2 on the jurisdiction of the county courts to grant freezing injunctions and search orders.

10 See Chapter 2 on the jurisdiction of masters and district judges to grant injunctions.

practice direction, to ensure that the correct procedure is being followed for each application.)

In summary, the general rules provide that a party wishing to make an application should file an application notice, along with any supporting evidence, at the court office where the claim was started. The court issues the application notice and allocates a hearing date for the application. The court then serves the application notice, along with any supporting evidence, on the respondent, who is given at least three clear days notice of the application hearing.

The application notice

Under the old rules, most interim applications in the High Court were made by way of a form known as a summons, although they could also be made by other methods, for example, by way of notice of motion, whilst in the county court there was no prescribed form, but applications were usually made by way of notice in Form N244. Under the CPR, the general rule is that in order to make an interim application, the applicant must file and serve an application notice. This is defined in the rules as a document in which the applicant states his intention to seek a court order (r 23.1). The practice followed in the county courts under the old rules has been adopted under the CPR, namely, that there is no prescribed form, but that new Court Form N244 may be used for making applications. However, in some cases, some other form, such as a letter, will suffice, for example, an application to extend a stay or to correct a court order under the 'slip rule'. Parties to an application are known as 'applicant' and 'respondent' (r 23.1).

Contents of an application notice

Part 23 simply provides that an application notice must state what order the applicant is seeking and briefly why the applicant is seeking the order (r 23.6). The Practice Direction supplementing Part 23 specifies further formal details that must be provided, namely, that the application notice must be signed and include:

- the title of the claim;
- the reference number of the claim;
- the full name of the applicant;
- where the applicant is not already a party, his address for service; and
- either a request for a hearing or a request that the application be dealt with without a hearing (PD 23, para 2.1).

It is also stated that Practice Form N244 *may* be used.

An applicant who makes an application using Form N244 must also indicate how any supporting evidence will be presented by ticking one of three options provided on Form N244, that is, witness statement or affidavit, statement of case, or a written summary set out on the back of the application notice itself. Form N244 also states that the application should provide a time estimate for the hearing and say whether this is agreed to by all the parties, state which level of judge is required, for example, district judge, and set out all the parties who need to be served. The form has been amended so that parties can also indicate whether they want the matter dealt with by way of a telephone conference (see Practice Form N244).[11]

Form N244 includes a box for the applicant to sign a statement of truth.[12] An application notice is not one of the documents which by Part 22 *must* be verified by a statement of truth. However, if an applicant wishes to rely on matters set out in his application notice as evidence, it must be verified by a statement of truth (r 22.1(3) and PD 23, para 9.7).

Filing the application notice

The general rule is that in order to make an application for a court order, the applicant must *file* an application notice at court (r 23.3(1)). Filing means delivering the application notice by post or otherwise to the court office (r 2.3(1)).[13] This will become the court copy of the application notice.

When a limited time is provided in the rules for the making of a particular application, receipt at the court office of the application notice will constitute the making of the application (r 23.5). Further, if the specified time ends on a day on which the court office is closed, the application will be made in time if it is received on the next day when the court office is open (r 2.8(5)).[14]

Applications made without filing an application notice

The rules provide for a party to make an application orally, without filing an application notice, if this is permitted by a rule, practice direction, or the court dispenses with the requirement for an application notice (r 23.3(2)).

If the application is extremely urgent, there may not be enough time to file an application notice before making the application. For instance, a party may need to apply for an urgent interim injunction.[15] In such a situation an application can be made without filing an application notice, but after the

---

11 See below, p 219.
12 See Chapter 11, Statements of Case, p 128.
13 See Chapter 2, Sources of Civil Procedure: Structure and Jurisdiction of the Civil Courts, p 21.
14 See *ibid*, p 18.
15 See Chapter 20, Interim Remedies.

hearing the applicant is obliged to file the application notice at the court office on the same or next working day or within another time ordered by the court (PD 25, para 4.3(2)).

There is also the flexibility for the court to dispense with the need for an application notice. This might be appropriate where, for instance, during the course of a case management conference,[16] a party discovers that they need to make an application for a particular remedy. If no injustice would be caused to the respondent, the court may allow the applicant to apply orally for the order during the course of the case management conference without the need for an application notice to be filed first.

Notifying the opponent of the application

The general rule is that if an application is sought against another person that person, the respondent, should be notified and served with a copy of the application notice (r 23.4(1)).

Serving the application notice

Part 6 of the CPR sets out the permissible methods for the service of documents.[17]

The general rule is that the court will serve the application notice (r 6.3(1)). The method of service the court will normally use is ordinary first class post (PD 6, para 8.1). Once the application notice is filed, the court will serve the application notice on the respondent and notify the parties of the date of the hearing (if any). Under r 6.3(1)(b) a party is free, however, to notify the court that he will serve the document himself. Also, the court will attempt service once; if it is not effective it will serve a notice of non-service on the applicant, who will then be responsible for serving the application notice (r 6.11).

Time limits for service

Rule 23.7(1) sets out the time limits for serving an application notice. This states, first, that it must be served as soon as practicable after it has been filed. The rule then goes on to state that in any event, except where another time limit is specified by a rule or practice direction, it must be served at least three days (under r 2.8(2) this means clear days)[18] before the court is to deal with the application. If an application notice is served without giving the specified

---

16 See Chapter 18, The Multi-Track, p 199.
17 See Chapter 9 on service of documents.
18 See Chapter 2, p 18, for a definition of clear days.

amount of notice, r 23.7(4) gives the court power, if the circumstances of the case warrant it, to reduce the amount of notice that the applicant is required to give the respondent (sometimes known as 'abridging the time for service'). In such a case, the court can treat whatever notice has been given as sufficient and hear the application.

Applications made without notice

In general, respondents are notified of the application and given an opportunity to attend and oppose it. Exceptionally, an application can be made without notice in the following circumstances:

- *If permitted by a rule, practice direction or court order*

  An application can be made without notice if this is permitted by a rule, practice direction or court order (r 23.4(2) and PD 23, para 3.6). An example of a rule permitting such an application is r 7.6(4)(b), which specifically provides that an application by the claimant to extend the period of time in which to serve the claim form may be made without notice. The reason for the rule for such an application is because at that stage, the defendant to the action has not even been served with the proceedings and if the order is refused, the claimant may not be able to bring the action at all. Moreover, if the order is granted, the defendant is then given the opportunity to apply for the order to be varied or set aside (r 23.10(1)).

  In Part 25, which deals with interim remedies,[19] r 25.3(1) provides that the court may grant an interim remedy on an application made without notice 'if it appears to the court that there are good reasons for not giving notice'. An example of a good reason for not giving notice to the respondent would be if the type of remedy needed required secrecy, such as a freezing injunction, which relies on a pre-emptive strike in order to be effective. The raison d'être for a freezing injunction is that the applicant believes that if the respondent has notice of court proceedings against him, he will try to hide or dissipate his assets in order to avoid paying any judgment debt. In such circumstances, the applicant has to secure and enforce the order for the freezing injunction before the respondent even knows that one has been applied for.

- *Urgent applications*

  An application can be made without notice where there is exceptional urgency (PD 23, para 3.1). An example might be where an interim injunction is needed urgently to stop a person acting so as to cause another irreparable harm. If the application is really urgent, it may even be made

---

19   See Chapter 20, Interim Remedies.

before the claimant has issued a claim form against the defendant. There may not be time to attend court for a hearing and so there is provision to make an emergency application over the telephone to the judge and, if it is necessary, to do so outside the normal court hours.[20]

Where an urgent application is made without giving notice to the respondent, although there may not be enough time to give the respondent formal notification of the application in accordance with the rules, the applicant must give the respondent as much notice as he can, unless the application is of a type which requires secrecy (PD 23, para 4.2). This is a practice followed from the old rules where often, the applicant would give telephone notification to the respondent on the day that an application was being made and the respondent would attend at the hearing, often without evidence to rebut the claimant's contentions or any instructions apart from those to resist the application.

- *Other circumstances*

Other circumstances when an application can be made without notice are where the overriding objective[21] is best furthered by doing so (PD 23, para 3.2). This obviously allows the court to exercise its discretion to deal with particular circumstances; also, if all the parties consent, or with the permission of the court (PD 23, paras 3.3 and 3.4)). There is also the further situation where a date for a hearing has been fixed and a party wishes to make an application at that hearing, but he does not have sufficient time to serve an application notice. In such circumstances, the applicant would be permitted to make the application orally at the hearing, so long as he notifies the respondent and the court (if possible in writing) as soon as he can of the nature of the application and the reason for making it (PD 23, paras and 2.10 and 3(5)).

Opportunity to set aside or vary orders made without notice

It is recognised that if the court grants an order after only hearing one side, there are obvious risks that injustice will be done. Therefore, if an order is granted on an application made without notice, the respondent has the right to return to court to try to vary or set aside the order (r 23.10(1)).[22] However, this right must be exercised by the respondent within seven days after the order was served on him (r 23.10(2)).

---

20 See Chapter 20, Interim Remedies.
21 See Chapter 5, Judicial Case Management: The Overriding Objective.
22 For an example of this rule in practice, see *Riverpath Properties Ltd v Brammall* (2000) *The Times*, 16 February, Neuberger J.

Service of application notice and evidence on the respondent where application made without notice

The CPR introduce a new rule that in those cases where an application is made without notice, even where the order applied for is not granted, the applicant has an obligation to serve the application notice and any supporting evidence on the respondent (r 23.9(2)). If the order is granted, the applicant also has an obligation to serve the order, application notice and supporting evidence on the respondent (r 23.9(2)). The latter situation is self-explanatory, since if the order is granted, the respondent should be notified of it, and often it would be in the applicant's interests to notify the respondent in any event, as the order may well require the co-operation of the respondent.

However, the former situation is new and was introduced because it was felt that where an applicant applied for a stringent order, such as a search order,[23] which requires proof of the respondent's wrongdoing, the respondent has an interest in knowing the basis on which the application was made. Judicial concern had been expressed that such remedies are applied for on improper grounds; that is, not because the respondent is threatening to misuse the applicant's property, but in order to stifle legitimate competition.[23a]

Court fees

The County Court Fees Order 1999[24] and the Supreme Court Fees Order 1999[25] currently set the fees for an application with notice at £50, and an application by consent, or without notice, at £25. In both cases this is subject to a different fee being specified. The fee is payable on filing the application notice at court. However, an individual in receipt of income-based state benefits (income support, family credit, disability working allowance or income based jobseeker's allowance), who is not represented by a solicitor under legal aid, may apply for an exemption from payment of the fee. Even if not in receipt of those benefits, an individual can apply for a reduction or remission of the whole fee if they can show that payment of the fee would cause them undue hardship owing to the exceptional circumstances of their case.

---

23 See Chapter 20, Interim Remedies.

23a See *dicta* of Hoffmann J in *Lock International plc v Beswick* [1989] 1 WLR 1268;[1989] 3 All ER 373.

24 SI 1999/689.

25 SI 1999/687.

SUPPORTING EVIDENCE

Types of supporting evidence

Under the old rules, evidence supporting interim applications had to be in the form of an affidavit. This is a sworn statement of facts which can be relied on as evidence. Affidavits are a relatively expensive way of presenting evidence for an application, as they need to be sworn before a commissioner for oaths (this includes solicitors,[26] barristers, and public notaries)[27] who charge a fee for each person swearing an affidavit and a fee for each exhibit referred to in the affidavit. Also, a solicitor or barrister involved in a case cannot take an affidavit for a party who he is acting for, so the party must go to the trouble of finding another commissioner for oaths before whom he can swear the affidavit.

It is still permissible to use affidavits[28] under the CPR and, in fact, for certain types of applications (such as search orders and freezing injunctions[29]) there is a requirement to support the application with affidavit evidence. However, now for all proceedings other than the trial, there are a number of other methods of presenting evidence.

The general rule is that at hearings other than trials, evidence should be presented by way of witness statements (r 32.6(1)). The intention is that witness statements, rather than affidavits, will become the standard method of presenting evidence at interim applications. However, a party may also rely on his statement of case or the application notice itself so long as these documents are verified by a statement of truth[30] (r 32.6(2)). So, if the evidence relied on is fully set out in the application notice, by including a statement of truth the party does not need to prepare any other document containing evidence for use at the hearing. However, it is only likely to be in very simple and straightforward applications that such a course can be followed.

The reason for the change is to reduce the costs involved in proceedings by taking away the requirement for a sworn affidavit. If a party does choose to use an affidavit where its use is not compulsory, he is unlikely to recover the extra costs involved in doing so. Yet, there remains a distinction between sworn evidence in an affidavit and other forms of evidence verified by a statement of truth. Swearing false evidence in an affidavit is punishable as

---

26 Solicitors Act 1974, s 81.
27 Courts and Legal Services Act 1990, s 113 and Administration of Justice Act 1985, s 65.
28 See Chapter 31, Evidence, p 358.
29 See Chapter 20, Interim Remedies.
30 See Chapter 11, Statements of Case, p 128.

perjury, whereas verifying a statement that the person knows to be false is punishable by contempt of court. Although both are ultimately punishable by imprisonment, only perjury is a criminal offence. The orders for which affidavit evidence is required under the CPR provide drastic remedies which presumably warrant the use of sworn evidence carrying with it the sanction of a criminal penalty if falsely made.

Function of supporting evidence

Although there has been a change to the standard form of supporting evidence from affidavits to witness statements, this was a change driven purely by questions of cost. The change does not bring about a change in the function of such supporting evidence. The purpose of the evidence is to prove the facts relied on in support of or for opposing the application. Although for certain applications there is a specific requirement for evidence – for example, in order to obtain judgment in default,[31] a party must prove that particulars of claim were properly served on the defendant – for others there are no specific requirements for evidence. For those other cases, the PD actually goes so far as to warn that the court will often need to be satisfied by evidence of the facts that are relied on in support of or for opposing the application (PD 23, para 9.1).

For some types of application, supporting evidence may not be necessary by way of a separate witness statement, if the original statement of case has been verified by a statement of truth and there is sufficient evidence in it to support the application, for example, an application to strike out a statement of case as an abuse for disclosing no claim or defence[32] or an application for summary judgment.[33]

Although, obviously, the court will need to be satisfied by evidence of the facts put forward in support of or against the application, this does not mean that the court will aim to resolve disputed contentions at this stage and there will not usually be, for instance, cross-examination of any witnesses. Even though the CPR place a greater emphasis on pre-trial resolution of issues in the case, what that means is that the court will strive to identify the real issues in the case and eliminate those which are not really being relied upon. It does not mean that during the course of an interim application, the court will attempt to resolve disputed questions of fact and hear detailed argument on points of substantive law underlying the issues in the case.

---

31 See Chapter 21, Judgment in Default.
32 See Chapter 23, Striking Out.
33 See Chapter 22, Summary Judgment.

Filing supporting evidence

If a party is relying on supporting evidence, it must be filed at court as well as served on the other parties (PD 23, para 9.6). However, exhibits should not be filed unless a party is specifically directed to do so (PD 23, para 9.6). Rule 23.7(2) states that if the court is serving the application notice, the applicant must also file a copy of any written evidence in support of his application at the same time as he files his application notice. If a party is relying on evidence for an application which has already been filed or served, there is no need to file or serve another copy of such evidence (r 23.7(5)).

The rules also provide powers for the court to exercise active case management functions when dealing with applications in the sense that there is also provision for the court to direct what evidence should be filed, the form it should take and when it should be served on the other party (PD 23, para 9.2).

Skeleton arguments

There are additional requirements for bundles of documents and skeleton arguments in the specialist divisions[34] of the court. So, for instance, in the Chancery Division, the general rule is that for applications made to a judge and any substantial applications made to the master, the parties must prepare a skeleton argument and submit it to the court in advance of the hearing (see the Chancery Guide, 8.31, 8.40). Documents must be made into a bundle if the number of pages of documents is more than 25 and they, too, must be filed in advance of the hearing (Chancery Guide, 8.19). Reference should be made to the relevant specialist division guides and practice directions for further details.

Although there is no specific requirement for a skeleton argument or bundles of documents for applications in Part 23, if the application is substantial then their use is advisable.

The draft order

Unless the application is extremely simple, the applicant should bring a copy of the draft order to the hearing. Also, if the case is proceeding in the Royal Courts of Justice, and the order is unusually long or complex, it should also be supplied on disk for use by the court office (PD 23, para 12). The draft order should also be served on the respondent along with the application notice and any supporting evidence (r 23.7(3)).

---

34 See Chapter 2, Sources of Civil Procedure: Structure and Jurisdiction of the Civil Courts, p 18.

METHODS OF DEALING WITH APPLICATIONS

Active case management includes: 'dealing with the case without the parties needing to attend at court' (r 1.4(j)) and 'making use of technology' (r 1.4(k)).[35] The new rules provide a number of options, apart from an oral hearing, for dealing with an application. As well as dealing with the application without the expense of an oral hearing, the CPR now also makes provision for telephone and video conferencing. Lord Woolf envisaged video and telephone conferencing as vital tools for case management.[36] He was not proposing that telephone conferencing would replace existing hearings or meetings, but instead that it would encourage greater, proactive communication where, in the past, there would have been silence.[37]

However, there is nothing in the rules to suggest that telephone and video conferencing is limited to certain types of application or case management functions of the court. Yet, despite their availability for a number of years, and even in the light of a number of pilot schemes to promote them, telephone and video conferencing have not proved popular with the legal profession. This may change now that suitable equipment for telephone conferences is now being supplied to more judges' chambers.

Applications dealt with without a hearing

Rule 23.8 sets out the circumstances where an application may be dealt with without a hearing; these are:

- if the parties agree as to the terms of the order sought (r 23.8(a));
- if the parties agree that the application should be dealt with without a hearing (r 23.8(b); or
- the court considers that a hearing would not be appropriate (r 23.8(c)).

Orders made by consent[38]

A respondent may agree to or not oppose the making of an order in the case. For instance, an applicant may seek an interim injunction,[39] but before the hearing the respondent agrees to the terms of the injunction. In those circumstances, the respondent can undertake to abide by agreed terms without the need for a contested application hearing. Therefore, there is

---

35 See Chapter 5, Judicial Case Management: The Overriding Objective.
36 See Final Report, Chapter 21, p 286, para 7. (*Ibid.*)
37 See Final Report, Chapter 21, p 291, para 21. (*Ibid.*)
38 See Chapter 32, Hearings and Judgments, p 367.
39 See Chapter 20, Interim Remedies.

provision, as there was under the old rules, for the court to enter and seal judgment by consent of the parties. In some circumstances, this can be achieved by simply presenting the agreed order to a court official without the need for the court to approve the consent order (r 40.6(2)). Otherwise, the party must apply for a consent order and the matter must be brought before the court for the order to be approved (r 40.6(5)). However, such a consent order can be dealt with without the need for a court hearing (r 40.6(6)).

With the introduction of case management, the court will take a more active role in ensuring that the terms of any order agreed are consistent with the ethos of the new CPR and in particular, the overriding objective.[40]Moreover, the parties cannot agree between themselves to the terms of an order which would have the effect of varying the 'case milestones', for example, the date for return of the listing questionnaire, trial period or trial date[41] (rr 28.4, 29.5). Practice Direction 23 reminds the parties of this as well as of the fact that if a consent order is made, the parties must inform the court so that any date fixed for the hearing of the application can be vacated (PD 23, para 10.5).

Agreement that application be dealt with without a hearing

The parties may agree that the application should be dealt with without a hearing. This may arise when the parties decide that the application would not justify the time and cost of a hearing and that their position can be protected by means of a written application and supporting evidence alone. If that is the case, the parties should inform the court in writing and each should confirm that all evidence and other material on which he relies has been disclosed to the other parties to the application (PD 23, para 11.1)

Court considers that a hearing would not be appropriate

The first request for information made to the applicant when filling out the application notice form N244 is whether he would like the application dealt with at a hearing. Indeed, this information must be provided whether Form N244 is used or not (see PD 23, para 2.1(5)). When making an application, the applicant, therefore, has to indicate his preference as to whether the application is dealt with at a hearing or on paper or by way of telephone conference.[42]

---

40 See Chapter 5, Judicial Case Management: The Overriding Objective.
41 See Chapter 17, The Fast Track, and Chapter 18, The Multi-Track.
42 See below, p 219.

However, in the absence of agreement with the other parties, the applicant cannot insist that the application be dealt with without a hearing. If the applicant makes that choice, the application notice will be sent to the master or district judge, who must consider whether the application is suitable for consideration without a hearing (PD 23, para 2.3). The master or district judge then has to be satisfied that it is suitable for the application to be dealt with without a hearing. If that decision is made, the court will inform the applicant and respondent and may give directions for the filing of evidence (para 2.4). If the master or district judge is not so satisfied, the court will notify the applicant and respondent of the time, date and place for the hearing of the application (para 2.5).

Despite the wording of r 23.8(c), the more detailed provisions of the Practice Direction supplementing Part 23 seem to suggest that on making an application, if the applicant asks for the application to be dealt with at a hearing, the court does not have the power to decide instead that the application will be dealt with without a hearing. Paragraph 2.2 of PD 23 states that on receipt of an application notice containing a request for a hearing the court *will* notify the applicant of the time and date for the hearing of the application. It is only if the application notice contains a request for the application to be dealt with without a hearing that the Practice Direction states that the application notice will be sent to a master or district judge for a decision whether the application is suitable for consideration without a hearing (para 2.3).

However, although there is this apparent limitation on the court's powers to decide that an application be dealt with without a hearing once the applicant has requested one, it should be borne in mind that if the court decides to make an order of its own initiative, which it has power to do under r 3.3, it can do so without hearing the parties or giving them an opportunity to make representations.[43] Moreover, if the court decides that the application is suitable to be dealt with without a hearing it will treat the application as if it were proposing to make an order on its own initiative (PD 23, para 11.2).

Applications by telephone or video conference

Making use of technology, an application can be heard without the parties being physically present before the court. Instead, an application can be made by means of a telephone or video conference. The evidence suggests that such methods are becoming more commonplace. However, the Commercial Court Guide positively discourages such applications, stating that 'in most cases applications in the Commercial Court are more conveniently dealt with in person' (See para F1.11 of the Commercial Court Guide).

---

43 See Chapter 5, Judicial Case Management: The Overriding Objective, for the court's powers to make orders of its own initiative.

Telephone hearings

PD 23, para 6.1 provides that the court may order an application, or part of one to be dealt with by a telephone hearing. The application notice was amended to include the opportunity for the applicant to request that the application be heard by telephone conference. Although the court has the power to order that the application is heard by way of a telephone conference, it is unlikely to be ordered unless all the parties consent (PD 23, para 6.2). Also if a party is acting in person, a telephone conference will not be ordered unless that party is accompanied by a responsible person who is known to the party and who confirms the identity of the party at the beginning of the hearing (PD 23, para, 6.3(1)). A responsible person includes a barrister, solicitor, legal executive, doctor, clergyman, police officer, prison officer or other person of comparable status (PD 23, para 6.3(2)).

The telephone hearing is set up by the applicant arranging a telephone conference through BT's (or other comparable telecommunications provider's) 'call out' system, which allows a three-way (or more) telephone conversation, for precisely the time ordered by the court (PD 23, para 6.5(1)). Each party will then be able to participate in the hearing as if they were before the court. The applicant must then arrange for the conference to be recorded on tape by the telecommunications provider whose system is being used and send the tape to the court (PD 23, para 6.5(5)). The costs of the telephone charges will be treated as part of the costs of the application (PD 23, para 6.5(9)).

Video conferencing

Part 23 also refers, in very general terms, to the availability of video conferencing facilities. Such facilities exist in some courts and can be used to make a live video application to another, more distant court. No detail is provided in the practice direction apart from the information that if the parties wish to use this facility, they should apply to the master or district judge for directions (PD 23, para 7).

CASE MANAGEMENT

Review of the whole case

Case management is a completely new concept for our civil justice system and it affects the operation of all of the new CPR.[44] Now, the parties must expect that whenever the case comes before the court, even for a specific remedy, the

---

44   See Chapter 5, Judicial Case Management: The Overriding Objective.

procedural judge may well take an opportunity to review the conduct of the case as a whole and give directions for its future conduct. Practice Direction 23 warns the parties that the court may well wish to make case management directions when an application is dealt with and that they should be ready to assist the court with this function and answer any questions the court may ask for this purpose (PD 23, para 2.9). Thus, it is important that the person who attends court is competent in this regard, failing which there may be a danger of a wasted costs order being made.[45]

Timing of the application hearing

Active case management by the court includes: 'dealing with as many aspects of the case as it can on the same occasion'[46] (r 1.4(2)(i). In accordance with this, and if appropriate, parties should issue any application they wish to make at the same time as they file their allocation questionnaire.[47] Any hearing set to deal with the application will also serve as an allocation hearing if allocation remains appropriate.[48] Alternatively, the applicant should make the application so that it can be considered at any other hearing for which a date has already been fixed, or for which a date is about to be fixed. If the court has fixed a case management conference, allocation or listing hearing or pre-trial review for the case, then the application should be heard at one of those hearings (PD 23, para 2.8).[49]

Obviously, if none of those hearings has been fixed for the case, if the application has to be made before any of those events occur (for example, extending the time for service of the claim form[50]), or the application is urgent, then the application will be heard at a separate hearing. Although the application should, if possible, be considered at the same time as any other scheduled interim court hearing in the case, the application itself should be made, and notified to the other party, as soon as it becomes apparent that it is necessary or desirable to make it (PD 23, para 2.7). The court will not look kindly on a party who delays making an application when the need for one has arisen.

---

45 Part 29, R 29.3(2) and PD 29, paras 5.2(2) and 5.3, and see *Baron v Lovell* (1999) *The Times*, 14 September, CA, and Chapter 33, Costs.
46 *Ibid*.
47 See Chapter 15, Judicial Case Management: Allocation.
48 *Ibid*.
49 See Chapter 17, The Fast Track and Chapter 18, The Multi-Track.
50 See Chapter 7, Starting an Action, p 79.

Duration of the application hearing

Even before the introduction of the CPR, there was judicial criticism of the use of interim applications for detailed consideration of evidence and extended legal argument (see the case of *Derby and Co Ltd v Weldon (No 1)* [1990] Ch 48, CA, where the hearing of the interim application took 26 days and the documents to appeal the judge's order consisted of several thousand pages of affidavits and exhibits). In that case, Parker LJ referred with approval to Lord Templeman's comments in *Spiliada Maritime Corporation v Cansulex Ltd* [1987] AC 460 where he said 'that [interim applications] should be measured in hours not days, that appeals should be rare and that [the Court of Appeal] should be slow to interfere' (p 465). He also advocated costs orders being made against parties who used interim applications to try to persuade the court to resolve disputed questions of fact or against those who made detailed arguments on difficult points of law relating to the underlying claim (p 58F–G).

Such sentiments have now been incorporated into the CPR. Part 1 of the CPR, the overriding objective, which governs the application and interpretation of all the rules, includes saving expense (r 1.1(2)(b)), dealing with cases in proportion to their value, importance, complexity and the financial position of each party (r 1.1(2)(c)). It is also recognised that court resources are limited and so, rather than allow the parties to decide how much time and money to expend on proceedings, the court will control this by only allotting an appropriate share of the court's resources to a case and taking into account the need to allot resources to other cases (r 1.1(2)(e)).

It will be interesting to see how this concept will be applied in practice – is this budgeting to be based on actual figures compiled from cases currently in the system, or simply based on a judge's impression as to the backlog of applications waiting to be heard and his feel as to how much time and money a case deserves to have devoted to it? What is clear is that with the court's new powers of case management, the procedural judge will be actively considering whether the time and money spent on each step of a case is proportionate and whether it is likely to produce a justifiable benefit.

OTHER PROCEDURAL MATTERS

Applications to be heard in public

Now, the general rule is that all hearings are held in public (r 39.2(1)). This includes interim applications and is, on the face of it, a major change from the old system where most interim applications were held in chambers. However, although technically in public, the court does not have to make special arrangements for accommodating members of the public (r 39.2(2)). Therefore, just on this basis alone, it is unlikely that many members of the public will observe interim applications, the majority of which will be heard in a master's or district judge's room which, owing to their size and location in court buildings, are not readily accessible.

Further, there are a number of circumstances in which the court can hold a hearing in private.[51] These include when publicity would defeat the object of the hearing (r 39.2(3)(a)) and when the court considers it necessary, in the interests of justice (r 39.2(3)(g)). Therefore, if the nature of the application relies on it being made secretly, such as a freezing injunction or search order, this would justify the court ordering that the application be heard in private.

Power of the court to proceed in the absence of a party

The court has the power, as it did under the old rules, to proceed with an application and make any order it thinks fit, even if one of the parties fails to attend the hearing. There is then provision for the court to re-list the application, to be heard again, either of its own initiative or by application of one of the parties (r 23.11).

COSTS OF THE APPLICATION HEARING[52]

The general rule is now that for application hearings lasting for less than one day, the procedural judge should make a summary assessment of costs at the end of the hearing unless there is good reason not to do so. A good reason can include where there is not enough time to make a summary assessment (PD 44, para 4.4). This general rule does not apply if the receiving party is legally aided or is a child or patient[53] whose solicitor has not waived the right to further costs (PD 44, para 4.9(1), (3)). Further, the parties have a duty to assist the judge in making a summary assessment of costs. In order to do so, if a party intends to claim costs, he must prepare a written statement of those costs, including specified information as to how they are calculated, file that statement at court and serve it on the party against whom he is claiming costs at least 24 hours before the hearing of the application (PD 44, para 4.5). Failure to do so may result in the court awarding only nominal costs or no costs at all.

However, if the court decides to make an order for 'costs in the case' at the end of the application hearing, there will not be a summary assessment of costs (PD 44, para 4.4(2)). Such an order will be made when the court thinks it

---

51 See Chapter 32, Hearings and Judgments, for provisions relating to hearings.
52 See Chapter 33, Costs, for detailed consideration of costs.
53 See Chapter 26, Special Rules for Children and Patients.

is appropriate to suspend its judgment as to who should pay the costs of the application until the end of the case. An order for 'costs in the case' means that the party in whose favour the court makes an order for costs at the end of proceedings is entitled to his costs of the application for which the order was made (PD 44, para 2.4).

If an order for the summary assessment of costs is not made, the court may make an order for the detailed assessment of costs under Part 47. Alternatively, the parties may agree the costs themselves. However, if at the end of the application the order made does not mention costs, no party is entitled to the costs of that application (r 44.13) This is a departure from the previous practice where costs would be costs in the cause (now known as costs in the case) if no order for costs was made.

CHAPTER 20

INTERIM REMEDIES

INTRODUCTION

The courts may make interim injunctions, declarations, and a variety of orders in relation to property, its preservation and its inspection, and to goods for their delivery. All interim remedies are now within one part, that is, Part 25.

An application for an interim remedy may be made at any time and, if urgent, or 'otherwise desirable in the interests of justice', before a claim has been made (r 25.2(1)). Importantly, a draft of the order sought must be filed with the application and, if possible, a disk containing the draft should be available (in Word Perfect 5.1) (PD 25, para 2).

SCOPE OF THE REMEDY

Interim remedies are listed in r 25(1) under three categories, namely: interim (formerly 'interlocutory') injunctions; declarations (for example, authorising and supervising emergency medical treatment); and orders. Basically, the main orders relate to the detention, custody, preservation or inspection of property (r 25.1(c)(i) and (ii)), for the sale or payment of income from property (r 25.1(c)(v) and (vi)), for entry for the purpose of those orders (r 25.1(d)), and for orders for delivery up of goods under s 4 of the Torts (Interference with Goods) Act 1977.

Interim orders may therefore be granted:

- for disclosure or inspection of property before a claim has been made;
- for interim payment which a defendant is held liable to pay, and for disputed funds to be paid into court;
- for payment into court on terms of release of property pending the outcome of proceedings relating to it;
- for accounts and inquiries.

The list provided by r 25.1(1) is not exhaustive (r 25.1(3)).

EVIDENCE

Unless otherwise ordered, any application for an interim injunction must be supported by evidence (see Part 23 and Chapter 19, Making Applications for

Court orders), and this must explain why notice has not been given if made without notice (r 25.3). Save that applications for 'search orders' and 'freezing injunctions' must be supported by affidavit,[1] other applications, provided they are verified by a statement of truth (see Part 22 and Chapter 11, Statements of case, p 126.), can suffice by themselves; otherwise they may be supported by evidence set out in a witness statement or in a statement of case verified by a statement of truth (PD 25, paras 3.1, 3.2 and 3.3).

INTERIM REMEDIES BEFORE CLAIM ISSUED

These can only be granted if the matter is urgent, or 'it is otherwise desirable to do so in the interests of justice' – a defendant must seek leave if his application[2] is to be made before filing an acknowledgement of service[2] or a defence[3] (r 25.2).

If an application is made before the issue of proceedings, applicants must undertake – subject to the court otherwise ordering – to issue a claim form immediately. This should, where possible, be served with the order (PD 25, IP, para 4.4(2)). However, a claim form may not necessarily be directed where the application is only for pre-action disclosure (see Chapter 29, Disclosure of Documents).

INTERIM PAYMENTS

Although more than one application for an interim payment can be made (r 25.6(2)), no application can be made until the period for filing an acknowledgment of service[4] has expired (r 25.6(1)). Where the applicant is a child or patient,[5] permission of the court must first be obtained (PD 25B, IP, para 1.2) The application must:

- be served at least 14 days before the hearing;
- be supported by evidence (r 25.6(3)).

PD 25B, IP, para 2.1 sets out what the evidence must deal with:

1   the sum of money sought by way of an interim payment,

2   the items or matters in respect of which the interim payment is sought,

3   the sum of money for which final judgment is likely to be given,

4   the reasons for believing that the conditions set out in r 25.7 are satisfied,

---

1   See Chapter 31, Evidence, p 358.
2   See Chapter 8, Responding to an Action.
3   *Ibid.*
4   *Ibid.*
5   See Chapter 26, Special Rules for Children and Patients.

5   any other relevant matters,

6   in claims for personal injuries, details of special damages and past and future loss, and

7   in a claim under the Fatal Accidents Act 1976, details of the person(s) on whose behalf the claim is made and the nature of the claim.

Any relevant documents should be exhibited, including, in a personal injuries case, the medical report (PD 25B, IP, para 2.2). Any response by way of written evidence must be filed and served at least seven days before the hearing (r 25.6(4)).

The court will only make an interim payment order if:

• liability is admitted either in whole or in part (r 25.7(1)(a)); or

• judgment has already been obtained (r 25.7(1)(b)); or

• the court is satisfied that if the matter went to trial, the claimant would obtain a 'judgment for a substantial amount of money' (r 25.7(1)(c)) (see position as to more than one defendant, below); or

• it is a claim for possession and the defendant would be liable to pay for use and occupation (r 25.7(1)(d)). Payment could be directed either to the landlord or into court (r 3.1(2)(m), 3.1(3), (5)).

Where the claim is for personal injuries, an interim payment can only be ordered if:

• the defendant is insured; or

• the Motor Insurers' Bureau are dealing with the claim; or

• the defendant is a public body (r 25.7(2)).

Where there is more than one defendant in a personal injury case, the court must also be satisfied that the claimant would obtain judgment against at least one of them (r 25.7(3)). Although the court can take into account contributory negligence and any set off or counterclaim (r 25.7(5)), nevertheless, the amount of the interim payment should not be more than 'a reasonable proportion of the likely amount of the final judgment' (r 25.7(4)).

Although the rule refers to 'judgment for a substantial amount of money' (r 25.7(1)(c)), the principal purpose of an interim payment is to avoid or relieve hardship that the claimant may otherwise suffer by having to wait for trial or final assessment of his damages. So a comparatively small payment may be justified for a specific purpose. Although the means of the parties are not mentioned in the rule, they may be relevant, as the court is obliged to deal with a case in a way which is proportionate to the financial resources of the parties under r 1.1(2)(c)(iv).[6]

---

6   See Chapter 5, Judicial Case Management: The Overriding Objective.

The fact that a defendant has made an interim payment, whether voluntarily or by court order, shall not be disclosed to the trial judge until all questions of liability and the amount of money to be awarded have been decided, unless the defendant agrees (r 25.9). The amount of the interim payment is taken into account on the final judgment and any necessary adjustments made (PD 25B, IP, para 5). Once an interim payment has been ordered, the court can make orders for repayment where necessary (r 25.8).

FREEZING INJUNCTIONS
(FORMERLY CALLED MAREVA INJUNCTIONS)

This is an order to restrain a party from removing from the jurisdiction assets located there, or from dealing with assets wherever located.

The High Court alone has jurisdiction, except if there is an authorised judge. The same applies to search orders (see below, p 225) (PD 25, para 1.1). However, there is jurisdiction for any master or district judge to make an order in the High Court if it is:

*   by consent;
*   in connection with charging orders and appointments of receivers;
*   in aid of execution (PD 25, para 1.3).

Therefore, if a freezing or search order is required in a county court case, the case should be transferred to the High Court to obtain the order. The case can then, if appropriate, be transferred back to the county court.

To succeed in such an application, the claimant must show:

*   a 'good arguable case' in relation to his substantive claim – it is not enough to show merely that there is 'a serious question to be tried' (see, for example, *Derby v Weldon* [1990] Ch 48, CA, *per* Parker LJ, p 57);
*   that the defendant has assets, whether in or outside the jurisdiction;
*   that there is a real risk that, if the court does not grant an order, the defendant will take the opportunity to dissipate those assets or otherwise put them beyond the reach of the court.

The applicant has to file an affidavit[7] or affidavits on which his application is relying. Undertakings as to damages if the court later finds loss has been caused to the respondent and bank guarantees will also be required. An affidavit will be called for giving the substance of what was said to the court by the applicant's counsel or solicitors. Practitioners are advised to refer to PD 25, paras 7 and 8 and the Annex giving specimens.

---

7   See Chapter 31, Evidence, p 358.

The court will have to balance between protecting the interests of the claimant in relation to the proceedings and respecting any lawful activity on the part of the defendant, bearing in mind the overriding objective[8] and the fact that, in the first instance, the application is made without notice to the defendant. Regard will also need to be had to Art 8 of the European Convention on Human Rights, which protects the right to private activities subject to certain exceptions.

A freezing injunction binds the person against whom it is given, as opposed to the assets themselves. It therefore gives the claimant no proprietary rights in the assets, but merely ensures that such assets will be available to meet a judgment in his favour.

A 'penal notice' is required to be appended to such 'freezing orders'. The wording is: 'Penal Notice – If you the within named disobey this Order you may be held in contempt of Court and liable to imprisonment or fined or your assets seized.' A third party notified of the freezing injunction is bound by it as soon as he is notified of it, even though the defendant may not yet be aware of it. Such a third party, if he does anything to assist the defendant to thwart the injunction, will be guilty of a contempt of court (*Z Ltd v A* [1982] 1 QB 558).

SEARCH ORDERS (FORMERLY ANTON PILLER ORDERS)

A search order compels the respondent to permit the applicant to enter and search his premises. It differs from a search warrant in that it is directed not at the premises themselves, but at the respondent or other person appearing to be in control of the premises and having authority to permit the search. If the respondent refuses to obey the order, the applicant is restricted to bringing proceedings for contempt of court. The European Court of Human Rights has held that the making of such an order in an appropriate case is not a breach of Art 8 of the ECHR (*Chappell v UK* [1989] FSR 617). As to the balancing act that the court has to undertake, see on freezing injunctions, above, p 228.

Note that the orders are also the preserve of the High Court (see above, p 228). The court has been empowered, most recently by s 67 of the Civil Procedure Act 1997, to make an order to secure the preservation of evidence or of property. Such an order can only be exercised by 'a supervising solicitor' experienced in their operation.

To obtain such an order, the applicant must show:

- that he has a strong *prima facie* case: the merits of his claim will certainly be scrutinised;
- that the danger that the order is to avert is serious;

---

8   See Chapter 5, Judicial Case Management: The Overriding Objective.

- that there is a real possibility that the material will be concealed, removed or destroyed if an order is not made;
- that the harm caused to the respondent by making the order will not be out of proportion to the value of the order to the applicant.

Hearing of applications for search orders

If after issue of a claim form, file the following:

- the notice of application;
- evidence in support – see above, p 221;
- draft order – see above, p 221.

All the above to be filed/lodged within two hours before the hearing if this is possible (PD 25, para 4.3(1)).

Before issue of a claim: all the above to be filed on the same day as the hearing, or next working day, or as ordered (PD 25, para 4.3(2)).

In both cases, the applicant should 'notify the respondent informally' of the application (PD 25, para 4.3(3)). In the second case above – application before issue – the applicant must undertake to issue a claim form immediately, or the court will give directions for the commencement of the claim (PD 25, para 4.4(1)).

CRITERIA FOR GRANTING INJUNCTIONS

In relation to all injunctions where there is a dispute of fact, the principles laid down in *American Cyanamid v Ethicon* [1975] AC 396 HL ought to be considered. These may be summarised as follows:

- the claimant must establish that he has a good arguable claim to the right that he seeks to protect;
- the court must not attempt to decide this claim on the evidence filed; it is enough for the claimant to show that there is a serious issue to be tried;
- if the claimant satisfies these tests, it is for the court to decide on the balance of convenience whether or not to grant an injunction.

To these principles, there must now be added consideration of the principles set out in the overriding objective[9] (r 1.1(2)).

---

9   *Ibid.*

Hearing by telephone

Provided the practitioner feels confident that these criteria are satisfied, application may be made by telephone as under PD 25, para 4.5:

(1) where it is not possible to arrange a hearing, application can be made between 10.00 a.m. and 5.00 p.m. weekdays by telephoning the Royal Courts of Justice on 020 7936 6000 and asking to be put in contact with a High Court Judge of the appropriate Division available to deal with an emergency application in a High Court matter. The appropriate district registry may also be contacted by telephone. In county court proceedings, the appropriate county court should be contacted;

(2) where an application is made outside those hours the applicant should either –

   (a) telephone the Royal Courts of Justice on 020 7936 6000 where he will be put in contact with the clerk to the appropriate duty judge in the High Court (or the appropriate area Circuit Judge where known), or

   (b) the Urgent Court Business Officer of the appropriate Circuit who will contact the local duty judge.

(3) where the facility is available it likely that the judge will require a draft order to be faxed to him,

(4) the application notice and evidence in support must be filed with the court on the same or next working day or as ordered, together with two copies of the order for sealing,

(5) injunctions will be heard by telephone only where the applicant is acting by counsel or solicitors.

CESSER OF INJUNCTION

A defendant may apply to discharge an interim injunction. However, where the application is made shortly before trial, the defendant is protected by an undertaking in damages and there is no evidence that additional damage may be suffered, the court may apply the overriding objective and refuse to hear the application (*Stephenson Ltd v Mandy*[10]).

An interim injunction ceases if the claim is stayed other than by agreement between the parties unless the court orders otherwise (r 25.10). If the court has granted an interim injunction and the claim is struck out under r 3.7 (sanctions for non-payment of certain fees[11]), the interim injunction ceases to have effect

---

10   (1999) NLD, 30 June, CA.
11   See Chapter 5, Judicial Case Management: The Overriding Objective, p 59.

14 days after the date that the claim is struck out unless the claimant applies to reinstate the claim before the interim injunction ceases to have effect. The injunction shall continue until the hearing of the application unless the court orders otherwise (r 25.11).

SECURITY FOR COSTS

An application for costs may be made by a defendant under r 25.12. It must be supported by written evidence (r 25.12(2)). Although the provision is only available to defendants, a claimant could apply for security for costs under rr 1.2(a) and 3.1(2)(m). Such an application by the claimant is likely to succeed only in exceptional circumstances.

The grounds for the application are set out in r 25.13(2):

(2) The conditions are –

    (a) The claimant is an individual –

        (i) who is ordinarily resident out of the jurisdiction; and

        (ii) is not a person against whom a claim can be enforced under the Brussels Conventions or the Lugano Convention, as defined by section 1(1) of the Civil Jurisdiction and Judgments Act 1982;

    (b) The claimant is a company or other incorporated body –

        (i) which is ordinarily resident out of the jurisdiction; and

        (ii) is not a body against whom a claim can be enforced under the Brussels Conventions or the Lugano Convention;

    (c) The claimant is a company or other body (whether incorporated inside or outside Great Britain) and there is reason to believe that it will be unable to pay the defendant's costs if ordered to do so;

    (d) The claimant has changed his address since the claim was commenced with a view to evading the consequences of the litigation;

    (e) The claimant failed to give his address in the claim form, or gave an incorrect address in that form;

    (f) The claimant is acting as a nominal claimant, other than as a representative claimant under Part 19, and there is reason to believe that he will be unable to pay the defendant's costs if ordered to do so;

    (g) The claimant has taken steps in relation to his assets that would make it difficult to enforce an order for costs against him.

The defendant may seek an order for security for costs against any other person, if the court considers it appropriate, if that person assigned their right to claim to the claimant to avoid a costs order being made against them (for example, a company assigning a right to a director who can apply for funding assistance) or has agreed to contribute to the claimants costs in return for a share in anything recovered (r 25.14). The court may also order security for costs of an appeal (r 25.15).

CHAPTER 21

JUDGMENT IN DEFAULT

INTRODUCTION

If a defendant fails to respond to proceedings, the claimant can apply for judgment to be entered in default. As judgment is entered in these circumstances without there being any trial of the merits, and is purely as a result of the defendant's failure to comply with the procedural requirements of the rules, the court has a discretion to set the judgment aside if good reason is shown, and particularly if the defendant has a good defence on the merits. However, the court may well make setting aside of the judgment conditional on the defendant complying with a condition, such as the payment of money into court or on the immediate payment of the claimant's costs incurred in entering and setting aside judgment.[1]

TYPES OF CLAIM WHERE JUDGMENT IN DEFAULT AVAILABLE

Judgment in default is available for most types of claim. However, there are some notable exceptions. Judgment in default is not available:

- if the claim is for the delivery of goods where the agreement is regulated by the Consumer Credit Act 1974;
- if the claim is brought under Part 8;[1a]
- if the claim is a mortgage claim (unless the permission of the court is obtained);
- if a practice direction provides that judgment in default is not available, for example, claims for provisional damages, or in some specialist proceedings[2] such as admiralty proceedings (r 12.2, PD 12, paras 1.2 and 1.3).

---

1   See Chapter 5, Judicial Case Management: The Overriding Objective, p 58.
1a See Chapter 14, Part 8 Claims.
2   See Part 49 and Chapter 2, p 18.

APPLYING FOR JUDGMENT IN DEFAULT

A claimant may obtain either:

- judgment in default of an acknowledgment of service: if a defendant has not filed an acknowledgment of service or a defence to the claim (or any part of the claim) and the time limit for doing so has expired, the claimant may obtain judgment in default (r 12.3(1)). The time limit for filing acknowledgment of service is 14 days after service of particulars of claim on the defendant;[3] or

- judgment in default of a defence: if a defendant has filed an acknowledgment of service, but has not filed a defence and the time limit for doing so has expired, the claimant may obtain judgment in default (r 12.3(2)). The time limit is 28 days after service of the particulars of claim.[4]

Therefore, if a defendant does not respond at all, judgment will be entered in default of an acknowledgment of service rather than in default of defence even if judgment is entered at a time when the time limit for filing the defence has expired.

If a defendant makes a counterclaim to the claimant's claim and the claimant does not file a defence to counterclaim within the time limit for doing so, the defendant may apply for judgment in default (r 12.3(2)). The time limit for the claimant to respond to the defendant's counterclaim is 14 days after service of the counterclaim (rr 15.4 and 20.3). For the purposes of judgment in default, a defendant who has made a counterclaim is in the same position as a claimant to an action (r 20.3) and references in this chapter to claimant and defendant include claimant and defendant to a counterclaim. However, it should be noted that there is no procedure for a claimant to acknowledge service of the defendant's counterclaim (r 20.4(3)).[5]

CIRCUMSTANCES WHEN A CLAIMANT CANNOT OBTAIN JUDGMENT IN DEFAULT

In those claims where it is possible to obtain judgment in default, it will *not* be available where:

- the defendant has applied to have the claimant's statement of case struck out under r 3.4[6] and that application has not been heard;

---

3   See Chapter 8, Responding to an Action, p 84.
4   *Ibid*, p 96.
5   See Chapter 12, Part 20 Claims.
6   See Chapter 23, Striking Out.

- the defendant has applied for summary judgment under Part 24[7] and that application has not been heard;
- the defendant has satisfied the whole claim (including any claim for costs); or
- the defendant has admitted liability to pay the *whole* of a money claim but requested time to pay (r 12.3(3)).[8]

PROCEDURE FOR APPLYING

Filing a request for judgment in default

Where a claimant is seeking the following remedies, he can apply for judgment in default by simply filing a request in the relevant practice form. That is where the claim is for:

- a specified amount of money (Form N205A or N225);
- an amount of money to be decided by the court (unspecified amount of money) (Form N205B or N227);
- delivery of goods where the claim form gives the defendant the alternative of paying the value of the goods (if value specified – Form N205A or N225; if value unspecified – Form N205B or N227);
- any combination of the above remedies; or
- a claim for costs only, being fixed costs (Form N205A or N225) (r 12.4 and PD 12, para 3).

JUDGMENT FOR A FINAL AMOUNT OR AN AMOUNT TO BE DECIDED

If a claimant obtains judgment in default by filing a request in the relevant practice form, the judgment will be either for a final amount, if the claim is for a specified amount or value, or for an amount to be decided by the court at a hearing, if the claim is for an unspecified amount or value.

---

7   See Chapter 22, Summary Judgment.
8   See Chapter 8, Responding to an Action, p 88.

Judgment for a final amount

Where the claim is for a specified amount of money, if judgment in default is entered, the claimant may specify in the request whether he wants payment to be made immediately or by a specified date, or may specify the time and rate of payment by instalments (r 12.5(1)). As a judgment in default for a specified amount will entitle the claimant to seek immediate payment of the amount claimed from the defendant, without the need for any further assessment, it is often referred to as judgment for a 'final amount'.

Judgment will be entered for the amount of the claim (less any payments made), interest (if entitled)[9] and fixed costs, as shown on the claim form, to be paid at the time and rate requested by the claimant, or if the claimant has not specified the time and rate of payment, judgment will be for payment to be made immediately (r 12.5(2)).

However, it should be noted that a default judgment obtained by filing a request in a claim for delivery of goods, where the claim form gives the defendant the alternative of paying their value, will be judgment requiring the defendant to deliver the goods or (if he does not do so) pay the value of the goods as decided by the court (less any payments made) and costs (r 12.5(4)).

Interest

On entering judgment in default, a claimant who is claiming a *specified* amount of money will be able to include an amount for interest up to the date of judgment when filing his request so long as the following conditions are met. These are:

- that the claimant has given the requisite details about interest in his particulars of claim;[10]

- that the request includes a calculation of interest from the date of issue of the claim form to the date of the request for judgment; and

- if interest is claimed under s 35A of the Supreme Court Act 1981 or s 69 of the County Courts Act 1984, so long as the rate claimed is no higher than that which was available under those provisions when the claim form was issued (r 12.6(1)).

Where the claimant is claiming an unspecified amount of money, or the above conditions are not met, judgment will be for an amount of money to be decided by the court (r 12.6(2)).[11]

---

9   See *ibid*, for entitlement to interest, p 89.
10 See Chapter 11, Statements of Case.
11 See below.

Judgment for an amount to be decided by the court

If a claimant claims an unspecified amount of money and applies for judgment in default, the judgment will be for an amount to be decided by the court and costs (r 12.5(3)).

The court will also enter judgment in default for an amount to be decided by the court when a request is made for judgment for the value of goods to be decided by the court or an amount of interest to be decided by the court.

Although r 12.7(2) states that when entering judgment for an amount to be decided by the court, the court will give any directions it considers appropriate, including allocating the case to a case management track, PD 26, para 12.7 states that on entering judgment in default under Part 12 without a hearing, the court will list a disposal hearing.[12]

Disposal hearings

Judgment in default for an amount of money to be decided by the court falls within the definition of a 'relevant order' for the purposes of of PD 26, para 12.1. Therefore, if that judgment is entered without a hearing, the court will list a disposal hearing (PD 26, para 12.7).

At the disposal hearing, the court will either decide the amount the claimant is entitled to on the judgment, or give directions for the matter to be decided and allocate the claim to a track. Evidence relied on at a disposal hearing should be in the form of a witness statement or statement of case and/or application notice if verified by a statement of truth (r 32.6).

If the financial value of the claim, as determined in accordance with Part 26,[13] is such that the claim, if defended, would be allocated to the small claims track, the court will normally allocate it to that track and may treat the disposal hearing as a final hearing in accordance with Part 27 (PD 26, para 12.8(2)).[14] This means that the hearing will be informal and the 'no costs rule' will apply.

Even if the claim is not within the small claims track, if the court is able to do so, it can decide the amount to be payable there and then without allocating the claim to any track or giving any other directions (PD 26, para 12.8(3)). However, the court will not exercise its power to decide the amount there and then unless any written evidence the claimant is relying upon has been served on the defendant at least three days before the disposal hearing (PD 26, para 12.8(5)).

---

12 See below.
13 See Chapter 15, Case Management: Allocation.
14 See Chapter 16 on small claims hearings.

In all other cases, the court will give directions as to how the amount is to be determined, which includes allocating the case to a track (PD 26, para 12.8).

Jurisdiction of masters and district judges

A master or district judge has jurisdiction to decide the amount to be paid to the claimant whatever the financial value of the claim, unless the court orders otherwise (PD 26, para 12.10).

Costs of the disposal hearing

The court has a discretion as to the costs of the disposal hearing. The court can also order a summary assessment of those costs. The usual order will be for the defendant to pay the claimant's costs of the disposal hearing, but the court can make other orders. However, if the claim has been allocated to the small claims track, the 'no costs rule' will apply (PD 26, para 12.9).

MAKING AN APPLICATION FOR JUDGMENT IN DEFAULT

For those claims where the claimant is seeking a discretionary remedy rather than damages, or where the parties fall into certain categories of litigant, the claimant must make an application for judgment in default. Therefore, the claimant must make an application (in accordance with Part 23)[14a] for judgment in default where:

- the claim consists of or includes a non-monetary remedy such as an injunction;
- the claim is for costs only, *not* being fixed costs;
- the claim is against a child or patient;[15]
- the claim is in tort by one spouse against the other;
- the claim is against the crown; or
- where the defendant is resident outside the jurisdiction,[16] the claim is against persons or organisations who enjoy immunity from civil jurisdiction under the provisions of the International Organisations Acts 1968 and 1981 (that is, diplomatic immunity) (r 12.4(2)) and PD 12, para 2.3).

In most cases, the application under Part 23 must be made on notice to the defendant.[17]

14a See Chapter 19, Making Applications for Court Orders.
15 See Chapter 26, Special Rules for Children and Patients.
16 See Chapter 10, Service out of the Jurisdiction.
17 See Chapter 19, Making Applications for Court Orders.

If a claimant expressly abandons his claim for any of the above, by so declaring in his request for judgment in the relevant practice form, he can obtain judgment in default by filing a request (r 12.4(3)).

When the claimant makes an application for judgment to be entered, the judgment that is entered in default is such judgment that it appears the claimant is entitled to on his statement of case (r 12.11(1)). That is, the court will not make any inquiry into the merits of the case and will simply grant such judgment as it appears the claimant is entitled to on his statement of case, so long as the procedural requirements of Part 12 have been complied with. The judgment in default is therefore conclusive of issues of liability in the statement of claim.

However, this is subject to the exception that if an application is made for judgment in default against a child or a patient,[18] the claimant must satisfy the court by evidence that he is *entitled* to the judgment claimed (PD 12, para 4.1). There are also special requirements for evidence where a defendant is served out of the jurisdiction and for applications against a State.[19]

Judgment for an amount to be decided by the court

When entering judgment for an amount to be decided by the court, the court will give any directions it considers appropriate, including allocating the case to a case management track (r 12.7(2)).

As the judgment is for an amount to be decided by the court under Part 12, it falls within the definition of a 'relevant order' for the purposes of PD 26 (see para 12.1).

Although the court does not have to list a disposal hearing because the judgment was entered after a hearing (PD 26, para 12.7) because the claim will not have been allocated to a track before judgment was entered, the court will normally order that the matter be dealt with at a disposal hearing (PD 26, para 12.3) (see above for disposal hearings).

However, if the amount payable appears to be genuinely disputed on substantial grounds, the court may allocate the claim to a track for the matter to be determined (PD 26, para 12.3). The court is also likely to give other directions on allocating the claim to a track, including directions for allocation questionnaires[20] to be filed by a specified date, a direction for a date to be fixed for a hearing, a direction specifying the level or type of judge before whom the hearing should take place and the purpose of the hearing, or an order that the claim be stayed while the parties try to settle the case by alternative dispute resolution or other means (PD 26, para 12.2).

---

18 See Chapter 26, Special Rules for Children and Patients.
19 See PD 12, paras 4.3 and 4.4.
20 See Chapter 15, Judicial Case Management: Allocation.

ESTABLISHING ENTITLEMENT TO JUDGMENT IN DEFAULT

In all types of claim where the court is requested to enter judgment in default, whether through the filing of a request or by application, the court must be satisfied that the requirements of Part 12 have been fulfilled.

However, in all cases (except for claims against a child or patient),[21] even the type of case where an application must be made under Part 23 and supported by evidence, the evidence required to enable the court to enter judgment on liability does not have to prove the merits of the substantive claim itself, but instead must simply prove that the correct procedure has been followed to serve the particulars of claim and show that the defendant has not responded to them.

Therefore, both on a request and on an application for default judgment, the court must be satisfied that:

- the particulars of claim have been served on the defendant (if the court has effected service, there is no need for further evidence; if the claimant has effected service himself, he must file a certificate of service);[22]

- the defendant has not filed either an acknowledgment of service or a defence and the relevant period for doing so has expired;

- the defendant has not satisfied the claim, and

- the defendant has not admitted liability to pay the whole of a money claim, but requested time to pay (PD 12, para 4.1).

When necessary, a party should provide a witness statement covering all these matters along with his application under Part 23.

Where an application is made for judgment in default, the claimant need not serve evidence in support of his application on a party who has failed to file an acknowledgment of service (r 12.11(2)).

In the case of an application for judgment against a child or patient, a litigation friend must be appointed to act on behalf of the child or patient before judgment can be obtained and the claimant must satisfy the court by evidence that the claimant is entitled to the judgment claimed (PD 12, para 4.2).

On an application for judgment for delivery up of goods where the defendant will not be given the alternative of paying their value, the evidence must identify the goods and state where the claimant believes the goods to be situated and why their specific delivery up is sought (PD 12, para 4.6).

In those cases where the defendant was served with the claim either outside the jurisdiction without leave under the Civil Jurisdiction and Judgments Act 1982, or within the jurisdiction, but when domiciled in

---

21 See above, p 239.
22 See Chapter 9, Service of Documents, p 109.

Scotland or Northern Ireland or in any other Convention territory, and the defendant has not acknowledged service, evidence, in the form of an affidavit, must establish that the claim is one the court has power to hear and decide, no other court has exclusive jurisdiction under the Act to hear and decide the claim and the claim has been served properly in accordance with Art 20 of Scheds 1, 3C or 4 to the Civil Jurisdiction and Judgments Act 1982.[23]

CLAIMS AGAINST MULTIPLE DEFENDANTS

Judgment in default by request

If the claimant's claim is for money or for the delivery of goods, and judgment in default can be obtained by filing a request in the relevant practice form,[24] if the claim is against two or more defendants, the claimant may obtain judgment in default (if Part 12 is made out) against one of the defendants and proceed with his claim against the rest (r 12.8).

If the claimant's claim is of a type, or against a defendant, where judgment in default can only be obtained by making an application,[25] and the claimant is proceeding against two or more defendants, if he applies for judgment in default against one of the defendants, so long as the claim against the other defendants can be dealt with separately, the court will enter judgment in default against one of the defendants and allow the claimant to continue proceeding against the other defendants (r 12.8(2)(a)). However, if the claim cannot be dealt with separately from the claim against the other defendants, the court will not enter judgment in default against only one of the defendants and the court must deal with the application for judgment in default at the same time as it disposes of the claim against the other defendants (r 12.8(2)(b)).

SETTING ASIDE DEFAULT JUDGMENT

Default judgment set aside as of right

Where judgment has been entered against a defendant in default in circumstances in which the necessary preconditions for the entry of judgment under Part 12 have not been satisfied, the court *must* set the judgment in default aside.

---

23 See Chapter 10, Service out of the jurisdiction.
24 See above, p 235.
25 See above, p 238.

Therefore, the court must set default judgment aside if:

- in the case of a judgment in default of acknowledgment of service, an acknowledgment of service has been filed, or if the time limit for filing an acknowledgment of service has not yet expired;
- in the case of a judgment in default of defence (whether to a claim or counterclaim) a defence has been filed, or if the time limit for filing a defence has not yet expired;
- the defendant has applied to have the claimant's statement of case struck out under r 3.4 or applied for summary judgment under Part 24 and the application has not been disposed of;
- the whole of the claim was satisfied before judgment was entered; or
- the defendant admitted liability for the whole of a money claim and requested time to pay (r 13.2).

Court exercising discretion to set aside or vary default judgment

In all other cases, apart from those where the court must set aside default judgment,[26] the court has a *discretion* to set aside or vary default judgment if:

- the defendant has a real prospect of successfully defending the claim; or
- it appears to the court that there is some other good reason why the judgment should be set aside or varied or the defendant should be allowed to defend the claim (r 13.3(1)).

It is also expressly provided that the court, when deciding whether to exercise its discretion to set aside default judgment, must consider whether the person seeking to set aside default judgment applied to do so promptly (r 13.3(2)).

The existence of a defence on the merits will be a powerful factor indicating that the court should exercise its discretion to set aside default judgment, as it would seem unjust to allow judgment to be entered for a claimant on an unmeritorious claim because a defendant has not responded to it in time. However, this must be weighed against the prejudice that can be caused to a party by excessive delay, a consideration which is given even more importance under the ethos of the new rules.

On the other hand, it is likely that in most cases, the court will not exercise its discretion to set aside default judgment if the defendant has no real prospect of successfully defending the claim. It would seem contrary to the overriding objective,[26a] as it would simply cause undue expense and delay for both parties and the court system, to set aside judgment entered in default if the defendant has no defence to the claim and will therefore inevitably be found liable to the claimant.

---

26 See above, p 241.
26a See Chapter 5, Judicial Case Management: The Overriding Objective.

However, just because a defendant has a real prospect of defending the claim does not mean that he will be entitled to have judgment in default set aside, after having let judgment be entered against him in the first place. The overriding objective puts an obligation on the court to ensure that cases are dealt with *expeditiously* as well as fairly (r 1.1(2)(d)).[27] The new culture introduced by the CPR emphasises that the parties must abide by the rules and not indulge in delay, or they risk sanctions being imposed which include the striking out of their statement of case. Therefore, if a defendant is guilty of excessive delay, particularly when this has caused prejudice to the claimant, the court in the exercise of its discretion may consider that it would be contrary to the overriding objective to set aside default judgment in those circumstances, even where the defendant has a reasonable prospect of defending the claim.

It should be borne in mind, however, that despite the emphasis on the avoidance of delay under the new rules, an *obiter dictum* of the court of appeal (given in a case dealing with the application of the old rules for setting aside judgment in default) stated that a defendant's failure to give any reason for delay would not be a 'knockout blow' to an application to set aside default judgment. Instead, this would be one consideration for a judge, applying the overriding objective, in deciding whether to exercise his discretion to set aside judgment in default.[27a]

Also, the rules do give the court a wide discretion to set aside or vary default judgment if there is some other good reason, apart from the defendant having a real prospect of defending the claim, for the judgment to be varied or set aside or for the defendant to be able to defend the claim.

The court may impose conditions, such as the payment of a sum of money into court, when it grants an order setting aside judgment in default[27b] (r 3.1(3)).

PROCEDURE FOR APPLYING TO SET ASIDE OR VARY DEFAULT JUDGMENT

An application to set aside or vary default judgment must be made by notice of application in accordance with Part 23.[27c]

An application to the court to exercise its discretion to set aside or vary default judgment must be supported by evidence (r 13.4(3)). In accordance with the general principle for evidence at hearings other than trial, the

---

27 *Ibid.*

27a See *obiter dictum* of Lord Brook in *Thorn plc v MacDonald* (1999) unreported, Case No CCRTI 1999/0439/2, CA.

27b See Chapter 5, Judicial Case Management: The Overriding Objective.

27c See Chapter 19, Making Applications for Court Orders.

evidence should be in the form of a witness statement rather than oral (r 32.6(1)). Moreover, if a party's statement of case or application notice is verified by a statement of truth,[28] this can be used as evidence at the hearing (r 32.6(2)).

The evidence should set out an explanation for the failure to respond to the particulars of claim in time and demonstrate that the defendant has a real prospect of successfully defending the claim.

Automatic transfer

The application to set aside or vary default judgment will be automatically transferred to be heard at the defendant's home court[28a] if the following conditions are met:

- the claim is for a specified amount of money;
- the judgment was obtained in a court which is not the defendant's home court;
- the claim has not been transferred to another defendant's home court either for the court to determine the rate of payment following an admission under r 4.12 or as a result of the operation of the rule of automatic transfer under r 26.2; and
- the defendant is an individual (r 13.4).

The above rules on automatic transfer will not apply if the claim was commenced in a specialist list.[29]

Circumstances where claimant must set aside default judgment

If the claimant enters judgment in default, but subsequently has good grounds to believe that the defendant did not receive the particulars of claim before judgment was entered, the claimant must either:

- file a request for judgment to be set aside; or
- apply to the court for directions (r 13.5(2)).

The claimant must take no further steps in the proceedings to enforce judgment until the judgment has been set aside or the court has disposed of the application for directions (r 13.5(3)).

---

28 See Chapter 11, Statements of Case, p 128.
28a See Chapter 15, Case Management: Allocation, for definition of defendant's home court.
29 See Part 49 and Chapter 2, p 18.

Abandoned claim restored when default judgment set aside

If a claimant abandoned a remedy for which judgment in default could only be obtained by making an application[30] in order to apply for judgment in default by filing a request,[31] and that judgment is set aside, the abandoned claim is automatically restored when the default judgment is set aside (r 13.6).

---

30 See above, p 238.
31 See above, p 235.

CHAPTER 22

SUMMARY JUDGMENT

INTRODUCTION

In some cases, a party will have no prospect of succeeding in bringing or defending an action and in those circumstances, it will be open to their opponent to apply, or for the court, acting on its own initiative,[1] to dispose summarily of an issue or issues, or sometimes the whole case, without the need for a full trial.

Lord Woolf stated that part of his aims in making his recommendations in his report was to encourage settlement 'by disposing of issues so as to narrow the dispute'.[2] In this way, the court, as well as the parties, has the power to initiate a summary judgment hearing. Also, the ethos of the new rules aims to discourage the tendency, particularly of lawyers, to include every possible issue as part of a party's case, meritorious or not. In order to discourage this practice, the court has a duty as part of active case management[3] to '[identify] the issues at an early stage' and to '[decide] promptly which issues need full investigation and trial and accordingly disposing summarily of the others' (r 1.4(2)(b) and (c)).

When describing this aspect of case management in making his proposals for reform of the former system, Lord Woolf imagined '[t]he legal profession ... performing its traditional adversarial role in a managed environment governed by the courts and by the rules which will focus effort on the key issues rather than allowing every issue to be pursued regardless of expense and time, as at present'.[4]

A party may make an application based on both Part 3.4[5] and Part 24 for early judgment in a matter and the court, acting of its own initiative, may exercise its powers under both these parts (PD 3, para 1.2).

---

1 See Chapter 5, Judicial Case Management: The Overriding Objective, p 59.
2 See *Access to Justice*, Final Report, Chapter 1, p 16, para 7(d) (www.lcd.gov.uk/civil/finalfr.htm).
3 See Chapter 5, Judicial Case Management: The Overriding Objective.
4 See Final Report, Chapter 1, p 14, para 3. (*Ibid.*)
5 See Chapter 23, Striking Out.

BY WHOM CAN AN APPLICATION FOR SUMMARY JUDGMENT BE MADE?

An application for summary judgment can be made either by a claimant or a defendant, or by the court of its own initiative. The availability of summary judgment against a claimant was a major innovation of the CPR, it not being formerly available under the old rules, and reflected the importance the new rules placed upon weeding out unmeritorious claims, defences and issues.[6]

AVAILABILITY OF SUMMARY JUDGMENT

It is available for 'any type of proceedings' (r 24.3) – this includes small claims. There is similar power to grant summary judgment in small claims under r 27.6(1)(b).

Application by claimant

A claimant can make an application for summary judgment against a defendant in any type of proceedings except residential possession proceedings against a mortgagor or a person with security of tenure under the Rent Act 1977 or the Housing Act 1988 or in proceedings for an admiralty claim in rem (r 24.3(2)).

Application by defendant

A defendant can make an application for summary judgment against a claimant in any type of proceedings (r 24.3(1)).

Summary judgment for single issue or whole claim

Summary judgment is available in respect of a whole claim or defence or part of a claim or defence or in respect of a particular issue or issues forming part of the claim or defence (r 24.2).

---

6   See *Access to Justice*, Interim Report, Chapter 6, paras 17–21 (www.lcd.gov.uk/civil/interfr.htm).

GROUNDS FOR SUMMARY JUDGMENT

Lord Woolf proposed that the test for summary judgment under the CPR should be easier for applicants to satisfy than the test under the old rules.[7] The old test was for the claimant to satisfy the court that the defendant had 'no defence to the claim'. Thus, summary judgment was only available where there was plainly no defence to a claim and, if the defendant could show a 'triable issue', he would succeed in avoiding summary judgment. The new test is for the applicant to satisfy the court that there is 'no reasonable prospect of succeeding in bringing or defending a claim'. However, it remains to be seen whether the courts will interpret this test more leniently than that applicable under the former rules for obtaining summary judgment.

The test the court will apply when deciding whether to grant summary judgment is whether it is satisfied, in the case of an application against the claimant, that he has no real prospect of succeeding on the claim or issue, and, for an application against the defendant, that he has no real prospect of successfully defending the claim or issue, *and*, in both cases, that there is no other compelling reason why the case or issue should be disposed of at trial (r 24.2).

Thus, in an application for summary judgment against a claimant under CPR 24.2, the correct test is not whether the claim is bound to fail, but whether the claimant has no real prospect of succeeding on the claim or issue.[8]

An application for summary judgment may be based either on a point of law (including the construction of a document), or the absence of evidence to prove a party's case, or a combination of these (PD 24, para 1.3).

The final aspect of the test leaves the court with a wide discretion to decide whether it is appropriate to grant summary judgment. For instance, it may be that although a respondent cannot establish a claim or defence at the time of the application, he may be able to do so if he can obtain discovery of documents from the applicant or trace a key witness who is not immediately available. In such circumstances, the court is likely to decide that the case should be disposed of at trial rather than summarily.

In *Swain v Hillman and Gay*,[9] Woolf MR said: 'The words "no real prospect of being successful or succeeding" do not need any amplification, they speak for themselves. The word "real" distinguishes fanciful prospects of success.' Pill LJ said: 'This is simple language, not susceptible to much elaboration, even forensically.' It was also said in that case that, in dealing with the

---

7   See Interim Report, Chapter 6, para 21. (*Ibid.*)
8   *Peter Robert Krafft v Camden LBC* (2000) LTL, 24 October, CA.
9   (1999) unreported, 21 October, CA.

application, the judge should not conduct a mini-trial of issues which would be better investigated at a trial.

However, although the description of the test does not need any elaboration, the application of it necessarily involves a value judgment as to what is a 'real' prospect of success and therefore leaves much scope for the court to exercise its discretion in a particular case.

The same test, 'real' prospect of success, is applied by the court when a defendant applies to have judgment in default set aside,[10] in a case in which the court has a discretion to set judgment aside (r 13.3).[11]

A claim which is really hopeless should not be allowed to continue.[12] In *S v Gloucestershire CC; L v Tower Hamlets LBC*,[13] the Court of Appeal declared that for an application for summary judgment to succeed where a strike-out application would not succeed, three conditions must be satisfied, namely:

(a) all substantial facts relevant to the claimant's case which were reasonably capable of being before the court, must be before the court;

(b) those facts must be undisputed or there must be no reasonable prospect of successfully disputing them; and

(c) there is no real prospect of oral evidence affecting the court's assessment of the facts.

Summary judgment ordering an account or inquiry

If a claimant's claim includes, or necessarily involves, a remedy involving the taking of an account or the making of an inquiry, any party to the proceedings can make an application under Part 24 for an order directing that any necessary accounts or inquiries are taken or made (PD 24, para 6).

Specific performance of agreements relating to land

An expedited procedure is provided for claimants seeking summary judgment in an action which includes a claim for:

- specific performance of an agreement for the sale, purchase, exchange, mortgage or charge of any property or for the grant or assignment of a

---

10 See also *Alpine Bulk Transport Co Inc v Saudi Eagle Shipping Co Inc* [1986] 2 Lloyd's Rep 221, CA.

11 See Chapter 21, Judgment in Default.

12 *Elizabeth Harris v Bolt Burdon (A Firm)* (2000) *The Times*, 8 December, CA.

13 [2000] 3 All ER 346; (2000) *The Independent*, 24 March.

lease or tenancy of any property whether damages are claimed in the alternative or not; or

- the rescission of such an agreement; or
- the forfeiture or return of any deposit made under such an agreement (PD 24, para 7.1(1)).

The claimant can apply for summary judgment in respect of such a claim at any time after the claim form has been served, even if particulars of claim have not been served, and even if the defendant has not acknowledged service, whether the time period for acknowledging service has expired or not (PD 24, para 7.1(2)).

This special procedure is provided for such actions as, in most cases, so long as an enforceable agreement is in existence, the defendant will have no defence to such a claim.

PROCEDURE FOR APPLYING FOR SUMMARY JUDGMENT

Stage when application for summary judgment can be made

Given the nature of the application, a defendant will be able to apply for summary judgment as soon as proceedings are served on him.

However, a claimant cannot apply for summary judgment until the defendant has filed an acknowledgment of service[14] or a defence,[15] unless the court gives permission or a practice direction provides otherwise (r 24.4(1)).

Normally, a file will not come to the judge's attention until allocation, unless a vigilant clerk spots something amiss, but on allocation, or possibly earlier, the court will always consider its powers under r 3.4(1) to consider sanctions or to dispose of a claim summarily.

Claimant making application before defence has been filed

If a claimant does make an application for summary judgment against a defendant before he has filed a defence, the defendant does not need to file a defence before the hearing (r 24.4(2)).

In most cases, it will be more sensible for a claimant to apply for summary judgment only after a defence has been filed as it is easier to make an application armed with the knowledge of what the defendant's defence will

---

14 See Chapter 8, Responding to an Action, for acknowledgment of service and time limits.
15 See *ibid*, for time limits for filing a defence and Chapter 11, Statements of Case, for the contents of a defence.

be. Also, if a defendant has a weak case, he may well not proceed with filing a defence after acknowledging service and then the claimant can apply for judgment in default of defence to be entered instead. Judgment in default of defence can, in some cases, be entered simply on the basis of the filing of a request by the claimant in the prescribed form. However, even if it is the type of case where an application must be made, in both types of request for judgment in default, unlike an application for summary judgment, the court will not consider the merits of the claim or defence.

The application notice

An application for summary judgment is made in accordance with Part 23.[16] The applicant should fill in a general form of application and the application notice must include a statement that it is an application for summary judgment under Part 24 (PD 24, para 2.2).

The application notice or the supporting evidence, whether contained in the notice or referred to by the notice or served with the notice, must set out concisely the basis of the application (PD 24, para 2.3). Therefore, the application must state:

- the point of law or provision in a document on which the applicant relies; and/or
- that the applicant believes that on the evidence, the respondent has no real prospect of succeeding on the claim or issue or of successfully defending the claim or issue (as the case may be);

and in all applications state:

- that the applicant knows of no other reason why the claim or issue should be disposed of at trial (PD 24, para 2.3).

The application notice should also draw the respondent's attention to r 24.5, which provides details as to how and when the respondent can file and serve evidence[17] in reply to the claimant's evidence (PD 24, para 2.5).

Evidence relied on to support application

In contrast to the old procedure, there is no general requirement for the applicant to serve evidence in support of the application in the light of the provision[18] which confirms that existing evidence, such as that in a statement of case, can be relied upon, if appropriate.

---

16 See Chapter 19, Making Applications for Court Orders.
17 See below, p 254, Filing and serving evidence in reply.
18 PD 24, para 2.4 – see below, p 253.

Under r 32.6(1), if there is evidence at a summary judgment application, it should usually be in the form of witness statements, unless the court orders otherwise. The witness statement should comply with r 32.8 which includes the requirement that if letters, documents and other evidence are also relied upon, they should form exhibits to the witness statement. However, as with all other applications made under Part 23, if all the evidence on which a party wishes to rely is contained within the application notice or a statement of case, a party can rely on these documents instead, so long as the document is verified by a statement of truth[19] (r 32.6(2)).

If the evidence to support the application is contained in a document other than the application notice itself, for example, a witness statement or statement of case, the application notice should identify the written evidence on which the applicant relies (PD 24, para 2.4).

In most applications for summary judgment, therefore, there will be no oral evidence at the hearing and no cross-examination on the content of witness statements. It can therefore be seen that if a party's case is based on the type of evidence which can only be challenged through cross-examination at trial, such as oral factual statements that the other party denies, it is likely to prove difficult to establish that the other party's claim or defence has no real prospect of success in the context of a summary hearing.

Where the court is considering an application for summary judgment on the ground that the claimant has no real prospect of succeeding in its claim, the court has to conclude that there is a real prospect of success in the claim before investigating the likelihood of establishing damages and causation.[19a]

Notice of hearing

The applicant must give the respondent at least 14 days' notice of the hearing and the issues which it is proposed that the court will decide at the hearing (r 24.4(3)). The effect, where the hearing is fixed of the court's own initiative, is to extend the three day period mentioned in r 3.3(3). The time is reduced to four days for a claimant's application in a claim for specific performance (PD 24, para 7.3). As a result of PD 24, para 7.1, an applicant for specific performance will not be permitted to rely on the provisions in r 24.4(3); and r 24.5 (see below) will clearly have no application.

However, if a practice direction provides for a different period of notice to be given for applications in certain types of proceedings, those notice periods must be followed instead (r 24.4(4)). This allows for flexibility in fixing the

---

19   See Chapter 11, Statements of Case, p 128.
19a *Kumarth Khalagy and Another v Alliance and Leicester plc* (2000) LTL, 23 October, CA (unreported elsewhere).

time period for notice and to resolve the conflict between this rule prior to its amendment and PD 24, para 7 (specific performance).

Filing and serving evidence in reply

If the respondent wishes to rely on written evidence at the hearing in reply, he should file a copy of the evidence at court and on every other party to the application at least seven days before the hearing (r 24.5(1)).

On receiving the respondent's evidence, if the applicant wants to rely on written evidence in reply, he should file a copy of the evidence at court and on every other party to the application at least three days before the hearing (r 24.5(2)).

However, if a party intends to rely on his application notice or statement of case as evidence at the hearing, and these documents have already been filed at court and served on the other parties in the course of the proceedings, there is no need for a party to re-file or re-serve those documents again for the purposes of the summary judgment hearing (r 24.5(4)).

Timing of application

As with all applications made in accordance with Part 23, an application for summary judgment should be made as soon as it becomes apparent that it is necessary or desirable to make it (PD 23, para 2.7).

Although not restricting applications for summary judgment to certain stages of the proceedings, Lord Woolf warned that:

> [I]n keeping with the new ethos which my recommendations will bring about, applicants will be expected to apply promptly as soon as they have sufficient information on which to act [and] [w]here an application is made late in the course of proceedings … the courts would impose sanctions on the applicant if he has delayed unnecessarily and allowed costs to escalate … [and] the court itself will be in a position to direct a hearing and determine issues summarily. There should, therefore, be only a few cases in which an opportunity for summary disposal is overlooked.[20]

A party is asked to indicate whether he intends to apply for summary judgment when completing his allocation questionnaire[21] and will be expected to make the application before or when filing his allocation questionnaire (PD 26, para 5.3(1)). If a party makes an application for summary judgment before the case has been allocated to a track, the court will not normally allocate the case before the hearing of the application (PD 26, para 5.3(2)).

---

20 See Interim Report, Chapter 6, para 20. (*Ibid.*)
21 See Chapter 15, Case Management: Allocation.

If a party indicates in his allocation questionnaire that he intends to make an application for summary judgment, but he has not yet made the application, the judge will usually direct that an allocation hearing is listed (PD 26, para 5.3(3)), the intention being that the application is heard at the allocation hearing, so long as the application has been issued and served giving the other party the requisite notice (PD 26, para 5.3(4)).

Where the court decides, at a hearing in which a party is applying for summary judgment, or where the court has ordered such a hearing of its own initiative, that the claim should continue, it will either treat the hearing as an allocation hearing, allocate the claim and give case management directions or give other appropriate directions (PD 26, para 5.5).

While the issue of an application by the claimant for summary judgment relieves the defendant from the need to file a defence, this rule makes no similar provision if the application is made by the defendant. Nevertheless, if the defendant makes an application under this Part, the claimant may not obtain default judgment against him until it is disposed of (r 12.3(3)(a)).

Court convening summary judgment hearing of its own initiative

The court has unlimited powers to make orders of its own initiative, whether following a hearing or without a hearing.[22] This therefore includes deciding whether to dispose summarily of issues or to order summary judgment against one of the parties.[23]

If the court decides to convene a hearing of its own initiative for the purposes of deciding whether to dispose summarily of issues or to enter summary judgment against one of the parties, it must give both parties at least 14 days' notice of the hearing and details of the issues that it is proposed the court will decide at the hearing (r 24.4(3)).

If the court sends the parties' notice of a summary judgment hearing fixed of its own initiative, any party who wishes to rely on written evidence must file a copy of it at court and on every other party to the proceedings at least seven days before the hearing (r 24.5(3)(a)).

Also, if a party wishes to reply to a party's evidence, he must file a copy of the written evidence in reply at court and on every party to the proceedings at least three days before the hearing (r 24.5(3)(b)).

However, the court may make a different order about the requirement of the parties to serve their evidence on each other (r 24.5(3)).

---

22 See Chapter 5, Judicial Case Management: The Overriding Objective.

23 *Peter John O'Donnell and Others v Charly Holdings Inc (A Company Incorporated under the Laws of Panama) and Another* (2000) Lawtel, 14 March, CA (unreported elsewhere).

Jurisdiction of masters and district judges

The master or district judge has jurisdiction to hear the application. However, the master or district judge can also refer the matter to be heard by a High Court judge or circuit judge respectively, if the nature of the case is such that the master or district judge thinks this appropriate (PD 24, para 3).

COURT'S POWERS ON SUMMARY JUDGMENT APPLICATION

Judgment for the claimant

If the applicant is the claimant and the court is satisfied that the respondent's defence (or any issues within it) has no real prospect of success and there is no other compelling reason why the case should proceed to trial, it can enter judgment for the claimant for the whole claim or on a particular issue or issues (PD 24, para 5.1(1)).

Judgment for the defendant

If the applicant is the defendant and the court is satisfied that the respondent's claim (or any issues within it) has no real prospect of success and that there is no other compelling reason why the case should proceed to trial, the court can strike out or dismiss the whole claim or a particular issue or issues within it (PD 24, para 5.1(2)).

Dismissal of the application

If the court decides that the application is an unsuitable one for summary judgment, it can dismiss the application (PD 24, para 5.1(3)).

On dismissing the application, the court will give case management directions as to the future conduct of the proceedings (PD 24, para 10), for example, direct that allocation questionnaires[24] be filed.

---

24 See Chapter 15, Case Management: Allocation.

Conditional orders

If it appears to the court that it is possible, but improbable, for the claim or defence to succeed, the court is likely to make a conditional order (PD 24, para 4). Such an order will be appropriate when the court is doubtful about the merits of a claim or defence, but is unable to decide conclusively that it has no real prospect of success without proper testing of the evidence at trial. The conditions the court can impose in such circumstances are an order for the party to:

- pay a sum of money into court; or
- take a specified step in relation to his statement of case; and in both cases
- provide for the claim to be dismissed or statement of case struck out if he does not comply (PD 24, para 5.2).

Case management directions

If an unsuccessful application for summary judgment is made, the court can give directions about the future management of the case at the hearing (r 24.6(b)). If the defendant has filed a defence but the case has not yet been allocated, the next direction would be for the claim to be allocated. If the court has enough information at this stage, it can allocate the case there and then, or it can treat the rest of the hearing as an allocation hearing. Alternatively, the court might make an order for allocation questionnaires to be filed by a specified date.

If an unsuccessful application for summary judgment is made by the claimant and the defendant has not yet filed a defence, the most likely direction for the court to make is for the filing and service of a defence (r 24.6(a)).

Costs of the application

In accordance with the general rule, the costs of a summary judgment application are in the discretion of the court. However, the most likely order is for the unsuccessful party to the application to pay the successful party's costs.[25]

CPR Part 45 sets out the fixed costs that the court will award to the applicant on the entry of judgment following an application for summary judgment (r 45.4).

---

25 See r 44.3 and Chapter 33 on costs.

If the court does not order fixed costs, it is likely to order summary assessment of the costs of the application (r 43.3).

However, it should be noted that, in accordance with the general rule, if the order for summary judgment does not mention costs, none will be payable (r 44.13). The onus is therefore on the successful party to ensure that costs are applied for.

SETTING ASIDE AN APPLICATION FOR SUMMARY JUDGMENT

If the applicant or respondent fails to attend the hearing, the court can proceed in his absence (r 23.11(1)). If the court makes an order at that hearing it may, on an application or of its own initiative, set aside the order and re-list the application for hearing (r 23.1(2)).

Practice Direction 24, para 8.1 also specifically provides that if an order for summary judgment is made against a respondent who did not appear at the hearing of the application, the respondent may apply for the order to be set aside or varied.

The court is only likely to consider setting aside or varying an order for summary judgment where the respondent can demonstrate a real prospect of successfully bringing or defending the claim. Also, the court is likely to impose conditions such as the payment of a sum of money into court or the payment of costs on the indemnity basis as the price for setting aside the order.

APPEAL AGAINST AN ORDER FOR SUMMARY JUDGMENT

If an order for summary judgment is made following a hearing at which both parties attended, a party who wishes to challenge the order must appeal against the order following the procedure in r 52.[25a]

SUMMARY POSSESSION OF LAND

Introduction

In many cases, proceedings for the recovery of land are lengthy and costly, with the court having wide powers to suspend orders for possession. However, where squatters occupy land in circumstances where there could be

---

25a See Chapter 35, Appeals.

no question of having the permission of the landowner to do so, it would be inequitable to require the landlord to pursue the usual route to regain possession even if accelerated possession procedures were utilised.[26] Therefore, for such situations, a landowner can use a summary procedure to obtain possession in a short period of time.

The summary procedure can be used against persons who enter onto or remain in occupation of land without the licence or consent of the owner, but is not available against a tenant who is holding over after the expiration of his tenancy (r 55.1(b)) other than an unlawful sub-tenant.[27] However, as the procedure is available against a person who entered into occupation with the permission of the owner, but remains in occupation of land without his licence or consent, it may be available against a licensee where the licence has been terminated.

Summary possession proceedings

The procedure for summary possession of land is contained in CPR Part 55 as from 15 October 2001 (see Chapter 14, Part 8 Claims).

County court procedure

Where summary possession proceedings are brought, the court will fix a day for the hearing when it issues the claim form (r 55.5(1)).

The proceedings must be commenced in the county court for the district where the land or any part of the land is situated (r 55.3(1)). In exceptional circumstances a claim may be commenced in the High Court (r 55.3(2) and PD 55, paras 1.1 and 1.3).

Even if the dispossessed landowner does not know the name of the occupants (which is likely to be the case in respect of squatters), he can still issue summary possession proceedings. In these circumstances, the occupiers are described as 'persons unknown' (r 55.3(4)).

The proceedings are commenced by way of a claim form in Form N5.[28]

The applicant must file particulars of claim (Form N121) which state:

- the applicant's interest in the land on the basis of his right to claim possession;

---

26 Such as that available in the case of an assured shorthold tenancy where the contractual term has expired and a notice requiring possession has been served.
27 *Moore Properties (Ilford) Ltd v McKeon* [1976] 1 WLR 1278.
28 In the High Court, the Part 8 claim form is used in Form N208.

- the circumstances in which the land has been occupied without licence or consent and in which his claim to possession arises (PD 55, para 2.6).

Service of the proceedings

Service is in accordance with Part 6. The claim form and any witness statements must be filed and served together (r 55.8(5)). (See Chapter 9, Service of Documents.)

Where all or any of the occupants are not named as respondents, the claim form must be served either by affixing a copy of the documents on the main door or other conspicuous part of the premises, and if practicable inserting a copy through the letterbox at the property in a sealed transparent envelope addressed to 'the occupiers', or by placing copies, addressed to the occupiers, in sealed transparent envelopes in stakes in the ground at conspicuous parts of the occupied land (r 55.6) (PD 55, para 4).

Hearing of claim

In most cases, the day fixed for the hearing by the court will, in the case of residential premises, be not less than five days after the day of service and in the case of other land, not less than two days after service (r 55.5(2). However, these periods can be shortened in the case of urgency or by permission of the court (r 3.1(2)(a)).

If there is no substantive defence to the claim for possession, the court must make an order for possession, which is usually to have immediate effect.[29]

Order of possession

The order for possession, in Form N36, will be an order *in rem*, that is, an order that the applicant recover possession of the land rather than an order for the occupants to give possession.

If an order for possession is made against squatters, the court is bound to make an order for possession to be given forthwith and has no discretion to suspend the order.[30] However, the court has the power to specify a date for possession as if it were exercising powers under ordinary possession proceedings if the original entry was lawful (CCR Ord 24 r 5).

---

29 See *McPhail v Persons, names unknown; Bristol Corporation v Ross and Another* [1973] 3 All ER 393.

30 *Ibid.*

Warrant of possession

Once an order for possession is made, a warrant of possession to enforce the order, in Form N52, can be issued without the court's permission (CCR Ord 24 r 6(1)). However, after the expiry of three months from the making of the order for possession, the permission of the court must be obtained to issue a warrant of possession (CCR Ord 24 r 6(2)).

As the order for possession is an order *in rem*, it is effective against all the occupiers of the premises, and the bailiff is entitled to evict everyone he finds on the premises, even though that person was not a party to the proceedings for possession.[31]

Interim possession orders

In respect of summary possession proceedings in the county court,[32] if certain conditions are fulfilled, the applicant can apply for an interim possession order.[33]

The conditions which must be fulfilled are:

- the only claim in the proceedings is for the recovery of premises;[34]
- the claim is made by a person with an immediate right of occupation and who has had such a right throughout the period of unlawful occupation;
- the claim is made against a person who entered the premises without consent and has not subsequently been granted consent;
- the claim is made within 28 days of the date when the applicant first knew, or ought reasonably to have known, that the respondent was in occupation (CCR Ord 24 r 9).

Issue of the application

The applicant files a claim form in N130, along with an affidavit or witness statement verifying that the applicant fulfils the conditions set out in Ord 24 r 9.[35] The applicant should also give suitable undertakings, such as an undertaking to reinstate the respondent and pay damages if it turns out that the order was not justified (CCR Ord 24 r 11(1) and CCR Ord 24 r 12).

---

31 See *R v Wandsworth County Court ex p London Borough of Wandsworth* [1975] 3 All ER 390.
32 An interim possession order is not available in the High Court.
33 Introduced by the Criminal Justice and Public Order Act 1994, ss 75 and 76.
34 Premises within the meaning of s 12 of the Criminal Law Act 1977, which does not include open land.
35 See above.

Service of the application

The proceedings should be served by fixing a copy of the documents on the main door or other conspicuous part of the premises and, if practicable, inserting them through the letter box at the premises in a sealed transparent envelope addressed to 'the occupiers' (PD 55, para 4). Additionally, but not alternatively, the applicant can fix copies of the documents, in sealed transparent envelopes, on stakes in the ground at conspicuous parts of the premises (PD 55, para 4).

The applicant must file a witness statement or affidavit of service in Form N135 at or before the time fixed for consideration of the application (CCR Ord 24 r 11(4)).

The respondent to the order may file a witness statement or affidavit in Form N133 in opposition to the making of the interim possession order (CCR Ord 24 r 11(5)).

The making of an interim possession order

The application may be dealt with by the judge in the absence of one or both of the parties (CCR Ord 24 r 12(3)).

The court shall make an interim possession order if:

- the conditions for the making of an interim possession order as specified in CCR Ord 29 r 9 are met;
- the court is satisfied that adequate undertakings have been given by the applicant;
- the applicant has filed a witness statement or affidavit of service (CCR Ord 24 r 12(4) and (5)).

The interim possession order

If the court makes the interim possession order, it is in prescribed Form N134 and compels the respondent to vacate the premises within 24 hours of the service of the order on them (CCR Ord 24 r 12(6)).

The interim possession order must be served on the respondent by the applicant within 48 hours of the court approving the terms of the order (CCR Ord 24 r 13(1)).

On making the interim possession order, the court will fix a return date for the hearing of the claim which is not less than seven days after the date on which the interim possession order is made (CCR Ord 24 r 12(7)).

In the meantime, the applicant can act on the interim possession order and if the respondent does not vacate the premises, the applicant must ask the police to enforce the order. The order cannot be enforced by the bailiffs under a warrant of possession.

The interim order expires on the return date and on that date, the judge must either make a final order for possession, dismiss the claim or direct that the proceedings continue as summary possession proceedings under CCR Ord 24 r 1 (CCR Ord 24 r 14(3)).

If the court holds that the applicant was not entitled to an interim possession order, the respondent may apply for enforcement of the undertakings given by the applicant which can include an assessment of any damages suffered (CCR Ord 24 r 14(5)).

CHAPTER 23

STRIKING OUT

INTRODUCTION

The court has the power to strike out a party's statement of case either on the application of a party or of its own initiative. Striking out is often described as a draconian step, as it usually means that either the whole or part of that party's case is at an end. The circumstances when a statement of case will be struck out can be divided into three broad types.

First, there is the situation where a party's case as pleaded is unmeritorious, unsustainable, or an abuse of process; secondly, where the party has failed to prosecute or defend their case with sufficient diligence and/or in accordance with the rules; and, thirdly, where the court has ordered striking out as an automatic sanction unless a party complies with a particular order of the court.

POWER TO STRIKE OUT A STATEMENT OF CASE

Rule 3.4 sets out specific circumstances where the court has the power to strike out a statement of case. These are where it appears to the court:

- that the statement of case discloses no reasonable grounds for bringing or defending the claim (r 3.4(2)(a));
- that the statement of case is an abuse of the court's process or is otherwise likely to obstruct the just disposal of proceedings (r 3.4(2)(b)); or
- that there has been a failure to comply with a rule, practice direction or court order (r 3.4(2)(c)).

These powers are in addition to any other power the court may have to strike out a statement of case (r 3.4(5)). So, for instance, the court could strike out a statement of case in the exercise of its inherent powers to protect its own process from abuse, this inherent jurisdiction of the court being expressly preserved by r 3.1.

Statement of case

Statement of case is defined in the rules to mean a claim form, particulars of claim (where these are not included in a claim form), defence, Part 20 claim or reply to defence. The term also refers to any further information given in relation to a statement of case, whether it is given voluntarily or in response to a court order (r 2.3(1)).

Any reference in the rules relating to the power to strike out a statement of case includes the power to strike out part of a statement of case (r 3.4(1)).

STRIKING OUT

The glossary at the end of the CPR defines striking out to mean the court ordering written material to be deleted so that it may no longer be relied upon.

STRIKING OUT UNMERITORIOUS CASES

As part of case management, the court has an active role in ensuring that those issues, whether pleaded as part of a claim or a defence, which can or should be disposed of summarily before trial, should be disposed of at as early as stage as possible rather than continue to go forward for full investigation at trial.[1]

The court has two distinct powers to achieve this. One is under r 3.4 where the court can strike out a statement of case (or part of one) if it discloses no reasonable grounds for bringing or defending a claim, or is an abuse of process of the court, or is otherwise likely to obstruct the just disposal of the proceedings. The other is under r 24, which gives the court the power to enter summary judgment against a claimant or defendant where that party has no real prospect of succeeding on his claim or defence. There is a substantial overlap between the two powers, and an application can be made under both rules.

It is expressly provided that if a party believes he can show without a trial that an opponent's case has no real prospect of success on the facts, or that his case is bound to succeed or the opponent's fail because of a point of law, he can apply either under r 3.4 or Part 24 or both as he thinks appropriate (PD 3, para 1.7). Indeed, it might be desirable when applying to strike out a case to add an application for summary judgment as an alternative.

The court can exercise its powers of summary disposal of issues either on an application by a party or of its own initiative (PD 3, para 1.2). Even if an application for strike out fails the court may, as part of its management

---

1   See r 1.4(2)(c) and Chapter 5, Judicial Case Management: The Overriding Objective.

powers, consider the question of summary judgment.[2] The following points emerge from the cases of *S v Gloucestershire CC; L v Tower Hamlets LBC*:[3]

- the court will only strike out a statement of case under r 3.4(2)(a) in the clearest case;

- for an application for summary judgment to succeed where a strike out application would not succeed, three conditions must be satisfied, namely:

  (a) all substantial facts relevant to the claimant's case (for example, negligence) which were reasonably capable of being before the court, were before the court;

  (b) those facts must be undisputed or there must be no reasonable prospect of successfully disputing them; and

  (c) there is no real prospect of oral evidence affecting the court's assessment of the facts.

The Practice Direction accompanying r 3.4 gives examples of the types of case when the court may strike out a statement of case on the basis that it fails to disclose any reasonable grounds for bringing or defending the action (PD 3, paras 1.4–1.6). For instance, if a claimant's statement of case states 'Money owed £5,000' and does not set out any facts indicating what it is about, it is liable to be struck out. In the same way, if the defendant's defence is simply a bare denial without any facts in support, that too is liable to be struck out. Thus, 'the defendant denies the claimant's claim and puts the claimant to strict proof' will not be acceptable.

A party's statement of case is also liable to be struck out if it is based on incoherent facts which make no sense or if based on facts which are coherent, but even if true would not amount to a legally recognisable claim or defence. It is stressed in the practice direction that these examples are given by way of illustration only (PD 3, para 1.8).

The type of case where a statement of case is likely to be held to be an abuse of the court's process or is otherwise likely to obstruct the just disposal of proceedings is said to be where the claim is vexatious, scurrilous or obviously ill-founded (PD 3, para 1.5). An example of this may be where an action is started to pursue a claim which has already been dealt with by way of full and final settlement between the parties.

---

2   *O'Donnell and Others v Charly Holdings Inc and Another* (2000) Lawtel, 14 March, CA (unreported elsewhere).

3   [2000] 3 All ER 346; (2000) *The Independent*, 24 March, CA.

The court's powers to sift out unmeritorious claims and defences

When a claim form is presented for issue or when a defence is filed, it will first be received by a court officer. A court officer[4] is a member of the court staff, but has no judicial function. However, in order to further the process of case management at all levels, court officers presented with documents by parties with a request for a step to be taken can, instead of taking that step, consult a judge instead. The judge can then decide whether that step should be taken (r 3.2).

Claims

Where it appears to a court officer that the claim form which is being presented for issue falls within r 3.4(2)(a) or (b) above, he is obliged to issue the claim form, but can then consult a judge before further steps are taken in the case. If the judge is satisfied that the claimant's statement of case is such that it does fall within r 3.4(2)(a) or (b), he has the power to order that the claim be stayed until further order. This can include the order that the claim form be retained by the court and not served on the defendant until the stay is lifted.

The judge can also order that no application to lift the stay be heard unless the claimant files further documents such as a witness statement or particulars of claim. The judge has the power to make such orders of his own initiative[5] or after giving the claimant the opportunity to attend a hearing before deciding whether to do so (PD 3, paras 2.1–2.4).

Defences

In the same way, the court officer may consult a judge about a defence filed which appears to fall within r 3.4(2)(a) or (b). If satisfied that the defence does fall within those provisions, the judge can make an order of his own initiative striking it out. However, it is more likely that the judge will make an order that unless the defendant file a properly formulated defence within a certain period, his defence will be struck out, or allow the defendant a hearing before deciding whether to strike out the defence.

The judge can also make an order that unless a defendant clarifies his defence or provides further information about it within a specified time, his defence will be struck out (PD 3, paras 3.1–3.5). Note that a defence which admits liability, but disputes the amount of damages (rather than damages as

---

4   See r 2.3.
5   See Chapter 5, Judicial Case Management: The Overriding Objective, p 59, for orders of the court's own initiative.

a whole), is likely to be treated by the judge as no defence at all, resulting in judgment being given to the claimant with disposal ordered as to the damages.[6]

STRIKING OUT FOR FAILURE TO COMPLY WITH A RULE, PRACTICE DIRECTION OR COURT ORDER

Under r 3.4(2)(c), the court has the power to strike out a party's case if that party has failed to comply with a rule, practice direction or court order. In most circumstances, the court is unlikely to order the striking out of a statement of case on a single occasion of failure to comply. Instead, the court is more likely to make an order that unless the party in default take the required step by a specified date, his statement of case will be struck out.[7] Note, however, that in the light of the fact that one of the matters that the court takes into consideration under r 3.9[8] when dealing with an application for relief from sanctions is whether there has been previous default by the applicant, it must be borne in mind that the more often a party breaks court orders in an action, the more likely they are to be struck out for continuing to do so.

Also, it would seem that the court is unlikely to exercise its power under this rule to strike out a statement of case where there has been a technical failure to comply with the rules but the party in default has provided all the necessary information about their case to the other party. In the case of *Hannigan v Hannigan*,[9] a party started proceedings in the wrong form and committed many other breaches of the rules in presenting their case. The Court of Appeal held in that case that as the defendant knew precisely what was being claimed, and as the interests of the administration of justice would have been better served if the defendant had pointed out the procedural defects to the claimant in accordance with the duty of the parties to help the court further the overriding objective, it would not be just to strike out the claimant's claim, notwithstanding the claimant's catalogue of procedural errors, as in the circumstances such a response would be disproportionate.[10] Where a middle course, such as limiting interest or damages, is more appropriate than strike out, that should be followed.[11]

---

6   See Chapter 21, Judgment in Default, p 237.

7   See below, p 271.

8   CPR, r 3.9(e) and see Chapter 5, Judicial Case Management: The Overriding Objective.

9   [2000] 2 FCR 650; (2000) *The Independent*, 23 May; [2000] ILR, 3 July, CA.

10 See also *Alexandra Helen Luttenberger v Margaret Joyce Ann Prince (T/A Prince and Co)* (2000) Lawtel, 3 April, QBD (Nelson J) and *Keith v CPM Field Marketing Ltd* (2000) *The Times*, 29 August, CA.

11 *Walsh v Misseldine* (2000) NLD, 29 February, CA.

Consideration should also be given to the impact of the Human Rights Act 1998[12] and a possible contention that striking out a statement of case for a single technical misdemeanour might amount to a breach of Art 6(1) of the European Convention on Human Rights – the right to a fair trial.

STRIKING OUT FOR DELAY

In the case of *Biguzzi v Rank Leisure plc*,[13] Lord Woolf gave some general guidance on the operation of the court's powers to strike out a statement of case under r 3.4(2)(c). He emphasised that while the court must not be lenient towards a party who had failed to comply with a rule, practice direction or court order, as the court had the scope to impose a wide range of sanctions to punish default, it should not be driven to resort to striking out when another sanction would be more appropriate. He believed that the drastic remedy of striking out would be most appropriate for the most serious breaches of the rules. Lord Woolf was also mindful that a lesser sanction than striking out was less likely to result in an appeal of the order. Other sanctions include the power to order a party to pay indemnity costs and to pay a sum of money into court.[14]

This decision should be considered in the light of *UCB Corporate Services v Halifax*[15] where the court made it clear, however, that just because the court had available a wide range of other sanctions short of striking out, that did not mean that the court could not order the striking out of a statement of case if it was justified in all the circumstances of a case.

It should be borne in mind that the above two decisions were both transitional cases where the conduct complained of, being the 'wholesale disregard of the rules' which led to the case being struck out, occurred under the old civil procedure rules, but the appeal against the striking out was heard after the CPR came into force. With active judicial case management, it is unlikely for a party to have the opportunity to indulge in 'wholesale disregard of the rules' and '[t]he delays which used to disfigure the conduct of litigation ought not to occur in future'.[16]

Under the CPR, at each stage of the proceedings the court is likely to impose an order threatening striking out if a party fails to carry out the required action within a specified time.[17] If such an order is made and not

---

12 See Chapter 37, The Human Rights Act 1988.
13 [1999] 1 WLR 1926; [1999] 4 All ER 934, CA.
14 See Chapter 5, Judicial Case Management: The Overriding Objective.
15 (1999) unreported, 6 December, CA.
16 See judgment of Brooke LJ in *Walsh v Misseldine* (2000) NLD, 29 February, CA.
17 See below, p 272.

complied with, the striking out of the statement of case will apply automatically, leaving a party to resort to applying for relief from that sanction.[18]

PROCEDURE FOR APPLYING FOR AN ORDER TO STRIKE OUT A STATEMENT OF CASE

In accordance with the general rule about the making of applications, an application for striking out a statement of case must be made as soon as possible and before allocation if possible.[19] The application should be made on Form N244, the general form of application, and supported by evidence if necessary. Some applications to strike out – those, for instance, based on the grounds that a party's case does not disclose a legally recognised cause of action – should not require evidence to support them, as it should be clear from their statement of case.

CONSEQUENTIAL ORDERS

As well as striking out the statement of case, the court can make other orders consequential on the striking out (r 3.4(3)). For instance, it is usually ordered that the costs of the other party are to be paid by the party whose case was struck out. Also, the court has the power to enter judgment for the other party.

Restrictions on resurrecting a struck out claim

If a claimant's statement of case is struck out and the court has also made an order for the claimant to pay the defendant's costs of the action, if the claimant fails to pay those costs, and in fact starts another claim against the same defendant based on facts which are the same or substantially the same as those relied on in the struck out statement of claim, the defendant can apply for the subsequent action to be stayed until his costs of the original action are paid (r 3.4(4)).

It is likely to be treated as an abuse of process in itself to start another claim based on the same or substantially the same facts as the claim that was struck out if the original claim was struck out on the grounds that it disclosed no reasonable cause of action or was an abuse of process. Moreover, given the court's obligation, in furtherance of the overriding objective, to consider the interests of all court users,[20] it may well decide that it is not an appropriate

---

18 See Chapter 5, Judicial Case Management: The Overriding Objective, p 62, for the principles and procedure relating to relief from sanctions.

19 See Part 23, Chapter 19, Making Applications for Court Orders.

20 See r 1.1 and Chapter 5, Judicial Case Management: The Overriding Objective.

use of court resources to allow a claimant to bring a fresh action based on the same grounds as one that has already been struck out on the grounds of delay even though the limitation period has not expired.

In considering this question in the case of *Securum Finance Ltd v Ashton*,[21] the Court of Appeal held that the court must consider, when deciding whether to allow a second action to proceed in those circumstances, whether the claimant's wish to have a second bite at the cherry outweighs the need to allot the court's own limited resources to other cases.

Also, if a claimant's statement of case is struck out and the limitation period[21a] for the cause of action has expired, if the claimant starts a new action against the defendant for the same matter, the defendant will be able to have that action struck out, either under r 3.4(2)(a) or under Part 24 on the grounds that the limitation period has expired.

Appealing order striking out statement of case

If a party's statement of case is struck out under r 3.4, and that party wishes to challenge that order or any consequential order, such as the entry of judgment in the other party's favour, this should be done by way of appeal of the order in accordance with the appropriate procedure under Part 52.[22]

ORDERS THREATENING STRIKING OUT

The court has the power to make an order for a party to do something backed by the sanction that if the party fails to comply, their statement of claim shall be struck out. Such an order is usually made in the first instance where a party has failed to comply with a rule, practice direction or court order and in effect gives the party a second chance to comply before their statement of case is struck out.

Judgment by request following striking out for non-compliance with order

If an order is made warning a party that if he does not comply by a specified time, his statement of case shall be struck out, and he does not comply, the statement of case will be automatically struck out. The other party can then, if certain conditions are met, apply for judgment to be entered for him with costs by simply filing a request for judgment (r 3.5).

---

21 (2000) *The Times*, 5 July.
21a See Chapter 3, Limitation of Actions.
22 See Chapter 35, Appeals.

For all parties, in order to be able to enter judgment in these circumstances by filing a request, the order threatening to strike out the statement of case must relate to the whole of the other party's statement of case (r 3.5(2)(a)). Where the party wishing to obtain judgment is the claimant, he can only do that by request if his claim is for one of the following remedies:

- a specified amount of money;
- an amount of money to be decided by the court;
- delivery of goods where the claim form gives the defendant the alternative of paying their value; or
- a combination of any of the above claims (r 3.5(2)(b)).

Form requesting judgment

The request must state that the right to enter judgment has arisen because the court's order has not been complied with.

Judgment by application following striking out for non-compliance with order

If either the order threatening to strike out the statement of case does not refer to the whole of a party's statement of case or, where the party seeking to enter judgment is a claimant, his case is not one set out in the list set in r 5(2)b, the party must instead make an application to the court under Part 23[23] to enter judgment.

Setting aside judgment entered after striking out

Where judgment has been entered after a party's statement of case has been struck out for non-compliance with a specified order, the party against whom judgment has been entered may apply to the court for judgment to be set aside (r 3.6(1)). An application should be made on Form N244 in accordance with Part 23.[24]

However, in order to apply for judgment to be set aside, the party must apply not more than 14 days after the judgment was served[25] on him (r 3.6(2)).

If judgment was entered in circumstances where the right to enter judgment in fact had not yet arisen, the court has no discretion and must set

---

23 See Chapter 19, Making Applications for Court Orders.
24 *Ibid*
25 See Chapter 9, Service of Documents, for deemed dates of service.

the judgment aside (r 3.6(3)). However, if judgment had been rightfully entered in accordance with the procedure set out in r 3.5, the party must apply to the court to exercise its discretion to set judgment aside, in accordance with its powers to grant relief from sanctions[26] (r 3.6(4)).

VEXATIOUS LITIGANTS

A vexatious litigant is a person who habitually and persistently without any reasonable ground brings vexatious civil proceedings or makes vexatious applications in civil proceedings or brings vexatious criminal prosecutions whether against the same person or different persons. Vexatious proceedings or applications include those that are frivolous and without any reasonable grounds. An order can be made against a vexatious litigant which prevents him from bringing or continuing with civil proceedings or from making applications within civil proceedings or from bringing criminal proceedings without first obtaining the leave of the High Court to do so.

The order may be either a 'civil proceedings order', 'criminal proceedings order' or 'all proceedings order' depending on whether civil, or criminal, or all proceedings are involved. Such an order can only be obtained on the application of the Attorney General. If a civil proceedings order or all proceedings order is in place against such a vexatious litigant, he will be unable to begin or continue or make any application in any civil proceedings without seeking the permission of the High Court.

The procedure for making such an application is set out in PD 3, paras 7.1–7.10. Given the importance of the right which has been restricted, namely the ability to bring or progress a civil or criminal action, only the High Court has jurisdiction to hear the application.

---

26 See above, r 3.

CHAPTER 24

OFFERS TO SETTLE AND PAYMENTS INTO COURT

INTRODUCTION

The system of Part 36 offers to settle and payments into court is designed to put pressure on parties to settle disputes rather than litigate them.

Lord Woolf said, in his Final Report:

> My approach to civil justice is that disputes should, wherever possible, be resolved without litigation. Where litigation is unavoidable, it should be conducted with a view to encouraging settlement at the earliest appropriate stage.[1]

Part 36 offers and payments are an important part of the new ethos introduced as a result of Lord Woolf's Report.

Avoiding litigation and early settlements fall within the 'saving expense' part of the overriding objective[1a] (CPR r 1.1(2)(b)) and Part 36 offers and payments can be seen as one of the main tools in bringing these results about. Part 36 provides a mechanism for a party, the offeror, to make an offer or payment to settle a dispute which, if rejected by the opponent, the offeree, and the case proceeds to trial, can be used as an indicator as to whether those proceedings were a waste of time and money.

If at trial judgment is given which is the same as or less than the terms or amount of the Part 36 offer or payment, then, on the face of it, the offeree will have wasted expense for both parties in litigating the matter rather than accepting the Part 36 offer or payment. Therefore, Part 36 provides that such a party will be penalised for the wasted expense in taking the case to trial through costs or interest penalties unless it would be 'unjust to do so'. The nature of the penalties imposed depends on whether the party is claimant or defendant. The risk of incurring those penalties operates as a tremendous pressure on parties to settle rather than litigate disputes.

However, as might be expected under the ethos of the new rules, the decision of the court as to whether a party should be subject or entitled to the costs and other penalties provided by Part 36 is not simply based on a 'mathematical' test of whether the offer or payment is better or worse than that ordered at trial. Rather, a Part 36 offer or payment will be viewed against the backdrop of the litigation as a whole and the conduct of the parties, particularly relevant in this context being the behaviour of the parties in

---

1 See *Access to Justice*, Final Report, Chapter 10, p 107, para 2 (www.lcd.gov.uk/civil/finalfr.htm).

1a See Chapter 5, Judicial Case Management: The Overriding Objective.

disclosing material matters. Therefore, a party can only be confident of obtaining the advantages provided by the system of Part 36 offers to settle and payments into court if they have given full disclosure of all relevant evidence and information about their case so that the other side can make an informed decision whether to make or accept such an offer.[2]

The position relating to Part 36 offers has been complicated somewhat by the fact that, under Part 44[3] the court, when dealing with costs, can consider any offer (or lack of offer) made in the action (not just as to costs) whether or not it is Part 36 compliant.[4]

Definitions and terminology

As with all other provisions under the new rules, the system for payments into court and offers to settle are identified by the part of the rules which governs them, in this case, Part 36. The types of offer that can be made under Part 36 are referred to as 'Part 36 offers' and 'Part 36 payments' (r 36.2(1)). The distinction between Part 36 offers to settle and Part 36 payments into court and the circumstances when each can be used should be clearly made.

A Part 36 payment is made only by parties in the position of a defendant and involves the payment of a sum of money into the Court Funds Office with notification to the claimant that this is the amount by which the defendant is prepared to settle the action (r 36.2(1)(a)). Parties in the position of a defendant include a claimant in his capacity as defendant to a counterclaim or third party claim under Part 20,[5] and the reference to a defendant in this chapter should be taken to include these parties (r 20.3).

A Part 36 offer involves a written offer to settle the action on terms which may include the offer of a sum of money, but without actually paying that sum of money to the party or into court. A Part 36 offer may also consist of or include a non-monetary remedy, such as the giving of an undertaking (r 36.2(1)(b)). Part 36 offers can be made both by claimants and defendants; for the latter, only in respect of non-money claims (r 36.3(1)).

The party who makes a Part 36 offer or payment is known as the 'offeror' (r 36.2(2)) and the party to whom it is made is known as the 'offeree' (r 36.2(3)).

---

2   For an indication as to how the court approaches such considerations, see *Ford v GKR Construction* [2000] 1 All ER 802, below, p 298.

3   See r 44.3(4)(a) and (c), r 44.5(3)(a) and Chapter 33, Costs.

4   See below, p 301.

5   See Chapter 12, Part 20 Claims.

General overview of the operation of the system

Part 36 payments and Part 36 offers can only be made once proceedings have started (r 36.2(4)). However, there is also provision to make a pre-action offer to settle, which will be taken into account by the court so long as it complies with the provisions of r 36.10, but only in relation to the question of costs.[6] Once proceedings have started, a party can make a Part 36 offer or a Part 36 payment at any time (r 36.2(4)(a)). A Part 36 offer or payment can also be made in appeal proceedings (r 36.2(4)(b)).

If the defendant makes a Part 36 offer or payment which is accepted by the claimant, or the claimant makes a Part 36 offer which is accepted by the defendant (in both cases within the specified timescale), the claimant will be entitled to his costs of the proceedings up to the date of acceptance of the Part 36 offer or payment (rr 36.13–36.15).

If a party makes a pre-action offer to settle or Part 36 offer or payment there is nothing to stop the other party making a counter-offer in response. Each offer or payment will then separately have the potential consequences provided for by Part 36 so long as it fulfils the necessary formalities.

Importance of procedure

If an offeror makes a Part 36 offer or payment which is not accepted by the offeree, if the case goes on to trial and the offeree fails to better the Part 36 offer or payment, costs and interest consequences are likely to follow (the particular consequence depending on whether the offeree is claimant or defendant). In general terms, if the offer or payment is in accordance with the rules it *will* have the costs or other consequences specified by Part 36 *unless* the court considers it unjust to make such an order (rr 36.20 and 36.21).

Although a party is free to decide not to follow the procedure under Part 36 and to make an offer to settle in whatever way he chooses, such an offer to settle will only have the costs or other consequences specified by Part 36 if the court so orders (r 36.1(2)). On the other hand, when exercising its discretion whether to order costs, the court must take into account any payment into court or admissible offer to settle which has been drawn to its attention, whether or not the payment or offer has been made in accordance with Part 36 (r 44.3(4)).[7]

However, once proceedings have started, if the claim is for money, in order to have the consequences set out in Part 36, a defendant who wants to

---

6   See below, p 278.
7   See Chapter 33, Costs and p 301, below.

make a Part 36 offer or payment must do so by way of a Part 36 payment (r 36.3(1)). In those circumstances, the court would have no power under the rules to order that the consequences provided for by Part 36 apply in favour of a defendant who makes a Part 36 offer where it is a monetary claim and therefore a Part 36 payment is required. Although a defendant can make a pre-action offer to settle a monetary claim, which obviously would not involve a payment into court, within a certain time after proceedings have started, the defendant must turn that offer to settle into a Part 36 payment for it to have the cost consequences specified by the rules (r 36.10(3)).

Small claims

A Part 36 offer or payment will not have the costs or other consequences provided for by that part while the claim is being dealt with on the small claims track, unless the court orders otherwise (rr 36.2(5) and 27.2). Therefore, although a party is not prohibited from making a Part 36 offer or payment in cases dealt with on the small claims track, it will depend on the exercise of the court's discretion whether the costs or other consequences would be ordered against an offeree who fails to better the offer. It is submitted that in the light of the 'no costs rule' applicable to cases heard on the small claims track, the court is only likely to make such an order in exceptional circumstances, perhaps when a party is guilty of unreasonable behaviour such as would justify the court making a costs order against the unreasonable party in any event.[8]

Rule 36.2(5) provides that the restriction on Part 36 applying to small claims hearings only applies while the claim is 'being dealt with' on the small claims track. This suggests that this restriction will cease to apply if the claim is subsequently reallocated to another track.

PRE-ACTION OFFERS TO SETTLE

Before proceedings have started, parties can make pre-action offers to settle which the court will take into account when making any order as to costs so long as the offer complies with the provisions of r 36.10. The provisions of r 36.10 are that the offer must:

- be expressed to be open for at least 21 days after the date it was made;

---

8   See Chapter 16, The Small Claims Track, for details of the costs rules for small claims track cases.

- if made by a person who would be a defendant if proceedings were started, include an offer to pay the costs of the offeree incurred up to the date 21 days after the date it was made; and
- otherwise comply with Part 36 (r 36.10(2)).

Rule 36.10 provides that the offer is made on the date it was received by the offeree (r 36.10(5)). Therefore, this will be the actual date of receipt without taking into account any deemed time for service. There is no requirement that a pre-action offer to settle must be in writing, although in practice most will be. The last requirement 'otherwise comply with Part 36' is vague, and it is uncertain what it means. However, it is submitted that it covers such matters as making clear whether the offer includes interest or whether it takes into account any counterclaim.[9]

Significance of pre-action offer once proceedings started

Therefore, if an offer to settle is made in accordance with r 36.10 but rejected by the offeree and proceedings are started, the offer to settle will be taken into account by the court when any order for costs is made even if no further Part 36 offer or payment is made. However, if the offeror is a defendant to a money claim, in order to have the consequences specified by Part 36, he must turn that offer to settle into a Part 36 payment within 14 days of service of the claim form. Further, the Part 36 payment must be for at least the same amount or more than the sum specified in the offer to settle (r 36.10(3).

If the defendant makes a pre-action offer to settle and the claimant subsequently starts proceedings, the claimant is restricted in his freedom to accept the offer or any Part 36 payment without the permission of the court (r 36.10(4)). The claimant would therefore need to have a good reason for wanting to accept the offer or payment after he had implicitly rejected it by starting proceedings; with all its attendant cost both to the parties and the court system. This rule gives the court the opportunity to decide whether starting proceedings was an unreasonable step for the claimant to take rather than accepting the offer or payment which he now seeks to take.

In these circumstances, the claimant would have to make an application to the court in accordance with Part 23[10] to accept the offer or payment, thus giving the court the opportunity to decide whether the claimant should be deprived of his costs or ordered to pay some or all of the defendant's costs. If the claimant simply thinks better of carrying on with proceedings, having originally rejected the defendant's pre-action offer to settle, the likely order the

---

9   For these and other requirements, see the following sections on Part 36 offers and payments.
10 See Chapter 19, Making Applications for Court Orders.

court will make is an order that the defendant be awarded costs from the time when the claimant rejected the pre-action offer to settle (although the claimant is likely to be awarded the costs incurred before then). On the other hand, it may be that a defendant only discloses relevant documents at a late stage after proceedings have been commenced which, if revealed earlier, would have caused the claimant to accept the offer. In the latter situation, it may well be reasonable for the claimant to seek to accept the offer after proceedings were commenced and be entitled to an award of costs on the basis that it was not unreasonable for the claimant to reject the earlier offer in the absence of the subsequently disclosed documents.

MAKING A PART 36 PAYMENT INTO COURT

The general rule is that, once proceedings have started,[11] if the claimant's claim is for money and the defendant would like to make an offer to settle which would have the costs consequences provided by Part 36, if not accepted by the claimant, the offer must be made by way of a Part 36 payment (r 36.3). This is a strict rule subject only to two minor qualifications.[12] Therefore, although the court has a discretion to take into account offers to settle which do not comply with the provisions of Part 36, if the claim is for money, the court would have no power to make the costs orders provided by r 36.20 if the sum offered in settlement by the defendant has not been paid into court in accordance with Part 36.

Where the claimant's claim includes both a monetary and non-monetary element and the defendant wants to settle the whole claim, there is a special procedure which must be followed,[13] but basically the defendant must make a Part 36 payment in respect of the monetary element (r 36.4(2)).

Like a Part 36 offer, a Part 36 payment can only be made once proceedings have started, but one can be made at any time after proceedings have started and one can be made in appeal proceedings (r 36.3(2)). A Part 36 payment can be improved at any time and as many times as required.

---

11 See above, p 278, for offers by the defendant to settle a money claim made before proceedings are started.

12 See below, p 283.

13 See below, p 287.

Procedural requirements

A defendant who wishes to make a Part 36 payment must file at court a Part 36 payment notice (r 36.6(2)) and the payment. Payment should usually be made by cheque and there are different formalities depending on whether the money is paid in to the county court/district registry or to the Royal Courts of Justice (See PD 36, para 4.1 for details). Form N242A may be used for the Part 36 payment notice, but it is not a prescribed form. However, in order to be a valid Part 36 payment notice, the notice must comply with the following requirements. It must:

- state the amount of the payment (r 36.6(2)(a));
- state that it is a Part 36 payment (PD 36, para 5.1(1));
- be signed by the offeror or his legal representative (PD 36, para 5.1(2)). If the Part 36 payment is made by a company or other corporation, in accordance with the general scheme under the CPR, a person holding a senior position in the company or corporation may sign on the offeror's behalf, but that person must state what position he holds (PD 36, para 5.5);
- state whether the payment relates to the whole claim or to part of it or to any issue that arises in it and if so, to which part or issue (r 36.6(2)(b)). Therefore, the defendant can either make a payment which relates to the whole of the claimant's case or just part of it. However, the defendant must state whether the payment is in whole or part settlement of the claimant's case and if it is in part settlement, he must specifically identify which issue or issues he is offering to settle;
- state whether it takes into account any counterclaim (r 36.6(2)(c)). If the defendant is making a counterclaim, the claimant would obviously need to know if the defendant is also offering to settle the counterclaim at the same time and whether the amount paid in is only in respect of the claimant's claim or is the difference between the claimant's claim and the defendant's counterclaim. If the defendant did not have to so specify, as a counterclaim is treated as an independent claim in its own right (r 20.3), the claimant may unwittingly accept the sum paid in without realising that this does not bring an end to the dispute, as he still has to defend the defendant's counterclaim against him;
- if an interim payment has been made, state that the defendant has taken into account the interim payment (r 36.6(2)(d)). If the defendant has already made an interim payment, a claimant would need to know if the sum paid in is a clear sum in addition to the interim payment or if it is a sum which includes the amount already paid by way of interim payment;
- if it is expressed not to be inclusive of interest, give the details relating to interest set out in r 36.22(2), (r 36.6(2)(e)). If the Part 36 payment notice is silent as to interest, the sum offered will be treated as inclusive of all

interest up until the last day it could be accepted without needing the permission of the court (r 36.22(1)). However, if the sum offered is expressed not to include interest, the Part 36 payment notice must state whether interest is offered, and if it is give the amount offered, the rate or rates offered and the period or periods for which it is offered (r 36.22(2));

• provide certain additional information when benefit received by the claimant is recoverable under the Social Security (Recovery of Benefit) Act 1997 (r 36.23). In those cases where a claimant has received certain State benefits covering losses for which a defendant is liable, for example, where a claimant has been unable to work due to a personal injury and has been receiving income support, if the defendant makes a payment into court to settle the action which is accepted by the claimant, the defendant will be liable to repay the benefit received by the claimant to the Secretary of State in accordance with the Social Security (Recovery of Benefits) Act 1997.

Therefore in those cases, if the defendant makes a Part 36 payment, the Part 36 payment notice must specify the amount of gross compensation paid, the name and amount of any benefit by which that gross amount is reduced and that the sum paid in is the net figure after deduction of the amount of the benefit (r 36.23(3)). If the claimant does not accept the Part 36 payment in, it will be the gross figure that the claimant has to beat in order to avoid the costs consequences under Part 36 (r 36.23(4)). In those cases where a claimant has or may have obtained recoverable State benefits, the defendant must obtain from the Secretary of State a certificate of recoverable benefits which specifies the type and amount of recoverable benefit the claimant has received. When making the Part 36 payment in, the defendant must file in court the certificate of recoverable benefits with the Part 36 payment notice (PD 36, para 10.1(2)).

Service of a Part 36 payment notice

There is a presumption that the court will serve a Part 36 payment notice on the claimant, unless the defendant elects to serve it himself. When the defendant files the notice and money into court, the court will serve the notice on the claimant unless the defendant informs the court that he will serve the notice himself (r 36.6(3). If the defendant serves the notice, he must also serve a certificate of service[14] (r 36.6(4)). The usual rules on service apply.[15]

---

14 See Chapter 9, Service of Documents.
15 *Ibid.*

Qualifications to Part 36 payment in monetary claims

As was stated above, the almost invariable rule is that where the claimant is making a monetary claim and the defendant wants to rely on the costs consequences provided by Part 36, he must make a Part 36 payment (r 36.3). However, this general rule is subject to two minor qualifications.

- *Interim payments*

  First, if a defendant has made an interim payment to the claimant and decides not to offer any further sum in settlement of the action, he can make a Part 36 offer based on the interim payment (r 36.5(5)). Clearly, this exception will be of limited use, as almost by definition, an interim payment is of a sum which is less than the amount that the defendant believes he is liable for. Also, if the defendant wants to offer more than the amount provided by the interim payment, he must make a Part 36 payment of that additional sum in order to comply with r 36.3 and the payment in must state that it takes into account the interim payment (r 36.6(2)(d)). Thus, when a defendant has already made an interim payment to the claimant and decides to make that payment the final offer in settlement, then the defendant can make an offer to settle by reference to that interim payment without making any further payment into court. That offer to settle will, for all intents and purposes, be treated as if it were a payment into court in the sum of the interim payment.

- *Certificate of recoverable benefits*

  Secondly, in those cases where recoverable benefits have been paid to the claimant and the defendant has applied for, but not yet received, a certificate of recoverable benefits,[16] the defendant can make a Part 36 offer to settle a monetary claim which will have the costs consequences provided by Part 36 so long as he makes a Part 36 payment of that amount not more than seven days after he receives the certificate (r 36.23(2)(b)).

Split trial on liability and quantum

Where liability is denied by a defendant, the court can order that there be a separate trial on liability and then (if the claimant is successful) a separate assessment of the quantum of damages. This will often save expense, as time and costs will not have to be spent on the issue of the amount of damages until it is established whether the claimant will be successful. Where such an order is made, a defendant can make a Part 36 offer limited to accepting liability up to a specified proportion (r 36.5(4)). However, once (or even before) the trial on liability has been decided, in a money claim, the defendant

---

16 See above, p 282.

must make a Part 36 payment in order to claim the consequences under Part 36 if the claimant fails to better the payment at any subsequent hearing to determine the amount of damages to which the claimant is entitled.

Provisional damages

Where there is a risk that as a result of personal injury, the claimant may develop a serious disease or suffer some serious deterioration in his physical or mental condition, the claimant may seek additional damages to compensate for this risk. Alternatively, the claimant may make a claim for provisional damages[17] against the defendant. These apply where the claimant seeks a sum in damages from the defendant on the basis that he will not develop the disease or suffer the deterioration, but with the opportunity to return to court for further damages to be assessed if, within a specified timescale, in fact he goes on to develop the disease or suffer the deterioration. A defendant may make a Part 36 payment even when the claimant is also seeking provisional damages. However, when making a Part 36 payment in this type of case, the Part 36 payment notice must specify whether or not the defendant is offering to agree to the making of an award for provisional damages (r 36.7(1)).

If the defendant is offering to agree to the making of an award for provisional damages, the Part 36 payment notice must also state:

- that the sum paid into court is in satisfaction of the claim for damages on the assumption that the injured person will not develop the disease or suffer the type of deterioration specified in the notice;
- that the offer is subject to the condition that the claimant must make any claim for further damages within a limited period and state what that period is (r 36.7(3)).

If the claimant does accept the Part 36 payment, he will also be entitled to his costs of the action as provided by r 36.13 (r 36.7(4)). However, if the claimant accepts a Part 36 payment which includes an offer to agree to the making of an award for provisional damages, he must apply to the court within seven days of accepting the payment for the court to make an order for the award of provisional damages under r 41.2 (r 36.7(5)). At the same time as making the order, the court will also direct which documents are to be filed and preserved as the case file, which will be the basis for any future application for further damages (PD 41, para 2.1). The money in court will not be paid out until the court has dealt with the claimant's application for an award of provisional damages (r 36.7(6)).

---

17 See Chapter 25, Provisional Damages.

Court Funds Office deposit account

If a Part 36 payment is made but not accepted by the claimant within the time specified,[18] the money paid into court will be automatically placed on deposit by the Court Funds Office (Court Funds Rules 1987 r 31(1)). On any later payment out of the money, unless the parties agree otherwise, interest accruing up to the date of acceptance will be paid to the defendant and interest accruing as from the date of acceptance until payment out will be paid to the claimant (PD 36, para 7.10).

However, money paid into court which is accepted within the time specified will not be placed on deposit and will not accrue interest (Court Funds Rules 1987 r 32(4)).

Treating money paid into court as a Part 36 payment

The court has power to order a party to pay money into court in a variety of circumstances. It may be on the grounds that a party has without good reason failed to comply with a rule, practice direction or pre-action protocol (r 3.1(5))[19] or it may be as a condition for defending the action (r 3.1(3)).[20]

Where a defendant has been ordered to pay money into court under r 3.1(3) or r 3.1(5), he is entitled to treat the whole or any part of that sum as a Part 36 payment (r 37.2(1)). In order to do this, the defendant must file a Part 36 payment notice which will then be served on the other parties (r 37.2(2). The payment into court will then be treated like any other Part 36 payment into court which the claimant can accept in settlement of the action (r 37.2(3)).

The same provisions apply to a payment in made in accordance with a defence of tender before action (r 37.3).

MAKING A PART 36 OFFER

Part 36 offers to settle can be made by both the claimant and the defendant once proceedings have started.

As stated above, however, if the defendant is defending a money claim, he must make a Part 36 *payment* rather than a Part 36 offer (r 36.3). If the claim is not for a monetary remedy but instead for another remedy such as an

---

18 See below, p 290.
19 See Chapter 4, Pre-Action Protocols.
20 See Chapters 21, 22, and 5, Judgment in Default, Summary Judgment and Judicial Case Management: The Overriding Objective.

injunction or a boundary dispute, a defendant can make a Part 36 offer on terms which, if not accepted by the claimant who goes on to receive an order on the same or less advantageous terms after trial, will have the costs and other consequences provided for by Part 36.

A claimant can make a Part 36 offer to settle his own claim. That is, the claimant can offer to accept less money or less advantageous terms than he is claiming in his action and, if the defendant rejects this offer, the consequences provided for by Part 36 will apply unless the unless the court considers it unjust to make such an order.

Procedural requirements

In order to have the consequences specified by Part 36, a Part 36 offer must fulfil the following requirements:

- it must be in writing (r 36.5(1)). There is no prescribed form and it could be contained in a letter;
- the Part 36 offer must state that it is a Part 36 offer and be signed by the offeror or his legal representative[21] (PD 36, para 5.1);
- it must state whether it relates to the whole of the claim or to part of it or to an issue that arises in it and if so to which part or issue (r 36.5(3)(a)). Like a Part 36 payment, a Part 36 offer must state whether it is an offer to settle the whole claim or just part of it, and if only part of the claim, it must specifically identify which issue or issues it relates to;
- it must state whether it takes into account any counterclaim (r 36.5(3)(b)). Again, if the defendant is counterclaiming, the offeror must expressly state whether the terms offered take the counterclaim into account;
- if it is expressed not to be inclusive of interest, it must give the details relating to interest set out in r 36.22(2), (r 36.5(3)(a));
- if the Part 36 offer is silent as to interest, the sum offered will be treated as inclusive of all interest up until the last day it could be accepted without needing the permission of the court (r 36.22(1)). However, if the sum offered is expressed not to include interest, the Part 36 offer must state whether interest is offered, and if it is, give the amount offered, the rate or rates offered and the period or periods for which it is offered (r 36.22(2));
- if the Part 36 offer is made at least 21 days before the start of trial, it must state that it remains open for 21 days from the date it is made and also state that if the offeree does not accept it within those 21 days, the offer can

---

21 See above, p 281, for details as to who can sign on behalf of a company or corporation (PD 36, para 5.5).

only be accepted if the parties agree the liability for costs or the court gives permission (r 36.5(6));

- if the Part 36 offer is made less than 21 days before the start of the trial, it must state that it can only be accepted if the parties agree the liability for costs or the court gives permission (r 36.5(7)).

CLARIFICATION OF A PART 36 OFFER OR PART 36 PAYMENT NOTICE

The offeror must provide certain prescribed information when making a Part 36 offer or payment. This includes such matters as whether the offer or payment is in settlement of the whole of the claimant's case or is made only in respect of certain issues in the case and whether the offer or payment includes interest. It may be that the Part 36 offer or Part 36 payment notice is not entirely clear as to the basis on which it is made. In these circumstances, the offeree can request the offeror to clarify the offer or payment so long as they make this request within seven days of the offer or payment being made (r 36.9(1)).[22]

If the offeror does not voluntarily provide the information in clarification, so long as the trial has not started, the offeree can apply to the court for an order that such information is provided (r 36.9(2)). An application for clarification should be made in accordance with Part 23 (PD 36, para 6.2)[23] and should state in what respects the Part 36 offer or Part 36 notice of payment needs clarification (PD 36, para 6.3).

If the court makes an order that the offeror clarify the offer or payment, it will also specify the date when the Part 36 offer or payment is treated as having been made (r 36.9(3)). Therefore, if the offer needs to be clarified and the court makes an order to this effect, the court is also likely to order that the offer or payment be treated as having been made from the date when the clarified Part 36 offer was received, or the clarified Part 36 payment served, on the offeree.

CLAIMS FOR A MONEY AND A NON-MONEY REMEDY

A claimant may claim both a money remedy and a non-money remedy such as an injunction. It would be open to a defendant to make a Part 36 payment to settle just the monetary part of the claim or a Part 36 offer just to settle the

---

22   See below p 290, for time limits.
23   See Chapter 19, Making Applications for Court Orders.

non-monetary part of the claim. As set out earlier, the defendant's intentions as to whether it was the whole or part of the claim, and which part, that he was offering to settle must be specified in the Part 36 payment notice or Part 36 offer.[24] However, a defendant may, on the other hand, wish to settle the whole claim by means of both a Part 36 payment in respect of the monetary element of the claim and a Part 36 offer in respect of the non-monetary element of the claim. If so, the defendant must follow the procedure set out in r 36.4 in order for the offer to settle to have the consequences set out in Part 36.

Procedure

In order to settle the whole claim by means of a money offer in respect of the money claim and a non-money offer in respect of the non-money claim, the defendant must make a Part 36 payment in relation to the money claim and a Part 36 offer in relation to the non-money claim (r 36.4).

The Part 36 payment notice must identify the document which sets out the terms of the Part 36 offer and state that if the claimant gives notice of acceptance of the Part 36 payment, he will be treated as also accepting the Part 36 offer (r 36.4(3)). Then, if the claimant gives notice of acceptance of the Part 36 payment, he shall also be taken as giving notice of acceptance of the Part 36 offer in relation to the non-money claim (r 36.4(4)). In other words, the claimant cannot accept the Part 36 payment without also accepting the Part 36 offer.

Rule 36.4(4) does not expressly provide the same consequences if a claimant accepts the defendant's Part 36 offer (that is, that the Part 36 payment is also automatically accepted). In fact, the Practice Direction to Part 36 states that if the claimant accepts a Part 36 offer which is part of a defendant's offer to settle the whole of the claim, the claimant will be deemed to have accepted the offer to settle the whole of the claim (PD 36, para 7.11).

TIME WHEN A PART 36 OFFER OR PAYMENT IS MADE AND ACCEPTED

Part 36 puts a time limit on the ability of the offeree to accept a Part 36 offer or payment without the need for the parties to either reach an agreement as to the liability for costs or for the permission of the court to be obtained. It is therefore important to know when the time limit starts to run and when acceptance has occurred.

---

24 See above, pp 282 and 287.

Time when a Part 36 payment is made

Rule 36.8(2) states that a Part 36 payment is made when written notice of the payment into court is served on the offeree. This is further explained in the Part 36 Practice Direction as meaning that the Part 36 payment is made when the Part 36 payment notice is served on the offeree (PD 36, para 3.2). The defendant can expressly elect to serve the Part 36 payment notice himself, but failing that it will be served by the court (r 36.6(3)).[25] The usual rules as to service will apply.[26]

If the defendant increases the amount paid into court, the increase in the Part 36 payment will be effective when notice of the increase is served on the offeree (r 36.8(4) and PD 36, para 3.3).

Time when a Part 36 offer is made

A Part 36 offer is made when received by the offeree (r 36.8(1)), that is, whenever the written document setting out the Part 36 offer is actually received by the offeree. Therefore, the rules for service of documents and deemed dates for service set out in Part 6 do not apply – the Part 36 offer is simply made when the document containing it is received by the offeree.

If the offeror decides to improve the Part 36 offer, the improvement to the offer will be effective when its details are received by the offeree (r 36.8(3) and PD 36, para 2.5).

Acceptance of a Part 36 offer or payment

A Part 36 offer or Part 36 payment is accepted when notice of its acceptance is received by the offeror (r 36.8(5)). A notice of acceptance must be sent to the offeror and filed at court (PD 36, para 7.6). Court Form N243 can be used to accept the Part 36 payment, but it is not a prescribed form and there is no court form for acceptance of a Part 36 offer. What is prescribed is the information that must be contained in the notice of acceptance. The notice of acceptance must:

- set out the claim number;
- give the title of the proceedings;
- identify the Part 36 offer or Part 36 payment notice to which it relates; and
- must be signed by the offeree or his legal representative (PD 36, para 7.7).

---

25 See p 282, above.
26 See CPR Part 6 and Chapter 9, Service of Documents.

TIME LIMITS FOR ACCEPTANCE OF
A PART 36 OFFER OR PAYMENT

If the offeror makes a Part 36 offer or payment into court at least 21 days before the start of the trial, the offeree can accept it without the court's permission if the offeree gives the offeror written notice of acceptance not later than 21 days after the offer or payment was made (r 36.11(1) and r 36.12(1)).

If the offeree does not accept the offer or payment within this 21 day time period, the offeree cannot subsequently accept it unless the parties agree the liability for costs, or failing that the offeree obtains the permission of the court (r 36.11(2)(b)) and r 36.12(2)(b)).

Further, if the offeror makes a Part 36 offer or payment less than 21 days before the trial, the offeree cannot accept it without the permission of the court unless the parties agree what the costs consequences of acceptance will be (r 36.11(2)(a) and r 36.12(2)(a)).

If the court's permission is needed, it is obtained either by an application under Part 23[27] if made before trial, or by an application to the trial judge if made once the trial has started (PD 36, para 7.4). The court will then make an order regarding the costs of the action. The court has the discretion to make any order as to costs and this expressly includes the usual costs order which results when the claimant accepts a Part 36 offer or payment in (PD 36, para 7.4(2)).

A well timed and well pitched offer or payment exerts a tremendous pressure on the offeree to accept the offer within 21 days after it was made. Having rejected an offer, the offeree may lose confidence about the strength of their case, but will not be able to simply change his mind about taking the offer without negotiating some obstacles. In the case of a claimant rejecting a defendant's Part 36 offer or payment, it may be that the defendant is not prepared to pay all the claimant's costs up to the date of acceptance if the defendant has incurred further costs defending the action following the claimant's initial rejection of the offer or payment.

Unless the claimant agrees some other division of the costs burden with the defendant, the claimant will have to seek the court's permission to accept the offer and the court will decide where the costs liability will lie. The court may decide it was unreasonable for the claimant not to accept the offer or payment within the 21 days after it was made and that therefore the claimant should pay the additional costs incurred by the defendant after the offer was rejected.

In the case of an offer or payment made less than 21 days before the start of the trial, the practical effect of the rule is that it prevents a claimant from

---

27 See Chapter 19, Making Applications for Court Orders.

offering or accepting a relatively low sum at a late stage after substantial costs may have been incurred, and also being automatically entitled to recover the whole costs of the action on acceptance. The rule allows the court to consider the circumstances of each case and consider whether it was reasonable for a claimant to pursue an action so far and perhaps incur substantial costs for a relatively small sum. Of course, it may be that the circumstances are such that the claimant should be entitled to his costs of the action on acceptance in the usual way, but the rule operates as a safeguard in those cases where it would cause injustice if the usual rule were to apply.

Obtaining payment out of a Part 36 payment

If a claimant accepts a Part 36 payment, the claimant obtains payment out of the sum paid into court by filing a request for payment with the court in Practice Form 243 (r 36.16 and PD 36, para 8.1).

Certain information must be provided on Form 243, such as the name, address and bank details of the legal representative acting on behalf of the claimant, or if the claimant does not have a legal representative, his own details. If the claimant is legally represented, the payment out can only be made to the legal representative. Additional requirements apply if the request for payment out is made to the Royal Courts of Justice (see PD 36, paras 8.1–8.5 for details).

Children and patients[28]

In the case of litigants acting under a disability, namely, a child[29] or a patient,[30] the court must approve any settlement made on their behalf (r 21.10). Therefore, if a Part 36 offer or payment is made in such proceedings, the court's permission must be obtained before it can be accepted. Further, a court order is needed before the sum paid into court can be paid out (r 36.18).

The application for approval is made in accordance with Part 23 (PD 36, para 7.8).

---

28 See Chapter 26, Special Rules for Children and Patients.

29 A person under 18 years old: r 21.1(2)(a).

30 A person who by reason of a mental disorder within the meaning of the Mental Health Act 1983 is incapable of managing and administering his own affairs: r 21.1(2)(b).

PRIVILEGE OF OFFER/PAYMENT

There are restrictions on disclosure to the court of the fact that a Part 36 offer or payment has been made, or its contents, until all relevant questions of liability and quantum have been decided. The basis for this rule is that it is public policy to encourage parties to settle disputes rather than litigate them and it is thought that a party would be reluctant to try and compromise an action if statements or offers made in the course of such negotiations for settlement could be relied upon at trial as admissions of liability and quantum. Negotiations for settlement are, therefore, protected from disclosure by privilege.

The details of any offer or payment are usually put in a sealed envelope in the court file so that any judge dealing with the matter, especially the trial judge, will not be aware of it, although, by seeing the envelope, he may well be aware that an offer or payment has been made. On a case management conference[31] the judge is likely, in any event, to ask if any offers or payments in have been made as part of his general case management powers and with a view to encouraging the parties to settle. If details are given, the judge should then disqualify himself from dealing with any trial if the action is not settled. Similarly, the court's computerised history of the action, a copy of which is often on the court file or called for by the judge, will not contain any details of any offer or payment.

Part 36 offer

A Part 36 offer is to be treated as 'without prejudice except as to costs' (r 36.19(1)). The glossary to the CPR is not very illuminating and explains the phrase as meaning 'the circumstances in which the content of those negotiations may be revealed to the court are very restricted'. This phrase has been held to mean that the privilege by which such an offer to settle is protected from disclosure is modified so that there is a right to refer to the offer on the issue of costs.[32] Further, it has also been established that such offers, not being unreservedly 'without prejudice', can also be admissible in other circumstances if the fact that such an offer had been made was relevant, for instance in interlocutory matters such as an application for security for costs.[33]

The nature of the protection given to such offers should be distinguished from fully 'without prejudice' offers. As a rule of evidence, the latter cannot be revealed to the court at all, at any stage of the proceedings, except with the

---

31 See Chapter 18, The Multi-Track, p 199.
32 See *Cutts v Head* [1984] 2 WLR 349.
33 See *Simaan General Contracting Co v Pilkington Glass Ltd* [1987] 1 All ER 345.

consent (or by waiver) of both parties or to prove that a settlement has been reached if this is disputed.[34]

Therefore, if a party makes a Part 36 offer, although it will not be admissible to the trial judge, until all questions of liability and quantum have been determined, it will be admissible when the issue of costs comes to be decided. It is also likely that it will be admissible at interim hearings, even before the question of liability and quantum have been decided, if it would be appropriate and relevant for it to be revealed to the court.

Part 36 payment

Rule 36.19(2) provides that the fact that a Part 36 payment has been made shall not be communicated to the trial judge until all questions of liability and the amount of money to be awarded have been decided. This restriction is equivalent to that applied to disclosure of an offer made 'without prejudice except as to costs'. Therefore, as the rule specifically refers to only the trial judge, it would seem there is no general restriction on communication to a judge at an interim hearing where the fact of a payment in may be relevant to such matters as whether security for costs should be ordered or the size of an interim payment. This would be consistent with the former practice under the old rules and the expected position with Part 36 offers.

Rule 36.19(3) also expressly modifies any privilege from disclosure in the following circumstances:

- where the defence of tender before claim has been raised;
- where the proceedings have been stayed because a Part 36 offer or payment has been accepted;
- where the issue of liability has been determined before any assessment of the money claimed and the fact that there has or has not been a Part 36 payment may be relevant to the question of the costs of the issue of liability.

COSTS CONSEQUENCES OF ACCEPTANCE OF A PART 36 OFFER OR PAYMENT

Where the defendant makes a Part 36 offer or payment or the claimant makes a Part 36 offer which is of a type which can be freely accepted within a 21 day period,[35] and it is accepted by the claimant or defendant respectively, the claimant will be entitled to his costs of the proceedings up to the date of

---

34   See *Unilever v Procter & Gamble* [1999] 2 All ER 691.
35   See above, p 290.

service of the notice of acceptance (rr 36.13(1) and 36.14). In these circumstances, a costs order will be deemed to have been made in the claimant's favour which, if necessary, the claimant can apply to enforce (r 44.12(b) and (c)).

If the Part 36 offer or payment can only be accepted if the parties agree the liability for costs or the court gives permission, and the parties fail to reach an agreement, if the offeree applies for permission which is granted, the court will also make an order as to costs (r 36.11(3) and r 36.12(3)). The court will have a discretion as to the costs order to be made in all the circumstances of the case (see Part 44).[36]

If the Part 36 offer or payment relates to part only of the claim and the claimant abandons the rest of the action, although usually the claimant will still be entitled to the costs of the action up to the date of service of the notice of acceptance, in the circumstances, the court can make another order as to costs (r 36.13(2)). This will cover the situation where a claimant abandons a substantial part of his case, as it may well not be reasonable to do that without incurring any costs liability if substantial costs have been incurred pursuing that part of the action.

The costs will include the claimant's costs in defending a counterclaim (if any) if the Part 36 offer or Part 36 payment notice states that it takes into account the defendant's counterclaim (r 36.13(3)). Obviously, if the counterclaim is not also settled at the same time, this will continue as a separate action with an independent costs liability.

If the parties cannot agree a figure for the claimant's costs, on acceptance of a Part 36 offer or payment, the claimant will be entitled to costs on the standard basis (r 36.13(4)).[37] In those cases where the court's permission is needed to accept the Part 36 offer and the court makes an order for costs, the court will also decide whether those costs are to be payable on the standard or indemnity basis (see Part 44).[38]

Interest on costs

The claimant is also entitled to interest on costs paid on acceptance of a Part 36 offer or payment under s 17 of the Judgments Act 1838 (for High Court cases) and s 74 of the County Courts Act 1984 at the statutory rate of interest which is currently 8%.[39]

---

36 See Chapter 33, Costs.
37 *Ibid.*
38 *Ibid.*
39 See the Judgment Debts (Rate of Interest) Order 1993 SI 1993/564.

THE EFFECT ON THE PROCEEDINGS OF ACCEPTANCE OF A PART 36 OFFER OR PAYMENT

If a Part 36 offer or payment which relates to the whole claim is accepted, the claim will be stayed (r 36.15(1)). As the glossary to the rules states, a stay imposes a halt on proceedings.

Although the claim has been stayed, it is expressly provided that this will not affect the court's power to enforce the terms of a Part 36 offer, order payment out of the sum paid into court, or to deal with any question of costs relating to the proceedings (r 36.15(5)).

Although the action has been halted, it must be remembered that it is not a final judgment in the action and a stay can always be lifted. However, it would only be in exceptional circumstances that the court would allow a claimant to lift the stay and continue pursuing an action once an offer or payment in compromise of the action has been accepted; an example being where an agreement to settle has been induced by fraud.

Part 36 payment

In the case of a Part 36 payment, as the money is securely in court, on acceptance the Court Funds Office will simply pay the money out to the claimant.[40] Having accepted money paid into court and the proceedings having been stayed, the claimant would be unable to continue pursuing the action unless the court lifted the stay. As stated above, this would only be granted in exceptional circumstances. Moreover, if the claimant started fresh proceedings based on the same action, the defendant would, in most cases, be able successfully to apply for the new proceedings to be struck out as an abuse of process.[41]

Part 36 offer

If a Part 36 offer which relates to the whole claim is accepted, the claim will be stayed (r 36.15(1)). Both parties can seek to enforce the terms of a Part 36 offer by simply applying to the court without the need to start a separate action to enforce the compromise (r 36.15(2)). Somewhat repetitively, r 36.15(6) provides that where a Part 36 offer has been accepted and one party alleges that the other has not honoured the terms of the offer, and he is therefore entitled to a remedy for breach of contract, he may apply to the court for the

---

40 See above, p 291.
41 See Chapter 23, Striking Out.

remedy without having to start a new claim (unless the court orders otherwise). Therefore, although the Part 36 offer and acceptance will be binding as a contract between the parties, if either side fails to abide by the terms, the other party can apply to the court to enforce them without having to start entirely separate proceedings based on breach of contract.

Acceptance of Part 36 offer or payment relating to part only of the claim

If the Part 36 offer or payment relates to part only of the claimant's claim, the claim will be stayed as to that part only and unless the parties agree the liability for costs, these will be decided by the court (r 36.15(3)).

MULTIPLE DEFENDANTS

Where a claimant is suing more than one defendant and the defendants' jointly make a Part 36 offer or payment, which the claimant accepts, the usual costs and other consequences will apply as if there was only one defendant to the claim. Therefore, the claimant will be able to enforce the Part 36 offer and the deemed costs order against one or all of the defendants. However, the position is more complicated when the claimant wishes to accept a Part 36 offer or payment made by one or more, but not all, of a number of defendants. The relevant rules which apply depend on whether, on the one hand, the defendants are sued jointly or in the alternative, or on the other hand whether they are sued on the basis of several liability.

If the defendants are sued *jointly* (that is, both deemed to be liable) or in the *alternative* (that is, either claimed to be liable), the claimant can accept the Part 36 offer or payment (within the specified timescale) without needing the permission of the court so long as he:

- discontinues his claim against those defendants who have not made the offer or payment; and
- those defendants give written consent to the acceptance of the offer or payment (r 36.17(2)).

On the other hand, if the defendants are sued on the basis of *several* liability, the claimant can accept a Part 36 offer or payment (within the specified timescale) made by one or more, but not all, of the defendants without needing the permission of the court and continue with his claims against the other defendants, if he is still entitled to (r 36.17(3)).

If the claimant wants to accept a Part 36 offer or payment made by one or more, but not all, of the defendants in other circumstances to those set out in r 36.17(2) and (3) or outside of the specified timescale for acceptance, the claimant must apply to the court for an order permitting a payment out to him of any sum in court and such order as to costs as the court considers appropriate (r 36.17(4)).

WITHDRAWING A PART 36 OFFER OR PAYMENT

An offeror is free to withdraw a Part 36 offer, before it has been accepted, but if it is withdrawn it will not have the consequences provided by Part 36 (r 36.5(8)).

However, once a Part 36 payment is made, it can only be withdrawn by the defendant with the permission of the court (r 36.6(5)). A defendant should, therefore, consider very carefully the timing and amount of any payment into court as, once made, the presumption is that the claimant will be free to accept it (within the time limits) along with payment of his costs. In the usual course of events, it will be very unlikely for a defendant to have any desire to withdraw his payment in. The most likely reason why a defendant would wish to do so is if new evidence comes to light or there is a change in the law which puts a different complexion on the claimant's case than it had at the time when the defendant made the payment in. In the case of new evidence, it is likely that the court will have to be persuaded that it is new evidence and not simply evidence that the defendant could have, but did not obtain, before he made the payment in.

Whatever the reason for wanting to withdraw a payment in, the court will have to be persuaded that, in accordance with the overriding objective (see Chapter 5, Judicial Case Management: The Overriding Objective), it would be fair to allow a defendant to withdraw money previously paid into court. The rule applies even if the claimant does not accept the payment in within the time allowed without needing the permission of the court. However, if the claimant has not accepted within that timescale, it will be easier for a defendant to justify withdrawing a payment, as the claimant cannot accept it in any event unless the parties agree the liability for costs or the court gives permission.

REJECTION OF A PART 36 OFFER OR PAYMENT

If the offeree rejects a Part 36 offer or payment, the action is pursued to trial and the offeree fails to better the offer or payment, the costs and other consequences as provided by Part 36 will then come into play. What those consequences may be will depend on whether the offeree is claimant or defendant. Often, both claimant and defendant will have made a Part 36 offer or payment and then various outcomes may be possible, depending on which party has beaten what.

Claimant fails to better defendant's Part 36 offer or payment

If, at trial, the claimant is successful, but in a money claim is awarded a sum in damages the same as or less than the defendant's Part 36 payment, or in a non-money claim the judgment is for the same or a less advantageous remedy than that offered by the defendant's Part 36 offer, the defendant will usually be entitled to the costs consequences provided by Part 36. Rule 36.20 provides that, unless the court considers it unjust to do so, the court will order that the claimant pay all of the defendant's costs incurred from the latest date on which the claimant could have accepted the Part 36 offer or payment without needing the permission of the court.

This is often referred to as a 'split' order as to costs. This means that although the defendant is likely to be ordered to pay the claimant's costs incurred up to the last date for acceptance of the Part 36 offer or payment, the claimant will usually be ordered to pay the defendant's costs incurred thereafter. As the defendant's costs will, at this stage, include the costs of trial, they are likely to be substantial.

Although the rule is in mandatory terms, that is, that the court 'will' order the claimant to pay the defendant's costs in these circumstances, this is subject to the qualification 'unless the court considers it unjust to do so'. This gives the court the scope to make a different costs order in relation to the defendant's costs incurred after the claimant rejected the defendant's Part 36 offer or payment.

An example of a case where the defendant made a Part 36 payment which exceeded the claimant's award of damages, but was nevertheless ordered to pay the claimant's costs, and not granted a 'split' order for costs under r 36.20 because the court decided that it would be unjust to grant the defendant such an order is *Ford v GKR Construction*.[42] This was a personal injuries action where the defendant took the opportunity, during an adjournment of the trial, to employ inquiry agents to carry out secret video surveillance of the claimant. This video evidence clearly showed that the claimant was able to do more things than she had admitted in her testimony. The defendants were given leave to adduce this evidence at trial and, as a result, the judge awarded the claimant less damages than the amount of the defendant's payment into court. However, when it came to making an order for costs, the judge refused to grant the defendant the split order as to costs provided by r 36.20. The judge

---

42 [2000] 1 All ER 802.

decided – and his decision was upheld by the Court of Appeal – that it would be unjust to make the costs order in the defendant's favour provided by r 36.20 because the defendant had behaved unreasonably in obtaining and disclosing evidence which undermined the claimant's case only at a late stage in the proceedings. In the absence of this evidence, the claimant was not in a position to assess whether she should accept the defendant's payment into court at the time when it was made.

The Court of Appeal emphasised in this case that the parties must provide each other with as much information about their case as possible as early as possible so that an offeree can make an informed decision as to whether to accept a Part 36 offer or payment. This case underlines the philosophy behind the CPR for openness and co-operation between the parties. It also places an onus on parties to prepare their cases fully at an early stage, or run the risk of being effectively penalised under the rules for late preparation.

However, it should be stressed that the presumption is that it will be quite rare for a defendant to be deprived of the costs penalties against a claimant under r 36.20 when the claimant fails to better a Part 36 offer or payment. Lord Woolf, in *Ford v GKR*, stated that the provisions of rr 36.20 and 36.21 provide the 'usual consequences of not accepting an offer which, when judged in the light of the litigation, should have been accepted'.

Defendant fails to better claimant's Part 36 offer

A defendant 'betters' a claimant's Part 36 offer by being ordered to pay less money to the claimant at trial or where the judgment awarded to the claimant is on less advantageous terms than the claimant's proposals in his Part 36 offer. If at trial the defendant is held liable to the claimant for more, or the judgment against the defendant is more advantageous to the claimant than the proposals contained in a claimant's Part 36 offer, the court will order the consequences against the defendant provided by r 36.21 unless it considers it unjust to do so (r 36.21(4)). It should be born in mind that the claimant will be entitled to damages from the defendant in any event and, in most cases, interest and costs as well if he is successful at trial, but when a defendant also fails to better the claimant's Part 36 offer, the defendant also becomes subject to the penalties provided by Part 36. The defendant may be liable for all or any of the following:

- in a money claim, the defendant may be ordered to pay the claimant interest on any sum of money awarded (not including interest) at a higher rate than usual, but not exceeding 10% above base rate, for some or all of the period starting with the latest date on which the defendant could have accepted the offer without needing the permission of the court (r 36.21(2));

- an order to pay the claimant's costs on the indemnity basis[43] from the latest date when the defendant could have accepted the offer without needing the permission of the court (r 36.21(3)(a)); and

- interest on those costs at a rate not exceeding 10% above base rate (r 36.21(3)(b)).

The powers to award such penal interest on sums recovered or indemnity costs are in addition to the court's usual powers to award interest to the claimant (r 36.21(6)). However, r 36.21(6) was subsequently amended to make it clear that where the court awards interest under this rule on the same sum and over the same period as it awards interest under a different power, the total rate of interest awarded may not exceed 10% over base rate. The enhanced rate of interest provided for by CPR 36.21 is not a penalty, nor is it *ultra vires* the Civil Procedure Act 1997. The power to award enhanced interest is a power to sanction a party for failing to accept a reasonable offer.[44]

The consequences in r 36.21 will apply unless the court considers it unjust to make the orders. There would, therefore, seem to be a presumption that the claimant is entitled to the further orders unless the court is persuaded that it would be unjust to make them. The introduction of such additional penalties where a defendant fails to better a claimant's Part 36 offer are a major innovation of the new rules. Although the effect can be quite onerous for a defendant, the courts have made it clear that they are prepared to apply the rule in appropriate cases, recognising that by doing so this will also act as a deterrent to other litigants.[45]

Rule 36.21 contains a list of what the court may take into account when considering whether it would be unjust to make the order. Rule 36.21 provides that the court will take into account all the circumstances of the case including:

- the terms of any Part 36 offer;

- the stage in the proceedings when any Part 36 offer or payment was made;

- the information available to the parties at the time when the Part 36 offer or Part 36 payment was made; and

- the conduct of the parties with regard to the giving or refusing to give information for the purposes of enabling the offer or payment into court to be made or evaluated (r 36.21(5)).

Although only r 36.21 specifies this list of circumstances which the court will take into account when deciding whether it is unjust to make the order, it

---

43 See Chapter 33, Costs.

44 *All-In-One Design and Build Ltd v (1) Motcomb Estates Ltd (2) Whiteswan (Worldwide) Ltd* (2000) *The Times*, 4 April, Technology and Construction Court.

45 See *Richard Little and Others v George Little Sebire and Co* (1999) *The Times*, 17 November.

seems, in the light of *Ford v GKR*,[46] that the court will in fact carry out this exercise whenever it has to decide whether it is unjust to apply the costs or other penalties under either Part 36.20 or Part 36.21.

The interaction of Part 36 and Part 44

Rule 36.1(2) states that nothing in this Part prevents a party making an offer to settle in whatever way he chooses, but if that offer is not made in accordance with this Part, it will only have the consequences specified in this Part if the court so orders. Those last words make it clear that the court has a discretion to waive Part 36 requirements. This is reinforced by r 44.3, which deals with the circumstances to be taken into account by the court when exercising its discretion as to costs. Sub-paragraph 4(c) states that in deciding what order (if any) to make about costs, the court must have regard to all the circumstances, including any payment into court or admissible offer to settle made by a party which is drawn to the court's attention (whether or not made in accordance with Part 36).

This rather wide approach to the court's discretion has been tempered somewhat by the Court of Appeal in *Amber v Stacey*[47] in which they stated that there are compelling reasons of both principle and policy why those prepared to make genuine offers of monetary settlement should do so by way of Part 36 payments rather than by way of written offers. The Court of Appeal said that Part 36 payments offer greater clarity and certainty about: (a) genuineness, (b) ability to pay, (c) whether the offer was open or without prejudice, and (d) the terms on which the dispute could be settled.

Effect of claimant's Part 36 offer to settle where summary judgment obtained

It has been held in the case of *Petrotrade Inc v Texaco Ltd*[48] that r 36.21 does not apply where summary judgment is given as the provisions of that rule only have effect 'where at trial' the defendant is liable for more than the proposals contained in a claimant's Part 36 offer. In giving the judgment of the Court of Appeal in this case, Lord Woolf recognised that this may act as a temptation to claimants not to seek summary judgment in cases where it could otherwise be obtained so that higher rates of interest could be obtained at trial instead. However, he warned that such a course would be 'entirely contrary to the whole ethos and policy of the Civil Procedure Rules' and he was confident

---

46 [2000] 1 All ER 802.
47 (2000) LTL, 15 November, CA.
48 (2000) *The Times*, 14 June.

that if it was shown that such a tactic had been used, the court would use its ample powers to ensure that the claimant did not benefit from it.

Lord Woolf also stressed that the court always had power to order costs on an indemnity basis and to award interest at such rate as it considered just, this power being re-enacted in Part 44.[49] If this case had been decided by Lord Woolf at first instance, he would have been inclined to award additional interest at the rate of 4% above base rate for a period of 12 months as well as making an order for indemnity costs from the time of the Part 36 offer.

As the wording of r 36.20 is the same as r 36.21 in referring to 'trial', it would appear that the same provisions would apply if the claimant obtained summary judgment against the defendant, but was awarded terms less favourable or a sum less than the defendant's Part 36 offer or payment into court. In such circumstances, it seems a defendant could not rely on obtaining the costs benefit provided by r 36.20.

Claimant betters defendant's Part 36 offer or payment but fails to better own Part 36 offer

Under the terms of Part 36, so long as the claimant betters the defendant's Part 36 offer or payment, he will not be subject to any penalty under Part 36 if he does not also better his own Part 36 offer. In those circumstances, the usual costs order is likely to apply, namely that the defendant pay the claimant's costs of the action.

A claimant therefore has this advantage over a defendant. If a defendant makes his Part 36 offer or payment too low and it is not accepted by the claimant, he will suffer a disadvantage as he will fail to secure the 'split' order as to costs and, in all likelihood, end up paying the claimant's costs of the action. However, the claimant suffers no similar disadvantage if he makes his Part 36 offer too high. If the defendant rejects the claimant's Part 36 offer and the claimant does not better his offer at trial, there is no adverse consequence provided by Part 36 for the claimant.

As the claimant will have succeeded at trial, he is likely to recover his costs of the action from the defendant regardless of whether he also betters his Part 36 offer. However, this is not to say that the court will not take into account the fact that the claimant recovered less than his own Part 36 offer when exercising its discretion as to the making of costs orders under Part 44, although it is expressly provided in para 8.4 of PD 44 that this circumstance alone will not lead to a reduction in costs awarded to the claimant.[50]

---

49 But see *Amber v Stacey* (2000) LTL, 15 November, CA.
50 See Chapter 33, Costs.

CHAPTER 25

PROVISIONAL DAMAGES

INTRODUCTION

Definition

Under s 32A of the Supreme Court Act 1981 and s 51 of the County Courts Act 1984, in an action including a claim for damages for personal injuries in which there is a chance that at some time in the future the injured person will, as a result of his injuries, develop some serious disease or suffer some serious deterioration in his physical or mental condition, the court has the power to make a judgment awarding damages to the injured person on the assumption that he will not develop the disease or suffer the deterioration, but with an order that further damages will be awarded in the future if he does so. Such an award of damages is known as provisional damages (r 41.1(2)(c)).

If a claimant to a personal injuries case obtains evidence to show that a consequence of his injuries caused by the defendant is that he runs a risk of developing another disease or of suffering a deterioration in the future, he can either claim damages on a 'once and for all basis', which includes a sum in compensation for carrying this risk, or he can seek an order for provisional damages. A claimant in such circumstances will have to weigh up the advantages and disadvantages in seeking damages in full and final settlement, which include an element to compensate him for this risk, or whether to seek an order for provisional damages which will not give him any additional sum immediately, but which would allow him to make an application for further compensation if the disease or deterioration occurs in the future.

OBTAINING AN AWARD OF PROVISIONAL DAMAGES

Conditions for making an award of provisional damages

The court may make an order for an award of provisional damages if the particulars of claim includes a claim for them[1] and if the court is satisfied that s 32A of the Supreme Court Act 1981 or s 51 of the County Courts Act 1984 applies (r 41.2(1)). Therefore, it is important when drawing up proceedings to

---

1   See Chapter 11, Statements of Case.

consider whether a claim for provisional damages should be included as, after issue, it will be too late to add one, and there is no guarantee that the court will entertain an amendment to include it.

Terms of the order for provisional damages

The order for provisional damages must specify the disease or type of deterioration in respect of which an application for compensation can be made at a future date, and specify the period of time within which the application can be made (r 41.2(2)(a) and (b) and PD 41, para 2.1). The time period must be specified, but can be expressed as being for the duration of the claimant's life (PD 21, para 2.3).

An award of provisional damages can be made in respect of more than one type of disease or deterioration, and for each can specify different time periods within which an application can be made (r 41.2(2)(c)).

The Annex to PD 21 sets out a form for the terms of a provisional damages judgment (PD 21, para 2.6).

The case file

If an order for provisional damages is made, the court will make an award of immediate damages for the claimant's existing injuries and specify which documents are to filed and preserved as the case file in respect of any application for further damages (PD 41, para 2.1). The case file is likely to include such documents as a copy of the judgment, the statements of case, medical reports and a transcript of relevant parts of the claimant's evidence. If further orders are made, for instance, extending the time within which an application for further damages can be made, a copy will be added to the case file (PD 41, paras 3.2, 3.4). The associate or court clerk will endorse the court file to show that it contains the case file documents and in order to identify the period of time within which the case file documents must be preserved and preserve them in the court office where the proceedings took place (PD 41, para 3.3).

The Practice Direction expressly reminds legal representatives of their duty to preserve their own case file, which is sensible given the time period which may elapse before an application for further damages may be made (PD 41, para 3.6).

Agreeing provisional damages by consent

If the parties agree to compromise an action on grounds which include provisional damages, they should apply under Part 23[2] for an order to approve judgment by consent. The order for judgment by consent should contain the matters which would be specified in any court order for provisional damages following judgment[3] and a direction should be given specifying the documents to be preserved as the case file, and the documents specified should be lodged at court by the claimant or his legal representative (PD 41, paras 4.2, 4.3).

Applying for further damages

Once the time period specified by the order has expired, the claimant cannot apply for further damages in respect of the disease or deterioration under the order for provisional damages (r 41.3(1)). However, the claimant can make a number of applications to extend the time period originally specified (r 41.2(3)). It is likely that the claimant will have to establish grounds to justify making an extension of time and a current medical report should be filed at the time of making the application (PD 41, para 3.5).

A claimant is limited to making one application for further damages under the order for provisional damages (r 41.3(2)).

Procedure for applying for further damages

The claimant must give the defendant (and his insurers if known) at least 28 days' written notice of his intention to apply for further damages (r 41.3(3) and (4)).

Within 21 days after the end of the 28 day notice period, the claimant must apply to the court for directions (r 41.3(5)).

An application for further damages is made under Part 23[4] and follows the same procedure as that for applications for an interim payment[5] (r 41.3(6)). Therefore, a copy of the application notice must be served on the respondent at least 14 days before the hearing of the application and must be supported by evidence. The evidence must establish the claimant's entitlement to the further damages. The respondent to the application must file and serve any written evidence on which he intends to rely at least seven days before the

2   See Chapter 19, Making Applications for Court Orders.
3   See above, p 304, Terms of the order for provisional damages.
4   See Chapter 19, Making Applications for Court Orders.
5   See Chapter 20, Interim Remedies.

hearing of the application. If the applicant wishes to rely on written evidence in reply, he must file and serve a copy at least three days before the hearing (see r 25.6).

JUDGMENT IN DEFAULT WHERE PROVISIONAL DAMAGES CLAIMED

If the defendant fails to respond to the claimant's particulars of claim, which include a claim for provisional damages, the claimant cannot enter judgment in default under Part 12, unless he abandons his claim for provisional damages. Instead, if the claimant wishes to continue his claim for provisional damages, he should make an application under Part 23[6] to the master or district judge for directions (PD 41, para 5.1). The master or district judge will then direct the issues to be decided being, in most cases, whether the claim is an appropriate one for an award of provisional damages and the amount of immediate damages. If an award of provisional damages is made, provisions for the preservation of the case file will be made (PD 41, paras 5.2 and 5.3).

---

6   See Chapter 19, Making Applications for Court Orders.

CHAPTER 26

SPECIAL RULES FOR CHILDREN AND PATIENTS

INTRODUCTION

There are special rules governing proceedings involving children and patients which take account of the fact that such parties are usually not able to act on their own behalf and to ensure that any settlement is in their interests and for their benefit. In general, a child or patient acts through a litigation friend, who is usually a parent or guardian or someone else who is responsible for their welfare. If there is no such party, the Official Solicitor will be appointed to act as litigation friend.[1]

Under the old rules, children were referred to as 'infants' and a distinction was made between a 'next friend' and a 'guardian *ad litem*', the former acting for a claimant and the latter for a defendant. In accordance with the ethos of the reforms, the CPR introduced simplified and modernised terminology for the rules relating to children and patients, so, for instance, both now act through a litigation friend, whether they are bringing or defending proceedings.

DEFINITIONS

Child

A child is a person under 18 (r 21.1(2)(a)), replacing the expressions 'infant' and 'minor'. It is possible for a child also to be a patient, which may be relevant if the condition persists after they have ceased to be a child, especially with regard to any money awarded to the child.

Patient

A patient is a person who, by reason of a mental disorder within the meaning of the Mental Health Act 1983, is incapable of managing and administering his own affairs (r 21.1(2)(b)). 'Mental disorder' is defined by s 1(2) of the Mental Health Act 1983 as 'mental illness, arrested or incomplete development of mind, psychopathic disorder and any other disorder or disability of mind'.

---

1 See below, pp 308 and 310.

Thus, the definition is very wide. There are basically three categories of people who come within the definition: those with a mental illness, learning disabilities or brain damage.

The evidence of a medically qualified person is required for a diagnosis of a mental disorder and the court should not take that burden upon itself just because someone appears to be a difficult litigant. It may be necessary to stay proceedings until this issue has been resolved, with the court conducting an inquiry, on notice to the party in question, with appropriate medical evidence. Where there are difficulties in obtaining such evidence, the Official Solicitor may be consulted.[2]

Litigation friend

A litigation friend is a person who brings or defends proceedings on behalf of a child or patient. There may not be more than one for the child or patient in any particular proceedings.

A litigation friend has a duty to conduct proceedings fairly and competently on behalf of the child or patient. He must not have any interest in the proceedings adverse to the child or patient and every step and decision he takes in the proceedings must be for the benefit of the child or patient (PD 21, para 2.1). He is required by para 2.3 of PD 21 to state in the 'certificate of suitability' that he consents to act and knows or believes that party to be a child or patient.[3]

A litigation friend may be a parent or guardian, the person with whom a child or patient resides or who has care of him, or a person who is authorised under Part VII of the Mental Health Act 1983 to conduct proceedings on behalf of a patient. Alternatively, the litigation friend may be the Official Solicitor (so long as provision is made for his charges) (PD 21, para 3.6).

PROCEEDINGS BY OR AGAINST PATIENTS

A patient *must* have a litigation friend to bring or defend proceedings on his behalf (r 21.1(1)).[4]

---

2   See below, p 310.
3   See below, p 312.
4   Compare with children, below, p 309.

Title of proceedings involving a patient

The title of any proceedings involving a patient should give the name of the patient followed in brackets by the name of the litigation friend and the words, 'his/her litigation friend' (PD 21, para 1.3).

PROCEEDINGS BY OR AGAINST CHILDREN

A child must have a litigation friend to conduct proceedings on his behalf unless the court makes an order allowing the child to act on his own behalf (r 21.1(2) and (3)).

Application for an order permitting a child to act on his own behalf

The application for an order permitting the child to act on his own behalf must be made by the child himself. The application should be made in accordance with Part 23[5] and, if the child already has a litigation friend, must be made on notice to him, otherwise it should be made without notice (PD 21, para 21.2(4)).

However, if the court makes an order permitting a child to act without a litigation friend, but it subsequently becomes apparent that it is desirable for the child to have a litigation friend, the court may appoint a person to be the child's litigation friend (PD 21, para 21.2(5)).

Title of proceedings involving a child

If the child has a litigation friend, the title of the proceedings should give the name of the child followed in brackets by the words, 'a child by x his/her litigation friend' (PD 21, para 1.5(1)).

If the child is conducting proceedings on his own behalf, the child should be referred to in the title by his name followed in brackets by the words 'a child' (PD 21, para 1.5(2)).

---

5   See Chapter 19, Making Applications for Court Orders.

BECOMING A LITIGATION FRIEND

A person may not become a litigation friend for either a child or patient, whether by court order or under any other entitlement, unless he satisfies the following conditions:

- he can fairly and competently conduct proceedings on behalf of the child or patient;
- he has no interest adverse to that of the child or patient; and
- where the child or patient is a claimant, he undertakes to pay any costs which the child or patient may be ordered to pay in relation to the proceedings (subject to any right he may have to be repaid from the assets of the child or patient) (r 21.4(3)).

Order appointing a litigation friend

Under r 21.6, the court has the power to appoint a person to be a litigation friend, of either a child or a patient, so long as it is satisfied that the person meets the requirements set out in r 21.4(3).[6] An application to appoint a litigation friend should be made in accordance with Part 23[7] and may be made by either the person who wishes to be the litigation friend or a party to proceedings (r 21.6(2),(4) and PD 21, para 3.2). The application must be supported by evidence, which can be in the form of a witness statement or within the application notice itself, if it contains a statement of truth that the person consents to act as a litigation friend and which satisfies the court of the matter referred to in r 21.4(3).[8]

In the event of difficulty in finding a suitable litigation friend, it may be necessary to approach the Official Solicitor. He can only be appointed to act if he consents and he will only consent if there is no one else suitable to take up the post. The Official Solicitor to the Supreme Court may be contacted at 81 Chancery Lane, London WC2A 1DD, telephone number 020 7911 7127.

The application notice must be served on the following specified people: in the case of a child, one of the child's parents or guardians, or if there is no such person, the person with whom he resides or in whose care the child is (PD 21, paras 2.4(1) and 3.3(1)). In the case of a patient, on the patient, unless the court orders otherwise (r 21.8(2) and PD 21, para 3.3(2)), and on the person authorised under Part VII of the Mental Health Act 1983 to conduct

---

6   See above.
7   See Chapter 19, Making Applications for Court Orders.
8   See above.

proceedings on his behalf, or if there is no such person, on the person with whom he resides or in whose care the patient is (PD 21, para 2.4(2) and 3.3(1)).

Stage when litigation friend becomes necessary

A claimant must apply for an order appointing a litigation friend for a child or patient he is proceeding against if the child or patient has no litigation friend (and the court has not made an order allowing a child to act for himself), and either, someone who is not entitled to be a litigation friend files a defence, or the claimant wishes to take some step in the proceedings (apart from issuing and serving a claim form) (r 21.3(2)(b) and 21.6(3)).

If a party becomes a patient during proceedings, no party may take any step in the proceedings, without the permission of the court, until the patient has a litigation friend (r 21.3(3)).

Also, a person may not make an application against a child or patient before proceedings have started without the permission of the court (r 21.3(2)(a)).

If a party takes any step in the proceedings before a litigation friend has been appointed, it shall be of no effect, *unless the court orders otherwise* (r 21.3(4)). Thus, it is possible for the court to make an urgent order in proceedings involving a child or patient before the appointment of a litigation friend, taking into account all the relevant circumstances and provided there will be no prejudice to the child or patient.

Procedure for becoming a litigation friend without a court order

If a person is authorised under Part VII of the Mental Health Act 1983 to conduct legal proceedings in the name of, or on behalf of, a patient, he is entitled to be the litigation friend of the patient in any proceedings to which his authority extends (r 21.4(2)). Such a person must file an official copy of the order or other document which constitutes his authorisation to act (r 21.5(2)).

A person who is not so authorised under the Mental Health Act 1983, or who wishes to act for a child, may become a litigation friend for a child or patient without a court order by filing a certificate of suitability stating that he satisfies the conditions set out in r 21.4(3).[9]

In either case, if he is acting for the claimant, the person who wishes to act as the litigation friend must file the authorisation or certificate of suitability at the same time as when the claim form is issued; if he is acting for the defendant, at the time when he takes a step in proceedings on behalf of the defendant (r 21.5(4) and (5)).

---

9   See above, p 310, Becoming a litigation friend.

The certificate of suitability must also be served on every person specified in r 6.6[10] and a certificate of service[11] must be filed at the same time (r 21.5(6)). The specified persons are those referred to above under PD 21, para 2.4.[12]

Contents of a certificate of suitability

The statement of suitability must be signed in verification of its contents and contain the following statements by the person wishing to be the litigation friend:

- that he consents to act;
- that he knows or believes that the litigant is a child or patient;
- in the case of a patient, the grounds of his belief as to why he is a patient and attaching any relevant medical opinion;
- that he can fairly and competently conduct proceedings on behalf of the child or patient and that he has no adverse interest to that of the child or patient; and
- where the child or patient is the claimant, an undertaking to pay any costs which the child or patient may be ordered to pay (subject to any right he may have to be repaid from the assets of the child or patient) (PD 21, para 2.3).[13]

Changing a litigation friend or preventing a person from acting as a litigation friend

The court has the power to terminate the appointment of a litigation friend or substitute a different person as litigation friend or make an order that a person may not act as litigation friend (r 21.7(1)).

An application for the court to exercise its powers in that way must be made in accordance with Part 23,[14] giving the reasons why the order is sought, and be supported by evidence (r 21.7(2) and PD 21, para 4.2).

Under r 21.7(3), the court may not substitute a new litigation friend unless it is satisfied that the proposed person is a suitable person to act as such in accordance with the requirements of r 21.4(3).[15]

---

10 See Chapter 9, Service of documents.
11 *Ibid.*
12 See above, p 310, Order appointing a litigation friend.
13 This is contained in Form N235, Certificate of Suitability of Litigation Friend.
14 See Chapter 19, Making Applications for Court Orders.
15 See above, p 310, Becoming a litigation friend.

The application must be served on the persons specified in para 2.4 of PD 21,[16] the person who is currently the litigation friend, or purporting to act as the litigation friend, as well as the person who it is proposed should be the litigation friend (unless he is the applicant) (r 21.8(4) and PD 21, para 4.4).

PROCEDURE WHERE A LITIGATION FRIEND IS NO LONGER NECESSARY

Children

Where a litigant who was formerly a child, who is not also a patient, reaches the age of 18, a litigation friend's appointment automatically ceases (r 21.9(1)).

Notice that appointment of litigation friend for a child has ceased

The litigant who was formerly a child must then serve notice on the other parties stating that he has reached full age, that the appointment of the litigation friend has ceased, giving his own address for service and stating whether or not he intends to carry on with the proceedings (r 21.9(4) and PD 21, para 5.2). When the litigant who was formerly a child reached 18, the litigant friend may also serve a notice on all the other parties stating that his appointment has ceased, whether or not the former child does (PD 21, para 5.4). The litigation friend may do so in order to avoid any further liability for the costs of the former child.[17]

Title of proceedings after litigation friend's appointment ceases

On reaching full age, if the child carries on with the proceedings, he shall subsequently be described in the proceedings by adding the following words in brackets after his name, 'formerly a child but now of full age' (PD 21, para 5.3).

Consequences of failure to serve the notice

If the child does not serve such a notice on the other parties within 28 days of the appointment of the litigation friend ceasing, an application can be made for the court to strike out the child's claim or defence (r 21.9(5)).

---

16 See above, p 310, Order appointing a litigation friend.
17 See below, p 314, Litigation friend's liability for costs.

Litigation friend's liability for costs

Once the litigation friend's appointment has ended, he has an incentive to ensure that the other parties are notified of this because until such time as he does, he will remain liable for the child's or patient's costs of the proceedings (r 21.9(6)). The litigation friend's liability for costs will only end when the child or patient serves the notice referred to in r 21.9(4)[18] or the litigation friend serves notice on the other parties that his appointment to act has ceased (r 21.9(6)).

Patients

When a patient recovers and ceases to be a patient, the litigation friend's appointment will not cease until it is ended by court order (r 21.9(2)).

The former patient, the litigation friend or a party may make the application to the court for an order ending the litigation friend's appointment (r 21.9(3)). The application must be supported by evidence in the form of a medical report indicating that the patient has recovered and is capable of managing and administering his property and affairs. If the patient's affairs were under the control of the Court of Protection, the application must include a copy of the order or notice discharging the receiver. If the application is made by the patient, it should include a statement indicating whether or not he intends to carry on with or continue to defend proceedings (PD 21, para 5.7).

Notice that appointment of litigation friend for a patient has ceased

If the order is made, it must be served on the other parties to the proceedings and the former patient must file and serve on the parties a notice stating that his litigation friend's appointment has ceased, giving his own address for service and stating whether or not he intends to carry on with or continue to defend the proceedings (r 21.9(4) and PD 21, para 5.8).

The same potential consequences apply to the former patient who fails to serve such a notice as apply to a similar failure by a former child and the litigation friend's liability for costs continues in the same way until such a notice is filed and served (r 21.9(5) and (6)).[18a]

---

18 See p 313, Notice that appointment of litigation friend for a child has ceased, and below, Notice that appointment of a litigation friend for a patient has ceased.

18a See above, p 313, Consequences of failure to serve the notice and above, Litigation friend's liability for costs.

COMPROMISE BY OR ON BEHALF OF A CHILD OR PATIENT

In the light of the potential vulnerability of a litigant who is a child or patient, any settlement or compromise of proceedings involving such a litigant will not be valid unless approved by the court (r 21.10(1) and PD 21, para 1.6). This will enable defendants to obtain a valid discharge from the claim; will protect children and patients from any lack of skill and experience on the part of their legal representatives;[19] and will ensure that the legal representatives are paid a proper and reasonable amount for their fees.

A settlement will include where the child or patient accepts a Part 36 offer to settle or payment into court[20] or provisional damages[21] for which, therefore, the court's approval must also be sought.

Also, under the common law, in many instances, a contract between a child and another person is not binding, unless the child ratifies the contract on reaching the age of 18. As a result of this, if a claim made by or against a child is compromised before proceedings are started, there is a procedure for the court to approve the settlement and if it is approved, the settlement is binding and enforceable (r 21.10(2)).

Court approval of compromise or settlement of proceedings

An application should be made in accordance with Part 23[22] and should include the following information:

- whether and to what extent the defendant admits liability;
- the age and occupation of the child or patient;
- the litigation friend's approval of the proposed settlement or compromise; and
- in a personal injury claim arising from an accident; details of the accident, copies of any medical reports, information required by the statement of case, evidence and details of police reports and criminal prosecutions (PD 21, para 6.2).

Counsel's opinion

Unless it is a very straightforward case, counsel's opinion should also be obtained as to the merits of the settlement or compromise. A copy of the

---

19 *Black v Yates* [1991] 4 All ER 722.
20 See Chapter 24, Offers to Settle and Payments into Court.
21 See Chapter 25, Provisional Damages.
22 See Chapter 19, Making Applications for Court Orders.

opinion including the instructions sent to counsel should also be supplied to the court when the application for approval is made (PD 21, para 6.3).

Court approval of compromise or settlement before proceedings have started

The same information and requirement for counsel's opinion is necessary for an application for approval of a compromise or settlement made before proceedings have started, as is required once proceedings have started.[23] However, the application is made in accordance with Part 8.[24] The Part 8 application must include a request for approval of the settlement or compromise and, in addition to the details of the claim, set out the terms of the settlement or compromise or attach a draft consent order in Practice Form N292 (r 21.10(2)(b) and PD 21, para 6.1).

Judge hearing the application

The application for approval of the compromise or settlement, both before and after proceedings have started, is normally heard by a master or district judge (PD 21, para 6.4). The hearing should normally be attended by the litigation friend and child or patient unless this is not practical or there is some other good reason.

Hearing in public or private

The general rule is that all hearings are to be held in public (r 39.2(1)). This accords not only with the CPR, but is also in accordance with Art 6 of the Human Rights Act 1998 and the European Convention on Human Rights. However, this general rule is subject to a power to order that proceedings be heard in private if appropriate (r 39.2(3)).

Although the court has the power to direct that a hearing be held in private where it involves the interests of a child or patient, including the approval of a compromise or settlement or an application for the payment out of court of money to such a person, there is no presumption that such a hearing will be in private. In fact, in *Beatham v Carlisle Hospitals NHS Trust*,[25] Buckley J held that the approval of a settlement on behalf of a child or patient would normally be given in public.

---

23 See above, p 315, Court approval of compromise or settlement of proceedings.
24 See Chapter 14, Part 8 Claims.
25 (1999) *The Times*, 20 May.

COURT CONTROL OF MONEY RECOVERED BY OR ON BEHALF OF A CHILD OR PATIENT

The court will take steps to ensure that money paid by or on behalf of a child or patient is administered for the benefit of the child or patient (r 21.11(1)). The money is usually transferred to the Investment Division of the Public Trust Office to be applied for the benefit of the claimant as the court sees fit. The court will normally give directions as to the investment of the money on Form CFO320. There is usually a choice between high interest or equity investment or, more popularly, a combination of the two.

Application may be made from time to time for payment out of moneys in the fund, but moneys should only be paid out if they are clearly for the maintenance, education or benefit of the child. This may include, for an example, money to buy a computer or to pay for a school holiday, but close scrutiny will be given by the court to ensure that the payment out is to benefit the child and not as an indirect means of benefiting the parent.

In the exercise of this power, the court may order that the money be paid into court and invested or otherwise dealt with (r 21.11(2)).

Rule 21.12 and PD 21, paras 8.1 to 12.3, should be consulted for details as to the court's power to order investments and as to the appointment of the Official Solicitor to be guardian of a child's estate.

In the case of a patient, if the moneys are substantial (over £30,000), the question of the administration of them should be left to the Court of Protection.

COSTS PAYABLE TO OR BY A CHILD OR PATIENT

There are special rules as to the assessment of costs payable by or to a child or patient (r 48.5).[26] This will usually be a detailed assessment (r 48.5(2)), but the court may decide that this should be dispensed with (PD on Costs, para 50.2).

SERVICE OF DOCUMENTS ON A CHILD OR PATIENT

The claim form

The claim form[27] must be served[28] on the following specified people: in the case of a child, one of the child's parents or guardians, or if there is no such

---

26 See Chapter 33, Costs.
27 See Chapter 7, Starting an Action.
28 See Chapter 9, Service of Documents.

person, the person with whom he resides or in whose care the child is; in the case of a patient, on the person authorised under Part VII of the Mental Health Act 1983 to conduct proceedings on his behalf, or if there is no such person on the person with whom he resides or in whose care the patient is (r 6.6(1)).

Any other document

Apart from the claim form,[29] a party wishing to serve a document on a child or patient in proceedings must serve it on the child's or patient's litigation friend (r 6.6(1)). Obviously, if the court has made an order giving a child permission to act on his own behalf, a party should serve the document on the child.[30]

STATEMENTS OF TRUTH IN PROCEEDINGS INVOLVING A CHILD OR PATIENT

The rules require that certain documents *must* be verified by a statement of truth,[31] such as a statement of case or a witness statement, and certain documents *may* contain a statement of truth, such as an application notice (see r 22).

Statement of truth[31a] by a litigation friend

If a litigation friend is appointed, a statement of truth in a statement of case, a response under r 18.1 providing further information, or an application notice, is a statement that the litigation friend (as opposed to the child or patient) believes that the facts stated in the document being verified are true (r 22.1(5)). The statement of truth must be signed by the litigation friend or his legal representative (r 22.1(6)(a)). However, it should be noted that the statement of truth in a witness statement should be made and signed by the person making the statement (r 22.1(6)(b)). Therefore, this will be the child or patient if they make a witness statement.

---

29 See above, p 317, The claim form.
30 See above, p 309, Application for an order permitting a child to act to act on his own behalf.
31 See Chapter 11, Statements of Case, p 128.
31a *Ibid.*

JUDGMENT IN DEFAULT AGAINST A CHILD OR PATIENT

If proceedings are brought against a child or patient, but he fails to respond to the particulars of claim within the time period specified by the rules, the claimant can only obtain judgment in default by making an application to the court under Part 23[32] (rr 12.4, 12.10). If a litigation friend has not been appointed for the child or patient, or the court has not made an order permitting a child to act on his own behalf, the claimant will have to apply for a litigation friend to be appointed before making the application to enter judgment in default (rr 21.3(2)(b) and 21.6(3)).

---

32 See Chapter 19, Making Applications for Court Orders.

CHAPTER 27

INTERPLEADER

INTRODUCTION

Where a person holds property to which he claims no ownership and two or more persons are in dispute as to who is the true owner of the property, the person holding the property may apply to the court to adjudicate on the disputed ownership so that he can safely deliver the property to the true owner. Such an application is for interpleader relief (RSC Ord 17, CCR Ord 33).

THE USE OF INTERPLEADER RELIEF

There are three instances where interpleader relief is commonly used. The first is where a bailee is in possession of goods and two or more people claim ownership of them and demand their return, for example, a repair shop or auctioneers. The second is where a stakeholder holds a fund of money, such as a bank or solicitor's firm on a conveyance, and two or more persons, such as the vendor and purchaser, both claim ownership of it. The third is where a sheriff or bailiff is about to take execution of goods under a writ of fi fa or warrant of possession and a person other than the execution debtor claims title to them.[1]

PROCEDURE FOR APPLICATION
FOR INTERPLEADER RELIEF

If one of the competing owners of the property sues the interpleader, he can make an application under Part 23[2] for interpleader relief within the proceedings. If the interpleader expects to be sued, he can make his own application by bringing a claim under the Part 8 procedure[3] joining the disputing owners as parties (RSC Ord 17 r 3(1) and CCR Ord 33).

Unless the application is by the sheriff or bailiff in respect of goods in execution of a writ of fi fa or warrant of execution, the application or claim

---

1 See Chapter 39, Enforcement of Proceedings, writ of *fi fa* and warrant of execution.
2 See Chapter 19, Making Applications for Court Orders.
3 See Chapter 14, Part 8 Claims.

must be supported by evidence showing that the interpleader claims no interest in the subject matter of the dispute (other than for charges or costs), does not collude with any of the claimants to that subject matter and is willing to pay or transfer that subject matter into court or to dispose of it as the court may direct (RSC Ord 17 r 3(4) and CCR Ord 33).

POWERS OF THE COURT

The purpose of making an application for interpleader relief is so that the interpleader can drop out of the proceedings and leave the disputing owners to resolve the issue of ownership of the property without involving himself in further cost, expense or liability.

The court has wide powers to order that the issue of the disputed ownership of the property be stated and tried and that the disputing parties become parties to this action and for the interpleader to take no further part in the proceedings, whilst protecting any claim to costs or expenses (RSC Ord 17 r 5 and CCR Ord 33).

CHAPTER 28

CHANGE OF SOLICITOR

INTRODUCTION

If a client retains a solicitor to act in a matter, a solicitor acting for another party, who knows the other party has retained a solicitor to act, should not communicate directly with the other party except with the consent of the other solicitor.[1] If a solicitor or his client has notified the other party that the solicitor is acting for him and given the solicitor's address for service, the solicitor will be the recipient for service of proceedings, known colloquially (but not in the CPR) as being 'on the record'. If a solicitor ceases to act for the client, there is a requirement to notify the court and the other parties accordingly, similarly if a party instructs a solicitor having formerly acted in person.

SOLICITOR ACTING FOR A PARTY

A solicitor is treated as acting for a party when the address for service of documents is the business address of the solicitor (r 42.1).

The address for service is that defined by r 6.5. Rule 6.5(2) requires a party to give an address for service within the jurisdiction. Where a solicitor is acting for a party, the address for service is the solicitor's business address. However, where the document to be served is the claim form, the address for service will only be the solicitor's business address if the solicitor is authorised to accept service (r 6.13).

Where a party or his solicitor changes his address for service, a notice of that change should be filed and served on every party (PD 42, para 2.3).

DUTY TO GIVE NOTICE OF A CHANGE OF SOLICITOR

A party or his solicitor (where one is acting) must serve on every party notice of a change of solicitor or that a solicitor has ceased to or started to act in the following circumstances, where:

---

1   See *Guide to the Professional Conduct of Solicitors*, 8th edn, The Law Society, Chapter 19.

- a party for whom a solicitor is acting wants to change his solicitor;
- a party having conducted the claim in person appoints a solicitor to act on his behalf (except where the solicitor is appointed only to act as an advocate for a hearing); or
- a party, after having conducted the claim by a solicitor, intends to act in person (r 42.2(1)).

Where a party changes his solicitor or, having conducted the claim by a solicitor, intends to act in person, the party or his solicitor (where one is acting) must also serve the notice on his former solicitor (r 42.2(2)).

It is only after the notice has been served on all the parties (and any former solicitor) that it should then be filed at court (PD 42, para 1.2).

NOTICE OF CHANGE OF SOLICITOR

Practice Form N434 should be used. This contains the following information:

- that a party has changed solicitor, or that a solicitor has ceased to or started to act for the party, as the case may be;
- the party's new address for service;
- that the notice has been served on all the parties and, where applicable, the former solicitor (r 42.2(3) and (4)).

Solicitor 'on record' until notice is served or court order made

Where a party has changed his solicitor or intends to act in person, the former solicitor will be treated as the party's solicitor unless and until a notice of change of solicitor is served or the court makes an order that the solicitor has ceased to act (r 42.2(5)).

Order that a solicitor has ceased to act

A solicitor may apply for an order that he has ceased to be the solicitor acting for a party (r 42.3(1)). The solicitor may do this when he has terminated the retainer in circumstances when he can show just cause to do so, for example, when the client fails or refuses to provide instructions or money on account or to pay an interim bill, but the client fails or refuses to file and serve a notice that his solicitor has ceased to act for him.

The former client must be served with notice of the application, unless the court orders otherwise. The application should be made in accordance with

Part 23[2] and supported by evidence (r 42.3(2) and PD 42, para 3.2). In straightforward cases, this can be dealt with by the court without the need for a hearing.[3] However, the application should not be served on any other party to the proceedings, as this may injure the client's interests.

If the court makes an order that the solicitor has ceased to act, a copy of the order must be served on every party to the proceedings. In accordance with the usual rule, service will be effected by the court,[4] but if the party or the solicitor serve notice instead, a certificate of service in Practice Form N215 must also be filed (r 42.3 and PD 42, para 4.3).

If the court makes such an order, the party must give a new address for service within the jurisdiction (PD 42, para 5.1). If the party does not notify the other parties of a new address, the address for service of that party will be determined in accordance with the table in r 6.5(6).[5] It would seem that a solicitor would be obliged to seek such an order if the client refuses to file and serve the necessary notice as, in these circumstances, the solicitor cannot sign the notice on the client's behalf, but would still be treated as the solicitor on the record for that client until a notice was served or order made.[6]

LSC funded client or assisted person

If the certificate of an LSC funded client or an assisted person is revoked or discharged, the solicitor's retainer ends on receipt of the notice of revocation or discharge of the certificate (reg 4 of the Community Legal Service (Costs) Regulations 2000 and reg 83 of the Civil Legal Aid (General) Regulations 1989).

If the LSC funded or assisted person wishes to continue with the proceedings, if he appoints a solicitor to act on his behalf he must file and serve a notice of change of solicitor in accordance with r 42.2(2). If he wishes to act in person, he must give an address for service (r 42.2(6)).

Where the LSC funded or assisted person's certificate is revoked or discharged and the solicitor therefore ceases to act and the former client wishes to act in person or to appoint another solicitor to act on his behalf, the former solicitor must also file and serve on every other party a notice of the change giving the last known address of the former LSC funded or assisted person (PD 42, para 2.2).

---

2   See Chapter 19, Making Applications for Court Orders.
3   *Miller v Allied Sainif (UK) Ltd* (2000) *The Times*, 31 October, Ch D (Neuberger J).
4   See Chapter 9, Service of Documents.
5   *Ibid.*
6   It would appear that the provisions regarding solicitor/client privilege would prevent a solicitor from volunteering his client's address.

APPLICATION BY ANOTHER PARTY
TO REMOVE A SOLICITOR

Where a solicitor who has acted for a party has died, become bankrupt, ceased to practice or cannot be found and the party has not given notice of a change of solicitor or notice of intention to act in person in accordance with r 42.2(2), any other party may apply for an order declaring that the solicitor has ceased to be the solicitor for the other party in the case (r 42.4(1)).

The application should be made in accordance with Part 23[7] and supported by evidence and served on the party to whose solicitor the application relates, unless the court orders otherwise (PD 42, para 4.2). Where the court makes an order, the same provisions apply as to service of the order as where the court makes an order following a solicitor's application for a declaration that he has ceased to act.[8]

Where a party seeks to remove solicitors acting for its opponent on the grounds of a conflict of interest,[9] the court has the power to order the solicitors be removed from the record, but it does not have jurisdiction to order a party to instruct further solicitors.[10]

COURT'S INHERENT POWER TO REMOVE A SOLICITOR

The court has an inherent power to remove a solicitor from the record where it is in the interests of fairness and justice to do so. However, it is recognised that the exercise of this power is in conflict with the right of a litigant to choose his legal representatives and is therefore exercised only with extreme caution.

The court exercised this power to remove solicitors from the record in the case of *Re L (Minors) (Care Proceedings: Cohabiting Solicitors)*[11] by making a declaration that those solicitors were no longer acting. The grounds for the declaration were that that solicitors on the opposing sides were cohabiting and it was felt that on discovering this, an unsuccessful lay client may believe that there would therefore be bias. Wilson J said in that case: 'It was not disputed that the court had power to determine whether a particular firm of solicitors should play a role in the forensic exercise of which it was the director.' Striking features in that case which led to the exercise by the court of this power included the fact that the application was for care orders and that

---

7 See Chapter 19, Making Applications for Court Orders.
8 See above, p 324, Order that a solicitor has ceased to act.
9 See example below, p 322, in the case of *Re L (Minors) (Care Proceedings: Cohabiting Solicitors)* (2000) *The Times*, 27 July.
10 *SMC Engineering (Bristol) Ltd v Alastair Duff Fraser and Another* (2001) *The Times*, 26 January, CA.
11 (2000) *The Times*, 27 July.

one of the cohabitants had conduct of the case on behalf of the local authority exercising powers as the arm of the State.

Court's power to refuse to hear a particular advocate

The court has an analogous power under s 27(4) of the Courts and Legal Services Act 1990 to refuse to hear a particular advocate as it has to remove a solicitor from the record.

CHAPTER 29

DISCLOSURE OF DOCUMENTS

INTRODUCTION

There has been a long tradition in our jurisdiction of an extensive obligation to disclose relevant documents in the course of proceedings. This includes disclosing documents which would not only be evidence of an issue in the action, but also those 'which, it is reasonable to suppose, contain information which *may*, either directly or indirectly, lead the party seeking disclosure to a train of enquiry which enables him to advance his own case or to damage that of his adversary'.[1] Moreover, a distinctive feature of our common law system, in comparison to that on the continent for instance, is an obligation to disclose documents damaging to one's own case.

The rules on disclosure were substantially reformed with the introduction of the CPR in an attempt to limit the extent of the process. Therefore, although in appropriate circumstances, extensive orders for disclosure can be made, most orders made under the CPR will be limited to *standard disclosure*.[2] Also, whereas an order for disclosure was made under the old rules in every case as a matter of course, this is not the position under the CPR. Furthermore, when an application for more extensive disclosure than standard disclosure is made, the court applies a cost benefit analysis when deciding whether to grant the order in a particular case.

It will be noted that the old expression 'discovery' has been replaced with 'disclosure' and that added to the obligation to disclose is the obligation to search for relevant documents.[3] Proportionality and reasonableness have also been added to the duty to search and disclose.

Proportionality and disclosure

Rule 31.3(2) enables a party to refuse to give inspection of documents if it would be disproportionate to do so.[4] This may apply, for example, where extricating requested documents from a vast quantity of documents may not

---

1   Paraphrasing Brett LJ in the case of *Compagnie Financière et Commerciale du Pacifique v Peruvian Guano Co* (1882) 11 QBD 55.
2   See below, p 333.
3   See below, p 334.
4   See below, p 338.

be properly viable having regard to all the circumstances of the case. Similarly, the duty to search contained in r 31.7 is tempered by the factors to be taken in consideration as set out in sub-s 2.[5] In the disclosure statement, reference may also be made to the question of proportionality when explaining why some documents were not searched for and disclosed.[6]

Applicability of rules

The rules about disclosure and inspection of documents apply to all claims except those allocated to the small claims track (r 31.1(2)).

Disclosure on the small claims track

The usual direction in relation to documents on the small claims track, if any, is for a party to file at court and serve only copies of those documents on which he intends to rely.[7]

DEFINITION OF DOCUMENT AND COPY OF A DOCUMENT

A document is defined as 'anything in which information of any description is recorded' (r 31.4). The definition of a document in Part 31 is therefore much wider than the ordinary meaning of the word would suggest. It is not confined to paper documents and will include such things as photographs, videos, computer disks and CDs.

A copy of a document means anything onto which information recorded in the document has been copied, by whatever means, whether directly or indirectly (r 31.4).

Definition of disclosure

A party discloses a document by stating that it exists or has existed (r 31.2). It should be noted, therefore, that it is not necessary for a party to provide a copy of the document or allow a party to inspect it in order to comply with disclosure. However, the obligation to disclose a document is usually accompanied by the right of the other party to inspect or obtain a copy of the document.

---

5   See below, p 334.
6   See below, p 335.
7   See Chapter 16, Small Claims Track.

Control of a document

Where a party is required to disclose documents, he is obliged to disclose documents which are or have been in his control (r 31.8(1)). This covers not just documents in his actual physical possession, but also those that were in his physical possession, documents he has or has had a right to possession of, or documents he has or has had a right to inspect or take copies of (r 31.8(2)). It should be remembered that disclosure involves a statement that a document exists or has existed and so the mere fact that a document has been sent to or is held by someone else or no longer exists does not mean that a party is excused from disclosing it.

Copies of documents

If there is more than one copy of a document, a party need only disclose one of them (r 31.9(1)). However, if a copy of a disclosable document contains a modification, obliteration or other marking or feature, it will be treated as a separate document and disclosable in its own right (r 31.9(2)).

DISCLOSURE IN STAGES

The court may direct, or the parties may agree in writing, that disclosure, or inspection, or both, shall take place in stages (r 31.13). Such an order may be made, for instance, when there is an order for a split trial on liability and quantum.

DUTIES OF LEGAL REPRESENTATIVES IN RESPECT OF DISCLOSURE

A legal representative acting for a party must endeavour to ensure that the party understands his duty to comply with disclosure (PD 31, para 4.4). A party is often surprised at the obligation to disclose documents adverse to his case and a legal representative must fully explain this to his client.

CONTINUING DUTY OF DISCLOSURE

A party has a continuing duty of disclosure throughout the course of the proceedings. If further disclosable documents come to a party's attention, he must disclose them to the other party immediately (r 31.11 and PD 31, para 3.3).

CONSEQUENCES OF FAILURE TO DISCLOSE DOCUMENTS OR ALLOW INSPECTION

If a party fails to disclose a document or fails to allow inspection of it, he cannot rely on that document in the proceedings, unless the court gives permission (r 31.21). Although it has been said that default in discovery would not normally lead to a denial of a trial, where there has been deliberate tampering with documents so as to prejudice the possibility of a fair trial the court may be more inclined to summarily dispose of the miscreant's case.[8]

If a party knows of a disclosable document which the disclosing party has not disclosed, he should apply to the court for an order for specific disclosure.[9] If a disclosing party refuses to allow inspection of a disclosed document, for which he has no right or duty to refuse inspection,[10] as the other party has a right to inspect disclosed documents,[11] he can apply to the court for an order that he be entitled to inspect that document.

SUBSEQUENT USE OF DISCLOSED DOCUMENTS

The general principle, subject to exceptions, is that a party to whom a document has been disclosed may use the document only for the purposes of the proceedings and not for any other purpose (r 31.22). The exceptions are where:

- the document has been read to or by the court, or referred to at a public hearing;[12]

- the court gives permission; or

- the person who disclosed the document and the person to whom the document belongs agree (r 31.22(1)).

However, notwithstanding these exceptions, the court has the power, on the application of a party or any person to whom the document belongs, to make an order restricting or prohibiting the use of a document which has been disclosed, even where it has been read to or by the court or referred to at a public hearing (r 31.22(2) and (3)).

---

8 *Arrow Nominees Inc v Blackledge and Others* (2000) *The Times*, 7 July, CA.
9 See below, p 336, r 31.12.
10 See below, p 339.
11 See below, p 337, r 31.3.
12 See *Smith Kline Beecham Biologicals v Connaught Labs Inc* [1999] 4 All ER 498, CA.

DISCLOSURE

Extent of disclosure

In most cases, a party will only be required to give standard disclosure. An order requiring a party to give 'disclosure' means that the party is required to give standard disclosure only unless the court expressly orders otherwise (r 31.5(1) and PD 31, para 1.1). Therefore, although where disclosure is ordered, it is usually standard disclosure, the court has the power to make a more extensive order for disclosure than standard disclosure if required, but it must expressly do so.

A party does not have the right to insist that an order for standard disclosure is made in proceedings as the court has the power to dispense with the need for standard disclosure altogether, or limit its extent (r 31.5(2)).

The parties may agree to dispense with or limit standard disclosure. If the parties agree to this, they should record their agreement in writing and lodge it at court (r 31.5(3) and PD 31, para 1.4).

Disclosure under pre-action protocols

Although a party will not be obliged to give disclosure unless there is a direction in this regard, in some types of action, for example, personal injuries or clinical negligence claims, a prospective defendant should have already provided disclosure of a significant number of documents without an order in accordance with the pre-action protocol. A party's non-compliance with a relevant pre-action protocol can be taken into account by the court when making orders for cost (r 44.3). (See Chapter 33, Costs.)

STANDARD DISCLOSURE

Scope of standard disclosure

Standard disclosure imposes an obligation on a party to disclose the following documents which are or have been in his control:

- documents on which a party relies;
- documents which adversely affect his own case;
- documents which adversely affect another party's case;
- documents which support another party's case; and
- any documents which he is required to disclose by a relevant practice direction (r 31.6).

Thus, documents which are purely 'neutral' need not, and should not, be disclosed, otherwise costs consequences may apply.

Duty of search

A party is required to carry out a reasonable search for documents which he is obliged to disclose as part of standard disclosure (r 31.7(1) and PD 31, para 1.2). Such a test leaves considerable scope for deciding what is reasonable in a particular case and issues of proportionality[13] will obviously be important (PD 31, para 2). If a party decides not to search for a category of documents on the grounds that to do so would be unreasonable, he must state this in his disclosure statement and identify the category of document involved (r 31.7(3)). A party who has made this decision should have born in mind the following factors when reaching a decision that a search was unreasonable:

- the number of documents involved. The more documents involved, the greater the efforts that should be made;
- the nature and complexity of the proceedings. A large sum or complex proceedings would justify more effort being made than in proceedings for a smaller sum in a straightforward matter;
- the ease and expense of retrieval of any particular document. It may be disproportionate to go to a great deal of effort and expense in searching for a document even if the dispute involves a large sum or complex issues; and
- the significance of any document which is likely to be located. Obviously, the more important the document, the more effort that should be made (r 31.7).

Although the disclosing party does not have to apply to the court for permission to limit his search in this way, the court will take these factors into account when hearing any application for specific disclosure[14] made by a party who challenges the disclosing party's decision not to conduct a search on the grounds of reasonableness.

Procedure for standard disclosure

List of documents

In order to comply with disclosure, a party should compile a list of disclosable documents in Practice Form N265 and serve it on every other party (r 31.10 and PD 31, paras 1.3 and 3.1).

---

13 See Chapter 5, Judicial Case Management: The Overriding Objective.
14 See below, p 336, Specific disclosure.

The documents must be identified in a convenient order and manner and a concise description of each document (or category of document) should be provided (r 31.10(3)). The PD to Part 31 sets out how a party can comply with these requirements. This provides that the documents should be listed in date order, numbered consecutively and given a concise description such as, 'letter, claimant to defendant'. If there are a large number of documents falling into the same category, for example, bank statements, a party can list those documents as a category, rather than individually, for example, by saying '50 bank statements relating to account number x, at bank x, dated x to x' (PD 31, para 3.2).

The list must indicate those documents in respect of which the party claims a right or duty to withhold inspection (r 31.10(4)(a)).[15]

The list must also indicate those documents which are no longer in the party's control, and what has happened to those documents (r 31.10(4)(b)).

Form N265 is divided into three sections. In the first section, the disclosing party must list the documents in his control which he has no objection to the other side inspecting. In the second section, the disclosing party must list the documents in his control which he objects to the other side inspecting. In the third section, the disclosing party must list the documents he once had, but no longer has in his control.

Disclosure statement

Under r 31.10(5) and PD 31, para 4.1, the list of documents *must* include a disclosure statement containing specified information. The disclosure statement *must* be made by the party personally (or a representative or employee of a party in the case of a company or firm) and *not* by his legal representative on his behalf. The form of the disclosure statement is set out in the Annex to PD 31. The disclosure statement must:

- set out the extent of the search that has been made to locate disclosable documents. The party must specify the earliest date of the documents involved in the search, the locations of the search and the categories of documents searched for. The party must also draw attention to any particular limitations on the extent of the search and the reasons for the limitations based on the grounds of proportionality;

- expressly state that the party believes the extent of the search to have been reasonable in all the circumstances;

- in the case of a party which is a company, firm, association or other organisation, give the name, address and position or office of the person making the disclosure statement and an explanation as to why that person is the most appropriate person to make the statement;

---

15 See below, p 339.

- if applicable, state that the party claims a right or duty to withhold an identified document from inspection,[16] or part of a document to which it relates, and give the grounds on which he claims that right or duty;
- if applicable, identify documents which are no longer in the party's control and state what has happened to them;
- if applicable, state that the party considers it would be disproportionate to the issues in the case to permit inspection of identified documents within a certain category;[17]
- certify that the party understands the duty to disclose documents; and
- certify that to the best of his knowledge, the party has carried out that duty (rr 31.3(2), 31.10(4), (6), (7), 31.19(3), (4), PD 31, paras 4.1–4.7 and Annex to PD 31).

False disclosure statements

If a person makes, or causes another person to make, a false disclosure statement, without an honest belief in its truth, he is liable to be proceeded against for contempt of court (r 31.23).

Disclosing documents without a disclosure statement

The parties may agree in writing to disclose documents without making a list and to disclose documents without the disclosing party making a disclosure statement (r 31.10(8)).

Supplemental list

A party has a continuing duty of disclosure throughout the course of the proceedings (r 31.11(1)). If, therefore, the existence of further disclosable documents comes to the attention of a party after he has served a list of documents, he should prepare a supplemental list of these further documents and serve it on every other party (PD 31, para 3.3). A party should comply with this obligation as soon as these additional documents come to his attention (r 31.11(2)).

SPECIFIC DISCLOSURE

A party to whom disclosure has been made may have grounds to believe that the disclosure is inadequate on the basis that documents or category of

---

16 See below, p 339.
17 See below, p 339.

documents which should have been disclosed have not been, or that a party has not properly searched for disclosable documents. Moreover, in some cases, a party may believe that disclosure wider than standard disclosure is necessary to do justice in a particular case. In those circumstances, a party can apply to the court for an order for specific disclosure of a document or category of documents (r 31.12(1) and PD 31, para 5.1). In the first instance, the party should request that the disclosing party provide such disclosure voluntarily. However, if the disclosing party refuses to comply, the other party can apply to the court for an order.

The application should be made in accordance with Part 23[18] and the application must be supported by evidence justifying the applicant's belief that documents have not been disclosed which should have been, or why wider disclosure than standard disclosure is necessary in this case, as opposed to treating the application as a 'fishing expedition'. The grounds must be set out either in the application notice itself or in any supporting evidence (r 5.3). The court will consider all the circumstances of the case in the light of the overriding objective,[19] but if the court is satisfied that a party has failed to comply with his obligation to give disclosure, whether through a failure to conduct a proper search or otherwise, it is likely to make an order remedying this failure (PD 31, para 5.4). If the application is successful, the court may order a party to:

- disclose documents or classes of documents specified in the order;
- carry out a search to the extent stated in the order;
- disclose any documents located as a result of that search (r 31.12(2)).

When making the order, the court is likely to make it subject to or conditional on a sanction, such as striking out of the party's statement of case, if it is not complied with.[20]

INSPECTION

Right of inspection of a disclosed document

A party has a general right (subject to exceptions) to inspect a document which has been disclosed to him (r 31.3(1)).

Also, even if not formally disclosed to him, a party may inspect a document which has come to his attention because it is referred to in:

---

18 See Chapter 19, Making Applications for Court Orders.
19 See Chapter 5, Judicial Case Management: The Overriding Objective.
20 *Ibid*.

- a statement of case;
- a witness statement;
- a witness summary;
- an affidavit; or
- an expert's report (r 31.14).[21]

Exceptions to right to inspect disclosed document

A party will have no right to inspect a disclosed document if:
- the document is no longer in the control of the party who disclosed it;
- the party disclosing the document has a right or duty to withhold inspection;[22] or
- it falls into a category which the party disclosing the document has stated he considers disproportionate to the issues in the case to permit inspection of (this *cannot* include any documents the disclosing party is relying upon) (rr 31.3, 31.6(b)).[23]

Inspection and copying of documents

Often, a party will send copies of the disclosed documents to the other parties with the disclosure list. Strictly, however, a party need only send the disclosure list and it will be up to the other party to request inspection or copying of the documents on the list which are available or the other party has no objection to inspection of. In the latter circumstances, the party wishing to inspect documents must send the disclosing party written notice of his wish to do so. The disclosing party must then permit inspection no more than seven days after the date of receiving the request. If a party prefers to receive copies rather than physically inspect the documents, the disclosing party must comply with this request so long as the other party has undertaken to pay his reasonable copying charges (r 31.15).

A party can choose to inspect the documents and also request copies which should be provided so long as there is an undertaking to pay reasonable copying charges.

---

21 However, see Chapter 30, Experts, for the provisions relating to documents referred to in the instructions to the expert.
22 See below, p 339.
23 But see below, Order for specific inspection, p 339.

Order for specific inspection

If the disclosing party has indicated that he objects to the other party inspecting a document or documents falling into a certain category on the grounds that it would be disproportionate to the issues in the case to allow inspection,[24] the other party can apply to the court for an order for specific inspection of that document or category of documents (r 31.12(3)). The application should be made in accordance with Part 23[25] and should indicate the grounds on which the party maintains it is important that he be allowed to inspect the document or documents.

PRIVILEGE FROM DISCLOSURE OR INSPECTION OF A DOCUMENT

There are certain types of document which a party can usually withhold from disclosure or inspection. These can be divided in to three broad categories:

- public interest immunity;
- legal professional privilege; and
- privilege against self-incrimination.

PRIVILEGE FROM DISCLOSURE

Public interest immunity

There is a well established principle that a party can claim to protect a document from disclosure on the grounds that otherwise, disclosure would damage the public interest.[26] Such a ground is obviously more likely to be used by the government and public bodies rather than private parties. However, it is not restricted to such bodies, and a claim to such immunity was successfully made by a charity.[27]

If a party believes that disclosure of a document, which would otherwise be disclosable, would damage the public interest he must apply to the court, without notice, for an order permitting him to withhold disclosure (r 31.19(1)). The court will balance the public interest in concealment against the public interest that the administration of justice should not be frustrated when

---

24 See above, r 31.3(2).
25 See Chapter 19, Making Applications for Court Orders.
26 See *Burmah Oil Co Ltd v Governor and Co of the Bank of England* [1980] AC 1090 and *Conway v Rimmer* [1968] AC 910.
27 See *D v NSPCC* [1978] AC 171.

deciding whether to grant the order. Given the nature of the application, the order of the court must not be served on, or open to inspection by, any other person, unless the court specifically orders otherwise (r 31.19(2)).

PRIVILEGE FROM INSPECTION

Legal professional privilege

This category can be divided into two types: communications between a lawyer and client for the purposes of obtaining legal advice, and communications between a client or his lawyer and third parties which come into existence after litigation is contemplated or commenced and are obtained with the sole or dominant purpose of obtaining advice, information or evidence for the purposes of the litigation. The first category has absolute protection so long as the documents do not relate to the furtherance of criminal or fraudulent acts.[28] The second category relies on being able to show that the dominant purpose for the existence of the document is to obtain advice, information or evidence for actual or contemplated litigation.[29]

A party who wishes to claim that he has a right or duty to withhold inspection of a document must identify the document and state that he has this duty or right and the grounds on which he claims it either in his disclosure list,[30] or, in a case where there is no disclosure list, in a written statement to the other party (r 31.19(3) and (4)). In the first instance, the party making the claim merely has to assert the right or duty, it will then be up to the other party to apply to the court, if need be, in order to challenge the disclosing party's claim to be able to withhold inspection of the document (r 31.19(5) and PD 31, para 6.1).

Privilege from self-incrimination

A party is not compelled to give discovery of documents which may tend to expose him or his spouse to a criminal penalty.[31] However, the right has been withdrawn in relation to compliance with orders for discovery relating to infringement of industrial property rights, such as patents and copyright, by s 72 of the Supreme Court Act 1981. Also, if the person can be adequately protected by some other means, such as an undertaking by the CPS not to prosecute, the privilege will not apply.[32]

---

28 *O'Rourke v Darbishire* [1920] AC 581.
29 *Waugh v British Railways Board* [1980] AC 521.
30 See above, p 334, for disclosure list.
31 See Civil Evidence Act 1968, s 14.
32 *ATT Istel Ltd v Tully* [1993] AC 45.

Application to withhold disclosure or permit inspection

The application by a disclosing party to withhold disclosure under r 31.19(1), or by the other party to permit inspection under r 31.19(5), should be made in accordance with Part 23[33] and supported by evidence (r 31.19(7)). In order to decide the application, the court may order that the document in question is produced to the court or invite any other person, whether or not a party, to make representations about the application (r 31.19(6)).

Inadvertent release of privileged document

If a party inadvertently allows a privileged document to be inspected, the party inspecting the document may only use it or its contents with the permission of the court (r 31.20).[34]

PRE-ACTION DISCLOSURE AND DISCLOSURE AGAINST NON-PARTIES

Pre-action disclosure

Normally, a party is only obliged to provide disclosure once proceedings have started. However, under s 33 of the Supreme Court Act 1981 and s 53 of the County Courts Act 1984, in appropriate circumstances, a person can apply for disclosure of documents from another person even before any proceedings have started. Previously, this power was only available for potential claims in personal injury and clinical negligence claims, but with the introduction of the CPR, the power was extended to potential claims in all areas of law.

Such an application can be made in relation to any type of matter so long as the following conditions are satisfied:

- the respondent to the application is likely to be a party to subsequent proceedings;
- the applicant is also likely to be a party to those proceedings;
- the document or classes of document for which the applicant seeks disclosure would be disclosable by the respondent in accordance with standard disclosure if proceedings had started; and
- pre-action disclosure is desirable in order to either:

  (a) dispose fairly of the anticipated proceedings;

---

33 See Chapter 19, Making Applications for Court Orders.
34 See *Breeze v John Stacey and Sons Ltd* (1999) *The Times*, 8 July, CA.

(b) assist the dispute to be resolved without proceedings; or

(c) save costs (r 31.16(3)).

Disclosure against a non-party

A party can compel a non-party to attend court to give relevant evidence or produce relevant documents (r 34.2). However, if a non-party holds relevant documents which can support a party's case, it may well be to that party's advantage to obtain those documents before any hearing. The party may, for instance, need the document to prove a vital part of their case or in order to persuade their opponent to settle. Therefore, under s 34 of the Supreme Court Act 1981 or s 53 of the County Courts Act 1984, if the following conditions are met, the court can make an order for disclosure of documents against a person who is not a party. These are:

• the documents are likely to support the case of the applicant or adversely affect the case of one of the other parties to the proceedings; and

• disclosure is necessary in order to dispose fairly of the claim or to save costs (r 31.17(3)).

Applications for pre-action disclosure and disclosure against a non-party

The application should be made in accordance with Part 23[35] and must be supported by evidence (r 31.16(2), (r 31.17(2)). If the application is successful, the order must specify the document or classes of document which the respondent is obliged to disclose and require the respondent to specify, when making disclosure, whether any of those documents are no longer in his control or whether he claims a right or duty to withhold inspection of any of those documents (r 31.16(4), r 31.17(4)). The court may also order the respondent to indicate what has happened to any documents no longer in his control and specify a time and place for disclosure and inspection (r 31.16(5), r 31.17(5)).

Therefore, in the case of a non-party, if the order is made he will be required to give disclosure of these documents in the same way as if he was a party to the proceedings.

Costs of an application for pre-action disclosure or disclosure

---

35 See Chapter 19, Making Applications for Court Orders.

against a non-party

The court will usually allow the person against whom such an order is made the costs of the application as well as the costs of complying with any order which is made for disclosure. However, if the court considers it unreasonable for a party not to have voluntarily disclosed a document, particularly if the document should have been disclosed in compliance with a pre-action protocol, and unreasonable for the party to oppose the application for disclosure, the court may make a different order for costs, including one which provides that the party applying for the order be allowed the costs (r 48.1).

COURT'S INHERENT POWER TO ORDER PRE-ACTION DISCLOSURE AND DISCLOSURE AGAINST A NON-PARTY

The rules as to pre-action disclosure and disclosure against a non-party do not limit any other powers the court may have, in the exercise of its inherent jurisdiction to control proceedings, to order pre-action disclosure or disclosure against a non-party (r 31.18).

Rule in *Norwich Pharmacal*

If a person, through no fault of his own, whether voluntarily or not, has got mixed up in the tortious acts of others so as to facilitate their wrongdoing, he may not incur any personal liability, but he comes under a duty to assist the person who has been wronged by giving him full information and by disclosing the identity of the wrongdoers. This principle laid down in the case of *Norwich Pharmacal v Customs and Excise*[36] gives the court the power to make an order for disclosure, known as a *Norwich Pharmacal* order, against a so called 'innocent wrongdoer'. This power of the court based on the court's exercise of its inherent jurisdiction to control proceedings has been expressly preserved by r 31.8.

---

36 [1974] AC 133.

CHAPTER 30

EXPERTS AND ASSESSORS

INTRODUCTION

Lord Woolf was particularly concerned with the role of experts in civil proceedings. There were several issues that needed to be addressed:

- there was a perception of a lack of objectivity on the part of experts. The concept had developed of 'hired guns' – experts who would tailor their evidence to the requirements of those instructing and paying them;
- cases often had unnecessary experts;
- the fees of experts were often unreasonable and/or out of proportion to the size of the dispute;
- the availability of experts to attend court or even carry out examinations or inspections was often very doubtful, resulting in considerable delays.[1]

As a result of the introduction of the Civil Procedure Rules, the adversarial nature of expert evidence in litigation is mitigated and now the expert's primary duty is to help the court, and to override any obligation to those who may have instructed or paid him. This process begins even before the litigation starts – where there are protocols, for example, the personal injury pre-action protocol. In *Baron v Lovell*,[1a] the court held that it was proper to debar expert evidence where the expert's report was only presented on the day of the hearing and the court pointed out the necessity for early pre-trial disclosure.

The previous practice of having one's own 'tame' experts must come to an end, the suggestion being that it distorts the true administration of justice. Experts, by their nature, will be expected to be neutral.

Even if both parties have obtained their own expert reports, the court is likely to consider a single joint expert. This is particularly so in fast track matters where oral evidence by experts is likely to be discouraged. In such matters, the expert's report is likely to be decisive, rather like the court welfare officer's report in children matters. The judge will not be bound to follow the conclusions in the report, but will have to give good reasons for not doing so.

Further, in those cases where strict time limits have been set down, for example, fast track, the 'elusive' expert will be on his way out and the response by the court to a request for more time is likely to be 'get another expert'.

---

1 *Access to Justice*, Final Report, p 137 (www.lcd.gov.uk/civil/finalfr.htm).
1a (1999) NLD, 27 July, CA.

Even if the court does not permit a party to use their own expert, there is nothing to stop them from doing so in order to advise them (that is, a 'shadow' expert) including advising on the questions to be put to a court-approved single joint expert, but their evidence cannot be given to the court, nor can their fees be claimed as part of costs awarded against the other party.

The rule that expert evidence cannot be adduced without the leave of the court is re-asserted, so that no party may call an expert, or put in evidence an expert's report, without the court's permission. When permission is sought, the expert's name, or else identity of the fields in which the applicant or party wishes to call evidence, must be provided (r 35.4). That permission is restricted just to that expert or the area of expertise mentioned. Furthermore, the court may vary or withdraw any permission given under this rule.

Rule 35.1 demands that:

> Expert evidence shall be restricted to that which is reasonably required to resolve the proceedings.

Most importantly, the duty of the expert to the court is the overriding duty. Rule 35.3 states:

(1) It is the duty of an expert to help the Court on the matters within his expertise.

(2) This duty overrides any obligation to the person from whom he has received instructions or by whom he is paid.

In *Stevens v Gullis*,[2] an expert who failed to comply with court orders was debarred from giving expert evidence and the Court of Appeal considered that it would also be wrong to allow him to give evidence of fact. Provided that his or her expertise and knowledge of the necessity for objectivity are demonstrated, there is no presumption that an employee of a party cannot be used as an expert under this Part (*Field v Leeds CC*).[3]

The court will not direct an expert to attend in fast track cases 'unless it is necessary to do so in the interests of justice'. This has much to do with the time constraints of fast track (see Chapter 17, The fast track). In small claims, neither written nor oral expert evidence may be adduced without the permission of the court (see Chapter 16, The small claims track). Experts' fees, if any, in small claims are limited to the amount specified in PD 27, para 7.3, that is, £200.

ACCESS TO THE COURT

Perhaps more fundamentally, the expert is now given direct access to the court to assist him carrying out his functions as an expert to the court. An

---

2 *Ibid.*

3 [1999] CPLR 833, CA.

expert has the right to seek directions from the court without giving notice to either party (r 35.14). However, the court may direct that a copy of the request and of the directions given be served on the parties when the directions are given.

SINGLE EXPERT

The court has an overriding power to decide that evidence before it should be given by a single joint expert rather than the party's individual experts (r 35.7). This rule also applies to fast track matters. This provision is likely to be particularly important in fast track cases. It is certainly the thrust of the personal injury pre-action protocol and the practice direction to it. However, in *S (A Minor) v Birmingham HA*[4] it was held that the usual CPR restrictions as to experts were inappropriate at the early stages of a complex clinical negligence action as they would hinder the proper pleading of the case. Indeed, the more complex and significant the case, the more likely is the need to have more than one expert.

Where two or more parties want to submit expert evidence on a particular issue, the court may direct that the evidence on that issue be given by one expert only. Where the parties cannot agree who should be the expert, the court will decide from a list prepared or identified by the parties or may choose an expert in some other manner (r 35.7(3)). Instructions for the single joint expert appointed in this manner comes from both parties. The parties must exchange their respective instructions (r 35.8).

The liability to pay the fees of the expert will be joint and several unless the court has ordered otherwise. The court has a right to give directions about the arrangements of the payment of the expert's fees and may limit the amount that can be paid by way of fees and expenses.

The 'written questions' provision[4a] is available, enabling the parties to raise and clarify points with the expert. This is particularly useful in fast track cases where the single joint expert is likely to be the rule rather than the exception.

FORM AND CONTENT OF REPORTS

See r 35.10 and PD 35, paras 1.1–1.6 for details. The contents reflect the new regime and remind the expert of both his duty to the court and the need to be neutral.

---

4   (1999) Lawtel, 23 November, Curtis J (unreported elsewhere).
4a   See below, p 348.

The report must (PD 35, para 1.2):

(2) give details of any literature or other material which the expert has relied on in making the report,

(3) say who carried out any test or experiment which the expert has used for the report and whether or not the test or experiment has been carried out under the expert's supervision,

(4) give the qualifications of the person who carried out any such test or experiment, and

(5) where there is a range of opinion on the matters dealt with in the report –

(i) summarise the range of opinion, and

(ii) give reasons for his own opinion,

(6) contain a summary of the conclusions reached,

(7) contain a statement that the expert understands his duty to the court and has complied with that duty (r 35.10(2)), and

(8) contain a statement setting out the substance of all material instructions (whether written or oral). The statement should summarise the facts and instructions given to the expert which are material to the opinions expressed in the report or upon which those opinions are based (r 35.10(3)).

The report should conclude: 'I believe that the facts I have stated in this report are true and that the opinions I have expressed are correct', and there must be a final statement in any report that the expert understands his duty to the court, and has complied with that duty.

Significantly, the report must also state the substance of all material instructions, including oral instructions, upon which the report was written. Instructions are, therefore, no longer privileged against disclosure (r 35.10(4)). However, the rules do provide that the court will not order disclosure of any specific document referred to or permit examination of the expert in relation to the instructions unless the court is satisfied that there are reasonable grounds to consider that the statement of instructions contained in the report may be incomplete. Parties will need to exercise extra judgment in respect of all communications with 'their' experts: there is no privilege in any such matters if they are material to the opinion and it will be for the expert to judge (with or without help from the court under r 35.14) what to disclose.

A party may use another disclosed report on which the instructing party does not rely to support their case if so desired (r 35.11).

QUESTIONS TO EXPERTS

By r 35.6, the Court may permit, or the parties may agree, to put pertinent questions to the expert about his report, but these must only be for the purpose of clarification (r 35.6(1) and (2) (see below)).

PD 35, paras 4.1 and 4.2:

> 4.1 Questions asked for the purpose of CLARIFYING the expert's report (see Rule 35.6) should be put, in writing, to the expert not later than 28 days after receipt of the expert's report (see paragraphs 1.2 to 1.5 above as to verification).
>
> 4.2 Where a party sends a written question or questions direct to an expert and the other party is represented by solicitors, a copy of the questions should, at the same time, be sent to those solicitors.

Note that the right under PD 25, para 4.2 to see a copy of the questions put by the other side is limited to those litigants who are represented and does not extend to litigants in person. In the first instance, the party who instructed the expert pays for the answers, whichever party puts the question (PD 35, para 4.3).

FURTHER DETAIL ON QUESTIONS

Rule 35.6:

> (1) A party may put to:
>
> > (a) an expert instructed by another party, or
> >
> > (b) a single joint expert appointed under Rule 35.7, written questions about his report.
>
> (2) Written questions under paragraph (1) –
>
> > (a) may be put once only;
> >
> > (b) must be put within 28 days of service of the expert's report; and
> >
> > (c) must be for the purpose only of clarification of the report;
> >
> > unless in any case –
> >
> > > (i) the court gives permission; or
> > >
> > > (ii) the other party agrees.
>
> (3) An expert's answers to questions put in accordance with paragraph (1) shall be treated as part of the expert's report.
>
> (4) Where –
>
> > (a) a party has put a written question to an expert instructed by another party in accordance with this rule; and
> >
> > (b) the expert does not answer the question,
> >
> > the court may make one or both of the following orders in relation to the party who instructed the expert –
> >
> > > (i) that the party may not rely on the evidence of that expert; or
> > >
> > > (ii) that the party may not recover the fees and expenses of that expert from any other party.

DISCUSSION BETWEEN EXPERTS
AND AGREEMENT OF ISSUES

The court may direct discussion between experts so as to identify the issues and where possible reach an agreement, and the court may itself specify the issues which the experts must address when they meet, including the need to deal with drafting of agendas for expert meetings, the draft guidelines for expert meetings, as well as requiring the experts to prepare a statement after they have met showing those issues on which they agree and those on which they disagree with a summary of their reasons for disagreeing.

While any document which they prepare is 'open', the contents of discussions between experts remain privileged (r 35.12(4)) at trial. Any agreement between the experts does not bind the parties unless the parties themselves expressly agree to be bound by it (r 35.12).

NON-DISCLOSURE (r 35.13)

Finally, perhaps the only thing which is not surprising is that non-disclosure of an expert's report means that it cannot be relied upon, nor can the party call the expert to give oral evidence. However, again, r 35.13 adds 'unless the court permits'.

THE COURT'S RIGHT TO APPOINT ASSESSORS

When a change in the rules was first being debated, there was a lot of support for the idea of court-appointed experts. However, the general feeling was this might lead to a loss of independence and restrict the numbers of experts who might be available. The right to appoint assessors was, however, put in, but it does not appear to have been much used. In a sense, a jointly instructed expert is very much in the same position as a court-appointed assessor.

Under r 35.19, the court has the right to appoint an assessor to assist the court in dealing with a matter in which the assessor has skill and experience. The assessor will take such part in the proceedings as the court directs and may at the request of the court prepare a report which can be disclosed to the parties and which they may use at trial (r 35.15(4)). The costs of the assessor will be determined by the court and the court has the power to order any party to deposit a sum of money in court in respect of the assessor's fees (r 35.15(5), (6)). Where the court does so, the assessor will not be appointed until the payment has been made (r 35.15(6)).

CHAPTER 31

EVIDENCE

INTRODUCTION

With the exception of the provisions with regard to expert evidence (and particularly the presumption in favour of single joint experts) rules on evidence are an area that was not significantly affected by the introduction of the CPR. The courts already had power to order witness statements and rely on them as evidence-in-chief. What the new rules did was to enhance the power of the courts to control evidence and increase the profile of witness statements to the detriment of affidavits.

The provision for statements of case to be confirmed by a statement of truth[1] means that such documents cannot stand as evidence.

COURT'S CONTROL OF EVIDENCE

The court now has an expanded power to control evidence

Rule 32.1:

(1) The court may control the evidence by giving directions as to –

(a) the issues on which it requires evidence;

(b) the nature of the evidence which it requires to decide those issues; and

(c) the way in which the evidence is to be placed before the court.

(2) The court may use its power under this rule to exclude evidence that would otherwise be admissible.

(3) The court may limit cross-examination.

Directions as to the control of evidence may be given at any stage, but more usually on allocation or at a pre-trial review.

The power to exclude admissible evidence is new. It enables the court to exclude evidence which, as a matter of law, is relevant to an issue in question. The court will no doubt bear in mind the overriding objective and, in particular, proportionality.[1a]

---

1   See Chapter 11, Statements of Case.
1a   See Chapter 5, Judicial Case Management: The Overriding Objective.

RELEVANCE AND ADMISSIBILITY

Evidence, for the purposes of civil proceedings, can be described as information which may be properly presented to the court to support the probability of facts being asserted before it. Evidence can only be presented if it is relevant, meaning logically probative or disprobative of the matter for which proof is required.

Evidence which is relevant is admissible, meaning receivable, by the court *unless* it is by some rule excluded from being received. Apart from public security, this comes down to 'privilege',[1b] that is, the exclusion of what may have passed between a party and his legal or medical advisers, or exclusion by agreement between the parties; this may arise where there has been a communication between parties where a dispute has arisen, or is likely to arise and the parties have written letters or continued negotiations in the knowledge that the courts will not order disclosure of them if a concluded agreement is not reached. That is, they are expressly or by implication, 'without prejudice'.[1c]

With regard to marking letters or other communications 'without prejudice', the following advice is offered, namely, that it is often better in the client's interests to write an open letter, so that it can be later produced. This in particular applies in respect of letters before action, setting out the claim.

However, marking a letter 'without prejudice' does not by itself prevent the document from production if there is nothing in the letter which is of a privileged nature. Note also that, in certain respects, the privilege in relation to communications between solicitors and their experts is lost if the expert is approved for use by the court (see Chapter 18, Experts).

HEARSAY EVIDENCE

This is now always admissible, but its value may be questioned.

The Rules (r 33.1) define hearsay as 'a statement made otherwise than by a person while giving oral evidence in the proceedings, which is tendered as evidence of the matters stated'; basically, then, not the direct evidence of a witness himself, but what someone else has been heard to say. If a statement is made – other than by a witness in the course of giving his evidence – evidence of it can be given to prove that the statement was made, and that is not hearsay; but it cannot be offered as proof of its contents – that would be hearsay. For a full discussion, see *Subramaniam v Public Prosecutor*.[1d]

1b See Chapter 29, Disclosure of Documents, p 339.
1c See Chapter 24, Offers to Settle and Payments into Court, p 293.
1d [1956] 1 WLR 965.

Section 1 of the Civil Evidence Act 1995 provides that in civil proceedings, evidence shall not be excluded on the grounds that it is hearsay. Section 2(1)(a) says that a party intending to adduce hearsay evidence 'shall' give notice of that fact; such has been the requirement since the Civil Evidence Act 1968.

But now, s 2(4) of the 1995 Act goes on to say that *failure* to give notice goes to costs, and weight, and not so as to make the hearsay evidence inadmissible. Thus, there is now no power to actually exclude evidence which is hearsay, assuming it is relevant, under any circumstances.

The 'hearsay notice'

There are two circumstances under which reliance on hearsay evidence needs to be considered.

Notice required:

33.2 (1) Where a party intends to rely on hearsay evidence at trial and either –

(a) that evidence is to be given by a witness giving oral evidence;

or

(b) that evidence is contained in a witness statement of a person who is

not being called to give oral evidence;

that party complies with section 2(1)(a) of the Civil Evidence Act 1995 by serving a witness statement on the other parties in accordance with the court's order.

(2) Where paragraph (1)(b) applies, the party intending to rely on the hearsay evidence must, when he serves the witness statement, inform the other parties that the witness is not being called to give oral evidence.

(3) In all other cases where a party intends to rely on hearsay evidence at trial, that party complies with section 2(1)(a) of the Civil Evidence Act 1995 by serving a notice on the other parties which –

(a) identifies the hearsay evidence; and

(b) states that the party serving the notice proposes to rely on the hearsay evidence at trial.

(4) The party proposing to rely on the hearsay evidence must –

(a) serve the notice no later than the latest date for serving witness statements; and

(b) if the hearsay evidence is to be in a document, supply a copy to any party who requests him to do so.

Notice not required:

33.3 Section 2(1) of the Civil Evidence Act 1995 (duty to give notice of intention to rely on hearsay evidence) does not apply –

(a) to evidence at hearings other than trials;

(b) to a statement which a party to a probate action wishes to put in evidence and which is alleged to have been made by the person whose estate is the subject of the proceedings; or

(c) where the requirement is excluded by a practice direction.

An opposing party's application to cross-examine in respect of hearsay may be made within 14 days after notice to rely on hearsay has been given; the power of the court extends to allowing the opposing party to call the maker of a hearsay statement (r 33.4(1) and (2)).

Where the party relying on the hearsay statement does not himself propose to call the maker of it, the opposing party can give notice of his intention to call his evidence to attack the maker's credibility (r 33.5(1)).

DIFFERENT TYPES OF EVIDENCE

Admissions[2] (r 14)

A fact may be admitted on the pleadings; an opponent may make use of the admittance by himself averring it with a different interpretation. Formal admissions may also be made in response to a notice to admit,[2a] or in answer to a request for further information (Part 18 – see Chapter 19, Statements of Case). Admissions may be made at any stage, as well as at the trial itself. Formal admissions made in civil proceedings are binding only for the purpose of those proceedings.

Non-expert evidence

This is set out in Part 32. Rule 32.1(1) states that it is for the court to give directions as to the issues on which evidence is required as to the nature of the evidence required on those issues and the way in which the evidence is to be placed before the court.

Rule 32.1(2) states 'the court may use its power under this rule to exclude evidence that would otherwise be admissible'.

The general principle is that evidence of witnesses is to be proved:

• at trial by oral evidence in public;

• at any other hearing by written evidence.

---

2 See also Chapter 8, Responding to an Action, p 86.

2a See p 358.

Evidence may be given by video link or by 'any other means' (r 32.3) (see below).

Witness statements

The court is given the power to order a party to serve on any other party a witness statement of the oral evidence which the party serving the statement intends to rely on in relation to any issues of fact to be decided at trial.

A witness statement is a 'written statement which contains the evidence and only that evidence which a person will be allowed to give orally at trial' (r 32.4). It must also be verified by a statement of truth: 'A certificate by its maker that he believes the statements of fact in it are true' (PD 32, para 20; see Part 22 and Chapter 11, Statements of Case). For the format of witness statements, see PD 32, paras 17–24. Failure to comply with the formalities may result in a refusal of the court to admit the document or to allow the costs of preparation (PD 32, para 25).

A person who makes a false witness statement, being a false statement in a statement of case or an application containing a statement of truth, without an honest belief in its truth is guilty of contempt of court (r 32.14) as well as perjury.

Rule 32.4(2) and (3): the court can give directions as to the order in which witness statements are to be served and whether or not witness statements are to be filed. The normal situation will be for a witness whose statement has been served to give evidence orally in court (r 32.5(1)). The written witness statement is to stand as the evidence-in-chief unless the court orders otherwise (r 32.5(2)).[2c]

In giving oral evidence at trial, the witness may, with the permission of the court (and if the court thinks there is good reason (r 32.5(4)):

- amplify the witness statement;
- give evidence in relation to new matters which have arisen since the witness statement was served on the other parties (r 32.5(3)).

The usual rule is that the maker of the statement must be called/tendered for cross-examination, his statement having stood as his evidence-in-chief. The balance between confining a witness to what is in the statement and permitting departure (save in respect of 'new' material) is in effect a balance between unnecessarily expensive and elaborate statements on the one hand, and the potential for 'ambush' on the other. Substantial injustice caused by the latter should result in the new evidence simply being excluded, and this is an adjunct to the wide general powers under r 32.1.

2c See the general observations of Woolf MR in *McPhilemy v The Times* [1999] 3 All ER 775, CA as to how statements of case and witness statements fit together.

If a party who has served a witness statement does not call the witness or put in the witness statement as hearsay (see above), the other party may put in the witness statement as hearsay evidence (r 32.5(5) and see *Society of Lloyd's v Jaffray and Others*).[3] This is a new provision, making witness statements similar to that of experts' reports. However, the court may limit the use of such a statement. A party seeking to put in a witness statement served but not used by the other side must accept the totality of the statement (*McPhilemy v The Times (No 2)*).[4]

Note r 32.12:

(1) Except as provided by this rule, a witness statement may be used only for the purpose of the proceedings in which it is served.

(2) Paragraph (1) does not apply if and to the extent that –

   (a) the witness gives consent in writing to some other use of it;

   (b) the court gives permission for some other use; or

   (c) the witness statement has been put in evidence at a hearing held in public.

A witness statement that has been used in a public hearing can therefore form the basis of separate proceedings, for example, defamation.

Statements of evidence given in public are available for inspection by any person unless the court orders otherwise in the interests of justice or the public, in respect of medical evidence or confidential information, or where there are persons under a disability involved (r 32.13).

Witness summaries as an alternative

Witness summaries may be served with the court's leave on application without notice where it is not possible to obtain a witness statement (r 32.9(1)). The intention is to be able to refer to brief notes obtained and prepared which do not go quite so far as the full statement but r 32.9(2)(b) provides the document may also be a summary of 'matters about which the party serving the witness summary will question the witness'. This will therefore apply in the hostile witness situation. The rules as to service, amplification and form are the same as for witness statements (r 32.9(4), (5)).

---

3   (2000) *The Times*, 3 August, QBD (Cresswell J).
4   (2000) 1 SLR 1732, CA.

FAILURE TO SERVE WITNESS STATEMENTS

The idea behind witness statements is clear and is to be encouraged. However, r 32.10 provides that if a witness statement for use at trial (or a witness summary) is not served in respect of an intended witness within the time specified by the court, then the witness may not be called to give oral evidence unless the court permits.

To what extent the court will allow the evidence to be called will depend on the circumstances. Where the default results in an adjournment of the trial date being requested, such an application is unlikely to succeed, and therefore the evidence will be excluded, in the light of the strict intention of the court to maintain the trial date at all costs (see Chapter 17, The Fast Track and Chapter 18, The Multi-Track). A more minor default which causes no prejudice may be treated more leniently. The court will also have to have regard to the provisions of Art 6(1) of the ECHR as to the effect on a 'fair trial' of allowing or disallowing evidence in a particular case.[5]

ATTENDANCE OF WITNESSES

A witness summons to secure attendance may be issued at any time except that where a party wishes to have a summons issued less than seven days before the date of the trial he must obtain permission from the court, and in certain other exceptional cases (r 34.3(1), (2)). A witness summons is to be issued in the court where the case is proceeding, or where the hearing will be held (r 34.3(3)).

Witness summonses are to be served by the court, unless the party on whose behalf it is issued indicates in writing when he asks the court to issue, that he wishes to serve it himself (r 34.6(1)). Where the court is to serve the witness summons, the party on whose behalf it is issued must deposit in the Court Office the money to be paid or offered to the witness under r 34.7 (see below) (r 34.6(2)).

At the time of service, the witness must be offered or paid a sum reasonably sufficient to cover his expenses in travelling to and from the court and such sum by way of compensation for loss of time as may be specified in the relevant practice direction (r 34.7) (see PD 34). It is important to note that a witness summons may be set aside by the court which issues it, and the person served with a witness summons may apply.

The position with regard to witness summonses is not, therefore, much different from that which applied previously.

---

5   See Chapter 37, The Human Rights Act 1998.

AFFIDAVITS

Apart from a few exceptions,[6] witness statements now replace affidavits as the normal way of giving evidence.

Evidence is to be given by affidavit if it is required by the court, practice direction or any other enactment or as an alternative to witness statements or in addition to it if the court requires it (r 32.15(1)). An affidavit may be used in circumstances where a statement would have sufficed, but the party putting it forward may not recover any additional costs of preparing it unless the court otherwise orders (r 32.15(2)). For the format of affidavits see PD 32, para 2.16. Failure to comply with the formalities may have the same result as with witness statements, above.

NOTICES TO ADMIT FACTS AND/OR DOCUMENTS

These are available as previously under rr 32.18 and 32.19. A notice to admit facts must be served no later than 21 days before trial (r 32.18(2)), while a notice to prove a document must be served by the latest date for serving witness statements or within seven days of disclosure of the document, whichever is later (r 32.19(2)).

PLANS, PHOTOGRAPHS AND MODELS

For trial, to ensure that plans, etc, can be received in evidence, notice of intention to make use of the plans, models, etc, must be given 14 days before date for serving witness statements if they are part of witness statements, or affidavits, or expert's reports; in other cases, 21 days before the hearing (r 33.6).

VIDEO

Video is expressly referred to in r 32.3:

32.3   The court may allow a witness to give evidence through a video link or
        by other means.

---

6   For instance, in the case of applications for a freezing injunction or search order, see
     Chapter 20, Interim Remedies.

Also, in the Practice Direction to Part 23, para 7:

Video Conferencing:

7   Where the parties to a matter wish to use video conferencing facilities, and those facilities are available in the relevant court, they should apply to the Master or District Judge for directions.

Video links are currently being considered by the court service as part of their overall IT strategy. See also QB Masters' PD 50, Applications to QB Masters by video conference.

CHAPTER 32

HEARINGS AND JUDGMENT

HEARINGS (PART 39)

Introduction

The new rules did not have a significant effect on the actual trials themselves, except with regard to fast track trials.[1] The main changes are in the preparation for trial and, in particular, the management of the case by the court.[2]

Hearings are now to be mainly in public. The court is proactive in setting timetables which it expects to be complied with. The new rules re-affirm the consequences on a party who fails to attend a hearing. Detailed provision is made for the preparation and delivery of trial bundles.

General

Note the provisions of r 39.2:

(1) The general rule is that a hearing is to be in public.

(2) The requirement for a hearing to be in public does not require the court to make special arrangements for accommodating members of the public.

(3) A hearing, or any part of it, may be in private if –

(a) publicity would defeat the object of the hearing;

(b) it involves matters relating to national security;

(c) it involves confidential information (including information relating to personal financial matters) and publicity would damage that confidentiality;

(d) a private hearing is necessary to protect the interests of any child or patient;

(e) it is a hearing of an application made without notice and it would be unjust to any respondent for there to be a public hearing;

(f) it involves uncontentious matters arising in the administration of trusts or in the administration of a deceased person's estate; or

(g) the court considers this to be necessary, in the interests of justice.

(4) The court may order that the identity of any party or witness must not be disclosed if it considers non-disclosure necessary in order to protect the interests of that party or witness.

1   See Chapter 17, The Fast Track.
2   See Chapter 5, Judicial Case Management: The Overriding Objective.

(RSC Ord 52, in Sched 1, provides that a committal hearing may be in private.)

As for those cases which are to be held in private, see PD 39, paras 1.5–1.14.

1.5 The hearings set out below shall in the first instance be listed by the court as hearings in private under rule 39.2(3)(c), namely:

(1) a claim by a mortgagee against one or more individuals for an order for possession of land,

(2) a claim by a landlord against one or more tenants or former tenants for the repossession of a dwelling house based on the non-payment of rent,

(3) an application to suspend a warrant of execution or a warrant of possession or to stay execution where the court is being invited to consider the ability of a party to make payments to another party,

(4) a re-determination under rule 14.13 or an application to vary or suspend the payment of a judgment debt by instalments,

(5) an application for a charging order (including an application to enforce a charging order), garnishee order, attachment of earnings order, administration order, or the appointment of a receiver,

(6) an oral examination,

(7) the determination of an assisted person's liability for costs under regulation 127 of the Civil Legal Aid (General) Regulations 1989,

(8) an application for security for costs under section 726(1) of the Companies Act 1985, and

(9) proceedings brought under the Consumer Credit Act 1974, the Inheritance (Provision for Family and Dependants) Act 1975 or the Protection from Harassment Act 1997,

(10) an application by a trustee or personal representative for directions as to bringing or defending legal proceedings.

(11) any other necessary documents.

1.6 Rule 39.2(3)(d) states that a hearing may be in private where it involves the interests of a child or patient. This includes the approval of a compromise or settlement on behalf of a child or patient or an application for the payment of money out of court to such a person.

1.7 Attention is drawn to paragraph 5.1 of the practice direction which supplements Part 27 (relating to the hearing of claims in the small claims track), which provides that the judge may decide to hold a small claim hearing in private if the parties agree or if a ground mentioned in rule 39.2(3) applies. A hearing of a small claim in premises other than the court will not be a hearing in public.

1.8 Nothing in this practice direction prevents a judge ordering that a hearing taking place in public shall continue in private, or vice versa.

1.9 If the court or judge's room in which the proceedings are taking place has a sign on the door indicating that the proceedings are private, members of the public who are not parties to the proceedings will not be admitted unless the court permits.

1.10 Where there is no such sign on the door of the court or judge's room, members of the public will be admitted where practicable. The judge may, if he thinks it appropriate, adjourn the proceedings to a larger room or court.

1.11 When a hearing takes place in public, members of the public may obtain a transcript of any judgment given or a copy of any order made, subject to payment of the appropriate fee.

1.12 When a judgment is given or an order is made in private, if any member of the public who is not a party to the proceedings seeks a transcript of the judgment or a copy of the order, he must seek the leave of the judge who gave the judgment or made the order.

1.13 A judgment or order given or made in private, when drawn up, must have clearly marked in the title:

'Before [title and name of judge] sitting in Private'

1.14 References to hearings being in public or private or in a judge's room contained in the Civil Procedure Rules (including the Rules of the Supreme Court and the County Court Rules scheduled to Part 50) and the practice directions which supplement them do not restrict any existing rights of audience or confer any new rights of audience in respect of applications or proceedings which under the rules previously in force would have been heard in court or in chambers respectively.

The intention to hold hearings in public may be frustrated by the layout of court buildings. Many have district judge chambers (where, for example, small claims disputes are heard) in suites behind locked doors for security. This may be circumvented by a notice inviting members of the public who wish to be present to ask the usher to allow them access.

Failure to attend trial (r 39.3)

On failure of a defendant to attend, the claimant may prove his claim and obtain judgment and, if there is a counterclaim, seek to have it struck out. Where the claimant fails to attend, the defendant may prove his counterclaim and, similarly, seek the striking out of the claim. In cases where neither party attends, the court may strike out the proceedings. This will mean that a party will be left to apply for restoration and, where appropriate, for any judgment given to be set aside.

Timetables for trial

Details of the power of the court to fix timetables and fix a date for a trial are set out in r 28.6 in relation to fast track[3] and r 29.8 for multi-track.[4] The timetable will be fixed in consultation with the parties (r 39.4).

Trial bundles

Directions for preparation and lodging are likely to be given at listing stage, but the Rules require a bundle to be lodged not more than seven and not less than three days before trial (r 39.5(2)), though for fast track the directions as given in the Appendix to PD 28 state that the trial bundles must be lodged at least seven days before trial. Where there is a trial window, these periods would no doubt be calculated from the start of the window.

It is important to remember that a claimant will need to compile bundles for each of all other parties, and another for use of the witnesses. Originals of documents in the bundle should be available for production (PD 39, para 3.3).

Format of bundles (PD 39, para 3.2)

Unless the court orders otherwise, the trial bundle should include a copy of:

    (1) the claim form and all statements of case,

    (2) a case summary and/or chronology where appropriate,

    (3) requests for further information and responses to the requests,

    (4) all witness statements to be relied on as evidence,

    (5) any witness summaries,

    (6) any notices of intention to rely on hearsay evidence under rule 32.2,

    (7) any notices of intention to rely on evidence (such as a plan, photograph etc) under rule 33.6 which is not –

        (a) contained in a witness statement, affidavit or expert's report,

        (b) being given orally at trial,

        (c) hearsay evidence under rule 33.2,

    (8) any medical reports and responses to them,

    (9) any experts' reports and responses to them,

    (10)any order giving directions as to the conduct of the trial, and

    (11)any other necessary documents.

    3.3 The originals of the documents contained in the trial bundle, together with copies of any other court orders should be available at the trial.

---

3   See Chapter 17, The Fast Track.

4   See Chapter 18, The Multi-Track.

3.4 The preparation and production of the trial bundle, even where it is delegated to another person, is the responsibility of the legal representative (see rule 2.3) who has conduct of the claim on behalf of the claimant.

3.5 The trial bundle should be paginated (continuously) throughout, and indexed with a description of each document and the page number. Where the total number of pages is more than 100, numbered dividers should be placed at intervals between groups of documents.

3.6 The bundle should normally be contained in a ring binder or lever arch file. Where more than one bundle is supplied, they should be clearly distinguishable, for example, by different colours or letters. If there are numerous bundles, a core bundle should be prepared containing the core documents essential to the proceedings, with references to the supplementary documents in the other bundles.

3.7 For convenience, experts' reports may be contained in a separate bundle and cross-referenced in the main bundle.

3.8 If a document to be included in the trial bundle is illegible, a typed copy should be included in the bundle next to it, suitably cross-referenced.

3.9 The contents of the trial bundle should be agreed where possible. The parties should also agree where possible:

(1) that the documents contained in the bundle are authentic even if not disclosed under Part 31, and

(2) that documents in the bundle may be treated as evidence of the facts stated in them even if a notice under the Civil Evidence Act 1995 has not been served.

Where it is not possible to agree the contents of the bundle, a summary of the points on which the parties are unable to agree should be included.

3.10 The party filing the trial bundle should supply identical bundles to all the parties to the proceedings and for the use of the witnesses.

Lever-arch files are desirable, otherwise use a ring file. A separate file is convenient for any expert evidence, and different coloured files, where there are more than one, should be used.

Settlement before trial

Note PD 39, para 4:

4.1 Where:

(1) an offer to settle a claim is accepted, or

(2) a settlement is reached, or

(3) a claim is discontinued,

which disposes of the whole of a claim for which a date or 'window' has been fixed for the trial, the parties must ensure that the listing officer for the trial court is notified immediately.

4.2 If an order is drawn up giving effect to the settlement or discontinuance, a copy of the sealed order should be filed with the listing officer.

Conduct of the trial

Opening speeches, as before, may be dispensed with whether on fast or multi-track (PD 28, para 8.2 and PD 29, para 10.2).

As for presentation of witness evidence, see Chapter 31, Evidence. A company can be represented by an authorised employee provided the court gives permission (r 39.6 and see PD 39, paras 5.2 and 5.3). It is to be presumed that the court will include in the definition of 'employee' that of a director. The court will be entitled, when considering whether or not to grant permission, the difficulty of the case and the individual's experience and position in the company (PD 39, para 5.3). In addition, the employee will be required to produce evidence of authority to speak on behalf of the company or give an undertaking to that effect.

Exhibits proved at the trial will be recorded by the court and kept by the court until conclusion of the trial, unless otherwise directed (PD 39, para 7).

Usually, the evidence will be recorded (PD 39, para 6.1) and a copy of any transcript will be available on payment of a charge (PD 39, para 6.3).

JUDGMENTS AND ORDERS (PART 40)

Introduction

Every judgment or order, including those made at trial, will be drawn up by the court unless:

• the court orders a party to draw it up;

• a party with the permission of the court agrees to draw it up;

• the court dispenses with the need to draw it up; or

• it is a consent order under r 40.6 (see below) (r 40.3(1).

Thus, the High Court has now adopted the county court practice of drawing up the orders itself. A judge has jurisdiction to reconsider his decision before an order is drawn up.[5]

---

5 *Charlesworth (Willis Arnold) (Claimant) v Relay Roads Ltd (In Liquidation) and Others (No 2)* [1999] 4 All ER 397.

Service of judgments or orders

Where a judgment or order has been drawn up by a party and is to be served by the court, the party who drew it up must file a copy and sufficient copies for service (r 40.4). The court may also order a judgment to be served on the party, notwithstanding that he is represented by a solicitor (r 40.5), although such an order is only likely to be made in exceptional circumstances, for example, where a penal notice has been attached.

Consent judgments and orders

The court officer may enter and seal an agreed judgment or order if it is basically for payment of an amount of money, delivery up of goods, dismissal of any proceedings, or their stay, or the stay of enforcement of a judgment, the setting aside of a default judgment, payment out of money which has been paid into court, the discharge from liability of any party, or the payment, assessment or waiver of costs (r 40.6).

However, this does not apply where the approval of the court is needed for an order to be made (r 40.6(2)(c)) – for example, to change a 'milestone' date[6] (see r 28.4 and Chapter 5, Case management), or where one of the parties is a litigant in person (r 40.6(2)(b)).

When does a judgment or order take effect?

From the day when it is given or made, or at such later date as the court may specify (r 40.7). This changes the previous position which was that judgment ran from the time judgment was entered.

Interest[7] on judgments

The interest shall begin to run from the date that judgment is given unless there is a rule or practice direction which makes a different provision, or the court orders otherwise, and this includes ordering interest to begin from a date before the date that judgment was given (r 40.9).

---

6   See r 28.4 and Chapter 5, Judicial Case Management: The Overriding Objective.
7   See Chapter 8, Responding to an Action, p 89.

Time for complying with a judgment or order

If for payment of an amount of money, including costs, compliance is required within 14 days of the date of the judgment or order unless that specifies a different date for compliance, or any of the Rules specify a different date, or the court has stayed the proceedings or judgment.

Under the previous position, if no date was given for complying with the order, it was unclear as to when compliance was required. Now, if the order is silent as to the date, it is 14 days by default.

'Slip' rule

The court may, at any time, correct an accidental slip or omission in the judgment or order and a party may apply for a correction without notice (r 40.12).

Judgment on claim and counterclaim

If specified amounts are awarded both to the claimant on his claim and against the claimant on a counterclaim, then whatever may be the balance in favour of the one of the parties may be subject to an order for the net loser to pay the balance, but the court may make a separate order as to costs (r 40.13).

Sale of land, etc

As to the court's power to order the sale, mortgage, partition or exchange of land, and the appointment of conveyancing counsel, see r 40.15.

CHAPTER 33

COSTS

INTRODUCTION

In his Final Report, Lord Woolf said that costs were 'central to the changes' he wished to bring about and that virtually all his recommendations for reform of the civil procedure system were 'designed at least in part to tackle the problems of costs'. He stated that his reforms were designed to reduce the amount of costs incurred by a party by controlling what was required of a party in the conduct of proceedings, to make the amount of costs more predictable and more proportionate to the nature of the dispute. He also recommended that costs be used more effectively as a method to control unreasonable behaviour and that litigants should be provided with more information about costs so that they could exercise greater control over their lawyer's expenditure of costs on their behalf.[1]

Although it seems true to say that parties and legal representatives are now much more aware of the incidence of costs when conducting proceedings than they were before the CPR were introduced, and much more afraid of being penalised in costs for their conduct in the course of proceedings, there is no clear evidence that the CPR have in fact reduced the level of costs that are incurred in conducting proceedings. In fact, a common criticism made of the new regime under the CPR is that it causes 'front loading' of costs, which can result in higher levels of costs than would previously have been the case under the old civil procedure system, particularly if a case settles at an early stage. Complaint is also commonly heard that the requirement to produce costs estimates and statements of costs throughout the course of proceedings, in order to keep the client, the opponent and the court informed of the level of costs being incurred, paradoxically increases the costs burden on a party in conducting litigation.

However, what the courts are very alive to is costs being in some way proportionate to the amount in issue and they have not hesitated to reduce bills which have fallen foul of this principle. In addition, misconduct by one of the parties is likely to be reflected in the award of costs.

---

1   See *Access to Justice*, Final Report, Chapter 7, para 5 (www.lcd.gov.uk/civil/finalfr.htm).

DEFINITIONS AND JURISDICTION

Definition of costs

The term 'costs' in the CPR costs rules[2] has a wide definition and includes fees, charges and remuneration including success fees in conditional fee agreements[3] as well as disbursements, expenses and any insurance premiums for legal expenses insurance.[4] Costs also includes remuneration allowed to a litigant in person and any fee or reward charged by a lay representative for acting on behalf of a party in proceedings allocated to the small claims track (r 43.2).

Base costs and additional liabilities

Since the changes to the rules about recovering the success fee and insurance premium[4a] associated with conditional fee agreements[4b] from another party, the amounts claimed in success fees and insurance premiums are known as 'additional liabilities' and all the other costs of the action are known as 'base costs' (r 43.2 and PD 43, para 2.2).

Proceedings other than court proceedings

The costs rules apply not only to the costs of parties involved in court proceedings, but also, where the court has the power to assess those costs, to the costs of proceedings before an arbitrator, tribunal or other statutory body (r 43.2(2)(a)).

Solicitor/client costs

The costs rules also apply to the costs payable by a client to his solicitor when the client seeks to challenge the amount of those costs (r 43.2(2)(a)).

Costs payable under a contract

The rules will also apply to the costs payable by one party to another under the terms of a contract where the court makes an order for the assessment of those costs (r 43.2(2)(b)).

---

2   CPR, rr 44–48 and supplementary practice directions.
3   See Chapter 38, Funding Litigation.
4   *Ibid.*
4a *Ibid.*
4b *Ibid.*

Counsel's fees

There is confusion as to whether 'certificates for counsel' still need to be requested on interlocutory hearings. The sensible view would appear to be that they do not and that, indeed, PD 44, para 2.6 provides a mechanism for a certificate only when the judge feels that the attention of the taxing officer needs to be drawn to it.

Costs draftsmen's fees

Costs draftsmen's fees can be included in the 'reasonable costs of preparing and checking the bill' (PD 43, para 2.16), although this does not apply to publicly funded family matters. Whether a costs draftsman is needed to prepare a summary bill of costs[5] or costs estimate[6] will depend on its complexity.

Who assesses costs?

Costs assessed by the court may be assessed by either an authorised court officer, being an officer of a county court, a district registry, the Principal Registry of the Family Division or the Supreme Court Costs Office who has been authorised to assess costs; a costs officer, being a costs judge, a district judge or an authorised court officer; or a costs judge, being a taxing master of the Supreme Court (r 43.2(1)).

Authorised court officer

There are jurisdictional limits to the claims for costs that can be assessed by an authorised court officer by way of detailed assessment in the Supreme Court Costs Office and the Principal Registry of the Family Division (PD 47, para 30.1(1)). Also, if all the parties to a detailed assessment hearing agree that it should not be conducted by an authorised court officer, if the receiving party notifies the court of this when requesting a hearing date, the court will list the hearing before a costs judge or a district judge instead (PD 47, para 30.1(3)). If the parties cannot agree, but a party would like to object nevertheless, the party can make an application to the court under Part 23[6a] and the court can decide, if sufficient reason is shown, to list the detailed assessment hearing before a costs judge or a district judge (PD 47, para 30.1(4)).

---

5   See below, p 389.
6   See below, p 385.
6a See Chapter 19, Making Applications for Court Orders.

Moreover, there are certain aspects of the rules in relation to detailed assessment that an authorised court officer has no power to make. These are wasted costs orders, orders in relation to misconduct, sanctions for delay in commencing detailed assessment proceedings, detailed assessment of costs payable to a solicitor by his client (unless it relates to costs in proceedings involving a child or patient) and when a party makes an application objecting to an authorised court officer carrying out a detailed assessment (r 47.3).

Types of orders for costs

Note PD 44, para 2.4: there are certain costs orders which the court will commonly make in proceedings before trial. The following table sets out the general effect of these orders. The table is not an exhaustive list of the orders which the court may make.

Term	Effect
Costs Costs in any event	The party in whose favour the order is made is entitled to the costs in respect of the part of the proceedings to which the order relates, whatever other costs orders are made in the proceedings.
Costs in the case Costs in the application	The party in whose favour the court makes an order for costs at the end of the proceedings is entitled to his costs of the part of the proceedings to which the order relates.
Costs reserved	The decision about costs is deferred to a later occasion, but if no later order is made the costs will be costs in the case.
Claimant's/defendant's costs in the case/application	If the party in whose favour the costs order is made is awarded costs at the end of the proceedings, that party is entitled to his costs of the part of the proceedings to which the order relates. If any other party is awarded costs at the end of the proceedings, the party in whose favour the final costs order is made is not liable to pay the costs of any other party in respect of the part of the proceedings to which the order relates.
Costs thrown away	Where, for example, a judgment or order is set aside, the party in whose favour the costs order is made is entitled to the costs which have been incurred as a consequence. This includes the costs of – a preparing for and attending any hearing at which the judgment or order which has been set aside was made;

Term	Effect
	b preparing for and attending any hearing to set aside the judgment or order in question;
	c preparing for and attending any hearing at which the court orders the proceedings or the part in question to be adjourned;
	d any steps taken to enforce a judgment or order which has subsequently been set aside.
Costs of and caused by	Where, for example, the court makes this order on an application to amend a statement of case, the party in whose favour the costs order is made is entitled to the costs of preparing for and attending the application and the costs of any consequential amendment to his own statement of case.
Costs here and below	The party in whose favour the costs order is made is entitled not only to his costs in respect of the proceedings in which the court makes the order, but also to his costs of the proceedings in any lower court. In the case of an appeal from an Administrative Court the party is not entitled to any costs incurred in any court below the Administrative Court.
No order as to costs Each party to pay his own costs	Each party is to bear his own costs of the part of the proceedings to which the order relates whatever costs order the court makes at the end of the proceedings.

COURT'S DISCRETION AS TO COSTS

By s 51 of the Supreme Court Act 1981, the costs of and incidental to proceedings in the High Court and any county courts are in the discretion of the court and the court has full power to determine by whom and to what extent costs are to be paid.

A successful party is not entitled to recover costs, the court having a discretion in every case as to whether costs are recoverable from another party (r 44.3(1)(a)). Moreover, although the general rule[7] is that the unsuccessful party must pay the successful party's costs, the court can make a different order (r 44.3(2)).

---

7 The general rule does not apply to certain family and probate proceedings in the Court of Appeal, see r 44.3(3).

Therefore, although in most cases the general rule will prevail, behind these rules is the message, running throughout the CPR, that the court is not just concerned with the 'ends' but also the 'means' to the ends, that is, the court cannot simply award costs to the successful party, without also considering the conduct of the parties over the course of the proceedings. As Lord Woolf put it in *PPL v AEI*,[8] the general rule is 'a starting position from which a court can readily depart'.[9]

Also, a party cannot rely on the operation of the general rule in the absence of a reference to costs in a court order, because if costs are not expressly mentioned in the order, no party is entitled to any (r 44.13(1)).

Circumstances to be taken into account when ordering costs

Rule 44.3(4) provides that, when deciding what order to make about costs, the court must have regard to all the circumstances. The rule then provides that when considering the circumstances, the court must include certain matters, but these are not the only considerations and the court can consider any others that are relevant. The matters the court must consider are:

- the conduct of all the parties;
- whether a party has succeeded on part of his case, even if he has not been wholly successful; and
- any payment into court or admissible offer to settle made by a party which is drawn to the court's attention (whether or not made in accordance with Part 36) (r 44.3(4)(a)–(c)).

All of these factors (and any other relevant factors) may persuade the court to make a different order as to costs other than one in accordance with the general rule, namely, that the unsuccessful party pay the successful party's costs.

The conduct of the parties

When making a decision as to whether to order costs, the court's view of the conduct of the parties will be informed by the overriding objective[10] and the parties must therefore ensure that they have shown themselves to be open and fair in exchanging information and to have taken steps to avoid the need for litigation. The parties must also show that they have conducted the litigation in a reasonable and proportionate way and that they have concentrated on the real issues in dispute between them.

8   [1999] 2 All ER 299.
9   See p 313j.
10 See r 1.1 and Chapter 5, Judicial Case Management: The Overriding Objective.

In accordance with this, r 44.3(5) provides that the conduct of the parties includes:

- conduct before, as well as during the proceedings and, in particular, the extent to which the parties followed any relevant pre-action protocol;
- whether it was reasonable for a party to raise, pursue or contest a particular allegation or issue;
- the manner in which a party has pursued or defended his case or a particular allegation or issue; and
- whether a claimant who has succeeded in his claim, in whole or in part, exaggerated his claim.

Success for part of a case

In recognition of the fact that the parties must aim to identify and concentrate on the real issues in dispute, and in order to discourage the 'scatter gun' approach to litigation (including every possible issue as part of a case regardless of merit), the court is expressly given the power to make costs orders in favour of a party who has been successful on only part of a case, or certain issues in the case. This has been described as 'the most significant change of emphasis of the new [costs] rules'.[11] Therefore, under r 44.3(6), the court may order that a party must pay:

- a proportion of another party's costs;
- a stated amount in respect of another party's costs;
- costs from or until a certain date only;
- costs incurred before proceedings have begun;
- costs relating to particular steps taken in the proceedings;
- costs relating only to a distinct part of the proceedings; and
- interest on costs from or until a certain date, including a date before judgment.

In the interests of a more straightforward calculation, rather than order a party to pay costs relating to a distinct part of the proceedings the court must, if practicable, order a party either to pay a proportion of another party's costs or costs from or until a certain date instead (r 44.3(7)).

In a Court of Appeal decision, Lord Woolf explained why he thought the former approach to deciding which party was entitled to costs based simply on which party was the overall winner in the case was wrong in the following terms:

---

11 *Per* Lord Woolf in *PPL v AEI* [1999] 2 All ER 299, pp 313–14.

The most significant change of emphasis of the new rules is to require courts to be more ready to make separate orders which reflect the outcome of different issues. In doing this, the new rules are reflecting a change of practice which has already started. It is now clear that a too robust application of the 'follow the event principle' encourages litigants to increase the cost of litigation, since it discourages litigants from being selective as to the points they take. If you recover all your points as long as you win, you are encouraged to leave no stone unturned in your effort to do so.[12]

In the case of *Firle Investments Ltd v Datapoint International Ltd*[13] the judge decided that in order to do broad justice in that case, the defendant should be ordered to pay only a modest contribution to the claimant's costs. The judge therefore decided to order that the defendant pay only a third of the claimant's costs up to the date of a realistic offer of settlement made by the defendant and only 15% of the claimant's costs after that date. Such an order was made notwithstanding the fact that the claimant had recovered more than the defendant's Part 36 payment into court on the grounds that this was a 'slim victory' and criticised the claimant for not responding to this offer of settlement in a more constructive and conciliatory way.

Also, in *Mars UK Ltd v Teknowledge Ltd (No 2)*,[14] Jacob J declared that one of the claims pleaded by the successful claimant 'had only barely been reasonable' and that therefore, the unsuccessful defendant should be given credit for the costs relating to that issue. The court estimated that on final assessment, the claimant would only recover 40% of its costs as it was also guilty of heavy handed pre-action conduct.

Paying the balance of costs due

If a party who is entitled to costs is also liable to pay costs, the court may assess the costs the party is liable to pay and either set off the amount assessed against the amount the party is entitled to be paid and direct him to pay any balance, or delay the issue of a certificate for the costs to which the party is entitled until he has paid the amount which he is liable to pay (r 44.3(9)).

Part 36 offers to settle and payments in

One of the matters which the court must take into account when deciding what order to make about costs is any payment into court or admissible offer to settle which is drawn to the court's attention, whether or not it was made in

---

12 *PPL v AEI* [1999] 2 All ER 299, p 314a.
13 8 May 2000, QBD, Court Service website (www.courtservice.gov.uk).
14 (1999) *The Times*, 8 July.

accordance with Part 36.[15] Part 36 provides for a number of sanctions and penalties if a party fails to better a Part 36 offer or payment at trial.[16]

However, a Court of Appeal decision, *Ford v GKR Construction Ltd (and Others)*[17] has made it clear that the test as to whether a party should be entitled to the costs and other penalties provided by Part 36 is not simply a narrow one of whether the offer or payment is better or worse than that ordered at trial, as the court will also consider all relevant aspects of the litigation and behaviour of the parties. That case highlighted in particular the need to give full and early disclosure of all relevant information so that the other party is in a position to assess whether to make or accept an offer to settle or payment into court.[17a]

The case of *Firle Investments Ltd v Datapoint International Ltd*, referred to above,[17b] is also an example of circumstances where the court may not follow the general rule as to costs even where judgment is for a greater sum than a Part 36 payment.

Part 36 does not provide any penalty for a claimant where he makes a Part 36 offer to settle, but fails to obtain a judgment which is more advantageous than that offer. It seems to be the intention of the rules to encourage claimants to make such offers by protecting them from any adverse consequences if they fail to better them, as PD 44, para 8.4 specifically provides that those circumstances alone will not lead to a reduction in costs awarded to the claimant.

TIME WHEN COSTS ORDERS ARE MADE

The court has the power to make an order about costs at any stage of a case (PD 44, para 8.3(1)). Apart from making an order at the conclusion of the proceedings, the court is likely to make costs orders when it deals with any application, makes any order or holds any hearing (PD 44, para 8.3(2)). However, it should be remembered that if the court does not make an order for costs, none are payable,[18] and it is therefore incumbent upon a party seeking costs to apply for an order for them. Also, the court cannot assess the amount of any success fee relating to a conditional fee agreement or any other additional liability[19] until the conclusion of the proceedings (PD 44, para 8.3(3)).

---

15 See Chapter 24, Offers to Settle and Payments into Court.
16 *Ibid.*
17 [2000] 1 All ER 802.
17a See Chapter 24, Offers to Settle and Payments into Court, p 294.
17b See above, p 376.
18 See above, r 44.13(1).
19 See Chapter 38, Funding Litigation.

Costs of interim applications

There are a number of different orders about costs the court will commonly make when dealing with the case before trial. In relation to an application or hearing, these range from an order that a particular party is to bear the costs of the application or hearing whatever the outcome of a case, that the party who is successful at trial will be entitled to the costs of it, or that neither party will be entitled to the costs of it, depending on the nature and outcome of the application or hearing.[20]

For instance, a party who applies for judgment to be set aside is likely to have to pay the costs of the other party which have been incurred as a consequence and the costs order is likely to be for that party's 'costs thrown away'. However, if the court convenes a case management conference, the order for costs following that hearing is likely to be 'costs in the case'.

In the case of *Desquenne et Giral UK Ltd v Richardson*,[21] a case involving an application for an interim injunction, it was held that when deciding whether to make a costs order following a hearing or application, the court should take account of the effect of the overriding objective to deal with cases justly. Therefore, if the nature of the application or hearing was such that neither party could be said to be the winner or the loser at that stage, because that would depend on the merits of the substantive case at trial, it would not be just for the court to make a costs order in favour of one party or to order summary assessment of those costs. The proper order in such circumstances would be to reserve costs to the trial judge or order costs in the case.

Costs in appeal hearings

A court hearing an appeal has the power to make costs orders in relation to the hearing below as well as in relation to the appeal hearing unless the appeal is dismissed (r 44.13(2)). Therefore, if a party successfully challenges a judgment on appeal which includes an order for the party to pay the other party's costs, the appeal court, when allowing the appeal, may also reverse the costs order made by the court below.

Solicitor's duty to notify client about costs order

If the court makes a costs order against a legally represented party, when the party is not present, the party's solicitor must notify his client in writing of the costs order and explain why it was made, no later than seven days after the solicitor receives notice of the order (r 44.2 and PD 44, para 7.2).

---

20 See above, p 372 for the different types of costs orders that can be made.
21 [2001] FSR 1, CA.

Such a rule obliging a legal representative to keep his client informed about the costs that are being incurred in bringing or defending proceedings is consistent with the ethos of the CPR with its emphasis on proportionality and the saving of expense. It may also serve to make a client aware of any shortcomings in the conduct of their case by their legal representative which has resulted in the client becoming liable for costs. However, this rule should be distinguished from the court's powers to make orders for costs against a party or a legal representative for misconduct (r 44.14) and wasted costs orders made personally against legal representatives (r 48.7).[22]

Practice Direction 44 draws attention to the fact that there is no sanction specified if a legal representative does not abide by this rule, but goes on to state that the court may require the legal representative to produce evidence to the court showing that he took reasonable steps to so notify his client (PD 44, para 7.3). In any event, a failure to comply would very likely be seen as a matter of professional misconduct.

Conditional fee arrangements and other funding arrangements[23]

Where a party has entered into a conditional fee arrangement (CFA) which provides for a success fee and/or has taken out a legal expenses insurance policy, both known as funding arrangements, there is a presumption that any order for costs will also include payment of the success fee and insurance premium, unless the court orders otherwise (PD 43, para 2.1). The success fee and insurance premium are known as an additional liability as opposed to the usual 'base' costs of the action.

However, if, when calculating the percentage of the success fee, a legal representative has included an element to compensate for the fact that he will receive no costs until the conclusion of the case, that element cannot be recovered from another party and is payable by the client instead (r 44.3B(1)(a)). Also, in order to be enforceable, a CFA must include a summary of the legal representative's reasons for setting the percentage increase at the level chosen. If a party fails to disclose these reasons when required in any assessment proceedings, he will be unable to recover the success fee from another party (r 44.3B(1)(d)).

Court assessment of the additional liability

In order to preserve the confidentiality of the level of the success fee and/or any insurance premium from an opponent, the court will not assess the

---

22 See below, p 413.
23 See Chapter 38, Funding Litigation, for details of CFAs and other funding arrangements.

amount of any additional liability until the conclusion of the proceedings, or part of the proceedings, to which the funding agreement relates (r 44.3A(1)). Proceedings are concluded when the court has finally determined the matters in issue in the claim, whether or not there is also an appeal (PD 43, para 2.4). However, the court may order, or the parties may agree in writing that, although proceedings are continuing, they will nevertheless be treated as concluded (PD 43, para 2.5).

The court may either summarily assess both the base costs and the additional liability, make a detailed assessment of both the base costs and the additional liability, or summarily assess the base costs and make a detailed assessment of the additional liability (r 44.3A(2)). Therefore, the court cannot make a detailed assessment of the base costs but summarily assess the additional liability.

A party may not recover the additional liability for any period of the proceedings during which he failed to provide specified information[24] about the funding arrangement (r 44.3B(1)(b)). However, a party will be able to apply for relief from this sanction under r 3.9.[24a]

If the court decides in assessment proceedings to disallow all or part of the legal representative's success fee which is part of a CFA, the disallowed amount will not be payable by the legal representative's client either, unless the court orders otherwise.[25] If the legal representative wants to continue to claim payment of the disallowed amount of the success fee from his client, he must make an application to the court for such an order. If the legal representative's client is not present at the time the court disallows some or all of the success fee, and the legal representative indicates his wish to apply for such an order, the court may adjourn the assessment hearing so that the client can be notified of the application (r 44.16).

DEEMED COSTS ORDERS

In certain circumstances, a party will have a right to receive costs from the other party. The defendant will have a right to receive costs where:

- the claimant's case is struck out under r 3.7 for non-payment of fees;[25a] and
- the claimant discontinues[26] his action.

A claimant will have a right to receive costs where:

---

24 See Chapter 38, Funding Litigation.
24a See Chapter 5, Judicial Case Management: The Overriding Objective.
25 See reg 3(2)(b) of the Conditional Fee Agreements Regulations 2000 SI 2000/692 and Chapter 38, Funding Litigation.
25a See Chapter 5, Judicial Case Management: The Overriding Objective.
26 See Chapter 34, Discontinuance.

- he accepts the defendant's Part 36 offer or payment; or
- the defendant accepts the claimant's Part 36 offer.[26b]

In the event that these steps are taken, and the party becomes entitled to costs, a costs order will be deemed to have been made on the standard basis (r 44.12(1)).

Also, interest payable pursuant to s 17 of the Judgments Act 1838 or s 74 of the County Courts Act 1984, will begin to run from the date on which the event which gave rise to the entitlement to costs occurred (r 44.12(2)).

AMOUNT OF COSTS

Having ordered costs to be paid by one party to another, if the costs to be paid are not fixed costs[27] and if the parties cannot agree on the amount to be paid, the court must then also assess the amount of costs to be paid under the order. There are two bases on which costs can be assessed by the court; either the standard basis or the indemnity basis (r 44.4(1)).

Standard basis

The test for assessing costs on the standard basis is:
- only costs which have been reasonably incurred will be allowed;
- only costs which are proportionate to the matters in issue will be allowed; and
- any doubt about whether costs were reasonably incurred, or were reasonable and proportionate in amount, must be resolved in favour of the paying party (r 44.4(1) and (2)).

This is the basis that the court will order in most cases when assessing the costs that one party must pay to the other. In fact, if, when making an order for costs, the court does not indicate the basis on which costs are to be assessed, or if it orders a basis other than the standard or indemnity basis, the costs will be assessed on the standard basis (r 44.4(4)). It is important to note that the court will take into account the question of proportionality when deciding on the amount of costs to be allowed under the standard basis.

Proportionality

When assessing the amount of costs to allow on the standard basis, the court's test of proportionality will be based on the factors set out in r 1.1(2)(c),

26b See Chapter 24, Offers to Settle and Payments into Court.
27   See below, p 399.

namely, the amount of money involved, the importance of the case, the complexity of the issues and the financial position of each party (PD 44, para 11.1).

However, PD 44 goes on to provide expressly that it is recognised that the relationship between the total costs incurred and the financial value of the claim may not be a reliable guide and that a fixed percentage should not always be applied to the value of the claim in order to ascertain whether or not the costs are proportionate. It is also expressly stated that solicitors are not required to conduct litigation at rates which are uneconomic and it is recognised that in a modest claim, the proportion of costs is likely to be higher than in a large claim and may even equal or possibly exceed the amount in dispute (PD 44, para 11.2).

The indemnity basis

The test for assessing costs on the indemnity basis is:

- only costs which have been reasonably incurred will be allowed; and
- any doubt about whether costs were reasonably incurred or were reasonable in amount must be decided in favour of the paying party (r 44.4(1) and (3)).

This is the usual basis for assessing the amount of costs to be paid by a client to his solicitor. It will only rarely be used as the basis for assessing costs to be paid by one party to another and will usually be ordered in those circumstances as a punishment for the behaviour of the paying party.

Factors to be taken into account when assessing costs

When assessing the amount of costs to be paid on either the standard or indemnity basis, the court must take all the circumstances of the case into account (r 44.5). The whole ethos behind the CPR is to reduce the amount of time and money spent litigating and to avoid the need for litigation if possible; the parties will, therefore, have to be aware of the need to justify incurring costs and of the amount incurred at every stage of the case both before and after proceedings have started.

The court must consider the following circumstances (as well as any other relevant circumstances) when assessing the amount:

- the conduct of all the parties, including in particular conduct before as well as during the proceedings and any efforts made before and during the proceedings to try to resolve the dispute;
- the amount or value of any money or property involved;

- the importance of the matter to all the parties;
- the particular complexity of the matter or the difficulty or novelty of the questions raised;
- the skill, effort, specialised knowledge and responsibility involved;
- the time spent on the case; and
- the place where and the circumstances in which work or any part of it was done (r 44.5(3)).

PROCEDURES FOR ASSESSING THE AMOUNT OF COSTS

There are two procedures by which the court can assess costs: either by summary or detailed assessment. Where the court is to assess costs, it may decide to make either a *summary* assessment of costs or a *detailed* assessment of costs, unless one of those methods of assessment is specifically provided for by a relevant rule or practice direction (r 44.7). An order for costs will be treated as an order for the amount of costs to be decided by detailed assessment, unless the court orders otherwise (PD 44, para 12.2).

Time for payment of costs

If costs are assessed summarily or fixed costs are payable, if the judgment or order ordering payment also states the amount of costs, the paying party must pay them within 14 days of the date of the judgment or order. If costs are to be assessed by detailed assessment, the costs are payable within 14 days of the date of the certificate[28] which states the amount. In either case, the court can specifically order a different period of time for payment of the costs (r 44.8).

SUMMARY ASSESSMENT

Summary assessment is the procedure whereby the court assesses costs at the end of the hearing and orders payment of a sum of money, instead of fixed costs and without a detailed consideration of each item claimed (r 43.3). The court can use a party's costs estimates[29] provided throughout the hearing to help it decide whether costs claimed are reasonable (PD 43, para 6.6) as well as a statement of costs.[30] There seems to be a preference towards summary assessment of costs in the CPR with PD 44, para 13 providing that whenever a

---

28 See below, p 396.
29 See below, p 385.
30 See below, p 384.

court makes an order about costs which does not provide for fixed costs, it should consider whether to make a summary assessment of costs. However, there are certain circumstances when summary assessment cannot take place, such as of the costs of a legally aided or LSC funded client, and others where summary assessment will not be appropriate. Also, if the court makes an order for costs to be assessed, and decides that this should be by way of summary assessment, this should be specified as otherwise the order will be treated as an order for detailed assessment (PD 44, para 12.3).

In any event, as a general rule, unless there is a good reason not to do so, the court will make a summary assessment of the costs of the following:

- the whole claim following a fast track trial;[31]
- any hearing which has lasted no longer than one day (and if the hearing disposes of the whole claim, the court may summarily assess the costs of the whole claim); and
- hearings in the Court of Appeal to which para 14 of PD 52 applies (PD 44, para 13.2).

An example of a good reason not to summarily assess costs is where the paying party shows substantial grounds for disputing the sum claimed for costs which cannot be dealt with summarily, or where there is not enough time for summary assessment. Also, the court cannot make a summary assessment of the costs of a receiving party who is an assisted person or LSC funded client (PD 44, para 13.9).

In respect of a hearing which has lasted no longer than one day, although, as a general rule, the court will summarily assess the costs of the hearing, this is only likely to be the case if the order for costs has determined that one party is to receive the costs of the hearing. Therefore, summary assessment will not take place if the order for costs is costs in the case or some other order where the costs liability depends on which party is successful at trial, or is to be decided at a later date.[32]

Statement of costs

Whenever a party is claiming costs which are likely to be summarily assessed, he must assist the judge in making a summary assessment of those costs by filing at court and serving on every other party a statement of costs (PD 44, para 13.5(1)). Form N260 is a model form and its use is encouraged (PD 43, para 3.2). The statement of costs should cover the following matters: the number of hours claimed; the hourly rate; the grade of fee earner; disbursements; solicitor's costs for attending or appearing at the hearing;

---

31 See Chapter 17, The Fast Track.
32 See *Desquenne et Giral UK Ltd v Richardson* [2001] FSR 1, CA.

counsel's fee for attending the hearing; and any VAT to be added to these amounts (PD 44, para 13.5(2)). The statement of costs need not reveal the level of the success fee of any conditional fee agreement or the amount of any other additional liability (PD 44, para 13.5(5)). It must be signed by the party or his legal representative (PD 44, para 13.5(3)).

Time for filing and serving the statement of costs

The statement of costs should be filed and served as soon as possible and in any event not less than 24 hours before the date fixed for the hearing (PD 44, para 13.5(4)).

Consequences of failure to provide a statement of costs

The court will take into account the failure to provide a statement of costs when it is deciding what order to make about the costs of the claim. Therefore, the court may well decide not to award costs to a party who would otherwise be entitled to them if he fails, without reasonable excuse, to file and serve a costs schedule within the time period specified. If, as a result of the failure to provide a costs schedule, the court is unable to assess costs and a further hearing is necessary to do so, or detailed assessment is necessary, the court will take this into account when deciding what order to make as to the costs of the further hearing or detailed assessment proceedings (PD 44, para 13.6).

Costs estimates

It is a general principle of the CPR that a party should keep the other party informed as to their potential liability, not only in respect of the claim or counterclaim, but also in respect of costs. In furtherance of this, PD 43 provides for the filing and service of costs estimates at various stages of the proceedings. Costs estimates are also used to assist the court to decide what, if any, order to make about costs and for the purposes of case management. It is also the intention that the exercise of providing a costs estimate encourages parties and their legal representatives to be aware of the costs that are being incurred and to take steps accordingly to limit them. If the court is assessing costs, it may take any previous costs estimate into account when deciding whether the costs claimed are reasonable (PD 43, para 6.6).

Form of costs estimates

A costs estimate is a summary of the costs which a party intends to seek from another party if he is successful in the case. It is divided into two main parts:

- an estimate of costs already incurred; and
- an estimate of costs to be incurred.

The costs set out in the estimate should be 'base costs' only, that is, those costs other than the amount of any 'additional liability'. An additional liability includes the success fee of a conditional fee agreement and any legal expenses insurance premium.[33] The estimate of costs should also include disbursements (PD 43, paras 2.2 and 6.2). The costs estimate should follow the form illustrated in Precedent H in the Schedule of Costs Precedents annexed to the Practice Direction supplementing Parts 43 to 48 (PD 43, para 6.5).

Under PD 43, paras 6.3 and 6.4, unless the court otherwise directs, a party, apart from a litigant in person, must file at court and serve on all other parties a copy of a costs estimate at the following stages:

- in a claim outside the financial scope of the small claims track, at the same time as filing the allocation questionnaire;[33a]
- in a claim on the fast or multi-track or under Part 8, at the same time as filing the listing questionnaire;[33b] and
- at any other time that the court orders, within 28 days of the date of the order or within a time specified by the court. The court may also order that a party demonstrate the likely effect on costs of the giving of a particular case management direction that the court is considering, such as an order for a split trial.

When filing and serving the costs estimate with the allocation questionnaire and listing questionnaire, the legal representative must also serve a copy on his client (PD 43, para 6.4).

DETAILED ASSESSMENT

Detailed assessment is the procedure whereby the costs of the receiving party are assessed in detail by a costs officer (r 43.4). Detailed assessment has replaced the former procedure of taxation, and any reference to taxation in an order will be taken to mean detailed assessment (PD 43, para 3.8).

The general rule is that detailed assessment will not be ordered until the conclusion of the proceedings, that is, when the court has finally determined the matters in issue, whether or not the court's decision is appealed.[34] Therefore, it is unlikely that the costs of any interim application will be assessed by way of detailed assessment. However, the court has a discretion to order detailed assessment at any stage (r 47.1).

---

33   See Chapter 38, Funding Litigation.
33a See Chapter 15, Judicial Case Management: Allocation.
33b See Chapters 17, The Fast Track and 18, The Multi-Track.
34   See PD 47, para 28.1.

In some cases, proceedings will reach a stage where, although the matter has not been finally decided, there is no realistic prospect of the claim continuing; for instance, where a party has secured an interim injunction which has effectively determined the issues in dispute between the parties. In such circumstances, the court may order, or the parties may agree in writing, that although the proceedings are continuing, they will nevertheless be treated as concluded so that detailed assessment can take place (PD 47, para 28).

Venue for detailed assessment proceedings

An application for detailed assessment should be made in the appropriate office, which is the county court or district registry where the case which gave rise to the right to detailed assessment was being dealt with, or to which proceedings were transferred, and in all other cases the Supreme Court Costs Office (r 47.4 and PD 47, para 31.1).

Proceedings can be transferred to another county court for detailed assessment to be carried out (r 30.2). Also, a party may apply for, or the court of its own initiative may direct, that another specified court, registry or office is to be the appropriate office to carry out the detailed assessment. However, the Supreme Court Costs Office is reserved for the largest and most difficult assessments and so, unless this was already the appropriate office for a case, the court will not direct that the detailed assessment be carried out there unless it would be justified given such relevant matters as the size of the bill of costs, the difficulty of the issues involved, the likely length of the hearing and the cost to the parties (r 47.4(2), (3) and PD 47, para 31.2).

Payment on account

If detailed assessment is ordered, the court may order a specified amount to be paid on account before the costs are assessed and, in fact, the court should always consider whether to exercise its power to do so when it makes an order for detailed assessment (r 44.3(8) and PD 44, paras 8.6, 12.3). A payment on account is often referred to as an interim payment. In *Mars UK Ltd v Teknowledge Ltd (No 2)*,[35] the court held that the court should generally make an order for an interim payment of a lower amount than the party would almost certainly recover, calculated on a rough and ready basis. However, it was recognised that the court must take all the circumstances into account before deciding to make such an order. Relevant considerations which would indicate that an interim payment should not be made may include the unsuccessful party's intention to appeal, the relative financial position of each party and the overriding objective to deal with cases justly.

---

35   (1999) *The Times*, 8 July.

Detailed assessment pending an appeal

Detailed assessment will not be stayed pending an appeal, unless the court so orders (r 47.2). The party who is appealing should apply either to the court whose decision is being appealed or to the court which is hearing the appeal for an order staying the detailed assessment until after the hearing of the appeal (PD 47, para 29).

Detailed assessment in relation to an additional liability[36]

Detailed assessment proceedings may be in respect of just base costs[37] where there is no additional liability[38] to assess, or where those costs have been agreed. On the other hand, detailed assessment may be in respect of just an additional liability where the base costs have been agreed or assessed summarily. Alternatively, detailed assessment may be in respect of both the base costs and the additional liability (PD 47, para 32.2).

Commencement of detailed assessment proceedings

In order to commence detailed assessment proceedings, the party in whose favour a costs order has been made, known as the receiving party, must serve a notice of commencement in Form N252, a copy of a bill of costs and copies of evidence in relation to counsel's fees and disbursements on the party who has been ordered to pay costs, known as the paying party (r 47.6 and PD 47, paras 32.3 and 32.8).

If the receiving party does not respond to the notice of commencement and the paying party becomes entitled to a default costs certificate, the paying party will also be able to claim fixed costs[38a] and the court fees on obtaining a default costs certificate. The paying party, therefore, must show on the notice of commencement these extra sums that will be claimed in fixed costs and court fees if a default costs certificate is obtained (PD 47, para 32.8).

---

36 See Chapter 38, Funding Litigation.
37 See above, p 370, for definition.
38 *Ibid*.
38a See below, p 399.

Commencement of detailed assessment proceedings in relation to an additional liability[39]

If the detailed assessment proceedings are only in relation to an additional liability,[40] such as the level of success fee in a conditional fee agreement,[41] the receiving party must serve a notice of commencement in Form N252, a copy of the bill of costs, relevant details of the additional liability and a statement giving the name and address of any person upon whom the receiving party intends to serve the notice of commencement (PD 47, paras 32.4 and 32.5). The relevant details about the additional liability are, in the case of a success fee, a statement showing the amount of costs which have been agreed or summarily assessed and the percentage increase claimed in respect of them and a statement of the reasons for the level of the percentage increase (as required by reg 3 of the Conditional Fee Agreement Regulations 2000).[42] In the case of an insurance premium, the receiving party must serve a copy of the insurance certificate showing the extent of the costs covered and the amount of the premium (PD 47, para 32.5).

If the detailed assessment proceedings are in respect of both the base costs and an additional liability, the receiving party must serve all the documents referred to in PD 47, paras 32.3 and 32.5, as set out above (PD 47, para 32.7).

Service on other relevant persons

The receiving party must also serve these documents on any other relevant person. This is defined as a person who was involved in the court proceedings and is directly liable for any costs orders made against him, a party who has notified the receiving party that he has a financial interest in the outcome of the detailed assessment proceedings and therefore wishes to be a party to them, and any other party the court orders should be served with these documents. A person so served will also become a party to the detailed assessment proceedings (r 47.6(2), (3) and PD 47, para 32.10).

Bill of costs

A party applying for detailed assessment should submit a bill of costs. Although model forms of bills of costs in Precedents A, B, C and D in the Schedule of Costs Precedents should be used, they are not compulsory;

---

39   See Chapter 38, Funding Litigation.
40   *Ibid.*
41   *Ibid.*
42   *Ibid.*

however, if a model form is not used, a party must give an explanation in the background information of their bill as to why the appropriate model has been departed from (PD 43, para 3.7). PD 43, paras 4.1–5.20 cover in detail how a bill of costs should be set out and which items should be shown and what can be claimed.

Time limit for commencing detailed assessment proceedings

A party must commence detailed assessment proceedings within three months after the date when the right to detailed assessment arose. The circumstances giving rise to a right to detailed assessment are either a judgment, direction, order, award or other determination, or where the claimant discontinues under Part 38[43] or on the acceptance of an offer to settle or payment into court under Part 36[43a] (r 47.7).

The parties can agree to extend or shorten the time specified for commencement of detailed assessment proceedings or a party may apply for such an order (PD 47, paras 33.1, 33.2).

Sanction for failure to commence detailed assessment proceedings in time

If the receiving party commences detailed assessment proceedings later than the time period specified, the only sanction the court may impose is to disallow all or part of the interest on the costs otherwise payable to the receiving party under either s 17 of the Judgments Act 1838 or s 74 of the County Courts Act 1984. However, this is subject to the court's powers under r 44.14 to disallow all or part of the costs being assessed or to order a party or his legal representative to pay costs on the grounds of misconduct (r 47.8(3)).

However, if a receiving party fails to commence detailed assessment proceedings within the time period specified by the rules or a direction of the court, the paying party can apply to the court for an order that unless the receiving party commence the application within a further time specified by the court, all or part of the receiving party's costs, to which he would otherwise be entitled, will be disallowed (r 47.8(1) and (2)).

Points of dispute

In order to challenge the amount of costs claimed by the receiving party in his bill of costs, the paying party must serve points of dispute on the receiving

43 See Chapter 34, Discontinuance.
43a See Chapter 24, Offers to Settle and Payments into Court.

party and every other party to the detailed assessment proceedings (r 47.9(1)). PD 47 provides details as to the contents of the points of dispute. The points of dispute must identify each item in the bill of costs which is disputed and state the nature and grounds of the dispute, where practicable a suggested alternative figure that should be allowed instead should be given and the document must be signed by the party or his solicitor (PD 47, para 35.3). In any event, the Practice Direction also provides that the points of dispute should be short and to the point and follow Precedent G of the Schedule of Costs Precedents as closely as possible (PD 47, para 35.2).

Time for service of points of dispute

Points of dispute must be served on the receiving party, and any other party to the detailed assessment proceedings, within 21 days after the date of service of the notice of commencement (r 47.9(2) and PD 47, paras 35.4, 35.5). The parties may agree to extend or shorten the time specified for service of points of dispute or a party may apply for an order to extend or shorten that time (PD 47, para 35.1). However, in the absence of such agreement or order, the paying party may not be heard in the detailed assessment proceedings unless the court gives permission (r 47.9(3)).

Reply to points of dispute

The receiving party has the option of serving a reply to the points of dispute if he thinks it necessary. Such a reply should be served within 21 days after service of the points of dispute on him (r 47.13).

Documents on disk

In recognition of the fact that a bill of costs or points of dispute can be long and detailed, and as a sign of the times, there is provision for the party in receipt of such documents to request a copy on computer disk. A paying party can request that a disk copy of the bill of costs be sent to him by the receiving party, free of charge, within seven days after receipt of such a request (PD 47, para 32.11). Likewise, a receiving party can request, within 14 days of receipt of the points of dispute, that a disk copy of the points of dispute be sent to him, free of charge, within seven days after receipt of such a request (PD 47, para 35.6).

Parties agreeing costs

If the parties agree a figure for costs, they can apply for an order that a certificate be issued in the terms of the compromise agreement. As the judgment is by consent, it can be dealt with by a court officer who can issue the certificate, whether it be an interim or final certificate (PD 47, para 36.1).

If the parties agree costs, but the paying party will neither pay them nor agree to a consent order, the receiving party can make an application under Part 23[44] for an interim or final certificate to be issued based on the agreement reached between the parties (PD 47, para 36.2). The receiving party must support the application with evidence and the paying party can rely on evidence in response which must be filed and served on the paying party at least two days before the hearing date. The application will be heard by a costs judge or a district judge (PD 47, para 36.3).

Default costs certificates

If a receiving party has commenced detailed assessment proceedings, but the paying party has not served points of dispute within the time specified (or applied for or agreed extra time for doing so), the receiving party may file a request in Form N254, at the appropriate office, signed by the party or his solicitor, for a default costs certificate (r 47.9(4) and PD 47, paras 37.1, 37.2).

On receipt of the application a default costs certificate in Form N255 will be issued which includes an order to pay the costs to which it relates and which is enforceable by the receiving party (r 47.11(1), (2) and PD 47, para 37). This procedure therefore allows the receiving party to obtain an order for payment of his costs in default of the paying party's challenge to the amount of costs detailed in his bill of costs. However, if, before the court has issued a default costs certificate, any party to the proceedings serves points of dispute, the court may not issue a default costs certificate (r 47.9(5)).

If a default costs certificate is obtained, the paying party must still obtain a detailed assessment of any costs payable out of the Community Legal Service Fund (PD 47, para 37.5).

Fixed costs of default costs certificate

The receiving party will be entitled to fixed costs of £80 plus payment of any court fees in applying for a default costs certificate which will be included in the default costs certificate when it is issued by the court (PD 45, para 25.1).

44 See Chapter 19, Making Applications for Court Orders.

Setting aside a default costs certificate

The court also has the power to set aside a default costs certificate. The court must set it aside if the party obtaining it was not entitled to it, for example, if the time period for filing points of dispute had not expired (r 47.12(1)).

The court has a discretion to set aside or vary the default costs certificate if it appears to the court that there is some good reason why the detailed assessment proceedings should continue (r 47.12(2)). The application to set aside must be supported by evidence and the paying party should file a copy of the bill of costs and default costs certificate and a copy of the points of dispute he proposes to serve, if his application is granted, in order to persuade the court that he has good grounds to challenge the bill of costs. When deciding to exercise its discretion to set aside the order, the court must consider whether the application was made promptly and the applicant should explain the reason for failing to serve points of dispute in time. If the application to set aside the default costs certificate is successful, the court will give directions for the management of the detailed assessment proceedings (PD 47, para 38).

The court may direct that the order setting aside the default costs certificate is subject to a condition, such as the paying party paying a sum of money into court. The court may also order that the paying party pay a proportion of the costs being claimed to the receiving party on account (rr 3.1(3), 44.3(8) and PD 47, para 38.3).

Receiving party applying to set aside default costs certificate

If, after a default costs certificate has been issued, the receiving party discovers that the notice of commencement did not reach the paying party at least 21 days before the default costs certificate was issued, the receiving party must either file a request for the default costs certificate to be set aside or apply to the court for directions. The receiving party must not attempt to enforce the default costs certificate or take any further step in the detailed assessment proceedings until the certificate has been set aside or the court has given directions (r 47.12).

If the receiving party simply applies for the default costs certificate to be set aside, this is a purely administrative act and can therefore be carried out by a court officer. However, if the receiving party applies for any other order or for directions, this will be dealt with by a costs judge or a district judge (PD 47, para 38.1).

DETAILED ASSESSMENT HEARING

Form of request for a detailed assessment hearing

Where the receiving party has served a notice of commencement and the paying party has served points of dispute, the receiving party must file a request for a detailed assessment hearing in Form N258 (r 47.14 and PD 47, para 40.2). A court fee is payable on the filing of the request.[45]

Form N258 must be accompanied by the following documents:

- a copy of the notice of commencement of the detailed assessment proceedings;
- a copy of the bill of costs;
- a copy of the document giving the right to the detailed assessment (for example, a court judgment or order, a notice of acceptance of a Part 36 offer or payment, a notice of discontinuance);
- a copy of the points of dispute for every party who has served points of dispute (which should be annotated by the receiving party to show which items have been agreed and which are in dispute and the value of these items);
- a copy of any replies served;
- a copy of all court orders relating to the costs which are to be assessed;
- a copy of the required evidence of counsel's fee notes, expert fees and of disbursements claimed exceeding £250;
- where there is a dispute as to the receiving party's liability to pay his solicitor's costs, a copy of any document provided by the solicitor to his client explaining how the solicitor's charges are to be calculated; and
- a statement, signed by the receiving party or his solicitor, giving contact details of the receiving party, the paying party and any other relevant party, as well as an estimate of the length of time the detailed assessment hearing will take (PD 47, para 40.2).

Time limit for filing request for a detailed assessment hearing

Rule 47.14(2)–(5) sets out the same time limits for the filing of a request for a detailed assessment hearing and the sanctions and possible court orders for failure to do so within the time period. These are the same as those provided for the commencement of detailed assessment proceedings (for details, see above).

---

45 See the Supreme Court Fees Order 1999 and the County Court Fees Order 1999 for the level of fee.

Interim costs certificate

Once a receiving party has filed a request for a detailed assessment hearing, he can apply to the court for an interim costs certificate (r 47.15(1)). The application is made in accordance with Part 23[46] (PD 47, para 41.1). The court has the power to decide that an appropriate sum should be paid in the interim pending the detailed assessment hearing. The court will take into account whether a payment on account has already been made following the order for detailed assessment.[47]

If the application is granted, the court will issue an interim costs certificate in Form N257 for an amount it considers appropriate. The interim costs certificate will usually include an order that the paying party pay the costs to which it relates (r 47.15(2)). However, the court can decide to order that the amount be paid into court instead (r 47.15(3)). The court may amend or cancel the interim certificate at any time (r 47.15(1)(b)).

Date for the hearing

On receipt of a request for a detailed assessment hearing, the court will either fix a date for the hearing, or if the costs officer considers it necessary, give directions or fix a date for a preliminary appointment (PD 47, para 40.5).

Only the receiving party and paying party and any other relevant person who has served points of dispute may be heard at a detailed assessment hearing and the court will give those parties at least 14 days' notice of the time and place of the detailed assessment hearing and a copy of the points of dispute annotated by the receiving party in the way referred to above (r 47.14(6) and PD 47, para 40.6(1), (2)).

Documents to be filed

The receiving party must file the papers in support of the bill of costs not less than seven, nor more than 14 days before the date of the detailed assessment hearing (PD 47, para 40.11). PD 47, para 40.12 sets out detailed provision for the papers to be filed and the order in which they are to be arranged for the purposes of the hearing.

---

46   See Chapter 19, Making Applications for Court Orders.
47   See above, Payment on account, p 387.

Nature of the hearing

The hearing will only be concerned with considering the items specified in the points of dispute, unless the court gives permission for other items to be considered (r 47.14(7)).

Amendment of documents for detailed assessment

A party may vary his bill of costs, points of dispute or reply without seeking permission to do so, but the court may subsequently disallow the variation or permit it only upon conditions such as the payment of costs caused or wasted by the variation. If a party does vary any of these documents, he must file a copy of the documents showing the variations with the court and serve a copy on every party to the proceedings (PD 47, para 40.10).

Settlement of the detailed assessment proceedings

If the parties settle the detailed assessment proceedings before the hearing, the receiving party must notify the court immediately. In order to ensure that the hearing date can be free for other parties, it is requested that the receiving party notify the court by way of fax if possible (PD 47, para 40.9(2)).

If the parties agree the amount of costs, either party can apply to the court that was due to hear the detailed assessment proceedings for a costs certificate, either interim or final, in the amount agreed (r 47.10).

Final costs certificate

At the detailed assessment hearing, the court will indicate any disallowance or reduction in the sums claimed by making an appropriate note on the bill of costs. The onus is then upon the receiving party to draw up a completed bill of costs which makes clear the correct figures agreed or allowed in respect of each item and which re-calculates the summary of the bill in accordance with what has been agreed or allowed following the detailed assessment. The receiving party must then file the completed bill of costs (along with receipted fee notes and receipted accounts in respect of disbursements) with the court no later than 14 days after the detailed assessment hearing (PD 47, paras 42.1–42.4).

So long as the receiving party has paid all court fees associated with the detailed assessment, the court will then issue a final costs certificate in Form N256 and serve it on the parties to the detailed assessment proceedings (r 47.16(3) and PD 47, para 42.5). The final costs certificate will show the amount of costs agreed between the parties or which were allowed on detailed assessment along with the amount of any VAT if applicable (PD 47, para 42.7).

The final costs certificate will include an order to pay the costs to which it relates unless the court orders otherwise (r 47.16(5)). Payment of the costs ordered is then enforceable in the same way as any other judgment. However, enforcement proceedings for either an interim or a final costs certificate may not be issued in the Supreme Court Costs Office (PD 47, para 42.12).

COSTS OF DETAILED ASSESSMENT PROCEEDINGS

Receiving party generally entitled to costs

As a general rule, the receiving party will be entitled to the costs of the detailed assessment hearing and the court will assess those costs and add them to the bill of costs (r 47.18(1) and PD 47, para 45.1).

Court's discretion as to costs of detailed assessment proceedings

However, when deciding what order to make about the costs of the detailed assessment proceedings, the court must have regard to the conduct of all the parties, the amount by which the bill of costs has been reduced and whether it was reasonable for a party to claim the costs of a particular item or to dispute a particular item (r 47.18(2) and PD 47, para 45.4). If the court orders costs of the detailed assessment to be paid by the paying party it will either summarily assess those costs or make an order for them to be decided by detailed assessment (PD 47, para 45.2).

Offers to settle without prejudice save as to the costs of the detailed assessment proceedings

A paying party or a receiving party can make a written offer to settle the costs of the proceedings which gave rise to the assessment and, if the offer is expressed to be without prejudice save as to the costs of the detailed assessment proceedings, the court will take it into account when deciding who should pay the costs of those proceedings (r 47.19(1)). Therefore, if a paying party offers to settle the claim for costs in a sum which is the same or greater than the amount ordered by the court, the court is likely to award the paying party the costs of the detailed assessment proceedings. Likewise, if the receiving party offers to settle his claim for costs for a lower sum than that ordered by the court, he is likely to be awarded his costs of the detailed assessment hearing.

As such an offer is without prejudice save as to costs of the detailed assessment hearing, it should not be revealed to the costs officer until the question of costs of the detailed assessment hearing comes to be decided (r 47.19(2)).

Contents of the without prejudice offer

The offer to settle should specify whether or not it is intended to be inclusive of the cost of preparation of the bill, interest and VAT. The offeree may include or exclude some or all of these items so long as this is made clear on the face of the offer. However, unless the offer specifies that these items are excluded, the offer will be treated as being inclusive of them (PD 47, para 46.2).

Acceptance of the offer

Where an offer to settle is accepted, either party may apply for a certificate in agreed terms (PD 47, para 46.3 and r 47.10).

LSC funded client or assisted person

Where the receiving party is an LSC funded client or an assisted person, the provisions about without prejudice offers save as to the costs of the detailed assessment proceedings will not apply, unless the court orders otherwise (PD 47, para 46.4).

Time limits for making the without prejudice offer

Although r 47.19 does not specify a time limit within which the without prejudice offer should be made, PD 47, para 46.1 states that the offer should be made either within 14 days after service of notice of commencement on a party or within 14 days after service of points of dispute (depending on whether the party is the paying or receiving party). The Practice Direction warns that offers made after these periods of time are likely to be given less weight by the court when deciding what order as to costs to make unless there is good reason for the offer not being made until the later time.

Discontinuing detailed assessment proceedings

The paying party may discontinue detailed assessment proceedings in accordance with the general rules about discontinuance (PD 47, para 36.5(1)).[48]

The receiving party can discontinue detailed assessment proceedings without permission before he has requested a detailed assessment hearing. However, the paying party can then apply to the appropriate office for an order about the costs of the detailed assessment proceedings (PD 47, para 36.5(2)); the likely order on costs being that the receiving party pay the paying party's costs of the detailed assessment proceedings.

However, where the receiving party has requested a detailed assessment hearing, he must apply to the court for permission to discontinue the proceedings (PD 47, para 36.5(3)). Once a hearing has been requested, if the paying party wishes to discontinue, it is very likely that he will be ordered to pay the receiving party's costs and may be subject to other penalties.

If agreement is reached, a bill of costs can be withdrawn by consent at any time, whether or not a detailed assessment hearing has been requested (PD 47, para 36.5(4)).

FIXED COSTS

In certain circumstances set out in Part 45, an amount of costs is specified to be recoverable in respect of solicitor's costs. On making an order for costs, if fixed costs are applicable, then there is a presumption that only those costs will be payable and the court will not assess the costs. However, the court has the power to make a different order and may, for instance, order that the costs be assessed instead (r 45.1). The relevant tables in Part 45 should be consulted for details of the amount of costs allowed.

Circumstances where fixed costs payable

Where a party claims a *specified* sum of money (which exceeds £25) and he obtains:
- judgment in default under r 12.4(1);
- judgment on an admission under r 14.4(3);
- judgment on a part admission under r 14.5(6);
- summary judgment under Part 24;

---

48   See Chapter 34, Discontinuance.

- an order striking out the other party's defence under r 3.4(2)(a) as disclosing no reasonable grounds for defending the claim; or
- judgment for delivery of goods where this was the only claim and the court gave a fixed date for the hearing on issuing the claim,

the party is entitled to recover an amount of fixed commencement costs, fixed costs on entry of judgment and certain other fixed costs in relation to solicitor's charges in bringing the action as well as any appropriate court fee (r 45.1).

Also, a defendant will be able to limit his liability to pay only fixed commencement costs, and no other costs, if either:

- the claimant claims a specified amount of money which the defendant pays within 14 days after service of particulars of claim on him, so long as he also pays the fixed commencement costs at the same time; or
- the claimant claims a specified sum of money and the defendant makes a Part 36 payment into court[49] within 14 days after service of the particulars of claim on him in satisfaction of the whole claim and the claimant accepts it.

However, the court can order that the defendant pay more than those fixed commencement costs in appropriate circumstances (r 45.3).

Fixed commencement costs

In order to recover the fixed costs, they must be specifically claimed. The claim form includes a section where an amount for fixed commencement costs can be inserted. The amount which can be claimed is regulated by tables set out in Part 45 which provide different levels of costs depending on the value of the claim and the method of service used to serve the claim form. If the court served the claim form or the claimant served it by a method other than personal service, a lower amount is allowed than if the claimant effected personal service on the defendant (r 45.2).

Fixed costs on entry of judgment

Where the claimant has claimed fixed commencement costs in his claim form in certain circumstances, the claimant may also recover fixed costs on entry of judgment as well as the fixed commencement costs. Those circumstances are where the claimant is able to enter judgment:

- in default of an acknowledgment of service under r 12.4(1);[49a]

---

49 See Chapter 24, Offers to Settle and Payments into Court.
49a See Chapter 8, Responding to an Action.

- in default of a defence under r 12.4(1);[50]
- on an admission under r 14.4 or a part admission under r 14.5 and the claimant accepts the defendant's proposals for payment;[50a]
- on an admission under r 14.4 or part admission under r 14.5 and the court decides the date and times of payment;[50b]
- following a successful application for summary judgment under Part 24[50c] or the striking out of a defence under r 3.4(2)(a);[50d] or
- on a claim for delivery of goods under a regulated agreement within the meaning of the Consumer Credit Act 1974.

The amount of the fixed costs on entering judgment is based on an ascending scale in the above order with two different amounts given for each circumstance, depending on whether the sum claimed is above or below £5,000 (r 45.4).

Miscellaneous fixed costs

Part 45 also provides an additional amount of fixed costs for a case where there is a requirement that a party serve a document personally, where service by an alternative method is carried out under r 6.8, and where a document is served out of the jurisdiction (r 45.5).

Fixed costs in small claims

If a claim is allocated to the small claims track, a party is unable to recover his legal costs from his opponent even if successful as a result of the operation of the so called 'no costs rule'.[51] However, if the successful party is the claimant, the court can award him fixed commencement at the rate set out in Part 45 as well as the court fees paid by the claimant (PD 45, para 24).

COSTS PAYABLE UNDER A CONTRACT

Where the court assesses (whether by the summary or detailed procedure)[51a] costs which are payable by the paying party to the receiving party under the terms of a contract (for example, mortgages), the costs payable under those

---

50   *Ibid.*
50a *Ibid.*
50b *Ibid.*
50c See Chapter 22, Summary Judgment.
50d See Chapter 23, Striking Out.
51   See Chapter 16, The Small Claims Track.
51a See above, p 383.

terms are, unless the contract expressly provides otherwise, to be presumed to be costs which have been reasonably incurred; and are reasonable in amount, and the court will assess them accordingly (r 48.3(1)). This rule does not apply where the contract is between a solicitor and his client (r 48.3(2)).

PD 48, para 50.1 provides that the court may make an order that all or part of the costs payable under the contract shall be disallowed if the court is satisfied by the paying party that costs have been unreasonably incurred or are unreasonable in amount.

Where the contract between the parties determines that any award of costs shall be on the indemnity basis, that would appear to be enforceable.[52] Indeed, in mortgage possession matters, should the lender not ask for assessment, then they are entitled to their costs as of right if the mortgage document so provides without the court conducting an assessment.[53]

COSTS PAYABLE OUT OF THE COMMUNITY LEGAL SERVICE FUND

Where costs are payable only out of the community legal service fund (CLS), to a Legal Services Commission (LSC) funded client, or the legal aid fund to an assisted person, additional provisions apply where the court is to assess costs.

The LSC funded client or the assisted person's solicitor may commence detailed assessment proceedings[54] by filing a request in Practice Form N258A (r 47.17(1)).

Form N258A must be accompanied by the following documents:

- a copy of the bill of costs;
- the document giving the right to the detailed assessment;
- a copy of all orders of the court relating to the costs which are to be assessed;
- a copy of the required evidence of counsel's fee notes, expert fees and of disbursements claimed exceeding £250;
- legal aid certificates, LSC certificates, and any amendments, authorities and certificates of discharge or revocation;
- the relevant papers in support of the bill under PD 47, para 40.12 (see above, Papers filed in support of the bill for the detailed assessment hearing) only if proceeding in the Supreme Court Costs Office; for cases proceeding in a district registry or county courts, such papers should be filed only if requested by the costs officer;

---

52 *Gomba Holdings v Minories Finance* [1993] Ch 171; *Church Commissioners for England v Ibrahim and Another* (1996) The Litigation Letter, 9 February, CA.

53 *Gomba Holdings v Minories Finance* [1993] Ch 171.

54 See above, p 394.

- a statement signed by the solicitor giving his contact details and, if the assisted person has a financial interest in the detailed assessment and wishes to attend, giving his postal address to which the court can send a notice of any hearing (PD 47, para 43.3).

Time limits for application for detailed assessment

The solicitor claiming costs from the CLS or legal aid fund must file the request in Form N258A within three months after the date when the right to detailed assessment arose (r 47.17(2) and PD 47, para 43.2).

Notifying the client

If the LSC funded client or assisted person has a financial interest in the outcome of the assessment (this will be the case if he has made a contribution to his certificate or if he has recovered or preserved property in the proceedings), the solicitor must also serve a copy of the request for a detailed assessment on his client (r 47.17(3)).

Provisional assessment

Where the LSC funded client or assisted person does not have an interest in the outcome or has indicated that he does not wish to attend an assessment hearing, the court will provisionally assess the solicitor's costs on receipt of a request for detailed assessment, without the attendance of the solicitor, unless it considers that a hearing is necessary (r 47.17(5) and PD 47, para 43.4).

After provisionally assessing the bill, the court will send a notice in Form N253 setting out the amount of costs the court proposes to allow as well as the bill of costs to the solicitor (r 47.17(6) and PD 47, paras 43.5). If the solicitor accepts the amount of costs allowed on provisional assessment, he must complete the bill by entering the correct figures allowed in respect of each item, recalculate the summary of the bill in accordance with what was allowed, and file it along with a completed Community Legal Service Assessment Certificate in Form EX80A (PD 47, paras 43.5, 43.9). If the solicitor does not accept the provisional assessment, he may ask for a detailed assessment.[55]

---

55 See above, p 394.

Detailed assessment of CLS costs

Where the solicitor has certified that the LSC funded client or assisted person with an interest in the outcome wishes to attend an assessment hearing, the court will fix a date for a hearing on receipt of the solicitor's request (r 47.17(4)).

The court will also fix a date for an assessment hearing if the solicitor informs the court within 14 days after he has received a provisionally assessed bill that he wants the court to hold such a hearing (r 47.17(7)). The court will give at least 14 days' notice of the time and place of the detailed assessment hearing to the solicitor and, if appropriate, the solicitor's client (PD 47, para 43.7).

APPEALS FROM DECISIONS MADE BY COURT OFFICERS IN DETAILED ASSESSMENT PROCEEDINGS

Right to appeal decision of authorised court officer

Any party to detailed assessment proceedings (apart from an LSC funded client or an assisted person) may appeal the decision of the authorised court officer without leave and by following the procedure laid down in r 47.20 and para 47 of PD 47 (r 47.20 and PD 47, para 47).

Court hearing appeal

An appeal from the authorised court officer is to a costs judge or a district judge of the High Court (r 47.21).

Procedure for appealing

If a party wishes to appeal, he must file a notice of appeal in Form N161 along with a record of the judgment appealed against within 14 days after the date of the decision he wishes to appeal. The court will then serve a copy of the notice on the parties involved in the detailed assessment proceedings and give notice of a date for the appeal hearing to those parties (r 47.22 and PD 47, para 48.1).

Court's powers on hearing an appeal

On hearing an appeal from an authorised court officer, the court will re-hear the proceedings which gave rise to the decision appealed against and make any order and give any directions it considers appropriate (r 47.23).

Other appeals

All other appeals from decisions made in detailed assessment proceedings, apart from decisions made by an authorised court officer, must follow the general procedure for appeals set out in Part 52.[56]

FAST TRACK TRIAL COSTS

Part 46 sets a limit to the amount of costs an advocate can recover for preparing for and appearing in a fast track trial. These are known as fast track trial costs (r 46.1(1)). A maximum set amount is recoverable for the advocate's costs, whether the costs of the proceedings are assessed summarily or by detailed assessment (r 46.2(1)). However, it should be born in mind that the usual rule is for the costs of proceedings on the fast track to be assessed summarily (PD 28, para 8.5).[57]

The rules for fast track trial costs only apply where, at the time of trial, the claim is allocated to the fast track. The rules do not apply to trials heard on any other track, whatever the financial value of the claim (PD 46, para 26.2). This restriction also applies to claims heard on the small claims track where the financial value exceeds the small claims track limit, but the parties agree that the case should be allocated to the small claims track. In those cases, the costs are in the discretion of the court. However, the amount of those costs cannot exceed the amount of costs that would have been awarded in fast track trial costs if the case had been allocated to the fast track (PD 46, para 26.3 and r 27.14(5)).

Fast track trial costs of a litigant in person

If a litigant represents himself at trial, if he can prove that he has suffered financial loss in so doing, he can recover two-thirds of the amount that would have been awarded if an advocate had conducted the fast track trial. If the litigant in person cannot show financial loss, then he will be entitled to recover

---

56 See Chapter 35, Appeals.
57 See Chapter 17, The Fast Track.

an amount in respect of the time he reasonably spent doing the work at the rate specified for litigants in person in the Costs Practice Direction, which is currently £9.25 per hour (r 46.3(5) and PD 48, para 52.4).

Definition of trial

For the purposes of fast track trial costs, the definition of trial includes a hearing where the court is to decide an amount of money or the value of goods following the entry of default judgment or judgment after an admission[58] other than a disposal hearing (PD 46, para 26.3).[59] However, 'trial' in these circumstances does not include the hearing of an application for summary judgment under Part 24[59a] or the court's approval of a settlement or compromise which involves a child or a patient[59b] (r 46.1(2)).

Amount of fast track trial costs

There is a table of amounts of fast track trial costs which increase in accordance with the value of the claim (r 46.2(1)). This sets the fast track trial costs, which can be recovered by a party's advocate whether acting for a claimant or defendant. There are three bands of costs. Where the value of the claim does not exceed £3,000, fast track trial costs of £350 may be awarded. Currently, where the value is more than £3,000 but not more than £10,000, £500 may be awarded and where the value is more than £10,000, £750 may be awarded.

The figures provided are for the advocate's costs alone and do not include VAT or any disbursements (r 46.1(2)).

The court cannot award more or less than the amounts specified unless it decides not to award any fast track trial costs, a party is guilty of improper or unreasonable behaviour or it falls within the circumstances providing for additional amounts. The court can also apportion the amount awarded between the parties if a party is successful on some issues but not others, in order to reflect their respective degrees of success (r 46.2(2)).

Additional amounts

There are a number of circumstances where the court can award additional amounts to those specified for fast track trial costs in Part 46.

---

58 See Chapter 8, Responding to an Action.
59 *Ibid.*
59a See Chapter 22, Summary Judgment.
59b See Chapter 26, Special Rules for Children and Patients.

Costs of attendance of legal representative

If, in a particular case, the court considers that it was reasonable for a party's legal representative to attend the trial to assist the advocate, if that party is awarded costs, the court can award an additional amount of £250 in addition to the fast track trial costs for the attendance of the legal representative (r 46.3(2)).

Separate trial of an issue

If the court directs a separate trial of an issue, the court can award an additional amount in respect of the separate trial. The additional amount for the separate trial must not exceed two-thirds of the amount of fast track trial costs payable for the claim, but is subject to a minimum award of £350 (r 46.3(3) and (4)).

Success fees

If an advocate in a fast track trial is acting under a conditional fee agreement[60] which provides for a success fee, the court also has the power to add the amount of the success fee onto the amount allowed for fast track trial costs (r 46.3(2A)). In the event of any dispute between the parties as to the amount of the success fee, in view of the limitation of time which applies to fast track cases, the judge may be tempted to order a detailed assessment. This will have extra costs implications as well as preventing the quick 'finality' which fast track hearings were originally designed to achieve.

Unreasonable and improper behaviour

Where the court considers that the party who is to pay the fast track trial costs has behaved improperly during the trial, the court has a discretion to award an additional amount in costs to the other party as it considers appropriate (r 46.3(8)).

If the court considers that the party who is to receive costs has behaved unreasonably or improperly during the trial, it may award that party a lower amount than the amounts usually paid in accordance with the value of the claim (r 46.3(8)).

---

60 See Chapter 38, Funding Litigation.

Value of the claim for fast track trial costs

Part 46 specifies how the value of a claim is to be calculated. If the claim involves only money, the value of the claim is naturally decided by a different method depending on whether the party to be awarded the costs is the claimant or defendant.

Money claims

In a claim involving the payment of money only, if the claimant is entitled to costs, whether the claim was specified or unspecified, the value of the claim is the total amount of the judgment but excluding interest, costs and any reduction for contributory negligence (r 46.2(3)(a)).

If the defendant is entitled to costs, the value of the claim is either the amount specified by the claimant in the claim form, excluding interest and costs or, if the claim is for an unspecified amount, the maximum amount the claimant reasonably expected to recover as stated in his statement of value on the claim form. However, if the claimant had stated in his claim form that he could not reasonably say how much he expected to recover, the value of the claim is deemed to be more than £10,000, which gives rise to the highest amount of fast trial costs (r 46.2(3)(b)).

Non-money claims

If a claim is for a non-money remedy only, the value of the claim is deemed to be more than £3,000 but not more than £10,000, the middle band of fast track trial costs. However, in an appropriate case, the court can order that a different method of calculating the value is carried out instead (r 46.2(4)).

Mixed claims

If a claim includes a claim for a money and a non-money remedy, the value of the claim is deemed to be the higher of either the money claim (as calculated above) or the non-money claim (as calculated above). However, in an appropriate case, the court can order that a different method of calculating the value is carried out instead (r 46.2(5)).

COSTS OF COUNTERCLAIMS IN FAST TRACK TRIAL COSTS

Claimant successful

If a defendant makes a counterclaim against the claimant which has a higher value than the value of the claimant's claim against him, but the claimant is successful at trial, both on his claim and the counterclaim, the value of the claim for the purposes of fast track trial costs awarded to the claimant will be the value of the defendant's counterclaim, calculated by the same method set out above for claims (r 46.2(6)).

Defendant successful

Where a defendant makes a counterclaim and the claimant is unsuccessful on his claim, but the defendant is successful on his counterclaim, as a counterclaim is treated as if it were a claim,[61] if the court awards the defendant costs it is likely to calculate the amount of fast track trial costs by reference to the value of the counterclaim as if it were a claim. However, if the claimant put the value of the claim at a higher amount than the counterclaim, the court may decide to assess the fast track trial costs in accordance with the value of the claimant's claim under the rules referred to above which apply where a defendant is to be awarded costs.

Both parties successful

Where a defendant makes a counterclaim against the claimant and the claimant is successful on his claim, but the defendant is successful on his counterclaim, the court will calculate fast track trial costs in the following way. The court will calculate the amount of fast track trial costs the claimant would be entitled to on his claim, but for the counterclaim, and calculate what the defendant would be entitled to on his counterclaim, but for the claimant's claim, and make one award of fast track trial costs, of the difference, if any, to the party entitled to the higher award of costs (r 46.3(6)).

Fast track trial costs where there are multiple parties

Where the same advocate is acting for more than one party, the court may make only one award of fast track trial costs for that advocate. The parties for whom the advocate is acting are then jointly entitled to the fast track trial costs that are awarded (r 46.4(1)).

---

61 See Chapter 12, Part 20 Claims, and r 20.3.

Multiple claimants with money only claims

If each of a number of claimants has a separate claim against the defendant, in a money only claim, the value of the claim for the purposes of calculating the claimants' fast track trial costs is the total amount of the judgment made in favour of all the jointly represented claimants. If the defendant is to be awarded costs in these circumstances, the value of the claim is the total amount claimed by the claimants (r 46.4(3)(a)).

Multiple claimants with non-money claims

Where the only claim of each of a number of claimants is for a non-money remedy, the value of the claim is deemed to be more than £3,000, but not more than £10,000 (r 46.4(3)(b)).

Multiple claimants with mixed claims

Where the claims of a number of claimants includes both a money and a non-money claim, the value of the claim is deemed to be either more than £3,000, but not more than £10,000, or the total value of the money claims if that is higher (r 46.4(3)(c)).

Multiple defendants

Where there is more than one defendant and any or all of them are separately represented, the court may award fast track trial costs to each party who is separately represented (r 46.4(4)).

Multiple claimants/single defendant

If there is more than one claimant, but only one defendant, the court can only make one award of fast track trial costs to the defendant for which the claimants are jointly and severally liable (r 46.4(5)). This means that the defendant can choose to recover the full amount of the costs from just one of the claimants or from both. The value of the claim is calculated in accordance with the rules for claims by multiple claimants set out above (r 46.4(6)).

Fast track case settles before trial

If a case allocated to the fast track settles before trial, when assessing the amount of costs to be allowed for a party's advocate for preparing for the trial, the court cannot allow a greater amount than that which the party would have recovered in costs if the trial had taken place (r 44.10(1)). The court will also take into account when the claim was settled and when the court was notified of this when assessing such costs (r 44.10(2)).

COSTS ON THE SMALL CLAIMS TRACK AND FAST TRACK

Where a claim is allocated to the small claims or the fast track, the special rules about costs which relate to those tracks[62] will apply to work done before as well as after allocation, unless an order in respect of that work was made before allocation (PD 44, para 15.1(2)). However, before a claim is allocated to one of those tracks, the court is not restricted by any of the special rules about costs which apply to that track (PD 44, para 15.1(1)).

Allocation to small claims track following an admission

If a claimant issues a claim for a sum outside the financial limit of the small claims track, but the claim is allocated to that track only because an admission of part of the claim by the defendant reduces the amount in dispute to a sum within the normal scope of that track, on entering judgment for the admitted part before allocation of the balance of the claim, the court may allow costs in respect of the proceedings down to that date (PD 44, para 15.1(3)).

Allocation from small claims track

If the court decides to allocate a claim from the small claims track to another track, before the case is allocated, it must decide whether to make an order that one party is to pay costs to another party in accordance with the rules about costs on the small claims track. If the court decides that such an order for costs should be made, it will also summarily assess those costs (PD 44, para 16.3).

RE-ALLOCATION OF A CLAIM TO ANOTHER TRACK

If a case is allocated to one track, but then subsequently re-allocated to a different track, any special rules about costs on the track that the claim was originally on will apply to the claim up to the date of re-allocation, but then

---

62 See Chapter 16, The Small Claims Track, and above, p 405 onwards, Fast track trial costs.

any special rules about costs applying to the track the claim has been allocated to will apply from the date of re-allocation (r 44.11(2)). An example of a special rule about costs applying to a track is the 'no costs' rule of the small claims track. Also, any costs orders made before a claim is re-allocated will be preserved on re-allocation (r 44.11(1)).

COSTS-ONLY PROCEEDINGS

A new rule, r 44.12A, was introduced to deal specifically with the issue of costs where a dispute is compromised without the need for proceedings. Therefore, where the parties have settled a dispute before proceedings have been started and have reached agreement, which is made or confirmed in writing, on all issues, including which party is to pay costs, but the parties cannot agree the amount of those costs, either party may start costs-only proceedings by issuing a claim form in accordance with Part 8[63] in the court which would have been the appropriate office[64] if proceedings had been brought in relation to the substantive claim. However, the court must dismiss the claim if it is opposed.

Contents of the claim form

The Part 8 claim form must identify the claim or dispute to which the agreement to pay costs relates, state the date and terms of the agreement on which the claimant relies, attach a draft of the order which the claimant seeks, state the amount of costs claimed and whether they are claimed on the standard or indemnity basis. The Part 8 claim form must be accompanied by a copy of the compromise agreement and copies of documents on which the claimant relies to prove the defendant's agreement to pay costs must be filed and served along with the claim form (PD 44, paras 17.3, 17.4).

Once the time period for the defendant to file an acknowledgment of service has expired, the claimant can request that an order be made in the terms of his claim, by sending a letter to the court to this effect and the court will make the order unless the defendant has filed an acknowledgment of service indicating that he intends to contest the claim or seek a different order (PD 44, para 17.6).

The court has the power to either make an order for costs or to dismiss the claim. The order for costs will be for an amount to be decided by detailed assessment (PD 44, para 17.8). The court must dismiss the claim if it is

---

63 See Chapter 14, Part 8 Claims.
64 See above, p 387.

opposed. The defendant can oppose the claim by filing an acknowledgment of service stating that he intends to contest the proceedings or seek a different remedy. As soon as such an acknowledgment of service is filed, the court will dismiss the claim (PD 44, para 17.9).

If the claim is dismissed, the claimant can issue a claim form under Part 7 or Part 8 to sue on the agreement made in settlement of a dispute where the agreement makes a provision for costs (PD 44, para 17.9, 17.11). In order to avoid the defendant being able to contest the application, the party in whose favour the agreement to pay costs is made should ensure that the terms of the settlement include an agreement by the paying party that the amount of costs will be decided by detailed assessment if not agreed.

COSTS ORDERS FOR MISCONDUCT

The court may make a costs order disallowing all or part of the costs being claimed by a party or ordering a party or his legal representative personally to pay the costs which have been incurred by another party if the party or legal representative is at fault because:

- the party or his legal representative fails to comply with a rule, practice direction or court order in relation to a summary or detailed assessment; or
- the party or his legal representative has behaved unreasonably or improperly before or during the proceedings which are the subject of the assessment (r 44.14(1) and (2)).

This rule gives the court a wide scope to punish a party or his legal representative for misconduct both before and during the course of proceedings or in relation to assessment proceedings. Misconduct includes the taking of steps which are calculated to prevent or inhibit the court from furthering the overriding objective (PD 44, para 18.2).

Moreover, if the court makes such an order and the client is not present, the legal representative has an obligation to notify his client in writing no later than seven days after the solicitor receives notice of the order (r 44.14(3)). Although no sanction is specified for breach of this rule, the court has the power to require the solicitor to produce evidence to the court that he has complied with it (PD 44, para 18.3).

WASTED COSTS ORDERS

The court has the power under s 51(6) of the Supreme Court Act 1981 to disallow a legal representative's costs or to order that the legal representative personally pay costs to another party. In exercising this power, the court may make a wasted costs order, being an order that the legal representative pay a specified sum in respect of costs to a party, or an order disallowing the costs of the legal representative relating to a specified sum or items of work (PD 48, para 53.9).

Where the court is considering making a wasted costs order, it must be satisfied that:

- the legal representative acted improperly, unreasonably or negligently;
- such behaviour caused another party to incur unnecessary costs; and
- it is just to order him to compensate the party for some or all of those costs (PD 48, para 53.4).

Applying for a wasted costs order

A party can apply for a wasted costs order against a legal representative by making an application in accordance with Part 23[65] or simply by making an application orally in the course of any hearing (PD 48, para 53.3). If an application is made in accordance with Part 23, the application notice and any evidence in support must identify what the legal representative is alleged to have done or failed to do and the unnecessary costs that he has thereby caused the other party to incur (PD 48, para 53.8).

The court has the power to make a wasted costs order of its own initiative (PD 48, para 53.2).

Hearing before order made

The court must give the legal representative a reasonable opportunity to attend a hearing to give reasons why the court should not make a wasted costs order against him (r 48.7(2)).

Orders for wasted costs can be made at any stage of the proceedings, but are usually left until after the end of the trial, as otherwise the proceedings are likely to be sidetracked by the wasted costs matter.

Evidence at the hearing

The case of *General Mediterranean Holdings SA v Patel and Another*[66] led to part of r 48.7 being held to be *ultra vires*. Former r 48.7(3) (which was subsequently

---

65 See Chapter 19, Making Applications for Court Orders.
66 [1999] 3 All ER 673.

removed from the rules) gave the court the power, for the purposes of wasted costs proceedings, to direct that privileged documents be disclosed to the court and to the other party to the application. The reason for the rule was to allow the court to fully investigate the conduct and advice given by the legal representative in the proceedings when considering whether to make a wasted costs order against him, as this might only be possible through access to privileged documents. However, the privilege in such documents belongs to the client and it may not be in the client's best interests for the documents to be disclosed.

However, although para 4 of Sched 1 to the Civil Procedure Act 1997 gave the CPR the power to 'modify the rules of evidence as they apply to proceedings in any court within the scope of the CPR', the judge held that legal professional privilege was not a mere rule of evidence, but a substantive and fundamental common law principle, and one on which the administration of justice rests. The Civil Procedure Rule Committee, exercising as it did a subordinate power in drafting r 48.7(3), could not abrogate or limit a person's right to legal confidentiality. Rule 48.7(3) was accordingly held to be *ultra vires*.

The court cannot, therefore, order that a legal representative disclose privileged documents for the purposes of wasted costs proceedings. The position is now as it was before the existence of the rule and the judgment of Bingham MR in *Ridehalgh v Horsefield*[67] should be followed, in which he warned judges considering making a wasted costs order to make full allowance for the lawyer's inability to tell the whole story as a result of the operation of legal professional privilege and therefore to give the lawyer the benefit of any doubt.

The conduct of the hearing

In general, the hearing will be conducted in two stages. At the first stage, the court must be satisfied that it has evidence which, if unanswered, would lead to a wasted costs order being made and that the wasted cost proceedings are justified notwithstanding the likely cost of them. The court will therefore have to be satisfied that there is a case to answer as well as considering issues of proportionality before deciding whether to make a wasted costs order. The court will then usually adjourn the hearing in order to give the legal representative an opportunity to be heard as to why a wasted costs order should not be made against him. At the second stage, the court will hear the legal representative and even if the court is satisfied as to the matters at the first stage, the court must also be satisfied that it is appropriate to make the wasted costs order (PD 48, para 53.6).

---

67 [1994] 3 All ER 848.

If a party makes an application under Part 23[68] for a wasted costs order against a legal representative, the court may proceed to the second stage without adjourning the hearing if it is satisfied that the legal representative has already had a reasonable opportunity to give reasons why the court should not make a wasted costs order (PD 48, para 53.7).

Investigating the circumstances

The court may direct a costs judge or a district judge to inquire into the matter and report to the court as to the nature of the legal representative's behaviour and the unnecessary costs incurred as a result, before it makes a wasted costs order (r 48.7(6)).

Notifying the client

The court may also order that the legal representative notify his client of any proceedings for a wasted costs order being brought against him and of any wasted costs order made against him (r 48.7(5)).

COSTS ORDERS IN FAVOUR OF OR AGAINST A NON-PARTY

If the court is considering making an order for costs in favour of or against a non-party, that party must be added as a part to the proceedings for the purposes of the decision about costs only and given an opportunity to a hearing for the matter to considered further (r 48.2(1)).

These provisions do not apply where the party against which an order may be made is the Legal Services Commission, when the court is considering making a wasted costs order[68a] and for applications for pre-action disclosure and disclosure against a non-party[69] (r 48.2(2)).

COSTS IN FAVOUR OF A TRUSTEE OR PERSONAL REPRESENTATIVE

A trustee or personal representative acting as such in proceedings on behalf of and for the benefit of the fund over which he has been appointed, in the

---

68 See Chapter 19, Making Applications for Court Orders.
68a See above, p 413.
69 See Chapter 29, Disclosure of Documents.

absence of a right to be paid his costs under a contract,[70] is usually entitled to be paid his costs arising from such proceedings out of the fund and for those costs to be assessed on the indemnity basis (r 48.4(1) and (2)). Obviously, this rule may not apply if the trustee or personal representative is not acting on behalf of the fund (r 48.4(3)).

COSTS WHERE MONEY IS PAYABLE BY OR TO A CHILD OR PATIENT[71]

Where a child or patient is a party to proceedings in which money is ordered to be paid to or for the benefit of, or to be paid by or on his behalf, as a general rule the court must order a detailed assessment of the costs payable to the child or patient by another party and of the costs payable by the child or patient to his solicitor (r 48.5(1) and (2)). However, the court may make a summary assessment of the costs payable by a child or patient to the other party (PD 44, para 13.11).

The general rule does not apply where there is no need to apply it in order to protect the interests of the child or patient, or where the solicitor acting for the child or patient has agreed to waive the right to claim further costs following an agreement for the payment of a specified sum in costs by another party or the summary assessment of the costs by the court, or where an insurer or other party is liable to pay the child's or patient's costs to his solicitor and the insurer or other party can afford to do so (PD 48, para 51).

LITIGANTS IN PERSON

A litigant in person may be awarded costs, payable by another person, of acting on his own behalf. The court can decide to assess those costs either by summary or detailed assessment (r 48.6(1)).

Definition of litigant in person

Neither the rules nor the glossary to the CPR define the phrase 'litigant in person', presumably on the grounds that it is self-explanatory. However, r 8.6(6) states that, for the purposes of the rules about costs, a litigant in person includes a company or other corporation which is acting without a legal

---

70 See above, p 401, Costs payable pursuant to a contract.
71 See Chapter 26, Special Rules for Children and Patients.

representative and a barrister, solicitor, solicitor's employee or other authorised litigator who is acting for himself.

Solicitor acting for his firm or represented by his firm

It should be noted, however, that under the CPR, a solicitor who, instead of acting for himself, is represented in the proceedings by his firm or by himself in his firm's name, is not a litigant in person (PD 48, para 52.5). This means that the solicitor would be able to recover costs at the usual rate charged by a solicitor of the appropriate grade to conduct the proceedings.

AMOUNT OF COSTS RECOVERABLE BY A LITIGANT IN PERSON

Financial loss

If a litigant in person can show that he suffered financial loss in acting for himself in the proceedings, he can recover an amount of costs to reflect this, but the amount must not exceed more than two-thirds of the amount that would have been allowed in legal costs if a legal representative had represented the litigant in person (r 48.6(2)).

Evidence of financial loss

A litigant in person should file at court and serve evidence of his financial loss on a party from whom he seeks costs at least 24 hours before any hearing at which his costs may be decided. If a litigant in person seeks detailed assessment, he should file that evidence with his notice of commencement (PD 48, paras 52.2 and 52.3).

Hourly rate

If a litigant in person cannot show that he suffered financial loss in acting for himself, the amount of costs he can be awarded will be based on the amount of time which was reasonably spent doing the work at a rate which has currently been set at £9.25 per hour (r 48.6(4) and PD 48, para 52.5).

Other costs

The litigant in person can also recover the costs of disbursements if they would have been incurred by a legal representative on his behalf and any payments reasonably made by him for legal services relating to the conduct of the proceedings, plus the costs of obtaining expert assistance, from someone who is legally qualified or qualified to calculate legal costs, in order to assess his claim for costs (r 48.6(3) PD 48, para 52.1).

A litigant in person who does not seek costs may apply for a witness allowance[72] for his expenses in attending court. However, a litigant in person is not entitled to claim both his costs for attending court and a witness allowance (r 48.6(5)).

CLIENT CHALLENGING SOLICITOR'S BILL

In certain circumstances, a client can apply to the court for a detailed assessment of his solicitor's bill under s 70 of the Solicitors Act 1974 but proportionality will not be an issue. In respect of non-contentious business, the client can challenge the bill by way of detailed assessment, unless he has entered into a non-contentious business agreement with his solicitor under s 57 of the Solicitors Act 1974. In respect of contentious business, the client can challenge the bill by way of detailed assessment, unless he has entered into a contentious business agreement with his solicitor under s 59 of the Solicitors Act 1974.

Solicitor and client costs are assessed on the indemnity basis and when assessing the costs, the court will take into account the matters in r 44.5. There is also a presumption that costs were reasonably incurred if they were incurred with the express or implied approval of the client and that the costs are reasonable in amount if their amount was expressly or impliedly approved by the client. However, if costs are of an unusual nature or amount and the solicitor did not warn his client that, as a result, he might not recover them from his opponent, they are presumed to have been unreasonably incurred (r 48.8(2)). Regard should be had to the Solicitors Practice (Costs Information and Client Care) Amendment Rules 1998, which amended Solicitors Practice Rules, r 15, by requiring a solicitor to keep the client informed about costs, with updating at regular intervals (at least every six months). Solicitors are prohibited from recovering any shortfall from their clients in fast track matters as far as fixed trial costs (r 46.2) are concerned unless there is a written agreement with the client that they may do so (s 74(3) of the Solicitors Act 1974).

---

72 See Chapter 16, The Small Claims Track.

Procedure for assessment

If the court makes an order for the assessment of costs payable to a solicitor by his client, the solicitor must serve a breakdown of costs on his client within 28 days of the order. The client can then serve points of dispute, but must do so within 14 days after service on him of the breakdown of costs. If the solicitor wishes to serve a reply, he must do so within 14 days of service of the points of dispute. Either party can file a request for a hearing date after points of dispute have been served, but no later than three months after the date of the order for costs to be assessed (r 48.10).

In respect of any item of costs relating to proceedings in the county court, the solicitor can recover an amount of costs from his client greater that that which his client could have recovered from another party to the proceedings only if the solicitor and client have entered into a written agreement which permits this (s 74(3) of the Solicitors Act 1974, CPR, r 48.8(1A)).

CHAPTER 34

DISCONTINUANCE

INTRODUCTION

If a party starts proceedings which for any reason he does not wish to continue with, he has the right to discontinue those proceedings, but he should comply with the procedure for discontinuance under Part 38. There is no similar provision for a defendant to discontinue a defence – he should make an admission on which a judgment can be entered.

ABANDONING REMEDIES

If a claimant claims more than one remedy in proceedings, such as a money remedy and an injunction, if he wishes to abandon one of those remedies but continue seeking the other remedies, he is not treated as discontinuing his claim (r 38.1). In those circumstances, the claimant should follow the procedure to amend a statement of case under Part 17[1] in order to abandon the remedy.

In the light of the provisions relating to costs of proceedings and, in particular, the court's power to make costs orders which reflect how successful the parties have been, consideration should be given to abandoning a remedy at an early stage if time and costs will need to be spent by the parties in dealing with it, where a claimant believes he will be unsuccessful in achieving it at trial.[2]

DISCONTINUANCE

A claimant may discontinue all or part of a claim at any time, but in some circumstances the court's permission is needed (r 38.2). The same considerations as to the potential costs implications of continuing with an unsustainable claim apply as referred to above in relation to the abandonment of a remedy.[3]

---

1   See Chapter 11, Statements of Case.
2   See Chapter 33, Costs, p 375.
3   See above.

Discontinuance without the permission of the court

In most circumstances, all the claimant needs to do is to file a notice of discontinuance at court and a copy on every other party in order to discontinue the proceedings (r 38.2(1) and 38.3(1)). Court Form N279 can be used, but in any event the notice filed at court must state that the claimant has served notice of discontinuance on every other party to the proceedings (r 38.3(2)).

Multiple defendants

Where there is more than one defendant, the claimant may discontinue all or part of the claim against all or any of the defendants (r 38.2(3)). The notice of discontinuance must specify against which defendants the claim is discontinued (r 38.3(4)).

Multiple claimants

Where there is more than one claimant to the claim, a claimant may not discontinue unless every other claimant consents in writing, or the court gives permission (r 38.2(c)). In these circumstances, a copy of the written consent of the other claimant(s) must be attached to the notice of discontinuance (r 38.3(3)).

Date when discontinuance takes effect

Discontinuance takes effect on the date that the notice of discontinuance is served[4] on the defendant (r 38.5(1)). Proceedings will be brought to an end against the defendant on that date, unless the defendant applies to have the notice set aside (r 38.5(2)).[5]

Discontinuance of part of a claim

If the claimant discontinues *part* of a claim, he will only be liable for the costs of the part of the proceedings which he discontinues. The court will not usually assess these costs until the conclusion of the rest of the proceedings (r 38.6(2)).

---

4   See Chapter 9, Service of Documents.
5   See below, p 423, Right to have notice of discontinuance set aside.

However, if in these circumstances the parties agree a sum as to costs that the claimant should pay, or the court does in fact order the costs to be paid before the conclusion of the proceedings, the court may stay the remainder of the proceedings until the claimant pays those costs (r 38.8).

Discontinuance with the court's permission

A claimant needs the court's permission to discontinue all or part of a claim in respect of which:

- the court has granted an interim injunction;
- any party has given an undertaking to the court; or
- the claimant has received an interim payment (unless the defendant who made the interim payment consents in writing) (r 38.2(a) and (b)).

If a court has ordered an interim injunction or a party has given an undertaking to the court, in the light of the fact that the party obtaining the injunction or undertaking must give an undertaking as to damages if it turns out that the injunction or undertaking was unjustified, permission must be applied for to discontinue the claim, or part of the claim to which it relates, so that the court can discharge the order and make any orders on the undertaking as to damages which might be appropriate.

If an interim payment has been made and a claimant subsequently abandons his claim, the court has the power to order repayment and so the court's permission must be obtained to abandon proceedings in these circumstances.[6]

Where the claimant needs the court's permission to discontinue all or part of the claim, he should make an application in accordance with Part 23.[7]

Right to have notice of discontinuance set aside

If a claimant discontinues proceedings, the defendant can apply, within 28 days of service of the notice of discontinuance on him, to have the notice of discontinuance set aside (r 38.4). This provision gives the court a wide discretion to consider whether discontinuance may cause injustice to the defendant. The defendant should make any application in accordance with Part 23.[8]

---

6   See Chapter 20, Interim Remedies, and r 25.8.
7   See Chapter 19, Making Applications for Court Orders.
8   *Ibid.*

Costs of the proceedings

The usual price a claimant pays for discontinuing all or part of a claim against the defendant is that he must pay the defendant's costs of the proceedings incurred up to the date of discontinuance (r 38.6(1)). The defendant will be automatically entitled to costs, unless the court orders otherwise (r 38.6(2)(b)), and when the claimant discontinues, a costs order will be deemed to have been made in the defendant's favour on the standard basis[9] (r 44.12) and will be assessed on a detailed basis (r 44.7). However, a defendant could apply, using Part 23,[9a] for costs to be on an indemnity basis, for example, where there are allegations of misconduct. Similarly, a claimant could apply for the costs provision not to apply where, for example, an injunction has satisfied the demands of the claimant.

As there is usually no liability to pay an opponent's costs even if unsuccessful in the case of claims allocated to the small claims track, the provisions on deemed costs orders on discontinuance are specifically excluded from such (r 38.6(3)). Therefore, where the action was allocated to the small claims track, the 'no costs' regime will apply, save for any pre-allocation costs and any allegations of 'unreasonable behaviour' pursuant to r 27.14(2)(d).

The court retains the power to make a different order as to costs to that which is deemed to have been made. It may be that it would not be just for the defendant to be entitled to costs or that the defendant should have costs on the indemnity rather than the standard basis. However, as a costs order under the terms of r 44.12 will be deemed to have been made, it is incumbent on a party who would like an order in different terms to either agree such a variation with the other party or apply to the court for a different order. Any application to the court should be made in accordance with Part 23.[10]

Subsequent proceedings

If a claimant discontinues proceedings at any stage after the defendant has filed a defence, he will need to seek the permission of the court to make another claim against the same defendant arising out of the same, or substantially the same, facts as those relating to the discontinued claim (r 38.7).

Although the claimant must seek permission to start fresh proceedings in these circumstances, as there has been no judgment in the original

---

9   See Chapter 33, Costs.
9a See Chapter 19, Making Applications for Court Orders.
10 *Ibid.*

proceedings, the defence of issue estoppel or *res judicata* will not be available in relation to the subsequent proceedings.[11] However, it is likely that in most cases, the court will consider it an abuse of process to commence fresh proceedings after discontinuing the first, and strike out the subsequent proceedings under r 3.4. The court may also decide, by analogy with the cases on striking out for delay,[12] not to allow the subsequent proceedings to proceed on the grounds that when applying the overriding objective[13] and considering the interests of all court users, it would not be an appropriate use of court resources to allow a claimant to bring a fresh action based on the same or substantially the same facts as that of the discontinued action.

---

11 However, if the parties have compromised the claim and the claimant discontinues the proceedings, the defendant would be able to rely on the existence of the contract of compromise to strike out any fresh proceedings as an abuse of process under r 3.4.

12 See *Securum Finance Ltd v Ashton* (2000) *The Times*, 5 July.

13 See Chapter 5, Judicial Case Management: The Overriding Objective.

CHAPTER 35

APPEALS

INTRODUCTION

The revision of the rules relating to appeals did not come into operation at the same time as the rest of the Civil Procedure Rules. They were brought into being by the Access to Justice Act 1999 and came into effect about a year after the CPR did. The new provisions for appeals in small claims cases came into effect even later. In a sense, the new provisions have greatly simplified the routes of appeal while toughening up the grounds and discouraging second appeals.

GENERAL

The rules as to appeals in Part 52 do not apply to an appeal against a detailed assessment of costs by an authorised court officer[1] (r 52.1(2)). The appeals procedure does apply to all other orders made by judges including against summary or detailed assessment of costs.[1a] As from 2 October 2000, the rules apply to small claims hearings – thus, the previous grounds have been replaced with the same grounds as for a final decision in other matters (see below) and permission to appeal is necessary.

The appeal will take the form of a review of the decision of the lower court (that is, not a *de novo* hearing) unless a practice direction provides otherwise (see PD 52, para 9.1) or the court feels a re-hearing is necessary (r 52.11(1)).

With very few exceptions (a committal order; a refusal to grant habeas corpus; or a secure accommodation order made under s 25 of the Children Act 1989), permission is now required to appeal from a decision of a judge (r 52.3). The application for permission may be made either to the court who made the decision or to the appeal court in an appeal notice (r 52.3(2)). The court may decide the application without a hearing (PD 52, paras 4.11–4.14) or at a hearing (PD 52, paras 4.15 and 4.16).

Unless the court orders otherwise, the notice of appeal must be filed no later than 14 days from the date of the decision appealed against (r 52.4(2)). The lodging of the appeal does not automatically operate as a stay on the order of the lower court unless the court orders otherwise (r 52.7). The

---

1   See Chapter 33, Costs.
1a   *Ibid.*

appellate court has power to strike out an appeal notice or a permission to appeal if there are 'compelling' reasons to do so. No doubt the court will bear in mind the overriding objective[2] in the exercise of its powers.

For details of the procedure to be followed and the documents required on an appeal, see the Practice Direction to Part 52. Note that on the appeal, unless the court orders otherwise, no oral evidence or evidence which was not before the lower court will be allowed (r 52.11(2)). For the procedure on statutory appeals, that is, where under any enactment an appeal (other than by way of case stated) lies to the court from a minister of State, government department, tribunal or other person, see PD 52, para 17. Appeals by way of case stated are dealt with by PD 52, para 18.

GROUNDS FOR APPEAL

It will be noted that the grounds for appeal differ depending on whether it is against a final decision or a case management decision. For a discussion as to what constitutes a 'final decision', see PD 52, paras 2A.3 and 2A.4 and *Tanfern v McDonald*.[3]

Permission

Permission to appeal will only be granted where the court feels that the appeal stands a reasonable prospect of success or there is some other *compelling* reason for the appeal to go ahead (r 52.3(6)). Having given notice to the parties of its intention to do so, the appellate court may deal with the application for permission without a hearing PD 52, paras 4.11–4.14. The court may, when granting permission, limit the issues to be dealt with on the appeal (PD 52, para 4.18).

Allowing an appeal

The appellate court will allow an appeal where it considers the decision of the lower court was *wrong*, or *unjust* because of a serious procedural or other irregularity (r 52.11(3)). Any grounds in the notice should therefore be stated as falling within one or both of those categories (PD 52, para 3.2).

---

2   See Chapter 5, Judicial Case Management: The Overriding Objective.
3   [2000] 2 All ER 801.

Appeal from a case management decision

Note PD 52, para 4.5:

> Where the application is for permission to appeal from a case management decision, the court dealing with the application may take into account whether:
>
> (1) the issue is of sufficient significance to justify the costs of an appeal;
>
> (2) the procedural consequences of an appeal (eg, loss of trial date) outweigh the significance of the case management decision;
>
> (3) it would be more convenient to determine the issue at or after trial.

A 'case management decision' is defined by PD 52, para 4.4 as decisions made under r 3.1(2) (general case management matters)[4] and decisions about:

- disclosure
- filing of witness statements or experts reports
- directions about the timetable of the claim
- adding a party to a claim
- security for costs.

ROUTES OF APPEAL

PD 52, para 2A.1 sets out the usual routes of appeal. Decisions of district judges go to the circuit judge; decisions of the circuit judge, master or district judge sitting in a district registry go to a High Court judge, and thereafter to the Court of Appeal.

However, where the decision is one made at the final hearing of a multi-track case or in specialist proceedings[5] (see r 49(2)), then appeal is straight to the Court of Appeal. There may be circumstances where the appeal can 'leapfrog' straight to the Court of Appeal. By r 52.14(1), where the court from or to which an appeal is made or from which permission to appeal is sought considers that:

- an appeal which is to be heard by a county court or the High Court would raise an important point of principle or practice; or
- there is some other compelling reason for the Court of Appeal to hear it,

the relevant court may order the appeal to be transferred to the Court of Appeal.

---

4   See Chapter 5, Judicial Case Management: The Overriding Objective.

5   See Chapter 2, Sources of Civil Procedure: Structure and Jurisdiction of the Civil Courts, p 18.

POWERS OF THE COURT ON APPEAL

Note r 52.10(2).The appeal court has power to:

- affirm, set aside or vary any order or judgment made or given by the lower court;
- refer any claim or issue for determination by the lower court;
- order a new trial or hearing;
- make orders for the payment of interest;
- make a costs order.

Where the appeal is from a trial with a jury, for example, false imprisonment or wrongful arrest, the appellate court may, instead of ordering a re-trial, award damages or vary an order for damages (r 52.10(3)). Note that, unless it is the subject of the appeal, the appellate court will not be told of any Part 36 offer[6] (r 52.12).

The appellate court can dispose of an appeal, that is, dismiss it, by consent unless the appellant is a child or patient[7] (PD 52, paras 12.1–12.4). Similarly, the appellate court can allow an appeal on the basis that the lower court was wrong and that both parties agree that the lower court was wrong, but not where one of the parties is a child or patient[8] (PD 52, para 13.1).

FURTHER APPEALS

Parties are now discouraged from having a second go at an appeal. Rule 52.13 provides that permission to appeal further from a decision of the lower court which was itself an appeal will only be given if the appeal raises an important point of principle or practice or there is some other compelling reason for the Court of Appeal to hear it.

COSTS OF APPEAL

Note PD 52, para 14.1. Costs are likely to be assessed by way of summary assessment[9] at the following hearings:

- contested directions hearings;

6　See Chapter 24, Offers to Settle and Payments into Court.
7　See Chapter 26, Special Rules for Children and Patients.
8　*Ibid*.
9　See Chapter 33, Costs.

- applications for permission to appeal at which the respondent is present;
- dismissal list hearings in the Court of Appeal at which the respondent is present;
- appeals from case management decisions; and
- appeals listed for one day or less.

Thus, parties attending an appeal under any of the above circumstances must be prepared for a summary assessment.[10] Where summary assessment does not take place, it is to be presumed that the court will order a detailed assessment.[11]

---

10 PD 52, para 14.2 and see Chapter 33, Costs.
11 See Chapter 33, Costs.

CHAPTER 36

JUDICIAL REVIEW

INTRODUCTION

Although it may seem that the updating of judicial review has come rather late in the day in relation to civil procedure reforms, the date of implementation is no coincidence – 2 October 2000, the same date as the commencement of the Human Rights Act 1998. Applications to challenge the actions of public authorities will continue to be by way of judicial review with the extra consideration now being given to compatibility with the European Convention on Human Rights.[1] The new provisions contain tight time limits which are not capable of being extended by agreement between the parties.

Judicial review is used to challenge the lawfulness of an enactment or a decision action or omission by a public authority (r 54.1(2)(a)) and, therefore, is fertile ground for 'vertical' challenges under the Human Rights Act. The claimant would normally be seeking either a declaration or an injunction (r 54.3(1)). A claim for damages may be included, but does not have to be (r 54.3(2).

Part 54 claims are dealt with by a newly named Administrative Court (PD 54, para 2.1) instead of the previous Divisional Courts, although the address remains the same – the Royal Courts of Justice (PD 54, para 2.2) – apart from the Welsh, who have their own Administrative Court in Cardiff (PD 54, para 2.3). Although the claim must be issued in London or Cardiff, the court may direct the hearing to take place at some other venue (PD 54, para 8.3).

There is a change of name for the type of orders sought to reflect the dropping of Latin expressions and reliance instead on plain English – 'mandamus' becomes 'a mandatory order'; 'prohibition' becomes 'a prohibiting order'; and certiorari becomes 'a quashing order' (r 54.1(2)).

MAKING A CLAIM

Permission to proceed is required (r 54.4) and the claim form must be filed within three months after the date that the grounds arose (r 54.5(1)) or such shorter period as may be provided for by any enactment (r 54.5(3)). This time limit is not extendable by agreement between the parties (r 54.5(2)).

---

1   See Chapter 37, The Human Rights Act 1998.

The claim form must contain the same information as is required for Part 8 claims[2] as well as details of any interested parties and the request to proceed under r 54.4 above (r 54.6(1)).

As for contents of the claim form, see PD 54, paras 5.6–5.8:

5.6 The claim form must include or be accompanied by –

    (1) a detailed statement of the claimant's grounds for bringing the claim for judicial review;

    (2) a statement of the facts relied on;

    (3) any application to extend the time limit for filing the claim form;

    (4) any application for directions; and

    (5) a time estimate for the hearing.

5.7 In addition, the claim form must be accompanied by –

    (1) any written evidence in support of the claim or application to extend time;

    (2) a copy of any order that the claimant seeks to have quashed;

    (3) where the claim for judicial review relates to a decision of a court or tribunal, an approved copy of the reasons for reaching that decision;

    (4) copies of any documents on which the claimant proposes to rely;

    (5) copies of any relevant statutory material;

    (6) a list of essential documents for advance reading by the court (with page references to the passages relied on); and

5.8 Where it is not possible to file all the above documents, the claimant must indicate which documents have not been filed and the reasons why they are not currently available.

The court does not involve itself in service at all. The form must be served by the claimant on the named parties within seven days of issue (r 54.7).

Any party who wishes to take part in the proceedings must file an acknowledgment of service not more than 21 days after service of the claim form and serve a copy on the claimant and any other named party within seven days of filing it (r 54.8(2)). Again, these time limits may not be extended by agreement (r 54.8(3)). Where a claim is one under the Human Rights Act 1998, the court may direct that notice be given to the Crown or that the Crown be joined as a party (PD 54, para 8.2).

In the acknowledgment of service, the person filing it must set out a summary of his grounds for contesting the claim and details of any other party he feels ought to be added to proceedings (r 54.8(4)). Failure by a party to file an acknowledgment of service bars him from involvement in the 'permission' process (r 54.9(1)(a)), but not necessarily from the review itself,

---

2 See r 8.2 and Chapter 14, Part 8 Claims.

provided he complies with directions of the court as to the filing of a response (r 54.9(1)(b)), as to which, see below.

PERMISSION

The request for permission will usually be considered without a hearing (PD 54, para 8.4). Any decision, together with reasons (r 54.12), will be served on the claimant, defendant and any other party who filed an acknowledgment of service (r 54.11). There is no appeal against the decision, but a party may request a hearing at which the decision may be reconsidered (r 54.12(3)) provided a request is made within seven days of service of the reasons (r 54.12(4). Only two days' notice of the hearing date will be given (r 54.12(5)). At such a hearing, if the defendant or any other interested party attends, the court will not generally make an order for costs against the claimant (PD 54, para 8.6). In any event, neither the defendant nor any other person served with the claim may apply to set aside the order giving permission (r 54.13).

When giving permission, the court may also give case management directions (r 54.10).

RESPONDING TO THE CLAIM

Any person served with the claim who wishes to contest it must serve a response containing their detailed grounds plus any written evidence with 35 days of service of the order giving permission (r 54.14(1)).

EVIDENCE

No written evidence may be relied upon unless it has been served in accordance with directions or any order of the court or the court gives permission (r 54.16). Disclosure[3] is not required unless the court orders otherwise (PD 54, para 12.1). For provisions as to skeleton arguments, see PD 54, para 15.

---

3   See Chapter 29, Disclosure of Documents.

THE HEARING

The court can hear a request from any person (not being a party) that they be allowed to file evidence or be heard at the judicial review hearing (r 54.17). This would particularly apply to special interest groups, such as Amnesty International, Greenpeace or Friends of the Earth, who may have an interest in the proceedings. This is in stark contrast to claims under the European Convention on Human Rights, where the only participants can be the 'victim' and the alleged wrongdoer.[4]

The court may dispose of the matter without a hearing if all the parties agree (r 54.18). As for an agreed final order, see PD 54, para 17.

In the event of a quashing order, the court may either consider the whole matter there and then or remit it to the decision maker with a direction to reach a decision in accordance with the judgment of the court (r 54.19(2)).

4　See Chapter 37, The Human Rights Act 1998.

THE HUMAN RIGHTS ACT 1998

INTRODUCTION

The Act came into force on 2 October 2000. It incorporates the Convention rights set out in the European Convention on Human Rights (the Convention) into English domestic law (s 1). It requires the courts to construe legislation 'so far as it is possible to do' in a way which is compatible with those rights (s 3). It places public authorities under a duty not to act in a manner inconsistent with those rights (s 6) and enables litigants to allege breaches of those rights in proceedings before the English courts or tribunals – whether as a cause of action or as a defence or counterclaim (s 7).

The Act is not retrospective. Subject to one exception, there is no right to challenge the acts of a public authority committed before 2 October 2000. The exception relates to proceedings brought by a public authority; the defendant in such proceedings can raise any violation of his Convention rights by the authority, regardless of when it took place (s 22(4)).

ECHR CASES

Cases decided by the ECHR are relevant when interpreting Convention rights (see s 2), but the decisions are not binding and, in the words of the Lord Chancellor, the courts may 'depart from existing Strasbourg decisions and, upon occasion, it might well be appropriate to do so ... However, where it is relevant, we would of course expect our courts to apply Convention jurisprudence and its principles in the cases before them'.[1]

COMPATIBILITY

A litigant can argue that the Act under which he is being prosecuted violates his Convention rights. Section 3 requires the court to construe primary and secondary legislation in a way that is compatible with Convention rights 'so far as it is possible to do so'. This applies to all legislation, whenever enacted, and the first challenges are likely to arise in criminal matters; it has, for

---

1   Parliamentary discussion during the passage of the Bill.

example, been suggested that some of the trespass provisions in the Public Order Act 1996 violate the right of assembly conferred by Art 11.

The High Court, Court of Appeal or House of Lords may make a 'declaration of incompatibility' (s 4). This will not affect the validity of the legislation, but s 10 provides machinery whereby a minister may correct the incompatibility by order if he or she considers that there are 'compelling reasons' for proceeding under this section. No doubt this will be taken into account by the original court when considering what sentence (if any) to impose. The Crown is entitled to be joined as a party if the court is being asked to make a declaration of incompatibility (s 5).

Note also s 19: before a second reading in either House, the minister in charge of the Bill must state in writing that (a) in his view the Bill is compatible with Convention rights, or (b) although he cannot make such a statement, the government nevertheless wishes the House to proceed with the Bill.

This procedure also applies to subordinate legislation if the court is satisfied that, disregarding any possibility of revocation, the primary legislation precludes the removal of the incompatibility.

PUBLIC AUTHORITIES

It is unlawful for a public authority to act in a way which is incompatible with a Convention right [s 6(1)].

There is no exhaustive definition of a 'public authority', but the term clearly includes central and local government, prisons, NHS hospitals, the police, immigration officers, the BBC (but not ITV or the press) and 'any person certain of whose functions are functions of a public nature' (s 6(3)(b)). The case law on the direct enforceability of EU Directives against 'emanations of the State' is clearly relevant here so that, for example, the term 'public authority' can include privatised utilities who still have public functions to perform. This sub-section will only apply to such 'quasi-public bodies' where the act in question is a public act (s 6(5)).

The court as a public authority

This is the so called 'horizontal' effect of the Act. Having stated in s 6(1) that a 'public authority' must respect Convention rights, s 6(3) provides that 'In this section "public authority" includes a court or tribunal'.

The State is bound to protect Convention rights and it can be in breach if, acting through the courts, it fails to do so. In the absence of judicial authority (and no doubt a decision will emerge before very long) the position appears to be as follows:

(a) There can be liability if rules of court, or orders of the court, violate the applicant's Convention rights, for example, court fees or the legal aid contracting scheme may be said to unlawfully hinder access to justice and it could be argued that very short time periods (for example, in fast track litigation) can undermine the right to a fair trial under Art 6. It should be noted that the CPR were drafted with reference to the Convention and subject to overriding objectives, and are unlikely to be found to be non-Human Rights Act-compliant.

(b) When the court is exercising a discretion it should, as a public authority, do so in a Convention-compatible way.

(c) Although the Act does not create a new cause of action as between private parties, a litigant can look to the court as a 'public authority' to protect his or her Convention rights. The court can do this by developing existing causes of action in a Convention-compatible way. Thus in *Halford v UK*,[2] the Strasbourg court found that the UK government were in breach of Art 8 when a public-sector employer had unlawfully tapped the applicant's telephone calls. As from 2 October 2000, such a claim can be brought in the English courts or tribunals. If the employer had been a private employer, the applicant might have asked the court to protect her Convention rights by reference to the implied duty of trust and confidence. Similarly, the unwanted activities of a photographer (interfering with a person's Art 8 rights) can perhaps be curbed by asking the court to develop the law of breach of confidence or copyright. Finally, there is the ever-expanding tort of negligence, on the basis that 'the categories of negligence are never closed'. For example, public authorities such as the police, who have hitherto enjoyed immunity for negligence arising out of the performance of their duties, may now find themselves vulnerable.[3]

RAISING CONVENTION VIOLATIONS

A person alleging violation of Convention rights by a public authority can bring an action or rely on the alleged violation (for example, by way of defence) in any legal proceedings (s 7(1)).

They must prove that they are (or would be) a 'victim' of the unlawful act (s 7(1)). The application must be a 'victim' under Art 34 (formerly Art 25) of the Convention. From the large body of Strasbourg case law, the following points emerge:

---

2   [1997] IRLR 471.
3   *Osman v UK* [1999] 1 FLR 193.

(a) Individual complainants do not have to show that their rights have been violated; they need only show that they run the risk of being directly affected by the measure in question (see, for example, *Norris v Ireland*[4] – Irish law prohibiting homosexual acts between consenting males – the applicant was a 'victim' even though he had not been prosecuted and the risk of prosecution was minimal). In another case from Ireland, a woman of child bearing age successfully challenged a law prohibiting information about abortion facilities abroad (*Open Door Counselling and Dublin Well Woman v Ireland*).[5]

(b) An applicant may be an indirect 'victim', for example, a close relative.

(c) A trade union can be a 'victim' in its own right, but not merely as representing its members.

(d) A company can be a 'victim' in appropriate cases.

(e) The 'victim' test is narrower than the right to bring proceedings for judicial review (so that representative bodies or pressure groups such as Amnesty International or Families Need Fathers will not qualify).

TIME LIMITS FOR CLAIMS

The period is one year, beginning with the date on which the act complained of was done, or such longer time as the court thinks equitable having regard to all the circumstances. This is subject to any shorter time limit under domestic law (for example, three months for judicial review in the UK).

REMEDIES FOR BREACH OF CONVENTION RIGHTS

A court or tribunal can grant such remedies within its jurisdiction as it considers just and appropriate (s 8(1)). However, the power to award damages is subject to a number of limitations, for example:

• only by a civil court;

• only if the court considers that damages are necessary to afford just satisfaction to the applicant.

The principles adopted by the ECHR under Art 41 of the Convention must be applied; damages are discretionary and modest. Claims often fail on the issue of causation and a finding of liability is often regarded as 'just satisfaction' without the need for compensation .

---

4   (1988) 13 EHRR 186.
5   (1992) 125 EHRR 244.

The remedy for judicial acts (for example, failure to give horizontal effect to the Convention) is appeal or judicial review, that is, no damages. There are no damages for judicial acts done in good faith except compensation under Art 5(5) which relates to the victims of unlawful arrest or detention. Note that 'court' in this context includes a tribunal. The potential impact of the Human Rights Act is likely to be far greater in cases of tribunals than for courts, and likely to be much greater in criminal as opposed to civil cases.

RAISING A CONVENTION POINT

Lord Woolf has twice warned against an overuse of the Act – first when sitting as Master of the Rolls in *Daniels v Walker*[6] and then at a press conference after being sworn in as Lord Chief Justice. Nevertheless, notwithstanding the contention that the CPR are Convention-compliant, there may be cases where a human rights challenge is both necessary and appropriate (and where solicitors could face a negligence claim for failing to do so) – hearings in public, court fees and fast track timetables are just three areas which may be vulnerable. It is a difficult area calling for the exercise of sound professional judgment.[7]

As for setting out a claim when seeking a remedy under the Act, see PD 16 para 16:

16.1 A party who seeks to rely on any provision of or right arising under the Human Rights Act 1998 or seeks a remedy available under that Act –

(1) must state that fact in his statement of case; and

(2) must in his statement of case –

(a) give precise details of the Convention right which it is alleged has been infringed and details of the alleged infringement;

(b) specify the relief sought;

(c) state if the relief sought includes –

(i) a declaration of incompatibility in accordance with section 4 of that Act, or

(ii) damages in respect of a judicial act to which section 9(3) of that Act applies;

(d) where the relief sought includes a declaration of incompatibility in accordance with section 4 of that Act, give precise details of the legislative provision alleged to be incompatible and details of the alleged incompatibility;

---

6   (2000) 19 BSD 151.
7   For further comment see 'Human rights and the Woolf reforms' (2000) Law Soc Gazette, 8 June, p 51.

(e) where the claim is founded on a finding of unlawfulness by another court or tribunal, give details of the finding; and

(f) where the claim is founded on a judicial act which is alleged to have infringed a Convention right of the party as provided by s 9 of the Human Rights Act 1998, the judicial act complained of and the court or tribunal which is alleged to have made it.

(The Practice Direction to Part 19 provides for notice to be given and parties joined in the circumstances referred to in (c), (d) and (f).)

16.2 A party who seeks to amend his statement of case to include the matters referred to in paragraph 16.1 must, unless the court orders otherwise, do so as soon as possible.

(Part 17 provides for the amendment of a statement of case.)

CHAPTER 38

FUNDING LITIGATION

INTRODUCTION

Lord Woolf was of the opinion that 'The problem of cost is the most serious problem besetting our litigation system'.[1] He believed that 'the unaffordable cost of litigation constitutes a denial of access to justice'.[2] In his exploration for the reasons for the excessive cost of litigating, Lord Woolf criticised traditional charging methods used by lawyers (by the hour for solicitors, and by the day for barristers) as having an inflationary effect on costs (as the more that is done, the more the lawyer is paid) and he urged the adoption of charging on a fixed fee basis instead whenever possible.[3]

Many aspects of the CPR are intended to reduce the cost of litigating. This includes measures to reform the system in order to make it more efficient, such as the introduction of judicial case management,[4] but measures have also been introduced in order to limit the recoverability of costs. For instance, the requirement to provide costs estimates at various stages of proceedings,[5] the rule about fixed trial costs for cases heard on the fast track[6] and, more generally, through the introduction of the concept of proportionality in the assessment of costs.[7] Despite Lord Woolf's criticisms and the introduction of the new measures, lawyers continue to charge on the traditional basis, it being very unusual for them to offer their services, in a matter involving litigation, on a fixed fee basis.

The Lord Chancellor's Department (LCD) also criticised the cost of litigation and the charging practices of lawyers, stating that the current system 'does not encourage legal representatives – who are paid the same, win, lose or draw – to weed out weak cases'.[8] The LCD was of the opinion that conditional fee agreements (CFAs) were better than traditional methods of charging because they 'ensure that the risks of litigation are shared with the lawyer and the client: clients do not pay their lawyers fees unless they win;

---

1   See *Access to Justice*, Interim Report, Chapter 25, para 1 (www.lcd.gov.uk/civil/ interfr.htm).
2   See Interim Report, Chapter 3, para 13. (*Ibid.*)
3   See Interim Report, Chapter 25, para 8. (*Ibid.*)
4   See Chapter 5, Judicial Case Management: The Overriding Objective.
5   Eg, on allocation and when filing the listing questionnaire. See Chapter 33, Costs.
6   See CPR, Part 46 and Chapter 33, Costs.
7   See CPR, Part 44, r 44.4 and Chapter 33, Costs.
8   See Lord Chancellor's Department, *Access to Justice with Conditional Fees*, Consultation Paper, March 1998 (www.lcd.gov.uk/consult/leg-aid/confrefr.htm).

and lawyers, when they win, receive a level of fees that recognises the risks they have taken'.[9]

As part of its reform of the civil litigation system, the Government was determined to limit and control the legal aid budget and produced various statistics showing that whilst spending under legal aid increased year on year, the number of cases brought and people helped under the scheme constantly reduced.[10] The Lord Chancellor, Lord Irvine, believed that making CFAs (backed by legal expenses insurance) more widely available, whilst on the one hand providing some justification for abolishing legal aid for negligence based personal injury actions, and effectively for most other civil actions, on the other also furthered his aim of increasing access to justice.

It was against this background that on 1 April 2000, two fundamental reforms were introduced which will have a profound effect on the way civil litigation is funded. On that date the Civil Legal Aid System, administered by the Legal Aid Board, was replaced by the Community Legal Service (CLS), administered by the Legal Services Commission. Under the CLS, public funding is now no longer available for negligence based personal injury actions and for most other civil actions apart from social welfare type cases. Also, for those entering into a CFA from that date, the success fee and any legal expenses insurance premium is now recoverable from the unsuccessful opponent along with the usual costs of the action.

By making CFAs more attractive in this way, the expectation is that they will allow any client, regardless of means, to bring or defend an action. At the time when Lord Woolf wrote his Final Report, CFAs and legal expenses insurance were 'available only in limited classes of cases' (personal injury, insolvency, human rights) and Lord Woolf believed they would only become more generally available 'if costs are firmly controlled in the ways that I am proposing'.[11] However, the removal of civil legal aid funding for personal injury actions and most other civil actions has, at a stroke, accelerated the likely increase in the use of CFAs quite unconnected to the rate of cost reduction brought about by the introduction of the CPR.

---

9   *Ibid.*

10   For Government statistics, see *ibid.*

11   See *Access to Justice*, Final Report, s 1, p 10, para 12 (www.lcd.gov.uk/civil/finalfr.htm).

CONDITIONAL FEE AGREEMENTS

Background

It is possible to enter into an enforceable CFA for all types of civil litigation,[12] except family proceedings.[13] CFAs are not permissible in criminal proceedings apart from those under s 82 of the Environmental Protection Act 1990.[14]

Historically, CFAs were held to be contrary to public policy on the basis that it was undesirable for legal representatives to have an interest in the outcome of the cases they were conducting. This long standing policy was changed by s 58 of the Courts and Legal Services Act 1990, which was the framework legislation paving the way for the introduction of CFAs. CFAs were initially introduced only for certain types of case to be specified by regulations made by the Lord Chancellor. In 1995, the Conditional Fee Agreements Order 1995[15] provided that CFAs were permissible for personal injury, insolvency and cases before the European Commission of Human Rights and the European Court of Human Rights. In July 1998, the Conditional Fee Agreements Order 1998 extended CFAs to all civil non-family proceedings.[16] It is anticipated that CFAs will eventually be extended to those aspects of family cases concerned with the division of matrimonial property.[17]

Although conditional fee agreements are lawful, they should be distinguished from contingency fee agreements, which are not lawful for contentious matters. Contingency fee agreements allow the legal representative to take a proportion of the damages recovered by the client if the case is successful. It is thought to be undesirable and therefore against public policy for a legal representative to have a direct interest not only in the outcome of litigation, but the amount of damages recovered by a client.

References to 'regulations' or 'regs' are references to the Conditional Fee Agreement Regulations 2000, unless otherwise stated.

---

12 See Courts and Legal Services Act 1990, s 58(1), as substituted by Access to Justice Act 1999, s 27.
13 See Courts and Legal Services Act 1990, s 58A(1)(b), as substituted by Access to Justice Act 1999, s 27.
14 Courts and Legal Services Act 1990, s 58A(1)(a), as substituted by Access to Justice Act 1999, s 27.
15 SI 1995/1674.
16 SI 1998/1860.
17 See proposals contained in the Government's White Paper, *Modernising Justice*, 2 December 1998 (www.lcd.gov.uk/consult/access/mjwpcon.htm).

CONDITIONAL FEE AGREEMENTS

A CFA (commonly known as a 'no win, no fee' agreement) is defined as:

> an agreement with a person providing advocacy or litigation services which provides for his fees and expenses, or any part of them, to be payable only in specified circumstances.[18]

The 'specified circumstances' will be defined in the written agreement constituting the CFA. For instance, in the Law Society model CFA for use in personal injury cases, the specified circumstances are if the party 'wins' their claim. This is further defined as meaning if the party's 'claim for damages is finally decided in [their] favour, whether by a court decision or an agreement to pay [their] damages'.[19]

The success fee

Most CFAs also provide for payment of a success fee to the legal representative in addition to his usual fees, the rationale being to 'reward' the legal representative for taking the risk of losing the case and recovering no fees and so having done the work for nothing. The element of the legal representative's fees which do not form part of the success fee are known as the base costs.[20]

However, a CFA does not need to provide for a success fee in order to fall within the definition. An agreement which provides for the legal representative to be paid usual costs if the case is won, but no or lower costs if the case is lost, is a form of CFA. This latter type of CFA has come to be known as a 'Thai Trading Agreement' after the name of the case where such an agreement was held to be lawful and not contrary to public policy.[21] In that case, it was recognised that such agreements are often entered into by solicitors on an informal basis with their clients, the agreement consisting of no more than an expectation that fees will be paid only if the case is successful. However, the Thai Trading decision was subsequently disapproved in *Awwad v Geraghty and Co (A Firm)*,[22] where it was held acting for a client under a CFA not sanctioned by statute is against public policy. Under the new provisions, in order to be enforceable, such an agreement will have to comply with the onerous formal requirements specified for CFAs

---

18 Courts and Legal Services Act 1990, s 58(2)(a), as substituted by Access to Justice Act 1999, s 27.

19 See Condition 3 of the Law Society Conditions of their model CFA agreement for PI (personal injury) cases.

20 PD 43, para 2.2, see Chapter 33, Costs.

21 *Thai Trading Co v Taylor* [1998] 3 All ER 65, CA.

22 [2000] 1 All ER 608.

under the Courts and Legal Services Act 1990 and accompanying regulations. However, such agreements entered into before the new legislation came into force are potentially unenforceable.

LEGAL EXPENSES INSURANCE

Although a client entering into a CFA will not have to pay any fees to their lawyer if their case is unsuccessful, owing to our 'indemnity costs' system, whereby the loser is usually ordered to pay the winner's costs, in order for CFAs to be a viable option for litigants they are usually supported by a legal expenses insurance policy to insure against the risk of having to pay the opponent's costs if the case is lost. This type of legal expenses insurance is known as 'after the event' insurance, as compared to legal expenses insurance policies, frequently attached to car and home insurance, which provide legal expenses insurance cover before any claim has arisen.

NEW FUNDING ARRANGEMENTS

There is now a presumption that where the court makes an order for the losing party to pay the winning party's costs, the costs payable include the success fee and any insurance premium unless the court orders otherwise.[23] If a CFA includes one or both of these so called additional liabilities[24] (success fee or insurance premium), it will fall within the definition of a funding arrangement.[25]

Before this new legislation came into force on 1 April 2000, a successful litigant taking on a CFA expected to pay the cost of any insurance premium and the success fee out of the damages they recovered. The Government hopes that this change will not only make CFAs more attractive to parties seeking compensation, as the compensation is no longer eroded by payment of the success fee and insurance premium, but also that defendants and litigants seeking non-monetary remedies will be more likely to use CFAs knowing that if they are successful, they can recover the insurance premium and success fee from their opponent. The justification for the new rule is that

---

23 See Courts and Legal Services Act 1990, s 59A(6), as inserted by Access to Justice Act 1999 s 27 and Access to Justice Act 1999, s 29; PD 43, para 2.1, PD 44, para 9.1.
24 See CPR, r 43.2(1)(o).
25 See CPR, r 43.2(1)(k).

the losing party, having caused the need for litigation, should pay all the winner's costs including the success fee and any insurance premium.[26]

In order to be enforceable, CFAs must comply with regulations prescribed by the Lord Chancellor.[27] Those regulations are now the Conditional Fee Agreements Regulations 2000,[28] made under ss 58 and 119 of the Courts and Legal Services Act 1990 (which revoked the earlier 1995 Regulations). Rules and Practice Directions under the CPR cover the procedure for recovering the success fee and insurance premium from an unsuccessful opponent.[29]

ENTERING INTO A CFA

Duties of the legal representative before the CFA is made

A CFA is a rather complex contract and the Conditional Fee Agreements Regulations 2000[29a] impose obligations on the legal representative to inform the client about certain matters and explain the effect of a CFA to the client before he enters into it. The legal representative is required to give any explanation in plain English, in order to ensure that the client fully understands the type of agreement he is entering into.

Information which must be given orally

The legal representative must orally inform the client before the CFA is made (whether or not this information is also given in writing):

- about the circumstances when the client may be liable to pay the costs of the legal representative under the agreement (for example, if the client's case is successful, but also, for instance, if the client terminates the agreement before the conclusion of the case) (reg 4(2)(a));

- about the circumstances where the client may, and the procedure for seeking assessment of the legal representative's fees and expenses (reg 4(2)(b));

- as to whether the legal representative considers that the client's possible liability for costs in respect of the proceedings is already covered by an existing contract of insurance (for example, before the event insurance as

---

26 For an account of the LCD's policy see Lord Chancellor's Department, *Access to Justice with Conditional Fees*, para 2.14. (*Ibid.*)

27 See Courts and Legal Services Act 1990, s 58(3)(c) as inserted by Access to Justice Act 1999, s 27.

28 SI 2000/692.

29 See below, p 455 and Chapter 33, Costs.

29a References in this chapter to regulations are references to the Conditional Fee Agreement Regulations 2000, unless otherwise stated.

contained in some household contents insurance policies or car insurance policies) (reg 4(2)(c)); but if none is in existence

- whether some other method of financing those costs is available to the client (for example, after the event legal expenses insurance (reg 4(2)(d)).

Information which must be given both orally and in writing

The following information must be given both orally and in writing to the client before the CFA is entered into:

- an explanation to the client of the effect of the CFA (reg 4(3));
- if the legal representative recommends a particular after the event insurance policy to cover payment of costs for which the client may become liable, information as to why he recommends such a policy and a statement as to whether he has an interest in doing so (reg 4(2)(e)).

Moreover, there is also a general requirement to provide as much further explanation, advice or information to the client about the CFA as the client reasonably demands (reg 4(1)(b)).

However, these obligations do not apply when a CFA is entered into between a solicitor and a barrister (reg 4(6)). Nor does such an agreement between legal representatives need to be in writing (reg 5).

The contents of a CFA

The Conditional Fee Agreements Regulations 2000 specify particular requirements which the contract containing the CFA must fulfil in order to make it enforceable. The regulations distinguish between CFAs where a success fee is payable and those where one is not. For all CFAs, there are general requirements which must be fulfilled. There are then additional requirements which must also be fulfilled for CFAs providing for a success fee.

General requirements for all CFAs

The CFA must:

- be in writing[30] and signed by both the client and the legal representative (reg 5(1));
- specify the particular proceedings (or parts) to which it relates (reg 2(1)(a)). Therefore, the CFA should contain sufficient information to identify the proceedings, such as the type of action involved, the relevant date of the incident or cause of action and the identity of the defendant;

---

30 Access to Justice Act 1999, s 27(3)(a).

- specify whether the CFA includes any appeal, counterclaim or proceedings to enforce any judgment or order obtained (reg 2(1)(a)). If a client wishes to take further action, such as an appeal against a decision, then if such proceedings are not covered by the original CFA, the original agreement will have to be amended,[31] or a separate agreement, which may be another CFA, will have to be entered into;

- specify the circumstances when the legal representative's fees and expenses are payable (reg 2(1)(b));

- specify what payment is due if those circumstances only partly occur; irrespective of whether those circumstances occur; and on the termination of the agreement for whatever reason (reg 2(1)(c));

- specify the amounts which are payable in all the circumstances or the methods used to calculate them (reg 2(1)(d));

- specify whether the amounts payable are limited by the damages which may be recovered on behalf of the client (reg 2(1)(d)). Before it became possible to recover the success fee and insurance premium from the losing opponent, the Law Society recommended that in no case should the success fee exceed 25% of the damages recovered by the client. Now that these sums are recoverable from the unsuccessful opponent, the Law Society no longer makes this recommendation of voluntary restraint;

- contain a statement that the duties of the legal representative under reg 4[32] to inform the client about various matters before the CFA is entered into have been complied with (reg 2(2)).

CFAs providing for success fees

A CFA with a success fee will specify a percentage, the 'percentage increase', by which the amount of the legal representative's fee can be increased in the event of success. The success fee is designed to reflect the degree of risk the legal representative has taken in entering into the agreement, so the weaker and less likely to succeed the case, the higher the percentage success fee and vice versa.

It is permissible to include a success fee in all CFAs allowed under the Act apart from proceedings under s 82 of the Environmental Protection Act 1990.[33] These are criminal proceedings which allow a person afflicted by a statutory nuisance to seek an order for the nuisance to be remedied. A common use of this provision is by a tenant against a landlord who has failed to maintain the rented accommodation in a habitable condition. Although it is

---

31 See below, p 452.
32 See above, p 448.
33 See Conditional Fee Agreements Order 2000 SI 2000/823, reg 3.

permissible to enter into a CFA for this type of action, it is the only type of action (of those permitted) for which a success fee is prohibited.

Additional formalities for CFAs providing for success fees

Where the CFA includes a success fee, the CFA must:

- briefly specify the reasons for setting the percentage increase at the level stated in the agreement (reg 3(1)(a)). There must, therefore, be a written record of the reasons for setting the success fee at the chosen percentage increase at the time the agreement was entered into. This provision anticipates any challenge to the level of the success fee at a later date and can be seen as a protection for the legal representative, as he has a contemporaneous record of the relevant factors which affected his judgment as to the level of risk which he can use to distinguish factors only discoverable with hindsight;

- specify how much of the percentage increase, if any, relates to the cost to the legal representative of the postponement of the payment of his fees and expenses (reg 3(1)(b)). When fixing the level of the success fee, some legal representatives take into account the effect CFAs have on their cash flow, due to the fact that payment of fees is only made at the conclusion of the case. This element of the success fee, the cost to the legal representative caused by postponement of payment of his fees, is not recoverable from the losing opponent (r 44.3B(1)(a)). However, there is no requirement to include such an element in the calculation of the success fee.

CFAs which provide for success fees and which relate to court proceedings must also include the following terms:

- that if the percentage increase becomes payable as a result of proceedings, and the fees subject to the increase are assessed, then the client or the legal representative is permitted to disclose the reasons for setting the success fee at the rate specified in the CFA if required to do so by the court (reg 3(2)(a));

- if the success fee is assessed[34] and any amount of the percentage increase is disallowed on assessment on the ground that the level at which the increase was set was unreasonable in view of facts which were or should have been known to the legal representative at the time it was set, the amount ceases to be payable under the agreement unless the court is satisfied that it should remain payable (reg 3(2)(b);

- if the fees are not assessed[35] but the legal representative agrees with the paying party to accept a lower percentage increase than that specified in

34 See Chapter 33, Costs.
35 *Ibid.*

the CFA, then the amount of the percentage increase specified in the CFA shall be reduced accordingly unless the court is satisfied that the full amount should remain payable (reg 3(2)(c)).

The court will therefore have the power in any assessment proceedings to disallow any amount in respect of the percentage increase on the grounds that the level was unreasonable in the light of facts which were known or should have been known to the legal representative at the time the success fee was set. This means that the success fee can be extinguished or reduced. Regulation 3(2)(b) provides that in these circumstances, this amount ceases to be payable under the agreement, unless the court orders otherwise. The same result will follow if the fees are not assessed, but simply agreed, and part of the agreement is for a reduction in the percentage of the success fee.

This ensures that if the losing opponent does not have to pay the success fee, or the full amount of the success fee set under the agreement, the client will not be left to pay it instead unless the legal representative can persuade the court that it would be reasonable for the client to pay it. Such provisions will obviously deter legal representatives from setting an unduly high success fee.

Amendment of a CFA

A CFA will often not extend to the bringing of an appeal against the decision at trial. In those circumstances, if the client loses his case at first instance and wishes to appeal, and the legal representative is prepared to act for the client under a CFA, then either a new CFA to cover those proceedings will have to be entered into or the original agreement amended. If the original agreement is amended, the amendments must be in writing and the amendments must comply with the formalities specified for the original agreement under regs 2, 3 and 5 (reg 6(a)). Also, the requirement under reg 4 to provide specified oral and written information to the client before a CFA is entered into must be complied with in so far as the information is relevant to the amendments (reg 6).

Limits on the success fee

The maximum percentage increase allowed for a success fee has been fixed at 100%.[36] When the success fee was payable by the winning client out of damages recovered, the Law Society recommended that solicitors voluntarily limit the uplift to an amount which did not exceed 25% of the damages recovered. Now that the success fee is recoverable from the opponent, this recommendation has been dropped.

---

36 See Conditional Fee Agreements Order 2000 SI 2000/823, reg 4.

Law Society model agreement for personal injury cases

The Law Society produces a model CFA for personal injury cases as well as guidance on compliance with the regulations. The Law Society intends to produce a model agreement for use in other types of case as CFAs become more common in other areas.

DISCLOSURE OF FUNDING ARRANGEMENTS

Disclosure of the funding arrangement

In accordance with the general principle that a party should be informed about the full extent of any potential liability he may have to meet if he is unsuccessful in bringing or defending a claim, a party who has entered into a funding arrangement must disclose this to his opponent at various stages of the proceedings. A failure to give the necessary disclosure will result in the additional liability being irrecoverable.

Pre-commencement disclosure

Paragraph 4A.1 to the Protocols Practice Direction provides in general terms that where a party enters into a funding arrangement within the meaning of r 43.2(1)(k), he should inform other potential parties to the claim that he has done so. This rule applies to all proceedings whether or not subject to a pre-action protocol (r 4A.2). Although the Practice Direction is not precise as to the stage at which notification should be given, it does provide a cross-reference to r 44.3B(1)(c), which sets out the consequences of a failure to provide the proper notification once proceedings have begun[37] (namely, that any additional liability will not be recoverable from the opponent). Therefore, to be on the safe side, a party should inform any other potential party as soon as the funding agreement is entered into.

Disclosure on commencement of proceedings

Where a party has entered into a funding arrangement before proceedings are started, if proceedings are started he is required to file at court and serve on the other parties a notice containing information about the arrangement as specified in Form N251 and which is signed by the party or his legal representative (PD 44, paras 19.1–19.2).

On issuing a claim form, the claimant must also file the notice at court at the same time as the claim form. If the court is to effect service of the claim

---

37   For details, see below.

form, and sufficient copies of the notice have been filed, the court will also serve the notice along with the claim form. Otherwise, the claimant must serve the notice on the other parties himself (PD 44, para 19.2(2)).

A defendant who has entered into a funding arrangement before filing any documents at court files the notice when he files his first document at court. The first document a defendant files at court is likely to be an acknowledgment of service or a defence. Again, if the court is to effect service of the defendant's documents, and sufficient copies of the notice have been provided, the court will also serve the notice at the same time (PD 44, para 19.2(3)).

In all other circumstances, for instance, if the funding arrangement is entered into after the claimant starts proceedings or after the defendant files his first document at court, a party must file and serve notice of the funding arrangement within seven days of entering into it (PD 44, para 19.2(4)).

Contents of the notice

The information that must be provided in the notice as set out in Form N251 is:

- whether the party has entered into a CFA providing for a success fee;
- if so, the date of the agreement and the claim or claims to which it relates;
- whether the party has taken out an insurance policy to insure against liability for costs;
- if so, the name of the insurer, the date of the policy and the claim or claims to which it relates.

If both a CFA providing for a success fee and an insurance policy have been entered into, one notice can contain all the relevant information (PD 44, para 19.4).

It should be noted that, at this stage, the requirements are to disclose the fact that a CFA providing for a success fee and/or an insurance policy have been entered into as well as other formalities, but not the amount of the percentage increase or cost of the insurance (rr 44.3A and 44.15, PD 44, para 19.1). A requirement to disclose the level of the percentage increase or the amount of the insurance premium would cause serious disadvantage to a party with a funding arrangement as it would allow the opponent to assess how the other party viewed the strength of their case, as obviously the higher the percentage increase the lower the perceived chance of success.

Notice of change of information

There is a duty on a party to give notice of any change if the information about the funding arrangement he previously provided is no longer accurate

(PD 44, para 19.3). For instance, if one insurance policy is cancelled and another entered into.

Failure to disclose the funding arrangement

A failure to disclose the required details of the funding arrangement at the time or times specified will result in the sanction that any additional liability over any period in which there was a failure to provide the information will be irrecoverable (r 44.3B(1)(c)).

However, a party who is in default would be able to apply under the provisions of rr 3.8 and 3.9 (which have general application) for relief from that sanction.[38] It is likely that if the failure to disclose is a pure oversight and is quickly remedied, a party will be unlikely to lose the benefit of the success fee in those circumstances. Such an application is made under Part 23[38a] and supported by evidence (PD 44, para 10.1).

RECOVERING THE ADDITIONAL LIABILITY

The general principle is that if an order for costs is made against an opponent, this will include payment of the additional liability (r 44.3A). However, this is subject to the court's general discretion to order otherwise (r 44.3). Also, a party will not recover the additional liability for any period in the proceedings during which he failed to comply with the disclosure requirements referred to above (r 44.3B(1)(c)). Further, a party will not recover the success fee if he fails, when required, to disclose in any assessment proceedings the reasons for setting the percentage increase of the success fee at the level specified in the CFA (r 44.3B(1)(d)). It should also be noted that a party cannot recover the additional liability on any costs incurred before the funding arrangement was entered into (PD 48, para 57.9).

Although in most cases the parties will agree costs, including the level of the success fee and insurance premium, if no agreement can be reached, a party can ask for these additional liabilities to be assessed[38b] by the court at the end of the proceedings.[39]

The court will not assess the additional liability until the conclusion of the proceedings to which the funding arrangement relates (r 44.3A(1)). The court can either:

- make a summary assessment of all costs, including any additional liability;

38 See Chapter 19, Making Applications for Court Orders.
38a See Chapter 5, Judicial Case Management: The Overriding Objective.
38b See Chapter 33, Costs.
39 See CPR, r 44.3A.

- make an order for detailed assessment of the additional liability but make a summary assessment of the other costs; or
- make an order for detailed assessment of all costs (r 44.3A(2)).

It should be noted that the court cannot make a detailed assessment of the base costs and a summary assessment of the additional liability.

Challenging the success fee

If costs are assessed and the opponent challenges the level of the percentage increase payable under the CFA, the party claiming the costs must disclose not only the CFA, but also the statement of the reasons for the percentage increase as required by reg 3 (PD 44, para 32.5).

When deciding whether the percentage increase is reasonable, the court may take the following factors into account:

- the chances of success of the case as they reasonably appeared to the legal representative at the time when the CFA was entered into;
- the legal representative's liability for disbursements;
- what other methods of financing the costs were available to the party who entered into a CFA.[40]

The court is also able to allow different percentage increases for different items of costs or for different periods during which costs were incurred (PD 44, para 11.8(2)).

However, the court is expressly restrained from applying principles of proportionality to reduce the amount of the percentage increase. Accordingly, PD 44, para 11.9 states that the court cannot reduce a percentage increase on the ground that when added to base costs which are reasonable and proportionate, the total appears disproportionate.

Challenging the amount of an insurance premium

The factors which the court must take into account when deciding whether the amount of an insurance premium is reasonable include:

- where the insurance cover is not purchased in support of a CFA, how its cost compares with the equivalent cost of funding the case with a CFA providing for a success fee and supported by insurance. It is possible to purchase after the event legal expenses insurance as a 'stand alone' policy which is not in support of a CFA. Such an insurance product insures against the risk of paying your own legal representative's costs as well as

40 See PD 44, paras 11.7 and 11.8.

those of your opponent, so if the case is unsuccessful, the insurance premium covers both sets of costs. Under such an arrangement, as the party's legal representative will be paid his costs whether the party's case is successful or not, the costs payable to the party's legal representative would be ordinary base costs and would not include any element of a success fee. As such a policy covers the risk of paying both sides' costs, as compared with a CFA legal expenses insurance policy which will only cover the risk of paying the opponent's costs, the premium is usually considerably higher than that for those policies which support CFAs;

• the availability of any pre-existing insurance cover. The legal representative is obliged to advise a client about the existence of alternative sources of funding his case, including pre-existing 'before the event' insurance which the client can rely upon.[41] If this alternative source of funding was ignored, the court would be likely to hold the cost of this insurance premium irrecoverable;

• the level and extent of the cover provided;

• whether any part of the premium would be rebated in the event of early settlement;

• the amount of any commission payable to the receiving party or his legal representatives or other agents.

The last three factors could be said to be an assessment of the 'value for money' aspect of the insurance premium. It could be argued that a seemingly expensive premium is in fact justified if it pays out on a higher level of legal costs.

Recovering the percentage increase from the client

If, on assessing costs, the court disallows or reduces the percentage increase payable under the CFA, the general rule is that the disallowed or reduced percentage increase ceases to be payable under the agreement. This means effectively that the client will not be liable to pay it. However, the legal representative can apply to the court for an order that his client continue to be liable for the percentage increase and the court can make such an order if it considers it a suitable order to make (PD 44, para 20).[42]

Client challenging the level of the success fee

A client who has entered into a CFA can apply for the assessment of either the base costs or the percentage increase of the success fee, or both (r 48.9).

---

41 See above, p 448, and reg 4(2)(c).

42 See PD 44, para 20 for details of the procedure for such an application.

A client who applies to the court for the percentage increase under the CFA to be reduced must set out in his application notice:

- the reasons why the percentage increase should be reduced; and
- what the percentage increase should be.

When deciding whether the percentage increase is reasonable, the court will have regard to all the relevant factors as they appeared to the solicitor or counsel when the CFA was entered into (PD 44, para 55.1). When assessing the percentage increase, the court will consider the following factors in the light of the circumstances as they reasonably appeared to the solicitor or counsel when the CFA was entered into:

- the risk that the circumstances in which the fees or expenses would be payable might not occur;
- the disadvantages relating to the absence of payment on account;
- whether the amount which might be payable under the CFA is limited to a certain proportion of any damages recovered by the client;
- whether there is a CFA between the solicitor and counsel;
- the solicitor's liability for any disbursements (PD 44, para 55).

TRANSITIONAL PROVISIONS

A CFA entered into before 1 April 2000 does not fall within the definition of a funding arrangement. The practical effect of this is that any success fee or legal expenses insurance attached to the CFA will not be recoverable from the losing opponent. This restriction cannot be avoided simply by ending the original agreement and entering into a new one after 1 April 2000.

In the circumstances where a party entered into a funding arrangement and started proceedings after 1 April 2000 but before 3 July 2000 (when the new Costs PDs came into effect) the party had 28 days to comply with the requirements of the new rules and PD in order that the additional liability be recoverable.[43]

MEMBERSHIP ORGANISATIONS

Certain membership organisations, such as trade unions, fund litigation on behalf of their members from their own resources. The nature and size of the

---

43   The Civil Procedure (Amendment No 3) Rules 2000 SI 2000/1317, r 39.

organisation is such that they self-insure rather than take our insurance against potential costs liabilities arising from the litigation. Under s 30 of the Access to Justice Act 1999 and provisions of the Access to Justice (Membership Organisations) Regulations 2000 (SI 2000/693), such membership organisations can now also recover, as part of an order for costs, a sum that reflects the provision the organisation has made against the risk of having to meet the liabilities of the member whose case it has underwritten. The membership organisations that qualify, the formalities that must be complied with and the method by which the sum is calculated are set out in the Access to Justice (Membership Organisations) Regulations 2000.

THE COMMUNITY LEGAL SERVICE

Introduction

The Community Legal Service (CLS) was launched on 3 April 2000. The CLS is administered by the Legal Services Commission, which is a non-departmental public body. The CLS is funded from moneys out of the CLS Fund.

The CLS replaces the civil and family legal aid system. The attitude of the government to the former legal aid system can be summed up in this quote from Lord Irvine in a statement he made to the House of Lords on the publication of a consultation paper, *Access to Justice with Conditional Fees*,[44] on 4 March 1998:

> At present the legal aid system is failing us all. It is failing the many millions of people on modest incomes who do not qualify for legal aid and who simply cannot contemplate going to law because of the potential legal costs if they lose. It is failing people on legal aid, because the Government cannot direct money to those who need it most and to those cases where there is a public interest in seeing justice done. Finally, it is failing the taxpayer who year on year is being asked to pay more and more, and yet can rarely get help from legal aid when it is actually needed.

The CLS is supposed to be more than a replacement for the previous legal aid system. It is intended to bring together and co-ordinate all the sources of information and advice so that a person with a legal problem can find the best and most appropriate source of help. In this sense, it provides a 'directory' service which is available to everyone. The idea being that a person looking for legal advice and assistance can find out which is the best body or person to approach for help or information. The Community Legal Service Directory provides details of all the approved sources of help and information and

---

44 www.lcd.gov.uk/consult/general/030400hd.htm.

copies are available in places such as libraries and solicitors' firms (who are part of the scheme) and on the dedicated website www.justask.org.uk and telephone line 0845 6081122. The Government believes that it will, therefore, improve access to legal and advice services.[45]

However, although anyone can access the CLS Directory to identify a source of help for their problem, this does not mean that everyone will qualify for State funding to bring legal proceedings. Although the availability of legal aid was, in practice, very limited, as in order to qualify, a case not only had to satisfy a merits test, but the individual concerned had to satisfy a means test set at a very low level, funding for a case under the CLS will be even more limited. Unlike the Legal Aid Fund, the CLS Fund has a limited amount of resources to spend on legal services. Also, whereas Legal Aid was available for most types of civil case (there were some exceptions, such as defamation), funding from the CLS depends not only on whether the person seeking the help meets the merits test (just as stringent as under Legal Aid), but also whether the case falls into one of the limited categories of types of case funded by the scheme.

The main change to the scope of cases qualifying for State funding is that personal injury actions arising from negligence (except clinical negligence cases) are expressly excluded from funding under the CLS along with conveyancing, boundary disputes, partnership, company and business issues, will making, defamation or malicious falsehood and trust law.[46] Also, all other civil money actions (apart from family cases) are effectively excluded on the basis that they can be funded instead via a CFA. On the other hand, 'social welfare' cases have been prioritised for help: these are said to include family, benefits, debt, employment rent and mortgage arrears, immigration and nationality issues. However, it should be borne in mind that personal injury and death claims which are not based on negligence, for example, cases of trespass to the person, are not excluded from CLS funding.

Community Legal Service partnerships

CLS partnerships are an important part of the CLS. The partnership consists of those bodies and organisations that fund legal and advice services (the principal funders being the Legal Services Commission and local authorities, but also local and national charities) and those CLS approved individuals and bodies who supply the legal services (such as legal representatives and advice centres).

---

45 See Lord Chancellor's Department, *The Community Legal Service Performance Indicators for Community Legal Service Partnerships*, Consultation Paper, available on the LCD website (*ibid*).

46 See Access to Justice Act 1999, Sched 2, s 1.

The CLS partnerships are to have responsibility for assessing the requirements for legal services in their area and ensure that a service is in place to meet previously identified priority needs for that area. CLS partnerships are designed to respond to local differences on the basis that different areas and communities will have different needs for legal and advice services. Funding at a set level will then be made available by the Lord Chancellor to meet those needs which have been identified. In this way, the Lord Chancellor hopes to control public funding for legal services by limiting it to identified priority needs in an area at a previously set level which cannot be exceeded. When the CLS was launched, partnerships had not been established over all areas of England and Wales although the plan is that they will eventually exist to cover every area of the jurisdiction.

The Community Legal Service Quality Mark

Organisations and individuals providing services under the CLS can qualify for the CLS Quality Mark. This will be awarded to legal service providers that achieve the specified minimum standards of the CLS. Once qualified, they can display and advertise their body as having the CLS Quality Mark logo. This Quality Mark is based on the Legal Aid Franchise Quality Assurance Standard that was introduced under the former legal aid system. Firms of solicitors who previously qualified for a Legal Aid Franchise automatically acquired the Community Legal Service Quality Mark when the CLS was launched.

However, in recognition that the CLS is not just about the provision of legal advice from legal representatives, the CLS Quality Mark is awarded for three different levels of service provided:

- information;
- general help;
- specialist help.

Information

Those organisations displaying the CLS Quality Mark for Information simply provide access to information about the provision of legal services in an area, but in order to qualify for the Quality Mark, are likely to be able to supply information such as leaflets and other reference material, access to the CLS Directory of Services and/or access to the CLS website. Places such as libraries are likely to deal at this level of the service.

General help

At this level, basic advice is provided in the form of information about rights and responsibilities and some services such as helping to fill in forms, writing letters and negotiating on behalf of the inquirer. This type of help is typically provided by organisations such as Citizens' Advice Bureaux, who offer advice and assistance for problems through volunteers who are trained, but not usually legally qualified.

Specialist help

At this level, help is provided for complex legal problems or where legal representation is required. Organisations offering this level of service will be solicitors' firms and law centres. Solicitors' firms who are approved providers of the CLS who have been awarded a contract by the Legal Services Commission and have achieved the CLS Quality Mark will be able to take on certain types of cases with funding from the CLS fund.

Scope of the Community Legal Service Fund

In order to secure funding from the Community Legal Service Fund, the application must fulfil certain requirements.

Funding is available for legal services in relation to the areas of law set out in s 4(2) of the Access to Justice Act 1999.

In very general terms funding will be available for social welfare type cases such as housing and benefit claims.

Funding is only available for individuals and not, therefore, for firms, companies or other corporate bodies.[47]

Excluded services

Under Sched 2 of the Access to Justice Act 1999, certain areas of law are expressly excluded from funding (apart from the provision of general information about the law, legal system and availability of legal services). These are:

- personal injury and death claims[48] (apart from clinical negligence claims) and damage to property claims *caused by negligence*. These claims are excluded on the grounds that most of these claims can be funded by a CFA;

---

47 Access to Justice Act 1999, s 4(1).
48 PI and death claims not based on negligence, eg, trespass to the person, are not excluded from CLS funding.

- conveyancing; boundary disputes; the making of wills; matters of trust law; defamation or malicious falsehood; matters of company or partnership law; and other matters arising out of the carrying on of a business. These claims are excluded on the grounds that they are not considered to have sufficient priority to justify public funding.

Exceptions to the exclusions

In some circumstances, cases in areas of law normally falling within the excluded category can receive funding from the Community Legal Service. These include cases which can be shown to have a wider public interest, proceedings against public authorities alleging serious wrongdoing, such as abuse of power or breach of human rights, and personal injury cases with very high investigative costs.[49]

---

49 Access to Justice Act 1999, s 6(8).

CHAPTER 39

ENFORCEMENT OF JUDGMENTS AND ORDERS

INTRODUCTION

Once an order is made or judgment is entered for a claimant, if the defendant fails or refuses to comply with that order or judgment, the claimant may then take further steps to enforce it. There are a variety of different methods of enforcing orders and judgments and a choice can usually be made as to which method to employ. However, there are some restrictions on the methods that can be employed, depending on the nature and size of the judgment and the capacity of the defendant.

All the methods of enforcement of orders and judgments under the CPR are contained in Scheds 1 and 2 of the CPR. However, the rules in the Schedule are substantially in the format of the old Rules and, therefore, different rules apply to proceedings in the High Court to those in the county court. The rules for the High Court are contained in the Rules of the Supreme Court and set out in Sched 1 and the rules for the county courts are contained in the County Court Rules and set out in Sched 2. Although the actual CPR themselves do not contain any rules on enforcement, the rules in the schedules have, to a certain extent, been amended to make them consistent with the CPR, so for instance any application under them is made in accordance with Part 23.[1] However, the old methods of commencement of enforcement proceedings have been retained, such as a writ or warrant. Enforcement is currently a subject of review by the Lord Chancellor's Department.[2]

WHICH COURT?

Usually, if a judgment or order is obtained in the High Court and it is necessary to enforce it, the judgment creditor will enforce it in the High Court and similarly judgments or orders obtained in the county court will be enforced in that court. However, the judgment creditor may wish to enforce a county court judgment or order in the High Court to take advantage of the apparently more effective methods employed by the Sheriffs than county court bailiffs in execution against goods, or a High Court judgment or order in the county court in order to obtain an attachment of earnings order. An

---

1 See Chapter 19, Making Applications for Court Orders.
2 See consultation papers on methods of enforcement at the LCD website, www.lcd.gov.uk.

important consideration in deciding whether to enforce a county court judgment in the High Court is that interest is payable on all judgments enforced in the High Court, but only on county court judgments over £5,000.[3] In most cases, it is possible to enforce a judgment or order in a different court from that in which it was obtained, but there are some limitations and restrictions.

Enforcement of High Court judgment in the county court

A judgment creditor can enforce a High Court judgment in the county court for the district where the judgment debtor resides or carries on his business (CCR Ord 25 r 11). In most cases, the judgment creditor must apply for an order under s 40 of the County Courts Act 1984 for a transfer of the proceedings from the High Court to the county court for the purposes of enforcement. However, if the proposed method of enforcement is by means of charging order[4] or attachment of earnings,[5] then an order for transfer is not required.

Enforcement of county court judgment in the High Court

Section 85 of the County Courts Act 1984 provides that as a general rule, a county court judgment may always be enforced in the High Court (subject to Art 8 of the High Court and County Courts Jurisdiction Order 1991,[6] see below).

In order to enforce a county court judgment in the High Court, a judgment creditor obtains a certificate of judgment from the county court and delivers it to the High Court (CCR Ord 25 r 13).[7] A certificate of judgment is obtained by making a request in writing to the county court, stating that it is required for the purposes of enforcing the judgment in the High Court (CCR Ord 25 r 8).

County court judgments which cannot be enforced in the High Court

It is not possible to enforce a county court judgment for less than £2,000 by means of execution against goods in the High Court. On the other hand, a judgment for £5,000 can only be enforced by means of execution against goods

---

3   See Judgments Act 1838, s 17 and County Courts Act 1984, s 74.
4   See below, p 481, Charging orders.
5   See below, p 485, Attachment of earnings.
6   SI 1991/724.
7   See Senior Master's Practice Direction [1998] 4 All ER 63.

in the High Court (see Art 8 of the High Court and County Courts Jurisdiction Order 1991[8] SI 1991/724 as amended by High Court and County Court Jurisdiction (Amendment) Order 1996 SI 1996/3141, Art 3, and enforcement by writ of *fieri facias* below).

Agreements regulated by the Consumer Credit Act 1974

A judgment or order of the county court for the payment of a sum of money arising out of an agreement regulated by the Consumer Credit Act 1974 can be enforced only in the county court (Art 8(1A) of the High Court and County Courts Jurisdiction Order 1991). Consumer credit agreements regulated by the Consumer Credit Act 1974 are those in which the amount involved is less than the consumer credit limit of £25,000 for agreements entered into on or after 1 May 1998 (Consumer Credit (Increase of Monetary Limits) (Amendment) Order 1998).[9]

LIMITATION

Section 24(1) of the Limitation Act 1980 provides that an action cannot be brought on any judgment after the expiration of six years from the date on which the judgment became enforceable, subject to an extension for part payment or otherwise under Part II of the Act. However, the right to issue execution of a judgment is a matter of procedure and not treated as an action on the judgment.[10] Therefore, although a judgment creditor must often apply for permission to issue enforcement proceedings where six years or more have elapsed since the date of the judgment, this is not because execution of the judgment is statute-barred.

ENFORCEMENT OF JUDGMENT
FOR THE PAYMENT OF MONEY

A judgment for the payment of money may be enforced by the following methods in the High Court or county court:

- execution against goods (writ of *fieri facias* in the High Court, warrant of execution in the county court);
- garnishee proceedings;

---

8   Senior Master's Practice Direction [1998] 4 All ER 63.
9   SI 1998/996.
10 See *WT Lamb and Sons v Rider* [1948] 2 KB 331.

- charging order;
- appointment of a receiver; and
- in the case of a judgment or order for an injunction (or an undertaking) by committal or writ of sequestration.

The following additional method is only available in the county court:

- attachment of earnings order.

This list of methods is expressly said in the High Court to be without prejudice to any other remedy available to enforce a judgment or order (RSC Ord 45 r 1(1)). Other remedies include service of a statutory demand followed by a bankruptcy/winding up petition.

The Debtors Acts 1869 and 1878

As a general rule, a person cannot be imprisoned for non-payment of a sum of money, even if there is a court order or judgment specifying payment within a particular time. However, there are still in existence powers to imprison a person under the Debtors Acts 1869 and 1878 in limited circumstances for making default in payment of a sum of money. Those circumstances include non-payment of maintenance orders in family proceedings, non-payment of certain taxes and default by any 'attorney or solicitor in payment of costs when ordered to pay costs for misconduct'. The maximum term of imprisonment is one year and imprisonment does not release the person from the obligation to pay what is due (ss 4 and 5 of the Debtors Act 1869). However, exercise of such a power by the court is rare and other methods to enforce compliance are used before it is resorted to, it being common, for instance, to make an attachment of earnings order against a party defaulting on payment of a maintenance order instead.

Examination of judgment debtor as to his means

Where an order or judgment for the payment of money has been obtained, the judgment creditor can apply for an order compelling the judgment debtor to attend court to be examined as to his means. Such an order allows the judgment creditor to obtain information to assist him to decide as to the most effective method of enforcement to employ against the judgment debtor and is available in respect of both High Court and county court proceedings.

The judgment creditor can apply, without notice to the judgment debtor, for such an order. The order will compel the judgment debtor to attend before a master or district judge or nominated court officer, to be orally examined by the judgment creditor as to what debts are owing to the judgment debtor and whether the judgment debtor has any, and if so, what other property or means of satisfying the judgment or order. The order may also compel the judgment debtor to produce any books or other documents in his possession relevant to his means (RSC Ord 48 r 1(1) and CCR Ord 25 r 3(1)).

In the case of an application for examination as to means in relation to a judgment or order in the county court (known as an oral examination), the application is on Form N316 for the judgment debtor to attend at the court for the district in which the judgment debtor resides or carries on business. If there is more than one judgment debtor, the application may be made in the court for the district in which any one of them resides or carries on business (CCR Ord 25 r 3(2)).

Service of the order

In the High Court, the order for examination as to the judgment debtor's means must be served personally[11] on the judgment debtor (RSC Ord 48 r 1(2)). In the county court, the order will be in Form N37 and the usual method of service[12] by the court by first class post to the judgment debtor at his address for service, or to his solicitor's address if he is legally represented, will be employed unless the judgment creditor notifies the court that he will effect service, in which case it must be served personally by the judgment creditor (CCR Ord 25 r 3(3), (3A)). However, if the court serves the order, the deemed date of service will be the seventh day after the date on which the order was sent to the judgment debtor (CCR Ord 25 r 3(3B)). No particular period of notice before the return date is prescribed, but presumably reasonable notice must be given.

The oral examination

The examination as to the judgment debtor's means should be by way of a thorough and searching cross-examination of the judgment debtor. In the county court, this is usually done by an authorised officer and not by a judge. The master, district judge or other authorised court officer should make a record of the judgment debtor's statement as to means, read it to him and ask him to sign it, and if he refuses the judge or court officer should sign the statement (RSC Ord 48 r 3).

The judgment creditor is entitled to be present and may cross-examine the debtor as to his means.

---

11 See Chapter 9, Service of Documents.
12 *Ibid.*

Non-attendance of judgment debtor

In the county court, if the judgment debtor fails to attend the examination, the court can adjourn the examination and make a further order in Form N39 for his attendance at the adjourned hearing. The court may also order that further payments are paid into court and not to the judgment debtor (CCR Ord 25 r 3(4)).

Committal for contempt

In the county court, where an examination has been adjourned, the judgment creditor must pay the judgment debtor a reasonable sum to cover his expenses in travelling to and from court to attend the hearing, if requested to do so by the judgment debtor not less than seven days before the day fixed for the adjourned hearing (CCR Ord 25 r 3(5A)). The judgment creditor must then file a certificate stating either that no such request has been made or that payment has been made in accordance with such a request not more than four days before the date fixed for the adjourned hearing (CCR Ord 25 r 3(5B)). If the judgment creditor fails to pay a reasonable sum in travelling expenses, the judgment debtor cannot be committed for contempt for failing to attend the adjourned hearing (CCR Ord 25 r 3(5C)).

Examination of defendant in respect of a non-money judgment

Provision exists in the county court for an order as to the examination of a defendant where the judgment or order is for some relief other than the payment of money (CCR Ord 25 r 4).

Costs of examination

These are usually at the discretion of any judge who conducts the examination (but not an authorised officer) and are likely to be in a similar amount to the fixed costs allowed on a judgment summons or attachment of earnings application.[13] If the examination does not produce any useful information, for example, the debtor is unemployed and has no other income or assets, it is unlikely that any costs will be allowed.

---

13   CCR Ord 38, Appendix B, Part III, para 6.

EXECUTION AGAINST GOODS, WRIT OF *FIERI FACIAS* (*FI FA*) AND WARRANT OF EXECUTION

Execution against goods by either a writ of *fieri facias* in the High Court (often abbreviated to a *fi fa*), or warrant of execution in the county court, is the most common method of enforcing a judgment debt. In executing the writ or warrant, the sheriff (High Court) or bailiff (county court) can seize the judgment debtor's goods and arrange for them to be sold, usually at public auction, but another method of selling the goods can be ordered instead. Certain goods of the judgment debtor are protected from seizure, such as tools and equipment necessary to carry out his employment, and clothes and bedding necessary for satisfying his and his family's basic domestic needs. The proceeds of the sale are sent to the judgment creditor in the amount necessary to satisfy the judgment debt, court fees and costs with any balance being returned to the judgment debtor (RSC Ord 47 r 6 and CCR Ord 26 r 15).

Jurisdiction of High Court and county court

Article 8(1) of the High Court and County Courts Jurisdiction Order 1991[14] provides that a judgment or order obtained in a county court for the payment of money which is for a sum of £5,000 or more can only be enforced by means of execution against goods in the High Court. Therefore, if this method of enforcement is required, the judgment must be enforced in the High Court by writ of *fi fa*. On the other hand, if a county court judgment is for a sum of less than £2,000, it can only be enforced by means of execution against goods in a county court. However, a High Court judgment for less than £2,000 can be enforced in the High Court. For amounts between £2,000 and £5,000 the judgment creditor can choose whether to enforce by means of execution against goods either in the High Court or county court.

Permission to issue writ of fi fa/warrant of execution

In most cases, the judgment creditor does not need permission to issue a writ of *fi fa* or warrant of execution, but there are exceptions. These include where six years or more have elapsed since the date of the judgment or order, or where there is any change in the parties, by death or otherwise; for others, see RSC Ord 46 r 2 and CCR Ord 26 r 5. The application for permission is made in accordance with Part 23[15] and supported by evidence, in the form of a witness

---

14 SI 1991/724 as amended by High Court and County Courts Jurisdiction (Amendment) Order 1996 SI 1996/3141, Art 3.
15 See Chapter 19, Making Applications for Court Orders.

statement or affidavit, which includes an explanation for the reason why permission is necessary; for instance, the reason for the delay or how the parties have changed (RSC Ord 46 r 4, CCR Ord 26 r 5(2)). The application need not be made on notice unless this is required by the district judge or it is an application concerning the assets of a deceased person when notice must be given.[16]

Procedure for issuing writ of *fi fa*

The judgment creditor must file a praecipe (request) for the issue of the writ of *fi fa*, signed by or on behalf of the solicitor of the judgment creditor, or the judgment creditor personally. The writ of *fi fa* will not be issued unless the judgment or order, or an office copy of it and, if necessary, the order granting permission to issue, is also produced to the court at the same time. The court officer authorised to issue the writ must also be satisfied that the time period, if any, specified in the judgment or order, for the payment of the money has expired. The writ of *fi fa* is issued when it is sealed by the court (RSC Ord 46 r 6).

Procedure for issuing warrant of execution

In the county court, the judgment creditor files Form N323 requesting the issue of a warrant of execution, on which he must certify the amount remaining due under the judgment or order, and, where the judgment or order is for payment by instalments, certifying that the whole or part of any instalment due remains unpaid and the amount for which the warrant is to be issued (CCR Ord 26 r 1(1)).

If the judgment creditor has obtained a judgment or order for payment by instalments and the judgment debtor has defaulted in payment of the whole or part of at least one of those instalments, the judgment creditor can request either that a warrant of execution is issued for the whole of the outstanding sum of money and costs remaining unpaid, or for a part of that amount so long as that is not less than £50, or the amount of one monthly instalment, or, as the case may be, four weekly instalments, whichever is the greater (CCR Ord 26 r 1(2) and (3)).

If the court issues the warrant, this will be in Form N42 and a court officer will send a notice, in Form N326, to the judgment debtor warning that a warrant has been issued, unless a district judge directs otherwise. The warrant will not then be levied against the judgment debtor until seven days after the warning notice has been sent to him (CCR Ord 26 r 1(4)).

---

16   *Re Shepherd* (1890) 43 Ch D 131, CA.

Duration of writ of *fi fa*/warrant of execution

A writ of *fi fa* or warrant of execution is valid for execution for a period of 12 months from the date of issue (RSC Ord 46 r 8(1) and CCR Ord 26 r 6(1)).

Renewal of the writ of *fi fa*/warrant of execution

If the writ or warrant is not wholly executed, it can be renewed for further periods of up to 12 months by application to the court. An application to renew the writ or warrant should be made before the expiration of the original 12 month period of validity or any renewed period (if a further extension is required). However, the court does have the power to grant an extension of its validity even outside that period (RSC Ord 46 r 8(2) and CCR Ord 26 r 6(1)).

Therefore, if, since the issue of the writ of *fi fa* or warrant of execution, the judgment debtor has agreed to repay the judgment debt in instalments over a period of time which exceeds the original 12 months validity of the writ or warrant, the judgment creditor may apply for it to be renewed so that the balance of the debt can be enforced if the judgment debtor defaults on repayment of the instalments.

Stay of execution of writ of *fi fa*

The judgment debtor can apply for a stay of execution of the writ of *fi fa* if he can establish special circumstances making it inexpedient to enforce the judgment or order or on the grounds that he is unable, from any cause, to pay the money. The court has the power to stay the execution of the writ of *fi fa* either absolutely or for such period and subject to such conditions as it thinks fit (RSC Ord 47 r 1(1)). The judgment debtor can apply for a stay of execution at the time the judgment or order is made, or subsequently by an application made under Part 23[17] (RSC Ord 47 r 1(2)).

When making an application for a stay of execution of the writ of *fi fa* under Part 23, the judgment debtor must set out the grounds for making the application in the application notice and a witness statement or affidavit must be filed substantiating those grounds. If the application is made on the grounds that the judgment debtor cannot pay, he must disclose his income, the nature and value of any property he owns and the amount of his liabilities. The application notice and witness statement or affidavit must be filed at court and served on the judgment creditor not less than four clear days before the hearing (RSC Ord 47 r 1(3) and (4)).

---

17 See Chapter 19, Making Applications for Court Orders.

The court has a wide discretion when dealing with applications to stay. There would have to be a good reason to deprive the creditor of an opportunity of satisfying his judgment.[18]

Stay of execution of warrant of execution

If a judgment creditor has applied for the judgment debt to be enforced by means of a warrant of execution, a similar procedure applies as that where a defendant admits payment of a claim and asks for time to pay,[19] thereby enabling the judgment debtor to offer terms of payment and thereby suspend execution of the warrant.

Application for stay of execution

The judgment debtor can apply to the county court in Form N245 for a stay of execution of a warrant of execution. When making the application, the judgment debtor should propose terms as to repayment of the judgment debt and include a signed statement of his means. The court will then send a copy of the application and the signed statement of means to the judgment creditor, who must notify the court on Form N246A within 14 days of service on him whether he accepts the judgment debtor's proposals as to payment (CCR Ord 25 r 8(1), (2) and (3)).

Order suspending warrant

If no such response is received from the judgment creditor, a court officer may make an order in Form N41 suspending the warrant on terms of payment. Alternatively, if the judgment creditor objects only to the terms offered, the court officer can determine the time and rate of payment and make an order suspending the warrant on terms of payment (CCR Ord 25 r 8(4) and (5)).

Application for order to be reconsidered

Both parties then have 14 days of service of the order within which to apply for the order suspending the warrant on terms of payment to be reconsidered by means of a hearing before the district judge. The district judge can confirm the order or set it aside and make such new order as he sees fit (CCR Ord 25 r 8(6)).

---

18 *Winchester Cigarette Machinery Ltd v Payne (No 2)* (1993) *The Times*, 15 December, CA.
19 See Chapter 8, Responding to an Action.

Failure to abide by terms of the suspended warrant

If the judgment debtor fails to abide by the terms of payment made when a warrant is suspended, the judgment creditor can re-issue the warrant by filing a request certifying the amount of money remaining due under the judgment and showing that the terms have not been complied with (CCR Ord 25 r 8(9) and Ord 25 r 5(3)).

Costs of the execution

In most cases, the costs and fees incurred in enforcing a judgment can be added to the judgment debt to be enforced by writ of *fi fa* or warrant of execution.[20] However, in the High Court, if the judgment debt is for less than £600 and does not entitle the claimant to costs against the defendant, the writ may not authorise the sheriff to levy any fees, poundage or other costs of execution (RSC Ord 47 r 4).

Seizure and sale of goods

Warrants are handed to the bailiff, an officer of the county court, for execution. When the bailiff levies, he hands to the execution debtor, or leaves at the place of levy, a notice of levy on Form N42(C) (Ord 26 r 7). A bailiff may not force his way into a judgment debtor's house in order to gain entry to levy, such as by pushing a front door against the resistance of the debtor,[21] but once the goods have been levied upon, forcible entry may be effected.

If the goods are saleable, the bailiff usually takes 'walking possession', the judgment debtor signing an agreement on Form N42(C) to this effect. The form need not be signed by the judgment debtor personally,[22] but it is preferable that he should do so. For a description of 'walking possession', see *Lloyds and Scottish Finance Ltd v Modern Cars and Caravans (Kingston) Ltd*.[23] For effect of 'walking possession' as regards third persons, see *Abingdon RDC v O'Gorman*.[24] Where the bailiffs already have walking possession of goods, they can break into premises to retrieve those goods even if the premises have not been deliberately locked against them.[25]

---

20 For warrants of execution see County Courts Act 1984, s 85(2).
21 *Vaughan v McKenzie* [1968] 1 All ER 1154.
22 *National Commercial Bank of Scotland Ltd v Arcam Demolition and Construction Ltd* [1966] 3 All ER 113.
23 [1964] 2 All ER 732.
24 [1968] 3 All ER 79.
25 *McLeod v Butterwick* [1996] 1 WLR 995, Ch D.

No possession fee is payable in the case of 'walking possession'. Appraisement is usually made after removal by the auctioneer who acts as broker for the court.

When the goods are removed, the bailiff gives or posts to the executioner debtor an inventory (Ord 26 r 12(1)). Notice of sale must be given to the debtor not less than four days before the time fixed for the sale.

Items exempt from levy

Basically, what is exempt are 'necessary items'. These will include such tools, books, vehicles and other items of equipment as are necessary to the debtor for use personally in his or her job or business and such clothing, bedding, furniture, household equipment and provisions as are necessary for satisfying the basic domestic needs of the debtor and his or her family (s 89 of the 1984 Act). The definition is worded in broad terms without any monetary limit, and allows bailiffs to exercise their discretion in ensuring a proper balance between the interests of the debtor and his family, and those of the claimant. Guidance has been given to bailiffs to help with this process.

If furniture, motor vehicles or any other goods are alleged to be subject to a hire purchase agreement, the bailiff asks for such evidence as there may be, for example, the HP agreement. If a claim is made to the goods by some other person, such as a wife, a claim in writing (see below) must be given to the bailiff unless it is obvious that the goods do not in fact belong to the debtor. As to caravans and houseboats, there appears to be no authoritative decision to say whether they may be seized under a warrant of execution while used as a dwelling or intermittently as a dwelling, or when they are fixed to the land.

In the event of a dispute between the defendant and the bailiff in applying these definitions, the matter will be referred in the first instance to the bailiff manager. A levy should be made if at all possible. If the bailiff manager is unable to resolve the dispute, he consults with the court manager, who decides whether the district judge's directions should be sought. If a district judge or bailiff refused to levy on such, a complaint might be made by way of summons (N366) to the circuit judge under s 124 of the 1984 Act and Ord 34 r 1 when an order might be made for the trial of the issue.

If payment is likely to be made, the bailiff may allow a reasonable time for payment and no further fees are payable.

Separate writ of *fi fa*/warrant of execution to enforce payment of costs

Where a judgment or order is made for the payment of money only, along with an order for the detailed assessment of costs, if at the time when the money becomes payable under the judgment or order the costs have not yet been assessed, the judgment creditor can issue a writ of *fi fa* or warrant of execution (as appropriate) to enforce payment of the judgment debt alone. Once the costs have been assessed, the judgment creditor can then issue a separate writ of *fi fa* or warrant of execution to enforce payment of the sum ordered on detailed assessment (RSC Ord 47 r 3, CCR Ord 26 r 1(5)).

In the case of a High Court judgment or order, the subsequent writ issued to enforce payment of costs must be issued not less than eight days after the issue of the writ to enforce payment of the judgment debt (RSC Ord 47 r 3).

APPLICATION FOR VARIATION OF PAYMENT OF JUDGMENT DEBT

In the county court, where a judgment or order has been made for the payment of money, the judgment debtor or judgment creditor may apply for a variation of the date or rate of payment (CCR Ord 22 r 10(1)).

Application by judgment creditor for payment at a later date or by instalments

The judgment creditor can apply without notice to the judgment debtor for an order that the money, if payable in one sum, be paid at a later date than that by which it is due or that it be paid by instalments instead, or if it is already payable by instalments, that it be payable by smaller instalments. A court officer has jurisdiction to make such a variation in the order unless no payment has been made under the judgment or order for six years before the date of the application, in which case it will be referred to the district judge (CCR Ord 22 r 10(2)). The application does not operate as a stay on enforcement unless a stay is specifically requested and granted.

A judgment creditor, having originally requested payment of the judgment or order in one sum, may wish it to be payable by instalments in order that an attachment of earnings[26] order may be obtained if the judgment debtor defaults in payment of any instalments.

Application by judgment creditor for payment at an earlier date, in one sum, or by larger instalments

The judgment creditor may also make an application to the district judge, on notice to the judgment debtor, for an order that the money, if payable in one

26 See below, p 485, Attachment of earnings.

sum, be paid at an earlier date than that by which it is due, or if the money is payable by instalments, that it is paid in one sum or by larger instalments. The judgment creditor must set out the proposed terms and the grounds on which the application is made (CCR Ord 22 r 10(3)). Such an application would be appropriate if the judgment creditor has evidence that the judgment debtor's financial circumstances have improved since the judgment or order was made.

Application by judgment debtor for payment at a later date, by instalments or by smaller instalments

If money payable under a judgment or order is payable in one sum, the judgment debtor can apply for an order that the money be payable at a later date than that by which it is due, or by instalments instead, or if it is already payable in instalments, that it be paid by smaller instalments (CCR Ord 22 r 10(5)). The same procedure applies as where a judgment debtor applies for a warrant of execution to be suspended (see above, application for stay of execution and CCR Ord 25 r 8).

GARNISHEE PROCEEDINGS

Where a judgment or order for the payment of money of at least £50 is obtained, the judgment creditor can apply for an order, known as a garnishee order, which is an order compelling a third party (known as the garnishee), who owes money to the judgment debtor, to pay the money owed to the judgment creditor (known as the garnishor), rather than the judgment debtor. The court has a discretion to make the order which will compel the garnishee to pay so much of the debt owed as will satisfy the judgment debt, as well as the costs of the garnishee proceedings, to the garnishor (RSC Ord 49 r 1(1) and (10), CCR Ord 30 r 1(1), Ord 30 r 13). The procedure is not available against the Crown, instead of which s 27 of the Crown Proceedings Act 1847 and Ord 42 r 14 must be used.

Procedure for obtaining an order

A garnishee order is obtained in two stages. In the first instance, the judgment creditor makes an application in the High Court in Practice Form No 72 and in the county court in Form N84,[27] for an order to show cause (often known as an order *nisi*) (RSC Ord 49 r 1(2) and CCR Ord 30 r 1(2)).

---

27   See CPR, PD 4, Table 2.

The application to show cause can be made without notice to the judgment debtor under Part 23[28] (RSC Ord 49 r 2(1) and CCR Ord 30 r 2). This safeguards against the judgment debtor being alerted of the impending application and removing the funds the intended subject of the garnishee order before the order can be made.

The application must be supported by a witness statement or affidavit which contains the following information:

- the name and last known address of the judgment debtor;
- the judgment or order to be enforced including its amount with the amount remaining unpaid at the time the application is made;
- a statement that to the best of the information or belief of the witness the garnishee is within the jurisdiction and is indebted to the judgment debtor and stating the sources of the witnesses information or the grounds for his belief; and
- if the garnishee is a deposit taking institution with more than one branch, the name and address of the branch at which the judgment debtor's account is believed to be held and the number of that account, or if this information is not known, a statement to this effect (RSC Ord 49 r 2(2) and CCR Ord 30 r 2).

Garnishees are commonly banks who may hold funds for the judgment debtor in a bank account. However, they are not restricted to such bodies and could be, for instance, a person who owes a trade debt to the judgment debtor, such information being obtained as a result of an examination as to means.[28a]

The effect of the *nisi* order is to create an equitable charge in favour of the creditor.

Service of the order to show cause

The order to show cause must be served personally on the garnishee at least 15 days before the hearing of the further consideration of the matter and on the judgment debtor at least seven days after the order has been served on the garnishee and at least seven days before the hearing of the further consideration of the matter (RSC Ord 49 r 3(1) and CCR Ord 30 r 3).

The order to show cause specifies a time and place for further consideration of the matter and in the meantime attaches the debt, which binds the money in the hands of the garnishee, so that the money is frozen and in particular not paid to the judgment debtor (RSC Ord 49 r 3(2) and CCR Ord 30 r 3).

---

28   See Chapter 19, Making Applications for Court Orders.
28a See above, p 468, Examination of judgment debtor as to his means.

Making of an order absolute

Where, on the further consideration of the matter, the garnishee does not attend or does not dispute the debt claimed to be due from him to the judgment debtor, the court may make an order absolute against the garnishee ordering him to pay the debt to the judgment creditor (RSC Ord 49 r 4(1) and CCR Ord 30 r 7(1)).

Dispute of liability of garnishee

If, on the further consideration of the matter, the garnishee disputes his liability to pay the debt due or claimed to be due from him to the judgment debtor, the court may summarily determine the issue at the hearing or order that it be dealt with at a separate hearing which may be before the master or district judge (RSC Ord 49 r 5 and CCR Ord 30 r 8).

In the High Court, if a third party claims to be entitled to the sum held by the garnishee, instead of the judgment debtor, the court may order that person to attend and summarily determine the matter or order that it be dealt with at a separate hearing which may before a master or district judge (RSC Ord 49 r 6).

If the garnishee fails or refuses to pay the sum the subject of the garnishee order to the judgment creditor, it can be enforced against the garnishee in the same manner as any other judgment debt (RSC Ord 49 r 4(2) and CCR Ord 30 r 7(2)).

Money in court

If money is paid into court to the credit of the judgment debtor, the judgment creditor can make an application under Part 23[29] for the sum in court, or so much of it as is necessary to satisfy the judgment debt and the costs of the application, be paid to the judgment creditor (RSC Ord 49 r 9(1) and CCR Ord 30 r 12(1)). If such an order is obtained, it is not a garnishee order, but has a similar effect.

In the High Court, the application notice must be produced at the office of the Accountant General (office which controls court funds) and if the application is dismissed, the applicant must give notice of this fact to the Accountant General (RSC Ord 49 r 9(2)). In the county court, on receipt of the application, the court officer retains the money in court until the application has been determined (CCR Ord 30 r 12(2)).

---

29 See Chapter 19, Making Applications for Court Orders.

The application notice must also be served on the judgment debtor at least seven days before the hearing (RSC Ord 49 r 9(3)).

Costs of judgment creditor

The fixed costs are those specified in Ord 38, Appendix B, Part III, Item 7; County Courts Act 1984, s 109 authorises a deposit taking institution to deduct from the account a sum (currently £30) in respect of its expenses deducted from the amount recovered.

CHARGING ORDERS

Where a judgment creditor obtains a judgment or order for the payment of money, the court has the power to make an order under s 1 of the Charging Orders Act 1979 imposing a charge on certain types of property of the judgment debtor to secure payment of the money due; such an order is known as a charging order (RSC Ord 50 r 1 and CCR Ord 31 r 1). The types of property against which a charging order can be made are land, stocks and shares, unit trusts, and funds in court. A charging order does not result in payment of the debt, but secures it against the property; an order for the sale of the property can then be made in a separate application.

The court has a discretion whether to make such an order and will consider all the circumstances of the case and, in particular, evidence of the personal circumstances of the judgment debtor and whether any other creditor of the judgment debtor will be unduly prejudiced by the making of the order (s 1(5) of the Charging Orders Act 1979). The court will also consider whether the size of the debt is so small as to make the granting of a charging order disproportionate, especially where there are other forms of enforcement available.

Procedure for applying for a charging order

An application for a charging order is made in two stages; in the first instance, an application to show cause is made. This must be made in accordance with Part 23,[30] but does not need to be served on the judgment debtor. This safeguards against the judgment debtor being alerted to the impending application and disposing of the property the intended subject of the charging order before the order can be made. The application must be supported by a witness statement or affidavit:

---

30 *Ibid.*

- giving the debtor's name and address (the address is frequently forgotten, which results in the application being returned and should be given even if it is the same as the property to be charged) and those of all known creditors;
- certifying the outstanding balance under the judgment and that the whole or part of any instalment remains unpaid;
- identifying the subject matter of the intended charge;
- verifying the debtor's beneficial interest (if the asset is held by a trustee, one of the grounds specified by s 2(1)(b) of the 1979 Act must be given and verified);
- where securities (other than those in court) are to be charged, giving the name and address of the person to be notified to protect the charge;
- where an interest under a trust is to be charged, giving the names and addresses of known trustees and beneficiaries (RSC Ord 50 r 1(3) and CCR Ord 31 r 1(2)).

If a charging order is granted, it will provide the judgment creditor with security for his judgment debt and, therefore, the court will consider the position of other known judgment creditors of the judgment debtor before making such an order. The judgment creditor, therefore, also has an obligation to notify the court of any other judgment creditors known to him.

Order to show cause

If the application is granted, it will be an order in Practice Form 75 in the High Court and Form N86 in the county court[31] to show cause, specifying the time and place for further consideration of the matter and imposing the charge in any event until that time (RSC Ord 50 r 1 and CCR Ord 31 r1(4)). Notice of the order to show cause and a copy of the witness statement or affidavit in support of the application must be served on the judgment debtor at least seven days before the date fixed for the further consideration of the matter (RSC Ord 50 r 2(1) and CCR Ord 31 r 1(6)). The court can also direct that service also be made on any other creditor of the judgment debtor (RSC Ord 50 r 2(2) and CCR Ord 31 r 1(6)).

To obtain the full value of the order *nisi* procedure, the judgment creditor should take such additional steps before the debtor learns of the order *nisi* as will ensure that the debtor is not able on so learning to deal with the property which is the subject of the provisional charge. Thus, as an example, it will be for the judgment creditor promptly to register the order *nisi* under the Land Registration Act 1925 or the Land Charges Act 1972. The creditor for such

---

31 See CPR, PD 4, Table 2.

purposes should, therefore, arrange with the court officer to collect a copy of the order *nisi* as soon as it has been drawn up.

Making of charging order absolute

On the hearing of the application to show cause, the court will either make the order absolute or discharge it (RSC Ord 50 r 3(1) and CCR Ord 31 r 2(1)). In other words, it cannot be adjourned generally, but to another date if necessary,[32] with the *nisi* being extended to the return date to prevent it lapsing.

If the order is made absolute, it will be made in Form No 76 in the High Court and Form N87 in the county court.[33]

The court must consider the debtor's personal circumstances and also other creditors (s 1(5) of the 1979 Act). Conditions may be imposed (s 3(1)), including an instalment order. Where there is dispute over the beneficial ownership of any property subject to the order *nisi*, the court has the power to order that the dispute be tried first and to adjourn the application for the order absolute until it has been decided.

If an order absolute is made, the court serves it on:

- the debtor and creditor;
- (where funds in court are charged) the Accountant General at the Funds Office; and
- where securities not in court are charged, the persons or body required by RSC Ord 50 r 2(1)(b), when a stop notice must be put in the order;
- unless otherwise directed, any person or body on whom a copy of the order *nisi* was served (Ord 31 r 2(2), (3).[34]

Discharge of charging order

On the application of the judgment debtor, or any other person interested in the property, the court may vary or discharge the charging order, either before or after it is made absolute, on such terms as to costs as it thinks just (RSC Ord 50 r 7 and CCR Ord 31 r 3).

An application to discharge or vary the charging order is likely to be made where the judgment debtor has satisfied the judgment debt.

---

32 *Harman v Glencross* [1986] 1 All ER 545, CA.
33 See CPR, PD 4, Table 2.
34 For form of notice, see RSC Ord 50 r 5(3); Form 76 in Appendix A to the Supreme Court Practice.

Costs

Although fixed costs[35] are provided for where land is registered, judgment creditors are also entitled to ask for all the incidental fees, including swearing and land registration fees, which are incurred as a result of the application (Ord 38 r 18(1)). Creditors should bring the details of costs claimed with them to court for scrutiny by the district judge. At the time of this edition, together with the said fixed costs, they can total almost £200.

Enforcing a charging order by sale

Once a charging order absolute has been made, the judgment creditor can apply for an order for sale of the property charged in order to enforce payment of the judgment debt (RSC Ord 50 r 9A and CCR Ord 31 r 4(1)). An application for sale of the charged property must be made using a Part 8 claim form.[35a] In the High Court, it must be issued out of Chancery Chambers (Royal Court of Justice) or one of the Chancery District Registries (RSC Ord 50 r 9A). In the county court, it should be issued out of the county court which made the charging order (CCR Ord 31 r 4(2)).

The claim is supported by affidavit or witness statement (and copy):

- identifying the charging order and the property;
- specifying the amount for which the charge was imposed and the outstanding balance;
- verifying the debtor's title to the property;
- identifying prior incumbrances and the amounts due to them;
- giving an estimate of the sale price (Ord 31 r 4(1)).

In the case of land, circumstances may favour either a sale by auction or a sale by private treaty. Time will be a factor, as also will be the clearing of the charge and prior incumbrances, with, if possible, a credit balance in hand for the debtor. The court will be inclined to give the debtor one more opportunity to pay the debt, for example, by instalments with an effective order for sale in default.

The order for sale of land is provided for by Form N436, but the Judicial Studies Board considers it inadequate and, in their bench books, district judges are provided with a much fuller order based on the general format used in the Chancery Division. Also, see form of order in *Chancery Practice and Orders* (by Robert Blackford *et al*, 1991, Longman).

---

35   See Chapter 33, Costs.
35a See Chapter 14, Part 8 Claims.

The venue for the sale proceedings is the county court which made the charging order. In any other case, it will be the court for the district in which the debtor resides or carries on business or, if none, in which the judgment creditor resides or carries on business (Ord 31 r 4(2)).

The county court has jurisdiction only where the capital value of the land does not exceed £30,000, or in the case of a sale, the purchase money does not exceed that figure (s 23(d) of the 1984 Act and the notes thereunder in the County Court Practice). A copy of the affidavit is served on the debtor (Ord 31 r 4(3)). The district judge may determine the proceedings (Ord 31 r 4(4)).

In the case of a charging order on land, the creditor is not thereby entitled to possession; a charging order has the effect of an equitable charge created by writing under hand.[37] When the debtor has an interest in a property of which he is joint owner with a non-debtor, judicial sale is not appropriate and an application under s 14 the Trusts of Land and Appointment of Trustees Act 1996 (replacing s 30 of the Law of Property Act 1925) is the alternative (see below).

However, the question whether an equitable chargee, for example a bank having a charging order over the interest of one only of two or more co-owners of land, can ask the court to sell the whole of the land to realise the share over which he has the charge, has been determined in *Midland Bank plc v Pike and Pike*.[37a] The chargee is entitled to apply under s 14 of the Trusts of Land and Appointment of Trustees Act 1996 for an order for the sale of all the land as 'a person interested' within the meaning of that section; the chargee's rights are also to apply for an order for the sale of the co-owners' beneficial interest only, or for the appointment of a receiver of that interest, though obviously this would not enable the chargee to obtain as much as he could by sale of the property itself.

If a sale proceeds, a contract for sale is required, title must be proved, the costs of the proceedings and costs on sale must be provided for, a final account taken, and the proceeds distributed. Any net proceeds received on sale must be paid into court for this purpose (Ord 22 r 9 and Ord 31 r 4(5)).

ATTACHMENT OF EARNINGS

General

The Attachment of Earnings Act 1971 and Ord 27 apply. A county court may make an attachment of earnings order to secure payments under a High Court or a county court maintenance order, payment of a judgment debt of not less

---

37 Charging Orders Act 1979, s 3(4) ; *Tennant v Trenchard* (1869) 4 Ch 537; Supreme Court Practice, note 50/1 9/9.
37a (1986) 2 FLR 143; [1988] 2 All ER 434.

than £50, or for the balance under a judgment for a sum of not less than £50 (Ord 27 r 7(9)), or payments under a county court administration order (s 1(2) of the 1971 Act).

Maintenance orders to which the Act applies are set out in Sched 1 to the 1971 Act, and include orders for periodical or other payments under the Matrimonial Causes Act 1973, Part II, and certain orders under the Children Act 1989 and other Acts. The term 'judgment debt' does not include a maintenance order or an administration order (s 2(c), above).

Section 24(1) and Sched 3 to the 1971 Act define attachable earnings and s 24(2) and (3) restricts earnings that may be attached, for example, the pay or allowances of members of HM Forces cannot be attached.

As part of the increased computerisation of the courts, a Centralised Attachment of Earnings Payment System (CAPS) has been introduced into the county court. Where this system is in force, the relevant forms will indicate accordingly by using the prefix of 'CAPS'.

The application

Application is made to the court for the district in which the debtor resides (Ord 27 r 3(1)). If the debtor does not reside within England or Wales, or if the creditor does not know where he resides, the application may be made to the court in which the judgment or order was obtained (Ord 27 r 3(2)). Where the creditor applies for attachment of earnings orders in respect of two or more debtors jointly liable, the application is made to the court for the district in which any of the debtors resides; but if the judgment or order was given or made by any such court, the application must be made to that court (Ord 27 r 3(3)).

In the case of a maintenance order made in a county court, the application must be made to that county court (Ord 27 r 17(2)). A High Court maintenance order may be enforced in the county court designated in the High Court order (Ord 27 r 17(7)). To enforce an order for divorce costs, the application must be made to the court where the debtor resides (Ord 27 r 3(1)).

The persons who may apply for an attachment of earnings order are the persons to whom payment under the relevant adjudication is required to be made (whether directly or through an officer of any court); in the case of an administration order, any one of the creditors scheduled to the order may apply, or the debtor, where the application is to secure maintenance payments: he may apply on the making of the county court maintenance order or on an order varying that order (s 3(1) of the 1971 Act; Ord 27 r 17(4)).

Where a creditor desires to make an application to a county court other than the county court in which the judgment or order was obtained, he must apply for the transfer of the proceedings to the appropriate court under

Ord 25 r 2(1)(c). A letter applying for transfer and stating the defendant's address should be written. No fee is payable. The court sends a certificate of judgment or order (see N313 for the endorsement – no longer in the County Court Practice) to the named court, and the district judge of that court gives the proceedings a fresh plaint number and sends notice of the transfer to both parties (N314 – no longer in the County Court Practice).

The requirements for the issue of an application are:

- application (N337) certifying the balances due and that the whole or any part of any instalment due remains unpaid (Ord 27 r 4(1));
- fee.

In addition, if the judgment is of the High Court, or of another court, or is an arbitration award enforceable as such, the requirements are also:

- office copy of judgment or order or other evidence;
- affidavit verifying amount due (N321);
- where a writ of execution issued, office copy of sheriff's return (Ord 25 r 11).

In addition, if to enforce a magistrates' court order, the requirements are also:

- a certified copy of order;
- affidavit verifying amount due (N321) or, if payments are required to be made to the clerk of the magistrates' court, a certificate by him to the like effect.

If the application is made against a partner in a debtor firm, see Ord 25 r 9 (or RSC Ord 81 r 5 if a High Court judgment).

If a county court debt is involved, the originating process is to be produced for receipt of the fee to be endorsed. The name and address of the employer should be stated in the application if known. The application issues for the balance of debt and costs in the case of a judgment debt (s 6(4) of the 1971 Act). The balance may not include the costs of an execution not recovered thereunder (Ord 27 r 9(1)). The figures are completed by the court.

An application under s 32 of the Matrimonial Causes Act 1973 for leave to enforce the payment of arrears under a county court maintenance order, which became due more than 12 months before the application, should be made in that application (Ord 27 r 17(3)). Unless the debtor himself applies in respect of a maintenance order, the debtor must be in default (s 3(3) of the 1971 Act). The court may make an attachment of earnings order when the maintenance order itself is made without the consent of the debtor (s 1(4)(b) of the Maintenance Enforcement Act 1991).

Service

Maintenance orders

The court prepares a notice (N55A) to the debtor and copy for the creditor which contains a date of hearing before the district judge. Notice of the application is sent to the debtor, together with a form of reply (N56), which the debtor is required to file within eight days of receipt. The summons is served as if it were a fixed date summons (Ord 7 r 10(5), Ord 27 rr 5(1), 17(3A)). The court officer may, at any stage, send an N338 (see above) to the debtor's employers, if known (Ord 27 r 6).

If the debtor attends the hearing, the district judge may make such order as is appropriate (see below, The order).

Non-maintenance orders

The court prepares a notice to the debtor and makes a copy. The form informs the debtor that unless he pays the total sum due into court, he must complete and send a reply to the court office to reach it within eight days after service. Notice of the application (N55) and a form of reply (N56) are served on the debtor as if the application were a default summons (Ord 27 r 5(1)). If the application is not served, notice of non-service (N216 – no longer in the County Court Practice) is sent to the creditor.

Unless the debtor pays the balance owing (Ord 27 r 5(2A)), he must, within eight days after service, file in the court office the form of reply setting out particulars of his expenditure and income and the name and address of his employer, if any. The court sends a copy of the reply to the creditor (Ord 27 r 5(3)). If the debtor does not reply in time and the judgment creditor knows the employer, the court (court officer) should be asked by letter to request the employer (N338) to give details of earnings (Ord 27 r 6).

Where a reply is filed by a debtor in compliance with Ord 27 r 5(2) within eight days, and he gives the name and address of his employer, the court officer can still send notice (N338) to the employer requesting him to file a statement of earnings (Ord 27 r 6). Such a notice may be sent to an employer if the debtor gives information as to his earnings, but the court doubts the debtor's statement.

If an employer does not send a statement of earnings in compliance with the request, the court may compel him to do so (ss 14(1)(b), 23(2)(c) of the Attachment of Earnings Act 1971; Ord 27 r 15 as to enforcement).

The order

Order 27 r 7(1) allows a court officer to make attachment of earnings orders (including consolidated orders), except on applications to secure arrears of maintenance when the order is made by the district judge (see above). Applications in relation to judgment debts will not have an initial hearing and the defendant will be required either to pay the amount due to the claimant or to complete and return the form of reply which includes a statement of means (see N56). If he has sufficient information to do so, the court officer will make an order on receipt of the form, sending a copy to the parties and to the employer (Ord 27 r 7(1)). Employers can obtain from the Publications Unit, Court Service Agency (020 7210 1700) a copy of the Employer's Handbook explaining how they should comply with any attachment of earnings order.

If the debtor fails to pay or to return the form, the court officer may and probably will order him to file a statement of means in Form N61. Failure to reply will then result in the issue of a notice to show cause which will be listed before the district judge (Ord 27 r 7(A)). Order 27 r 19 provides for an application for a consolidated order to be made in any proceedings in which an attachment of earnings order (except a priority order) is in force.

Order 27 r 19(4) enables a court officer to make a consolidated attachment of earnings order where a further attachment of earnings order is applied for (see below, p 488).

The judgment creditor or the debtor may, within 14 days of service of the order on him and giving his reasons, apply on notice for the order to be reconsidered and the court officer shall fix a day for the hearing of the application and give to the judgment creditor and the debtor not less than two days' notice of the day so fixed (Ord 27 r 7(2)). The district judge may confirm the order or set it aside and make such new order as he thinks fit, or instead, a day may be fixed for hearing by the district judge (Ord 27 r 7(5)).

No reply filed by debtor; non-attendance

If a reply has not been filed, a variety of courses are open, the procedures differing depending on whether a maintenance order or any other form of judgment is involved, thus.

Maintenance orders

If the debtor fails to attend, then, subject to the creditor producing sufficient evidence, the district judge may either make an attachment of earnings order (Ord 27 r 17) or, more usually, adjourn the application to a specified date before the district judge in chambers and order the debtor to attend on threat of imprisonment (s 23(1) of the 1971 Act) (Ord 27 r 8(1)). Notice of the adjourned hearing (N58) must be served personally on the debtor unless an order for substituted service is made (Ord 27 r 8(1)). At the same time as serving N58, the bailiff may give the debtor an opportunity of completing a form of reply (N56), a copy of which should be attached to the order.

If the debtor attends at the adjourned hearing, the district judge can obtain the relevant information and make an appropriate order (see below) (N65). If, however, he fails to attend, the district judge may either commit the debtor to prison (N59) for a specific period not exceeding 14 days (s 23(1) of the 1971 Act) (Ord 27 rr 7A(3), 17) or order him to be arrested (N112) and brought before the court either forthwith or on a specified date (s 23(1A)). The judge or district judge can order that any committal order be suspended so long as the debtor attends at the time and place specified in the committal order. However, if he fails to attend, a certificate to that effect given by a court officer will be sufficient authority for the issue of a warrant of committal, although the authority for such is endorsed on the attachment of earnings file by the judge or district judge (Ord 27 r 7B).

The debtor may apply to the circuit or district judge without notice in writing for the revocation of the committal order. If in custody, the debtor applies to the circuit or district judge *ex parte* in writing attested by the governor or a principal officer, otherwise by affidavit. The debtor must undertake to attend when so ordered (see Ord 27 r 8 generally).

Other judgment debts

If it is desired to obtain from the debtor a statement of earnings, he must (a) be proved to have been served personally with N55, the form of reply and N337, or the court must be satisfied that they came to his notice in time for him to have complied with the instructions in N55 (Ord 27 r 5(2) proviso) and (b) he must be personally served with N61 (Ord 27 r 15) which warns him of the consequences of failing to obey the order, to which he must reply within eight days with his statement of means. In default, he commits an offence under ss 14(1) and 23(2)(c) of the 1971 Act and may be personally served with notice to show cause (N63) why he should not be imprisoned and a date is fixed for him to be brought before the circuit or district judge to be dealt with for that offence (Ord 27 r 7A(2)). At any stage, an N338 can be sent to the debtor's employers if they are known (see above) (Ord 27 r 6).

If the debtor does not attend, the circuit judge or district judge may commit him to prison (N59) under s 23(3) of the 1971 Act for a period not exceeding 14 days or fine him a sum up to £250 or commit him to prison for contempt under Ord 29 r 1 (N79/80) (Ord 27 r 7A(3)). If the debtor attends, however, and satisfactorily completes an N56, a court officer can make an appropriate order (see below, p 487). The suspended committal procedure is the same as for maintenance debts.

If the debtor has failed to supply sufficient information for the court officer to make an order, the papers are referred to the district judge (Ord 27 r 7(4)), who may either make an order (N60) if he feels that there is sufficient information, or direct a hearing in which case the parties are given at least eight days' notice (Ord 27 r 7(5)). If the debtor attends the hearing and gives sufficient information, the district judge can make an appropriate order (N60). If, however, the debtor does not attend, the district judge may adjourn the hearing under s 23(1) of the 1971 Act.

The court officer serves notice of the adjourned hearing (N63) (or if asked, delivers to the creditors for service) not less than five days before the hearing. If the debtor fails to attend or is unco-operative, the district judge may either order him to be imprisoned for not more than 14 days (N59) (s 23(1) of the 1971 Act) or order the bailiff to arrest him and bring him to court either forthwith or on a date to be fixed (N112A).

If, however, the debtor does attend the hearing or is arrested in response to N112A, and satisfactorily completes Form N56, a court officer can make an appropriate order (N60) as above. If, on arrest under N112A, the debtor does not satisfactorily complete N56, the district judge may commit him (N59) for up to 14 days (s 23(1) of the 1971 Act).

Form of order

The form is N60, or N65 (priority maintenance) (as amended by the County Court (Forms) (Amendment) Rules 1996 SI 1996/2811 (L9)) for maintenance. These must specify the normal deduction rate and a protected earnings rate. 'Normal deduction rate' is defined in s 6(5)(a) of the 1971 Act and is the rate at which the court thinks it reasonable for the debtor's earnings to be applied to meeting his liability. 'Protected earnings rate' is defined in s 6(5)(b) and is the rate below which, having regard to the debtor's resources and needs, the court thinks it reasonable that the earnings actually paid to him should not be reduced. Protected earnings are normally calculated by reference to the rates as amended from time to time of supplementary benefits under the National Insurance Acts and to rent or mortgage payments.

An attachment of earnings order is sent by post to the debtor (or his solicitor) and to the employer unless personal service is asked for (Ord 27 r 10(2). If the debtor is employed by a corporation which has so requested, the order may be sent to the address given by it. If the order is to enforce a judgment or order of the High Court or a magistrates' court, a copy of the order is sent to the court officer of those courts (Ord 27 r 10(3)). The order to the debtor states that he must inform the court of any change in employment.

An order may be made, but suspended while the debtor himself pays (N64). This is a common practice when the debtor is not anxious for his employer to know of the judgment. Should the debtor get into arrears with his payments, the creditors can apply *ex parte* to remove the suspension.

Deductions by the employer from the debtor's earnings are made in accordance with Sched 3 to the 1971 Act. Priority as between orders is set out in this Schedule. The employer is allowed on each deduction to deduct from the debtor's earnings, in addition, £1 towards his administrative costs.[38]

The employer is under no liability for non-compliance with the order until seven days have elapsed since the service (s 7(1)). If he does not have the debtor in his employment, or if the debtor ceases to be in his employment, he must give notice of the fact to the court within 10 days of service of the order or cesser (s 7(2)). If an employer ceases to have the debtor in his employment, the order lapses, but the court may direct it to another employer (s 9(4)). There appears to be no provision that the court should notify the judgment creditor if a debtor leaves his employment.

The employer pays the sums deducted from the debtor's earnings to the court and the sums in court are paid out to the creditor under normal procedures. There are no rules which prescribe that the court should notify a creditor when an employer makes no payment into court. The court does not act on its own initiative to inquire from the employer any reason for payments not being received. In such cases, the creditor should write to the court requiring an inquiry to be made, and should request the court to take action where an employer refuses or neglects to give the information required. Under such circumstances, the court may consider serving notice to the employer (N449), making an order to the employer for production of a statement of earnings (N61A) or issuing a summons against the employer for an offence under the 1971 Act (N62) for which a payment of a fine not exceeding £250 or committal to prison for a period up to 14 days may be ordered.

Consolidated attachment orders

These orders are made to secure the payment of a number of judgment debts (s 17 of the 1971 Act). Order 27 rr 18–22 apply.

They may be made by the court officer, where:

- two or more attachment of earnings orders are in force to secure the payment of judgment debts by the same debtor; or

- on an application for an attachment of earnings order to secure a judgment debt or for a consolidated attachment order, it appears that an attachment of earnings order is already in force (Ord 27 r 18).

A consolidated attachment order in respect of maintenance orders may be made in a magistrates' court (s 17(1)) or by the district judge.

Consolidated attachment orders (N66) may be made:

---

38 Attachment of Earnings Act 1971, s 7(4) and Attachment of Earnings (Employer's Deductions) Order 1991 SI 1991/356.

- on an application by the judgment debtor (Ord 27 r 19(1)(a));
- on an application by a judgment creditor who has obtained or is entitled to apply for an attachment of earnings order (r 19(1)(b));
- on the request of an employer (r 19(4)); or
- by the court of its own motion.

The judgment debtor may apply:

- in the proceedings in which any attachment of earnings order is in force; or
- on the hearing of an application for an attachment of earnings order (Ord 27 r 19(2)).

The requirements are:

- application (N244) and copies for service;
- copies of the application are to be served by post on the judgment creditor in the proceedings and also on any other judgment creditor who has obtained an attachment of earnings order which is still in force, giving not less than two clear days' notice (Ord 27 r 19(2); Ord 13 r 1(2); Ord 27 rr 3, 4 and 5 do not apply).

Fees are deducted from payments into court.

A judgment creditor's application must:

- if the judgment which he seeks to enforce was given 'by the court to which the application is made', be made in accordance with Ord 13 r 1, in the proceedings in which the judgment was obtained (Ord 27 rr 3, 4 and 5 do not apply);
- in any other case, the judgment is automatically transferred to the court which made the attachment of earnings order (Ord 27 r 19(3)).

The application must certify the amount of money due under the judgment or order and that the whole or part of any instalment due remains unpaid (Ord 27 r 19(3A)). The court officer notifies any party who may be affected by the application and requires them, within 14 days of receipt of notification, to raise any objections (r 19(3B)). If no objections are received within that time period, the court officer makes the consolidated order (r 19(3C)). If there are any objections, the matter is referred to the district judge for his consideration (r 19(3D)).

An employer to whom two or more attachment of earnings orders are directed to secure the payment of judgment debts by the same debtor may himself by a request in writing ask the court to make a consolidated attachment order. On receipt of such a request, the court must fix a hearing at which the request will be considered and give notice thereof to the debtor and the judgment creditors (Ord 27 r 19(4)).

Where an application is made for an attachment of earnings order and there is another order already in force, the court may of its own motion make a consolidated attachment order after giving all persons concerned an opportunity of being heard (Ord 27 r 20).

Where a consolidated attachment order is already in force, any creditor to whom another judgment debt is owed may apply to the court by whom the order was made for the consolidated attachment order to be extended to secure the payment of his judgment debt. Such an application is to be treated as an application for a consolidated attachment order (Ord 27 r 21, applying rr 19 and 20). It would appear that the debtor need not be in arrears for the creditor to be entitled to apply.

Cesser, discharge and variation

In the case of a judgment debt where the whole amount has been paid, the court gives notice to the employer that no further compliance is required (s 12(2) of the 1971 Act). In the case of a maintenance order where it appears to the court that the total payments made by the debtor (whether under the order or otherwise) exceed the total payments required up to that time by the maintenance order, and the normal deduction rate (or where two or more such orders are in force, the aggregate of such rates) exceeds the rate of payments required by the maintenance order, and no proceedings for the variation or discharge of the attachment of earnings order are pending, then the 'collecting officer' (the district judge) sends a notice (N341 – no longer in the County Court Practice) to the creditor and to the debtor (s 10(1) and (2); Ord 27 r 17(9)). The notice informs all parties that unless he applies to the court within 14 days after the date of the notice for an order discharging or varying the attachment of earnings order, the court will make an order varying the attachment of earnings order by reducing the normal deduction rate to the rate of payments required by the maintenance order or a lower rate.

When an attachment of earnings order ceases to have effect on the making of an order of commitment or the issue of a warrant of commitment for the enforcement of the debt, the court gives notice of the cesser to the employer (Ord 27 r 12).

The court may make an order discharging (N339 – no longer in the County Court Practice) or varying an attachment of earnings order (s 9(1) of the 1971 Act) and any party may apply on notice. An attachment of earnings order may be discharged (N339) by the court of its own motion:

- where it appears that the employer or person to whom the order is directed does not have the debtor in his employment (but the court may redirect the order to another employer if known) (Ord 27 r 13(2) and (3));

- where the court makes, or is notified of, another such order which is not to secure a judgment debt or payments under an administration order (r 13(4));
- where an administration order is made or an order made for the debtor to produce a list of his creditors with a view to the making of an administration order (r 13(5)) (but the court may vary the order to secure payment under the administration order);
- where the court makes a consolidated attachment of earnings order (r 13(6));
- where the defendant has been made a bankrupt (r 13(7));
- where the court grants leave to issue execution (r 13(8));
- where the maintenance order being enforced has ceased to have effect (r 17(10)).

Notice is to be given by the court to the debtor and judgment creditor of the time and place at which the question of any discharge or variation will be considered unless the court considers it unnecessary in the circumstances to do so (Ord 27 r 13(1)–(9)). If the debtor, at any time, satisfies the court that he is unemployed or self-employed, the court may, accordingly, stay or dismiss the application for an attachment of earnings order or, where one has already been made, dismiss it.

Administration orders

Order 39 applies. A person with multiple debts totalling not more than £5,000 can put all of the debts in the hands of the court, which collects a regular payment from him and distributes it proportionally. A debtor can apply for an order provided at least one judgment has been obtained against him. The debtor completes a request form which includes details of his debts (N92 or N93) (attachment of earnings) and a return date is fixed by the court. The request also contains provision for the debtor to ask the court to make a 'composition order' (so much in the pound). The application form is N92 and notes for guidance N270. The application form requires information about the applicant's income and outgoings and the notes for guidance provide information and examples to help the debtor complete the application form. Council tax arrears should not be included, nor any other debts which are enforceable in the magistrates' court.

Not less than 14 days' notice of the hearing is given to the debtor and creditors (Ord 39 r 5), the latter of whom have to raise any objections at least seven days before the return date (Ord 39 r 6(1)).

At the hearing, the district judge decides what order should be made. Creditors have the right to attend and, if necessary, raise objections (Ord 39 r 7(a)). A 'reasonable period' for repayment of the debt should be calculated, usually not more than about three years, if the court is inclined to make an administration order.

The order is subject to review at any time on debtors and creditors being given seven days' notice (Ord 39 r 8), including on a subsequent objection by a creditor who was not on the original list (Ord 39 r 10). Such a creditor may also ask to be included in the order (Ord 39 r 11). A 'court officer' can decide whether or not an administration order should be made or revoked and the rate of payment thereunder.

Any composition orders, reviews or objections to any part of the procedure are dealt with, however, by the district judge. Thus, where there is default by the debtor, the court officer may require the debtor to bring payments up to date or give an explanation as to why payments are not being made (Ord 39 r 13A(1)). If the debtor does not respond, the court officer may revoke the order (r 13A(2)). If the debtor gives reasons for default in payment, this will be referred to the district judge to decide whether or not to revoke or suspend the order or fix a review (r 13A(3)). On the review of an administration order, the court may suspend the order on terms, vary any provision of it, revoke it or make an attachment of earnings order (r 14(1)).

An attachment of earnings order should automatically be made to secure payments under an administration order unless there are good reasons for not doing so. Administration orders are registered at the Registry of County Court Judgments.

APPOINTMENT OF A RECEIVER

Where the judgment debtor has a business operating as a going concern, the judgment creditor may apply for the appointment of a receiver, in order to effect a sale of the business in order to provide payment of the judgment debt. When deciding whether to appoint a receiver, the court will determine whether it is just or convenient that the appointment should be made having regard to the amount claimed by the judgment creditor, the likely amount to be obtained by the receiver and the probable costs of his appointment (RSC Ord 51 r 1).

COMMITTAL FOR CONTEMPT

Contempt of court includes disobedience to a court judgment or order restraining an act or requiring an act to be done within a time specified in the judgment or order. The ultimate sanction is committal of a person to prison for contempt of court for a period of up to two years, but a fine of up to £2,500 can also be imposed (s 14 of the Contempt of Court Act 1981). The usual purpose of an application for committal is to enforce compliance with the order.

Enforcement of injunctions and undertakings

The remedy a claimant seeks may be an order requiring the defendant to do or abstain from doing an act, for example, to refrain from infringing copyright in property owned by the claimant or to shore up a party wall. Such a remedy is known as an injunction and can be obtained as an interim measure before trial and/or as a final remedy.

If a court order, requiring a person to do or abstain from doing a specified act within a specified period of time, is disobeyed, this is a contempt of court and as such may be enforced by an order for committal to prison, by the imposition of a fine, or, with the permission of the court, by a writ of sequestration against the person's property, or, where the person is a body corporate, against the property of a director or officer of the body corporate (RSC Ord 45 r 5(1) and CCR Ord 29 r 1(1)).

Service of injunction

Order requiring an act to be done

As the methods of enforcement for breach of an injunction are potentially very serious, in order to be able to enforce an injunction requiring a person to do a particular act through committal proceedings or sequestration of assets, a copy of the injunction must be served personally on the person required to do the act in question, unless the court orders otherwise (RSC Ord 45 r 7(2), (7) and CCR Ord 29 r 1(2)).

In the case of a body corporate, such an injunction must be served personally on the officer against whose property permission is sought to issue a writ of sequestration or against whom an order for committal is sought, unless the court orders otherwise (RSC Ord 45 r 7(3) and (7)).

Order specifying time within which act is to be done

If the original judgment or order for an injunction does not specify a time within which the act is to be done, the court has the power to make an order requiring the act to be done within a specified time (RSC Ord 45 r 6(2)). The party seeking such an order should make an application in accordance with Part 23 (RSC Ord 45 r 6(3)).[39]

---

[39] See Chapter 19, Making Applications for Court Orders.

Order requiring a person to abstain from doing an act

An order requiring a person to abstain from doing an act may be enforced through committal proceedings or sequestration of assets even if the injunction has not been personally served on that person so long as the court is satisfied that pending such service that person had notice of the order because they were present when the order was made, or were notified of the terms of the order by another method such as telephone or telegram (RSC Ord 45 r 7(6) and CCR Ord 29 r 1(6)). Again, in any event, the court can dispense with service of a copy of the order (RSC Ord 45 r 7(7) and CCR Ord 29 r 1(7)).

Penal notice

The injunction must also carry a penal notice prominently displayed on the front of the copy of the order. A penal notice is a warning to the person on whom the copy is served that disobedience to the order is a contempt of court punishable by imprisonment. In the case of a body corporate, the warning is in terms that the assets of the body corporate may be subject to sequestration and any individual director responsible may be imprisoned (RSC Ord 45 r 7(4)).

Undertakings

If a person agrees to provide an undertaking to the court rather than have an injunction ordered against him, if the undertaking is breached this will be enforceable in the same way as if an injunction had been ordered (RSC Ord 52) (CCR Ord 29 r 1A). Moreover, as an undertaking is voluntarily provided, in the High Court it will be enforceable even though an order in the terms of the undertaking has not been served with a penal notice so long as the court is satisfied that the party gave the undertaking and understood its effect. However, it is good practice personally to serve a copy of the terms of the undertaking with a penal notice on the person who gave it. In the county court, the undertaking will not be enforceable unless it is recorded in a document and served on the party who provided it (CCR Ord 29 r 1A).

Committal applications

Where the alleged contempt is contempt of a county court order, the application for committal must be made to the county court in question. Where it is contempt of a High Court order, it must be made to the High Court (PD 52, paras 1.1–1.3).

Procedure for committal applications

Where the application is made in existing proceedings, that is, to enforce an interim injunction, it should be made in accordance with Part 23[40] (RSC, PD 52, para 2.2 and CCR Ord 29 r 1(4)). If the application is made to enforce a final injunction, it must be commenced by issue of a Part 8 claim form[41] (RSC, PD 52, para 2.1 and CCR Ord 29 r 1(4)). The application form or Part 8 claim form must set out in full the grounds on which the application is made, identify separately and numerically each alleged act of contempt and be served personally on the respondent (PD 52, paras 2.5, 2.6 and CCR Ord 29 r 1(4A)).

Evidence in support

Written evidence in support or opposition to a committal application must be by way of affidavit[42] and, therefore, cannot be by way of witness statement[43] (PD 52, para 3.1). The affidavit must be filed and served personally on the other party (PD 52, para 3.2).

In the light of the seriousness of the allegation, the breach must be proved on the criminal standard 'beyond reasonable doubt'.[44] What must be proved is deliberate failure to comply with a court order rather than a negligent omission to comply.

Committal hearing

The applicant for the committal order must, when lodging the claim form for issue or application notice for filing, obtain a date from the court for the hearing of the committal application. Unless the court otherwise directs, the date for the hearing shall be not less than 14 clear days after service of the claim form or application notice on the respondent. On the hearing day, the court can either give case management directions for the hearing of the application at a future date, or, if the committal application is ready to be heard, proceed to hear the application (PD 52, paras 4.1–4.4).

The committal hearing should normally be heard in public in accordance with the general rule.[45] However, if it is heard in private and the court finds

---

40 *Ibid.*
41 See Chapter 14, Part 8 Claims.
42 See Chapter 31, Evidence.
43 *Ibid.*
44 *Dean v Dean* [1987] 1 FLR 51.
45 See CPR, r 39.2 and Chapter 32, Hearings and Judgments.

the respondent guilty of contempt, the judge shall state in public the name of the respondent, the nature of the contempt and any penalty imposed (PD 52, para 9).

Jurisdiction to hear a committal application

A committal application can, in most cases, only be heard by a circuit judge for proceedings in the county court or a High Court judge for proceedings in the High Court. However, there are exceptions where the master or district judge will have jurisdiction. For example, the district judge will have jurisdiction in respect of assaults on court officers[46] or disruption of court proceedings[47] (PD 52, para 11).

Orders on committal

The court has various options open to it. It may:
- imprison the respondent for up to two years (s 14(1) of the Contempt of Court Act 1981);
- make a suspended order for committal for a specified period including on terms;
- order an unlimited fine;
- take security for good behaviour;
- grant an injunction;
- adjourn sentencing to a specified date;
- make no order.

Specific performance of a contract

If the court makes a judgment or order directing a party to execute any conveyance, contract or other document or to indorse a negotiable instrument and that party refuses or fails to do so, the court can use its powers to punish the disobedient party for contempt (RSC Ord 45 r 5). Alternatively, in such circumstances, or if the party who should execute the document or indorse the negotiable instrument cannot be found, the court can nominate another person for that purpose (s 39 of the Supreme Court Act 1981). The court can also order that the cost of obtaining such execution or indorsement be borne by the disobedient party (RSC Ord 45 r 8).

---

46 County Courts Act 1984, s 14.
47 Ibid, s 118.

Enforcement of judgment for possession of land

In the High Court, except in the case of mortgage proceedings, a party must seek the permission of the court to issue a writ of possession in order to enforce a judgment or order for the giving of possession of land (RSC Ord 45 r 3(2)). The court will only grant such permission if it is satisfied that every person in actual possession of the whole or any part of the land has received sufficient notice of the proceedings to enable them to apply to the court for any relief that they may be entitled to. In the case of an order for possession against long leaseholders, the court must additionally be satisfied that no application for relief has been made by the tenant under s 16 of the Landlord and Tenant Act 1954 (RSC Ord 45 r 3(3)).

In the county court, if an order for the recovery of land is made by the court, this can be enforced by warrant of possession which is issued following the filing of a request in Form N325 which certifies that the land has not been vacated in accordance with the judgment or order granting possession (CCR Ord 26 r 17(1) and (2)).

In the High Court, if permission is granted to issue the writ of possession, it will be executed by the Sheriff, while in the county court the warrant of possession will be executed by the bailiff. In both courts, the writ or warrant may include provision to enforce payment of any money which is also ordered to be paid by the judgment or order (RSC Ord 45 r 3(4) and CCR Ord 26 r 17(3)).

Enforcement of judgment for delivery of goods

Writ/warrant of specific delivery

If a claimant obtains a judgment or order for the delivery of specific goods which does not give the defendant the option of paying the assessed value of the goods instead, the judgment or order can be enforced in the High Court by a writ of specific delivery (RSC Ord 45 r 4(1)(a)), the equivalent in the county court being a warrant of specific delivery (CCR Ord 26 r 16(2)).

Writ/warrant of delivery to recover goods or their assessed value

If the judgment or order is for the delivery of specific goods or payment of their assessed value, the judgment or order can be enforced by a writ of delivery (or warrant of delivery in the county court) to recover the goods or their assessed value.

In the High Court, if the judgment or order is for delivery of specific goods or payment of their assessed value, the claimant cannot issue a writ of specific delivery of the goods without first obtaining the permission of the court (RSC

Ord 45 r 4(2)). Such an application should be made in accordance with Part 23[48] and served on the defendant against whom such an order is sought (RSC Ord 45 r 4(2)).

In the High Court, a judgment or order for the payment of the assessed value of any goods may be enforced by the same means as any other judgment or order for the payment of money (RSC Ord 45 r 4(4)). A writ of specific delivery or a writ of delivery to recover any goods or their assessed value may also include provision for enforcing the payment of any money which is also ordered to be paid (RSC Ord 45 r 4(3)).

In the county court, a warrant of delivery entitles the judgment creditor to execution against the judgment debtor's goods for any money payable under the judgment or order which is to be enforced by the warrant of delivery (CCR Ord 26 r 16(4)).

RECIPROCAL ENFORCEMENT OF JUDGMENTS

Under various conventions and treaties, reciprocal enforcement is available both for a foreign judgment to be enforced in this jurisdiction and for a judgment obtained in our jurisdiction to be enforced in a foreign court.[49] For details of the procedure to be followed, see RSC Ord 71 and CCR Ord 35.

---

48 See Chapter 19, Making Applications for Court Orders.
49 See the Administration of Justice Act 1920, the Foreign Judgments (Reciprocal Enforcement) Act 1933 and the Civil Jurisdiction and Judgments Act 1982.

CHAPTER 40

TRANSITIONAL ARRANGEMENTS

INTRODUCTION

The CPR came into force on 26 April 1999.[1] The CPR apply in full to all proceedings issued after that date. The rules in existence before the CPR came into force were the Rules of the Supreme Court 1965 (RSC), which applied to proceedings in the Supreme Court, and the County Court Rules 1981 (CCR), which applied to proceedings in the county courts. The CPR are a single code applying to proceedings both in the Supreme Court and the county courts. Although the RSC and CCR were abolished on the coming into force of the CPR, some of the RSC and CCR were brought back into force and added as schedules to the CPR; Sched 1 containing the remaining RSC and Sched 2 containing the remaining CCR.

PROCEEDINGS ISSUED BEFORE COMMENCEMENT OF CPR

Practice Direction 51 contains general principles as well as detailed provision for the application of the CPR to proceedings issued before the CPR came into force (Part 51 and PD 51, para 1.1).

GENERAL PRINCIPLES RELATING TO
THE TRANSITIONAL ARRANGEMENTS

When a new step is to be taken in any existing proceedings after 26 April 1999, it is to be taken in accordance with the CPR (PD 51, para 11).

However, the general scheme is to apply the previous rules to undefended cases commenced before 26 April 1999, allowing them to progress to their disposal but to apply the CPR to defended cases as far as possible (PD 51, para 2).

The overriding objective[2] applies to all existing proceedings from 26 April 1999 whether or not steps are taken under the CPR or under the previous rules (PD 51, para 12).

---

1 SI 1998/3132, as amended by the Civil Procedure (Amendment) Rules SI 1999/1008, SI 2000/221, SI 2000/940, SI 2000/1317, SI 2000/2092, SI 2001/256 and SI 2001/1388.
2 See Chapter 5, Judicial Case Management: The Overriding Objective.

APPLICATION OF THE OLD CIVIL PROCEDURE RULES

Initiating steps under the old rules

Where an initiating step, such as the issue of proceedings or the making of an application, has been taken in a case before 26 April 1999, in particular if it involves the use of forms and documents required by the previous rules, the case will proceed in the first instance under the previous rules. If a step is required in response to something done by the other party in accordance with the previous rules, it must also be taken in accordance with those rules (PD 51, para 3).

If a party is served with an old type of originating process, such as a writ or summons, on or after 26 April 1999, the other party must respond in accordance with the previous rules following the instructions served with the originating process (PD 51, para 4).

Where a case has been begun by an old type of originating process, whether served before or after 26 April 1999, filing and service of pleadings (equivalent to statements of case) should be carried out in accordance with the previous rules (PD 51, para 5).

Extending the validity of a writ

If a party commences proceedings before 26 April 1999, and applies for an order to extend the validity of the originating process (for example, writ or summons) on or after that date, he must make the application in accordance with CPR, Part 23,[3] but the court will decide whether to allow the application in accordance with the principles under the previous law (PD 51, para 13.3).

Automatic directions/discovery

Where the timetable for automatic directions under RSC Ord 25 r 8 or CCR Ord 17 r 11 had already begun to apply, or a notice of directions under CCR Ord 17 r 11 had been sent out (even if the timetable did not start until after 26 April 1999) or automatic discovery under RSC Ord 24 had already begun to apply, to proceedings before 26 April 1999, those directions will continue to have effect on or after 26 April 1999 (PD 51, paras 6.1 and 6.2).

---

3   See Chapter 19, Making Applications for Court Orders.

No automatic strike out

Although automatic directions under CCR Ord 17 r 11 given before 26 April 1999 may continue to apply after that date,[4] the automatic direction under that order, providing for automatic strike out of proceedings for failure to request a hearing to be fixed within 15 months of deemed date of close of pleadings, no longer applies (PD 51, para 6(3)). This rule providing for automatic strike out of pleadings generated much case law and was generally thought to have failed in achieving its objective to encourage the fast and efficient disposal of proceedings.

Judgment in default/on admission

If a party to proceedings started under the old rules wishes to enter judgment in default or on admissions, he must do so in accordance with the old rules (PD 51, paras 7.1 and 8.1). Entry of judgment in such circumstances is an administrative act which can be carried out by a court officer. However, where there are outstanding issues to be decided, such as the assessment of damages, the court officer may refer the case to a judge for case management decisions to be carried out. The judge will apply the principles set out in para 15 of the Practice Direction,[4a] which gives him a discretion as to whether to disapply any provisions of the CPR, but with the general presumption that the CPR will apply to the proceedings from then on (PD 51, paras 7.2, 8.2 and 15).

If permission is needed to enter judgment in default or on admissions, in proceedings started under the old rules, the application for permission must be made in accordance with the procedure set out in Part 23 (PD 51, paras 7.3 and 8.3).[5]

In the case of judgment in default, the provisions under the CPR about applying to set aside or vary such judgment (Part 13) and about proceedings being stayed if not defended or admitted within a specified period of time (r 15.11) applies to these proceedings (PD 51, paras 7.4 and 7.5).

Obligation to comply with court orders made under the old rules

Where a court order has been made in proceedings before 26 April 1999, that order must still be complied with after 26 April 1999 (PD 51, para 9). However, if the proceedings come before a judge for the first time after that date, he has the power to make a different order under the CPR (PD 51, para 15).

---

4   See above, p 504, Automatic directions/discovery.
4a   See below, p 506, Cases coming before the court for the first time after 26 April 1999.
5   See Chapter 19, Making Applications for Court Orders.

Validity of steps previously taken in proceedings before 26 April 1999

If a party has taken a step in proceedings under the old rules, that step will remain valid under the CPR. Also, a party will not normally be required to carry out effectively the same step under the CPR that has already been complied with under the old rules. So, for instance, if discovery has been provided under the old rules, it will not be necessary for a party to provide disclosure under the CPR (PD 51, para 10).

APPLICATION OF THE CPR

Commencing proceedings after 26 April 1999

Only CPR claim forms will be issued after 26 April 1999. If a request to issue an old type of originating application, such as a writ or summons, is received at the court office on or after 26 April 1999, it will be returned unissued.

Case coming before the court for the first time after 26 April 1999

When a case started under the old rules comes before a judge (whether at a hearing or on paper) for the first time on or after 26 April 1999, the judge in the exercise of his discretion can direct how the CPR are to apply to the proceedings, and disapply certain provisions of the CPR. The judge may also give case management directions for the case, including allocating it to one of the case management tracks (PD 51, para 15.1).[6]

However, the general presumption is that the CPR will apply to the proceedings from then on (PD 51, para 15.2). If an application is issued before 26 April 1999 with a hearing date after that date, or the first occasion a case started under the old rules comes before a judge after that date is for trial, the presumption is that the application or trial will be heard in accordance with the CPR (PD 51, para 15.3 and 15.4).

Applications to the court after 26 April 1999

In general, all applications made to the court after 26 April 1999 must be made in accordance with Part 23[7] and in accordance with the rules under the CPR

---

6   See Chapter 15, Case Management: Allocation.
7   See Chapter 19, Making Applications for Court Orders.

relating to the application in question (for example, application for summary judgment under CPR, Part 24[8]), unless PD 51 provides otherwise (application to extend the validity of originating process[8a] and costs).[9] The other relevant rules under the CPR will also apply if appropriate, such as rules about court forms in CPR, Part 4 and rules about service of documents under CPR, Part 6 (PD 51, para 14). However, this general principle will not apply.

Note that since 26 April 1999, there have been many decisions of the Court of Appeal which have confirmed that case law which predates the introduction of the CPR is hardly of any relevance to cases dealt with after that date because the court now applies the principles contained in the overriding objective.[10]

Close of pleadings after 26 April 1999

Under the old rules, in the High Court, pleadings (equivalent to statements of case) were deemed to be closed 14 days after service of any reply, or if none, 14 days after service of the defence to counterclaim, or if none, 14 days after service of the defence. In the county court, pleadings were deemed to be closed 14 days after delivery of the defence, or where a counterclaim was served with the defence, 28 days after delivery of the defence (PD 51, para 16.6).

Where pleadings are deemed to be closed on or after 26 April 1999, the case management provisions in CPR Part 26 will apply to those proceedings and the court will serve an allocation questionnaire[11] on the parties in order to allocate the proceedings to one of the case management tracks (PD 51, para 16.2).[12]

If a defence is filed at court on or after 26 April 1999, the court will serve an allocation questionnaire on the parties (PD 51, para 16.3).

Agreement to apply the CPR

The parties to proceedings may agree in writing that the CPR will apply to the proceedings from the date of the agreement. All the parties must agree, the CPR must apply in their entirety, the agreement is irrevocable and the claimant must file a copy of the agreement at court (PD 51, para 17).

---

8   See Chapter 22, Summary Judgment.
8a   See above, p 504, Extending the validity of a writ, r 13.3.
9   See below, p 508, Costs, r 18.2.
10   See, eg, *Biguzzi v Rank Leisure plc* [1999] 1 WLR 1926; [1999] 4 All ER 934, CA.
11   See Chapter 15, Case Management: Allocation.
12   *Ibid.*

Costs

The court's decision as to whether to allow costs for work undertaken on or after 26 April 1999 will generally be in accordance with the CPR costs rules (Parts 43 to 48). Any assessment of costs which takes place on or after 26 April will also be in accordance with Parts 43 to 48. However, there is a general presumption that no costs for work undertaken before 26 April 1999 will be disallowed if they would have been allowed under a costs taxation under the old rules (PD 51, para 18).

When preparing a bill of costs for a period which consists of work done both before and after 26 April 1999, it is advisable to split the bill between pre and post 26 April 1999 work, as the court can apply the proportionality to the latter, but not to the former.

Existing proceedings after one year

If any existing proceedings (those other than for which final judgment has been given) have not come before a judge, at a hearing or on paper, between 26 April 1999 and 25 April 2000, those proceedings shall be stayed. Any party to those proceedings may then apply for the stay to be lifted (PD 51, paras 19.1, 19.2 and 19.4).

This provision does not apply to proceedings which have been given a fixed trial date after 25 April 2000, personal injuries cases where liability is not in issue, but the court has adjourned proceedings to determine the prognosis, where the court is dealing with the continuing administration of an estate or a receivership, or in respect of applications relating to funds in court (PD 51, para 19.3).

INDEX